D0712798

MAY 2 3 2022

THE STRATEGY OF DENIAL

ELBRIDGE A. COLBY

The Strategy of Denial

AMERICAN DEFENSE IN AN AGE OF

GREAT POWER CONFLICT

Yale

UNIVERSITY PRESS

NEW HAVEN & LONDON

Published with assistance from the foundation established in memory of
Philip Hamilton McMillan of the Class of 1894, Yale College.

Yale University Press books may be purchased in quantity for
educational, business, or promotional use. For information, please e-mail
sales.press@yale.edu (US office) or sales@yaleup.co.uk (UK office).

Epigraph: Republished with permission of Princeton University Press, from
Carl von Clausewitz, *On War,* ed. and trans. Michael Howard and Peter Paret
(Princeton, NJ: Princeton University Press, 1976, revised 1989), 88–89,
606–607; permission conveyed through Copyright Clearance Center, Inc.

Set in Times Roman and Scala Sans type by IDS Infotech, Ltd.
Printed in the United States of America.

Library of Congress Control Number: 2021932610
ISBN 978-0-300-25643-7 (hardcover : alk. paper)

A catalogue record for this book is available from the British Library.

This paper meets the requirements of ANSI/NISO Z39.48-1992
(Permanence of Paper).

10 9 8 7 6 5 4 3 2 1

This book is dedicated to my father, Jonathan,
with profound respect and gratitude
for his example and encouragement

The first, the supreme, the most far-reaching act of judgment that the statesman and commander have to make is to establish . . . the kind of war on which they are embarking; neither mistaking it for, nor trying to turn it into, something that is alien to its nature. This is the first of all strategic questions and the most comprehensive. . . .

Nothing is more important in life than finding the right standpoint for seeing and judging events, and then adhering to it. . . . Policy is the guiding intelligence and war only the instrument.

Carl von Clausewitz, *On War*

CONTENTS

PREFACE

WHAT IS THE BEST DEFENSE STRATEGY for America?

In other words, for what purposes should the United States be prepared to fight, and how should US military forces be readied to fight such wars? Because these questions involve life and death and loss on a great scale, they cannot be answered sensibly without a clear sense of the purposes such a strategy should serve.

For many years, these questions were not so pressing or pointed. Following the collapse of the Soviet Union, the United States was so much more powerful than any plausible rival that it could readily best any opponent over any interest for which it might realistically care to contend. While the United States might not have been able to seize Beijing or Moscow without suffering a nuclear retort, it had no reason to try. It enjoyed global preeminence without going to such lengths. For anything it might care to fight over—against Russia over NATO or against China over Taiwan, the South China Sea, or Japan—it needed only to apply the resources required to prevail.

That world is gone. The "unipolar moment" is over.[1]

Above all, this is because of the rise of China. Napoleon is supposed to have remarked that, when China rose, the world would quake.[2] China has now arisen—and is continuing to rise. And the world is quaking. For the first time since the nineteenth century, the United States no longer boasts the world's indisputably largest economy. As a result, we are witnessing a return to what is commonly referred to as "great power competition." This is a euphemism for an almost physical reality: an object so large must have the greatest consequence for any system that must accommodate it. China's enormous size and

sophistication mean that its rise will be of the utmost significance. It is one
thing to describe the phenomenon; it is another thing to understand how to react
to it.

This book seeks to explain what this reality means for the defense of the
United States and its important interests. It is motivated by the concern that
Americans and those interested in America's defense strategy do not yet have a
framework to answer these questions in a way that is at once comprehensive,
rigorous, and sound. There are, of course, contemporary works on strategy—
many superb—but they are mostly concerned with grand strategy. Few lay out
a single, coherent framework that provides clear guidance on what the nation's
defense strategy should be as an outgrowth of its grand strategy.[3]

The absence of such a framework is a serious problem. In the unipolar era,
Americans could make decisions about strategic questions without too much
fear of the consequences; America's preponderance of power buffered it from
the results of its decisions becoming too painful.

This is no longer the case. Power is now more diffuse, and the places to
which it is diffusing—especially China—are not established US allies. Ten
years ago, the United States spent more on defense than the next eighteen countries combined, and most of the immediately trailing countries were close allies. Today, that margin has shrunk; it spends as much as the next seven
combined, and China, which has leapt into second place, has increased its defense spending by around 10 percent every year for the past twenty-five years.
And the margin is likely to shrink further as China grows.[4]

It is not only the structure of global power that has changed. In the 1990s or
2000s, one could imagine that the world was becoming more peaceful and co-
operative; states such as China and Russia appeared largely to accept the international lay of the land. Recently, however, the world has become more tense,
if not rivalrous, in ways that reflect not just structural changes but also the
reemergence of a more overtly competitive attitude. This has meant that major
war, which once seemed a thing of the past at least in certain parts of the world,
now seems considerably more plausible.

How should the United States orient itself to all this? The fundamental reality
is that there are now structural limitations on what the United States can do—it
cannot do everything at once. Thus it must make hard choices. And with hard
choices, a framework for making them—a strategy—is crucial. A state can mud-
dle through without a conscious strategy when the consequences are minor, when

others determine its fate, or when it is already servant to an existing strategic framework. But, given their newfound limits, Americans now need to reconcile their international aspirations and commitments with their ability and willingness to follow through on them. To make intelligent decisions under such conditions, Americans need a basis for determining what is important and what is not, what the primary threats to the nation's interests are, and how best to serve those interests in a way that is attentive to the costs and risks they are willing to bear.

Importantly, a strategy is a framework, not a master plan. It is predicated on a coherent view of the world and provides a logic within which to make choices and prioritize. It is, at its heart, a *simplifying logic* to deal with a complex world that would otherwise be bewildering. Strategy, in this sense, is like any good theory meant to help explain the world—it should be as simple as possible, but no simpler. Without such a logic, there is no coherent way to discern what is truly important and needs to be specially prepared for versus what can be managed or ignored. In the situation of scarce resources in which the United States now finds itself, this is a recipe for frustration or disaster.

A strategic framework is especially necessary in times of transition like today, when the ideas and frameworks of yesteryear become increasingly mismatched with reality. The generation of post–Cold War primacy unmoored some Americans, or at least some of their leaders and eminent thinkers, from underlying realities, giving them a highly exaggerated sense of what the United States could and should accomplish in the international arena. This has had a number of sorry results. Moreover, many of America's leading thinkers on international affairs retain this heady sensibility, as if hoping the nation can will itself back to unipolarity, even as many ordinary Americans sense that things have changed profoundly. At the same time, there is a powerful strain, especially in the academy, of arguing that the United States should retrench and adopt a dramatically less engaged foreign policy than it has pursued since the Second World War.

My aim in this book is to describe how Americans can deal with this new reality and can pursue and protect their important interests abroad at levels of risk and cost they can realistically and justifiably bear. In particular, I am concerned with how they can be prepared to wage war for very important interests and do so in a sane way. This is a defense strategy book; it is rooted in a grand strategy, but its focus is on military affairs. War is not just another province of human activity; I argue that military affairs are in important respects determinative. But they are not comprehensive, and if defense strategy is done right, they can be made marginal. Success for the strategy in this book would be precisely this result: a situation in which the threat of war is *not* salient. But attaining this goal, paradoxically, requires a clear and rigorous focus on war. Readers will not find here any discussion of how to compete with China economically, how most international institutions should evolve, or any number of other problems in international politics. This is not because these are not important issues—they are—but because if Americans do not have the right defense strategy, these other considerations and interests will be forced to take a backseat. Figuring out that strategy is the task of this book.

Although this is a book about war—why it happens, for what purposes it should be fought, and how it should be waged—it is designed to promote peace, particularly a decent peace. But a decent peace compatible with Americans' freedom, security, and prosperity does not spontaneously generate.[5] It is an achievement. This book is designed to try to show how Americans might achieve such a peace at a level of cost and risk they can bear in an era when a decent peace can no longer be taken for granted.

Plan of the Book

This book proceeds deductively, beginning from first principles and presenting conclusions only after the logic leading to them has been established. The idea is to allow the reader to see the logical progression clearly, rather than starting from conclusions and then justifying them. I provide the plan below for those who wish to have a clear sense of where they are heading or who want to read selectively. Chapters 1 through 4 lay out the broad geopolitical strategy that should guide American defense strategy. Chapters 5–11 present the military strategy needed to uphold that broader strategy. Chapter 12 is a short conclusion.

Chapter 1 lays out the fundamental purposes of American grand strategy and how they shape US defense strategy. It introduces the central role of balances of power, with an emphasis on the core objective of denying any other state hegemony over one of the world's key regions in order to preserve Americans' security, freedom, and prosperity. It explains why Asia is the world's most important region, given its wealth and power, and why China is the world's other most important state. Like other very powerful states, China has a most potent interest in establishing hegemony over its region, and, predictably,

Beijing appears to be pursuing this goal. Denying China hegemony over Asia is therefore the cardinal objective of US grand strategy.

Chapter 2 explains why favorable regional balances of power matter for US strategy. It describes the role of anti-hegemonic coalitions in upholding such balances, namely, by leaguing together enough states to agglomerate more power than an aspiring regional hegemon and its confederates can muster. This chapter describes the challenges to forming and sustaining such coalitions in the face of an aspiring regional hegemon, especially when the aspirant employs a focused and sequential strategy designed to short-circuit or break apart any such coalition. Such a strategy allows the aspiring hegemon to focus on and isolate coalition members in sequence, progressively weakening the coalition until the aspirant is able to achieve its hegemony. This problem points to the importance of a cornerstone balancer—especially an external cornerstone balancer—and the United States' unique ability to play this role. Last, the chapter explains why the United States must focus on playing this role in Asia, given that an anti-hegemonic coalition is unlikely to form against China without America doing so and the much better prospects that such coalitions will form and sustain themselves in other key regions with a more modest American contribution.

Chapter 3 outlines the importance of alliances—formal commitments to fight for other states—within an anti-hegemonic coalition, which can itself be a more informal grouping that includes both alliances and less entangling partnerships. Alliances provide reassurance to states that might otherwise bandwagon with an aspiring hegemon such as China, especially in the face of its focused and sequential strategy. But, for participants, they also present the risk of entanglement in unnecessary or too costly wars. This is especially because defense of an ally, especially by a cornerstone balancer such as the United States, needs to be both effective and credible, which may not be easy to achieve. What matters most, however, is not American credibility in some general sense—that is, upholding every pledge or promise the United States has ever made, however imprudent—but US differentiated credibility in Asia: the degree to which important actors in the region believe that the United States will defend them effectively against China. The primary importance of this differentiated credibility, in turn, permits the United States to make difficult but important choices in other theaters without undermining its differentiated credibility in Asia.

Chapter 4 is about defining the US alliance, or defense, perimeter. Because the success of the anti-hegemonic coalition depends on America's protecting and husbanding its differentiated credibility, the United States must carefully select which states to include and exclude. If it undercommits, the coalition will be too weak; if it overcommits, it risks overextension, defeat, and the loss of its differentiated credibility. While some states, such as Japan and Australia, should obviously be included, whether others should be is less clear-cut. Because of the delicacy and competitiveness of the power balance, the United States should seek to include as many states as it can defend while excluding those it cannot. But this question of defensibility cannot be answered without an understanding of the best military strategy for the United States. Thus we must apprehend what America's best military strategy is before we can identify its optimal defense perimeter.

Chapter 5 begins the discussion of the best military strategy for the United States in light of this broad geopolitical challenge. It discusses the problems of conducting a limited war against China, given that both sides possess survivable nuclear arsenals, and explains why the United States must prepare to fight a limited war in this context. The chapter lays out why, in any war between the United States and China, both sides have the strongest incentives to keep the conflict limited, including most fundamentally by taking steps to avoid a large-scale nuclear war. Because neither side can reasonably contemplate a total war over partial (even if very important) stakes, the prevailing side will be the one that fights more effectively under whatever constraints emerge. This means that the victor will be the one that can achieve its goals while leaving such a heavy burden of escalation on the other side that the opponent either practically cannot or will not escalate its way out of a partial defeat.

Chapter 6 argues that, in its defense planning, the United States needs to focus on China's best military strategies rather than simply pleading ignorance and preparing for all eventualities or focusing on China's likeliest or most destructive potential strategies.

Chapter 7 argues that China's best military strategy is likely to be a fait accompli strategy against an exposed member of the anti-hegemonic coalition, especially one connected by an alliance or quasi-alliance to Washington. This is because strategies that rely on persuading a targeted country to give up core goods such as autonomy—as China would need to do to establish its regional hegemony—are likely to fail. Instead, China is likely to rely primarily on brute force to subordinate targeted states while depending on persuasion to deter that state's allies from coming effectively to its defense. The optimal form of this strategy is the fait accompli whereby China seizes vulnerable US confederates such as Taiwan or the Philippines while deterring a sufficiently strong defense by the United States and any other states that might participate. Applied sequentially, this strategy could undermine US differentiated credibility and weaken the coalition until it collapses, opening the way for China to become the regional hegemon. China's first target for this strategy is likely to be Taiwan, given its proximity to China and status as a US quasi-ally.

Chapter 8 lays out the optimal US response to China's best strategy. Restoring military dominance over China is infeasible, given its size and growth trajectory. Horizontal or vertical escalation is likely to fail or result in destruction out of proportion to any gains. Accordingly, America's best military strategy is a denial defense, or a strategy that seeks to deny China's ability to use military force to achieve its political objectives. China's strategy of subordinating targeted states through a fait accompli requires more than seizing peripheral territory: it must seize and hold the target state's key territory. With this leverage, Beijing could impose its terms; without it, it is unlikely to persuade even moderately resolute states to forgo their autonomy. Accordingly, the United States and any other engaged coalition members should seek to deny China the attainment of this standard. They can do so either by preventing China from seizing a target state's key territory in the first place or by ejecting the invaders before they can consolidate their hold on it.

Chapter 9 argues that if a Chinese invasion of Taiwan or the Philippines can be defeated in one of these ways, then Beijing will bear a heavy burden of escalation. China is very unlikely to be able to escalate its way to victory from such a defeat, since any such effort is likely to catalyze an effective coalition response. In such circumstances, the defenders can either settle in for a protracted war on an advantageous basis or attempt to coerce China's acceptance of defeat, most effectively through a strategy mixing elements of denial with cost imposition. If the defenders can defeat China's best military strategy even in the case of Taiwan, the anti-hegemonic coalition will very likely succeed in blocking Beijing's pursuit of regional hegemony.

Chapter 10 begins by emphasizing that conducting such an effective defense of Taiwan, while feasible, is by no means easy; China may be too powerful or the participating elements of the coalition too ill prepared for the defenders to mount an effective resistance. In this case, the defenders may have to substantially expand the war to conduct an effective denial defense, in effect assuming a heavy burden of escalation. Alternatively, if the defenders cannot prevent a successful Chinese invasion, the coalition might even be forced to recapture a lost ally. In this case, the key question is how the coalition, which should—if it is to serve its purpose—constitute a network of states with greater total power than China and its confederates, can muster the resolve to take the costly and risky steps needed to prevail. The solution to this problem is a binding strategy. This is an approach that deliberately positions the coalition members, including the United States, such that China's ability to employ its best military strategy would catalyze the coalition members' resolve to defeat it. The logic is to ensure that China, by putting its best strategy into effect, will make clear to the coalition members that they are better off defeating it now rather than later. This can be done if China's actions make the coalition members believe that it is more aggressive, ambitious, cruel, unreliable, powerful, or disrespectful of their honor than they had previously thought.

Chapter 11 lays out the implications for US defense strategy that follow from the book. The top priority for the US defense establishment should be ensuring that China cannot subordinate a US ally or quasi-ally in Asia, with the first priority being developing and maintaining the ability to conduct a denial defense of Taiwan. In light of this, the United States should maintain its existing defense perimeter in Asia. It should generally seek to avoid assuming additional alliances, particularly on the Asian mainland, but, if conditions require it, consider selectively adding a small number of Asian states as allies. The United States should also maintain a strong nuclear deterrent and a focused but effective counterterrorism posture; it should also maintain a missile defense shield against North Korea and Iran if this is not too costly. On the other hand, in order to focus its scarce resources, the United States should not size, shape, or posture its military to deal simultaneously with any other scenario alongside a war with China over Taiwan. Its first, overriding priority must be the effective defense of allies in Asia against China. If the United States does want additional insurance, however, it can make some provision for the one other scenario in which the United States might not realistically be able to defeat an opponent's theory of victory after defeating a Chinese assault on an ally in Asia: defeating a Russian fait accompli attempt against an eastern NATO ally, which is the only other scenario in which the United States could find itself facing a great power armed with a survivable nuclear arsenal and able to seize and hold allied territory. That said, the United States should seek to have European states assume the greater role in NATO. Last, this chapter considers what to do if both a denial defense and binding strategy fail; in this event, selective friendly nuclear proliferation may be the least bad option, though this would not be a panacea and would be dangerous.

In chapter 12, the book ends by emphasizing that the ultimate goal of this strategy is to be able to come to a decent peace and an acceptable détente with China. Achieving this, however, requires firm and focused action, and acceptance of the distinct possibility of war with China.

ACKNOWLEDGMENTS

I OWE A GREAT DEBT OF gratitude to many people for the support, illumination, and camaraderie that made this book possible. Naturally, the arguments and findings are my own and no one else's responsibility (or culpability), but I would never have come to them without the help of many friends, mentors, colleagues, and supporters.

In this vein, I give special thanks to: James Acton, Michael Albertson, Michael Allen, Ross Babbage, JR Backschies, Dennis Blair, Susanna Blume, Arnaud de Borchgrave, Shawn Brimley, Linton Brooks, Christian Brose, Curtis Buckles, Christopher Burnham, Tucker Carlson, Amy Chua, Ralph Cossa, Patrick Cronin, Abraham Denmark, Chris Dougherty, Ross Douthat, Thomas Ehrhard, Andrew Erdmann, Chris Estafanous, Ryan Evans, David Feith, Joe Felter, Thomas Fingar, Julie Finley, Ben Fitzgerald, Michèle Flournoy, Richard Fontaine, Aaron Friedberg, Mike Gallagher, Frank Gavin, Brett Gerry, Michael Gerson, Paul Gewirtz, Brad Glosserman, David Goldman, Michael Gordon, Alexander Gray, Boyden Gray, Chris Griffin, Jakub Grygiel, David Halberstam, David Hale, Rylan Hamilton, Jacob Heilbrunn, Kate Heinzelman, Jerry Hendrix, Larry Hirsch, Samuel Hornblower, Reuben Jeffery, David Johnson, Boleslaw Kabala, Andrew Krepinevich, James Kurth, Daniel Kurtz-Phelan, Burgess Laird, John Langan, Jeffrey Larsen, Ronald Lehman, Thomas Lehrman, Austin Long, Kent Lucken, Edward Luttwak, John Lyons, Harvey Mansfield, Roman Martinez, William McCants, Michael McDevitt, Brent McIntosh, Renny McPherson, Bronwen McShea, Richard Mies, Frank Miller, Louis Miller, Siddharth Mohandas, Mark Montgomery, Colin Moran, Grayson Murphy, Justin Muzinich, John Negroponte, Paul Nitze,

William Odom, Steven Ozment, Jonathan Page, George Perkovich, Richard Posner, Matthew Pottinger, Michael Reisman, Andres Reyes, Charles Robb, Carl Robichaud, Matthew Rojansky, William Rosenau, Joel Rosenthal, Boris Ruge, Reihan Salam, Eric Sayers, Nadia Schadlow, Paul Scharre, Thomas Schelling, Randy Schriver, Paul Schulte, John Shea, David Shedd, Laurence Silberman, Kristen Silverberg, Peter Swartz, Sugio Takahashi, Ashley Tellis, Bruno Tertrais, Jim Thomas, Michael Thompson, Jessie Tisch, Ashley Townshend, Michael Urena, Dustin Walker, John Warden, Ted Warner, David Weiss, Reed Werner, Peter Wilson, Ted Wittenstein, Jeffrey Wolf, Shirley Woodward, Robert Work, Thomas Wright, Dov Zakheim, Roger Zakheim, and Robert Zarate. I am particularly grateful to those who not only influenced my thinking but also took the time to review and comment on drafts of parts or all of the book: Jonathan Burks, Dale Copeland, Billy Fabian, Jonathan Finer, Josh Hawley, Larry Hirsch, Robert Jervis, Robert Kaplan, Adam Klein, Michael Leiter, Paul Lettow, Jim Miller, Wess Mitchell, Jim Mitre, Evan Montgomery, David Ochmanek, Ely Ratner, Kaleb Redden, Brad Roberts, Thomas Shugart, Walter Slocombe, Jonathan Solomon, Evan Thomas, and Daniel Tobin.

I especially thank and acknowledge those who shaped and enabled my thinking during my time at the Pentagon working on the National Defense Strategy—most of all former Secretary of Defense James Mattis. It was an extraordinary honor to work for him on this critical effort, and his vision and leadership made it possible. I also thank, in addition to those already mentioned, David Allvin, Jack Arthaud, Krista Auchenbach, James Baker, Phil Davidson, Anthony DeMartino, Michael Donofrio, Michael Duffey, John Ferrari, Dan Folliard, Tom Goffus, Clint Hinote, William Hix, Frank Hoffman, Justin Johnson, Paul Lyons, Stuart Munsch, David Norquist, Buzz Phillips, Patrick Shanahan, Rob Soofer, Cliff Trout, Greg Weaver, Rob Weiler, Katie Wheelbarger, and the superb NDS/SFD team.

Special thanks to those who helped make this book possible with Yale University Press, especially Bill Frucht, whose editing has greatly improved the manuscript and whose support has been invaluable, as well as Laura Jones Dooley, Margaret Otzel, and Karen Olson. Working with Yale has been a great pleasure.

Thanks also to my agent, Henry Thayer, an excellent counselor and advocate.

I also thank The Marathon Initiative, especially my partner Wess Mitchell, and the Center for a New American Security, especially Richard Fontaine and Ely Ratner, for enabling and supporting my work on this book, and the Hirsch

Family and Smith Richardson Foundations for critical support for my ability to write it.

I am grateful to Andrew Rhodes, who contributed the very helpful and creative maps.

Yashar Parsie and Carsten Schmiedl provided excellent aid with the endnotes; Yashar also did superb conceptual work researching numerous difficult questions that arose and played a critical role in finalizing the manuscript.

This book would simply not be what it is without Alexander Velez-Green, to whom I owe an inestimable debt. Alex's brilliance, rigor, care, and effort were invaluable in helping transform a rough and often jumbled manuscript into this final product. A great many of the ideas, structure, and logical constructs of this book—their heart—bear Alex's profound imprint. I cannot thank him enough.

Last, I thank my family—my mother, Susan; sister, Emily; brother, George; and extended family, especially my uncles, Paul, Carl, and John; my aunts Christine and Amie; my cousin Arthur; my grandparents; and my mother-in-law, Ana Maria, for their wonderful support, encouragement, and many years of patience and good nature in putting up with all my eccentric interests.

To my wife, Susana, my true partner in all things, I owe inexhaustible thanks for her loving support, inspiration, and counsel. She never flagged in her support for and valuing of this consuming project. To our boys, Orlando and Thomas, I hope that this book helps in some small way to bring about a decent peace that they and their contemporaries may enjoy and use to good effect.

THE STRATEGY OF DENIAL

The Purposes of American Strategy

A DEFENSE STRATEGY IS A WAY of employing, posturing, and developing military assets, forces, and relationships to attain a set of goals that are derived from and designed to serve broader political aims. My purpose in this book is to consider what America's defense strategy should be.

The Fundamental Purposes of American Strategy

Charting such a strategy must begin with identifying America's overall national objectives. These are, of course, subject to debate and not susceptible to precise definition; it is in the nature of a free society that these core questions are never fully settled. Yet certain fundamental political goals are very likely to command broad agreement among Americans. These are to maintain the nation's territorial integrity and, within that territory, security from foreign attack; sustain a free, autonomous, and vigorous democratic-republican political order; and enable economic flourishing and growth. In simpler terms, our basic national objectives are to provide Americans with physical security, freedom, and prosperity.[1]

Physical security is the cornerstone of all other interests and values; without it, people cannot take advantage of either freedom or prosperity and may lose them entirely. But physical security alone is not sufficient. To fulfill even the most basic understanding of America's political purposes, Americans must be free enough to determine their national life—to choose their own fate. Last,

Americans must be sufficiently prosperous, not only for its own sake but to undergird confidence in their society's fairness. Americans may elect to pursue ends beyond these three, but they may plausibly do so only if they are sufficiently secure, free, and prosperous.

The Central Role of the Balance of Power

The international arena in which the United States pursues these objectives remains anarchic, in the sense that there is no global sovereign to make and enforce judgments in a dispute.[2] In this context, security, freedom, and prosperity cannot be taken for granted; they are not self-generating. This is for two reasons. First, in an ungoverned situation, actors may rationally seek advantage and profit by using force to take from or undermine others. Second, inherently vulnerable actors may find it prudent to take preventive action against potential threats: the best defense may be a good offense. These factors mean that the prospect of force shadows Americans' pursuit of these goals.

To ensure its security, freedom, and prosperity, any country, including the United States, has a most powerful interest in ensuring *a favorable balance of power* with respect to its key interests. This is simply another way of saying that the most effective way to check another from doing something one does not want to abide is to be more powerful than the other is with respect to that interest. If one fails to maintain a favorable balance, one's enjoyment of these goods will be at the sufferance of the one who enjoys the advantage.

Ensuring America's security, freedom, and prosperity thus requires us to address the foundational role of power. To fulfill its core purposes, the United States should seek sustainably favorable military-economic balances of power with respect to the key regions of the world. In this chapter I will lay out the following key principles:

- Power in this context is composed of military-economic strength.
- The actors that matter most are states.
- Balances of power particularly matter in the key regions of the world, which are those where military-economic strength is clustered.
- The purpose of balancing is to deny another state hegemony over one of the key regions of the world.
- The favorable balance should be sustainable over time.

What Is the Balance of Power?

Physical force, especially the ability to kill, is the ultimate form of coercive leverage. While there are other sources of influence, such as wealth, persuasiveness, and charisma, they are all dominated by the power to kill. One with the ability to kill another can, if willing, escalate any dispute to that level and thus prevail. Although hard power is not the only form of power, it is dominant if effectively employed; hard power always has the capacity to dominate soft power. Left unaddressed, might trumps right. Therefore, to protect its interests, the United States must be especially concerned about the use of physical force.

In stable societies, the sovereign monopolizes the legitimate use of violence: this is law and order. But because there is no global sovereign, war—violence at a large and organized scale—is the final court of appeal in the international arena; if a disputant resorts to force, differences will ultimately be resolved in favor of the side that more effectively musters enough military power. To protect their interests in the international sphere, states such as the United States must therefore actively address the threat of violent force.

This is not to say that violence is always the most visible element of power. To the contrary: other elements of power—political, commercial, intellectual, ideological, spiritual—are usually more prominent, and mutually beneficial co-operation is normal and natural. But this is true only when the threat of violence is confined and regulated, and because of its capacity to dominate, this in turn requires the threat of violence itself. In other words, precisely to allow these softer instruments of power to be more influential, the threat of violence needs to be constrained. And because violence is the most important element of power, military power is ultimately necessary to constrain it.

Who Matters for the Balance of Power?

This reality means that US strategy for the world must first and foremost reckon with those with the power to wield large-scale violence, which means those that can muster military power. Less powerful actors, particularly those with some means of wreaking catastrophic violence (such as weapons of mass destruction), can pose a serious threat, but their weakness, by definition, means that more powerful parties have ways to deal with them. Specifically how the United States can do so is addressed later in this book.

In the modern world, military power derives from the ability to raise and command capable armed forces. Modern militaries, especially the more advanced and effective ones, are highly sophisticated, complex, and often large. They are therefore expensive and must be supported by advanced, robust economic and technological bases. Further, they are administratively and logistically demanding and need highly capable administrative structures to enforce the cohesion and command the obedience needed for effective war making.

In the contemporary era and for the foreseeable future, the only entities able to generate such modern militaries are *states*. The ultimate form of power in the international system, then, results from a state or group of states leveraging violence. And the states that have the most of this fundamental coercive leverage are those with the most wealth and internal cohesion. Thus, in practice, the states with the most military power are those with the greatest economic resources.

If the United States were more powerful in this sense than any combination of other states, it would enjoy a favorable power advantage under any conceivable circumstances. In such a situation, no state could meaningfully coerce it. To maintain such a favorable distribution, it would need only to tend to its own power base to at least stay abreast of other states' growth.

The United States does not, however, enjoy such a preponderance of power—nor will it. Rather, although it is very powerful, its power is substantially outweighed by that of the rest of the world.[3] If enough of the rest of the world's power were aggregated against it, the United States could be coerced with respect to its security, freedom, and prosperity; others could compel it to accept things Americans really do not want to tolerate. Accordingly, the United States should not allow such an unfavorable balance of power to form against it.

Where Does the Balance of Power Matter?

The states that matter most—the ones whose economies can support the generation of significant military power—are not randomly distributed but are clustered in particular regions. These key regions boast the vast majority of the active or latent military power that constitutes the most coercive form of leverage. In addition to North America, there are two regions—Asia and Europe—that have as much or more economic capacity that could be translated into military power as the United States and one subregion—the Persian Gulf—of notable significance.

The key regions of the world, ranked in order of geopolitical importance, are:

- *Asia.* Asia comprises approximately 40 percent of global gross domestic product (GDP), and given that it is the locus of about two-thirds of global growth, its share of global economic activity is rising.[4] Taken together, the Asian economies are already far larger than that of the United States and are increasingly advanced economically and technologically. From a geopolitical perspective, Asia is therefore the world's most important region.
- *Europe.* Europe comprises nearly one-quarter of global GDP, and its economies are on the whole considerably more advanced than most of Asia's.[5] For the United States, it is therefore the critical secondary external region after Asia.
- *North America.* North America is geopolitically important because of the United States. According to widely used estimates, the United States accounts for just under one-fifth of global GDP in purchasing power parity (PPP) terms. Largely because of this, most assessments rank the United States first in global power, though some indicate that China has surpassed it.[6] The rest of North America is modest in power and share of global economic activity, making the region unique in that it is overwhelmingly dominated by a single state.
- *The Persian Gulf.* The Persian Gulf is a far smaller and less important region than the others, comprising less than 5 percent of global GDP.[7] The Persian Gulf is home, however, to roughly 40 percent of the world's oil and natural gas reserves.[8] Control over these resources would provide a large source of power that could be readily leveraged, given their centrality in the carbon-based world economy. This strategic concern does not, however, extend to the remainder of the Middle East and North Africa; the power of this area would not make a material difference to American security, freedom, or prosperity.[9] The United States has a direct interest in preventing transnational terrorism against itself or its allies, but this is a more limited concern that can be addressed more narrowly.

The rest of the world is considerably less important in terms of military-economic power. If all of Latin America were to be agglomerated, it would represent approximately one-half of the total power of the United States.[10] This is significant, but by itself it would be manageable. The United States could not be meaningfully coerced by a grouping representing just half its power. Africa, the world's remaining major inhabited continent, is the least developed part of the world. Sub-Saharan Africa represents roughly 3 percent of global GDP, so gathering its power together would not result in a major threat to the United States.[11] Central Asia has some wealth and natural resources, but not nearly enough to plausibly contest core US purposes.[12] The rest of the world offers little power. Oceania is exceptionally small in population and economic power, and the poles are unoccupied. The fates of these regions are essentially completely determined elsewhere. The same is true of outer space for the foreseeable future.

Asia in particular and then Europe and North America are thus the decisive theaters for global politics; Asia alone is a larger economy than Africa, Latin America, Central Asia, and Oceania combined.[13] If a state could leverage the wealth of one of those decisive theaters, it could dominate a state ascendant in one of the other regions. It was this recognition that led Winston Churchill to remark, "If we win the big battle in the decisive theater, we can put everything straight afterwards."[14] For this reason, the United States has long been focused on what George Kennan famously identified in the early Cold War as the key "centers of military and industrial power."[15]

What Is Balancing Supposed to Do?

The mere existence of power in key regions is not what the United States should fear. Instead, it should care about the use of the power of these regions to materially impair America's security, freedom, and prosperity.

American concern should therefore focus on a state or states that could direct or marshal the power of one of these key regions. This is because no single state in the current environment—not even China, the world's other most powerful state—possesses sufficient power on its own to plausibly coerce the United States over its fundamental purposes; only some conglomeration of other states could gather the power to do this. Thus the only way the United States could face a situation in which other states were substantially stronger than America over the issues it really cares about would be if the power of one or more of these key regions were agglomerated.

The most plausible form by which a state could accumulate such power is *hegemony,* meaning that a state exercises authority over other states and extracts benefits from them, but without the responsibilities or risks of direct control. In

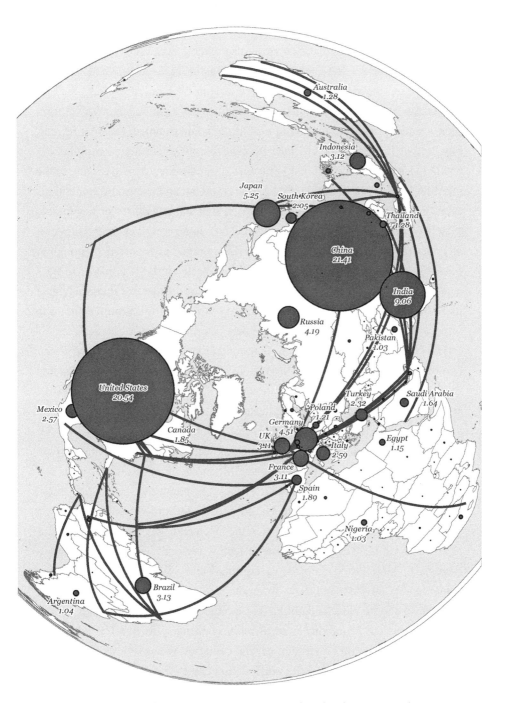

Global distribution of economic power. Proportional circles depict national GDP in USD trillions, at 2018 PPP rates. Economies over $1 trillion are labeled with total GDP value. Lines depict direct flight paths of top global long-haul air routes. Lambert Equal Area Projection. Original map by Andrew Rhodes.

this book I will use the term *predominance* interchangeably with *hegemony*.[16] (Empire, the other way that states exercise control over other states, is much more costly because it requires direct administrative control by the imperial center. Direct imperial control tends to be rarer in the modern world.)

It is almost invariably a unitary state that can aspire to hegemony over a region. In theory, a group or coalition of states could establish regional hegemony, but such a group would face tremendous collective action problems in trying to establish and sustain a joint form of predominance. This is due to the question of who would decide if the group could not agree on some contentious issue. Because of this, it is very difficult to find stable empires or hegemonic systems that involve shared state power. Thus an aspiring hegemon is, generally speaking, a state located or active in the region that is powerful enough to plausibly establish hegemonic control. More particularly, it is likely to be a state that is the most powerful within a region by a considerable margin. A state that is the strongest by only a modest degree will find it much more difficult to impose its predominance over its neighbors, for reasons I will discuss later.

The United States has reason to fear another state pursuing hegemony over one of the world's key regions because regional hegemony is highly alluring; there are potent incentives for a state to seek it, especially if it does not face a sufficient counterforce. Because of these advantages, the strongest states within a region almost always seek predominance at some point. The history of modern Europe is a catalog of attempts by very powerful states to gain regional hegemony: the sixteenth-century Habsburg Monarchy, France under Louis XIV and then Napoleon, Second and Third Reich Germany, and the Soviet Union. China held regional sway in East Asia for much of recorded history, and Japan sought it after it leapt ahead of China in the nineteenth and early twentieth centuries. The United States established effective regional hegemony in Central America and the Caribbean in the nineteenth century. We should not expect the contemporary environment to be different.

Because of Asia's size and military-economic potential, ensuring that it is not subjected to such hegemony is of primary importance for the United States. Asia is once again, after a lapse of several centuries, the area of the world with the greatest total wealth and the greatest capacity to translate that wealth into military power. That another state might establish hegemony over significant parts of Asia is therefore the most concerning possible regional scenario for the United States.[17]

Moreover, Asia also contains the world's most plausible aspirant to hegemony over one of the world's key regions: China. The People's Republic of China is by far the most powerful state, other than the United States, in the international system, and it is much more powerful than other states in Asia. China is a rising giant with a GDP that is nearly one-fifth of the global total; most assessments rank China as the world's second most powerful state, behind the United States, with some judging that it is more powerful than America.[18] China even rivals the total power of the other states within its region. Estimates of its power relative to the other Asian states suggest that it represents roughly half of Asia's power potential, placing it in a prime position to pursue regional predominance.[19] More to the point, there is much evidence that China *is* pursuing regional hegemony.[20]

Europe follows Asia as the other decisive theater for the United States. It has a smaller total economy than Asia but still accounts for about a quarter of global GDP.[21] Unlike Asia, however, no state in Europe is clearly preeminent. The state most commonly thought to be interested in regional predominance is Russia, and during the Cold War hegemony by the Soviet Union was a realistic prospect. Russia's economy, however, is only the second largest in PPP terms within Europe, behind Germany, and only slightly larger than those of the United Kingdom, France, or Italy.[22] No European state is anywhere near as powerful and wealthy relative to its neighbors as China is in Asia.

The Persian Gulf is a distant third in priority. While its natural resource wealth is highly leverageable for coercive purposes, it is the smallest economy of the key regions, and no state in the region is overwhelmingly stronger than its neighbors. Iran may aspire to regional hegemony, but it does not enjoy a commanding power advantage even within the region.[23]

The United States is effectively a hegemon in North and Central America, and it will not have any difficulty sustaining this position. For reasons I will discuss later, US hegemony over this region is compatible with and indeed beneficial for many other countries' interests.

There are two essential, related reasons for the United States to be very concerned about another state's establishing hegemony over Asia, Europe, or the Persian Gulf. These reasons are not self-evident because these regions are far from the United States, across great oceans.

The most straightforward reason is that, once it had secured such hegemonic power, a state could consolidate and leverage it to project violent force elsewhere, including into North America, and perhaps even occupy or subordinate the United

States. This of course would directly violate the most fundamental goods and purposes of American life. If Germany had won the Second World War in Europe or the Soviet Union had prevailed in the Cold War, either might very well have sooner or later sought to project military force against the United States.

This concern, though serious in principle, is rather remote. The United States lies behind two great oceans and is enormously rich and powerful. It can defend itself and its strategic sphere with the military afforded by the world's most sophisticated large economy, ultimately backed by a survivable nuclear arsenal that can impose the most punishing costs on an invader. Thus the United States has enormous resources for defense of its immediate sphere.

Moreover, the benefits of actually invading or aggressively projecting power into North America may not appear compelling to an established hegemon in Asia or Europe, considering the risks and costs it would entail. Given the influence and eminence afforded by ascendancy over one or both of these key regions, venturing to assault the North American continent might not add enough benefit to outweigh the costs. Hegemonic powers, especially more commercially oriented ones, often recognize the value of bounding their conquests. Even the Romans drew a limit to their power at the Danube and Rhine.

The more plausible and thus compelling reason why the United States should be so concerned about regional hegemons is less direct but nonetheless implicates the fundamental purpose of ensuring a free and uncoerced national life and prosperity. If a state such as China could establish hegemony over a key region such as Asia, it would have substantial incentives to use its power to disfavor and exclude the United States from reasonably free trade and access to these wealthy regions in ways that would undermine America's core purposes, shift the balance of power against the United States, and ultimately open the country to direct coercion in ways that would compromise Americans' freedom, prosperity, and even physical security.[24]

This is because, if China could establish hegemony over Asia, it could then set up a commercial and trading bloc anchored in the world's largest market that would privilege its own and subordinates' economies while disfavoring America's.[25] The resulting drain on American businesses, large and small, would be most keenly felt by the workers, families, and communities who rely on those businesses for jobs, goods, services, and the other benefits that come with a vibrant economy. The steady erosion of America's economic power would ultimately weaken the nation's social vitality and stability.

This kind of disfavoring is hardly a theoretical concern; China today appears to be seeking to shape the economic map in just this way.[26] Nor is it especially unusual; this sort of policy has a powerful appeal and internal logic and is a regular feature of how aspiring and established hegemons behave.[27] Essentially every aspiring hegemon in history has sought or planned to establish an economic system favoring itself, in order to enrich itself, sustain its predominance, and exclude or disfavor potential competitors. Examples range from Napoleon's Continental System to imperial Germany's Customs Union to Japan's Greater East Asia Co-Prosperity Sphere.[28] The United States itself has historically sought to create an economic sphere in North and Central America, including, most recently, through such arrangements as the North American Free Trade Agreement and the US-Mexico-Canada Agreement.

An aspiring hegemon like China would have at least three reasons to pursue an economic bloc approach privileging its own economy and prejudicing the American one: economics, geopolitics, and status.

First, China's leaders might—and indeed appear to—think that such a bloc is the most prudent way to advance their state's economic strength.[29] They might judge a trading or regulatory bloc anchored in Asia that they can control or substantially influence preferable to exposure in a competitive global market that they do not control.[30] Dominating an economic bloc with large internal flows of trade, capital, and labor would help insulate Beijing from global economic shocks and the attendant risk of slowing growth. Disfavoring the United States might seem necessary in order to form and sustain a cohesive bloc of China's own and resist what Beijing might regard as disruption by the United States and others.

Such a bloc could enable China to more effectively shape its own social and political future. State economic policies are not merely technical matters of maximizing growth and standards of living; they have deep implications for how societies evolve and are structured. Some societies may prefer political stability over uneven growth, or equality over wealth generation.[31] To achieve their goals, however, states must have the economic power to shape their societies in the face of enormously potent international economic forces. In light of this, China would be in a much stronger position to shape its own social-political destiny if it could dominate a large economic bloc; this would allow it to compete from a position of strength and more effectively regulate flows of trade, capital, and labor to promote its own preferred goals.

There are also more strictly economic reasons for China to pursue such a bloc. High-end economic activity is not randomly distributed; rather, it is clustered in North America, Europe, and East Asia. China might wish to channel this kind of economic activity to its own companies and workers in order to place itself at the forefront of the global economy, with all the benefits that would bring.[32] It might do this by nurturing industries it regards as important and by generating a large enough domestic market to enable its firms to grow and eventually gain the commanding heights of the global economy. An economic bloc that China controlled would offer a favorable basis for developing such industries.[33]

This, too, is hardly theoretical; in key respects it simply describes China's behavior over the last generation. The economy of the People's Republic of China, though in some respects a free market, involves a level of state involvement that the United States judges to be unfair and inimical to its interests.[34] In China's efforts to ascend the ladder of economic activity, shifting from a low-wage, labor-intensive economy to more capital-intensive forms of production, it has acted in ways the United States regards as discriminatory or worse. It appears clearly to be pursuing policies designed to shape its regional environment to insulate and promote its own preferred model.

Nor does Beijing seem to be changing this approach. China's pattern over the past decade has been to resist fundamental changes to this model in the face of both blandishments and pressure.[35] If extensive global economic engagement and growing wealth have not already persuaded China to change its behavior, it is unclear why it would be more likely to do so as it grows stronger and thus less susceptible to outside pressure. A state like China, with a deeply entrenched economic model that is fundamentally different from—and in key respects antithetical to—that of the United States, seems more likely to continue the course that has brought it wealth and power.

A second reason why a state like China might seek to develop an economic bloc that disfavored the United States is geopolitical: precisely to weaken the primary threat to its predominance.[36] One of the cardinal challenges of politics, and certainly of ascendancy over other states and peoples, is how to maintain one's power and the preferences it secures. China is no exception.

China would therefore have a most potent interest in reducing the power of any state that could challenge its predominance—and no state is stronger in the international system than the United States. Beijing could weaken the United States by wholly or partially excluding it from or disfavoring its engagements within important markets over which China exercised control or influence.[37] An arrangement that burdened America's ability to trade with Asia, which is the world's largest market and includes many of the world's most advanced economies, would depress the relative wealth of the United States. This in turn would weaken American power and consequently its ability to influence events.[38] A diminished United States would be less able to disrupt or challenge China's influence, and Beijing would be increasingly able to influence Washington's policies more through its growing power advantage and consequent leverage.[39]

A third and final key reason why a hegemon like China might pursue a discriminatory regional economic system is for status. Germany under Kaiser Wilhelm II yearned for a place in the sun, and twentieth-century China wished to stand up and once again be a great power in the world. China might thus see preeminence as a crucial benefit in its own right, and knocking the mighty United States down a peg would be a natural part of attaining it. In establishing its economic policy, a hegemon like China might favor a discriminatory market system precisely in order to reduce America's relative standing vis-à-vis China.

The consequences for the United States of being disfavored or excluded from Asia's vast markets would over time be very significant. Such a situation would result in the decline of Americans' prosperity and progressively weaken the United States' ability to resist being further disadvantaged, telling on the core purposes of American life. By undermining Americans' prosperity and expectations of future growth, China would make American society worse off and more susceptible to internal disputes over a stagnant economic pie.

Even more, a weakened United States riven by internal disputes would be more vulnerable to external pressure and even coercion, especially by an increasingly powerful China. Such a China would have far greater leverage to exercise influence in US internal affairs, whether through economic incentives and penalties, support or opposition to political groups, or propaganda and support—or outright ownership—of opinion-shaping outlets. China has already demonstrated a clear willingness to intervene in the United States' internal political affairs; there is every reason to think it will intensify that treatment if it gains the power to do so.[40]

Moreover, once established, such Chinese hegemony and its baleful influence would be difficult and costly for the United States to reverse. By definition, an established hegemon, able to direct the relevant policies of subordinate states, is harder to eject from its position than a state still grasping for hegemony.

This means that the United States must be concerned with even the possibility that a regional hegemon might pursue such disfavoring policies. Although a state like China, once so established, *might* pursue a more open-handed approach toward the United States, it also very well might not. Whether it did would be Beijing's choice, and there are more than enough reasons to think that it would not be respectful of US interests.

Especially because of this last point, US strategy must primarily be concerned with a potential hegemon, not only a declared or overtly aspiring hegemon, let alone an established one. This counsel is rooted in several reasons. First, intentions can change. Even a state that genuinely does not seek regional hegemony could later decide to. This might be because of new leadership: France under Louis XVI, for instance, was relatively content to maintain the status quo, but France under Napoleon a few years later was not. Or a state's perception of its strategic environment might alter: Mao's China in 1950 was rabidly hostile to the United States and aligned with the Soviet Union; just two decades later, Beijing had reversed itself.

Second, a state may want regional hegemony but conceal its aspirations behind lies, deceit, and distractions, as the Crowe Memorandum famously pointed out in the context of imperial Germany. Given the allure of regional hegemony, the United States should be skeptical of protestations of innocence regarding its pursuit. Contemporary China, governed by a Communist Party with a long record of dissimulation, is certainly no exception to this counsel.[41]

Third, preventing a capable state such as contemporary China from attaining regional hegemony is likely to be difficult and time-consuming; it is therefore necessary to act while the threat is still aborning. Even more, the United States is far less likely to be able to muster the power to reverse Chinese regional hegemony once established if Beijing does decide to pursue a more discriminatory course. Therefore the United States should err on the side of caution by seeking to prevent such a state from establishing predominance rather than waiting to be sure.

This is important because, even though it seems increasingly clear that China is pursuing regional hegemony, this assessment remains subject to debate. Given how powerful China is and will be, however, even if Beijing were not seeking regional hegemony, or if some future leadership decided not to do so, the United States would still need to ensure that China could not achieve regional hegemony at some later point.

This approach, of course, risks exacerbating a security dilemma with China. But so long as US efforts are clearly directed at denying Beijing hegemony rather than dismembering China, occupying it, or forcibly changing its government, the security dilemma should be manageable. The United States has no interest in dictating to China, only in blocking it from attaining regional hegemony. If a state genuinely does not seek hegemony, it should not fear efforts clearly limited to preventing it from doing so.[42] At the same time, the costs and risks of blocking a state from attaining regional hegemony that is genuinely uninterested in it should be low. Thus the risk of overpreparing is modest compared to the risks of failing to act in time.

It is important to emphasize that America's issue with a potential regional hegemon is primarily structural. The United States is fundamentally concerned about the condition of hegemonic domination of a key region because the incentives to exclude the United States exist for states of all kinds. It should be considerably less concerned about precisely which or what kind of state does establish such predominance. The United States should of course be *more* concerned if a state such as Nazi Germany or Soviet Russia were to gain regional hegemony because of such governments' violence and aggressiveness and their hostility to American preferences and values. But hegemony by any state, of whatever political complexion, would be a grave concern. China's achievement of hegemony would pose a serious challenge to US interests under any circumstances; that it would do so while governed by the Chinese Communist Party exacerbates the threat.

Over What Time Period?

The issue of state behavior changing over time casts into relief a crucial element of US interest: its fundamental strategic purpose is to sustainably avoid another state's hegemony over one of the world's key regions. Avoiding regional dominance today would not be very useful if it is going to happen in the future.

To summarize, then, the fundamental and primary objective of US strategy must be sustainably avoiding another state's hegemony over one of the key regions of the world. Because Asia has the largest economy of the key regions and China by far the largest other economy in the world, ensuring that China does not establish hegemony over Asia must be the United States' cardinal strategic aim.[43]

The Favorable Regional Balance of Power

THE WAY FOR THE UNITED STATES to ensure that another state does not establish hegemony over a key region is by maintaining favorable *regional* balances of power. Regional hegemony can be denied to a state such as China if enough other states in or active in the key region can league together to wield more power than the aspiring hegemon. If they are sufficiently strong, these other states can ensure that their important interests are respected. This balancing behavior is normal; safeguarding one's independence and autonomy is among the most basic impulses of state action, and since any hegemon threatens to compromise or eliminate states' self-determination, states naturally tend to seek to avoid falling under a hegemon's power. They thus have an incentive to collaborate with each other as well as with extraregional states that share their interest in averting another state's regional hegemony.

A group of states leaguing together to prevent another state from achieving such hegemony is an *anti-hegemonic coalition.* Such a coalition can include states both within and outside a region and may take many forms—formal or informal, open or quiet. The members of such a coalition need not even regard themselves as being in league. In the early modern period, for instance, France and the Protestant powers did not regard themselves as formally in league with the Ottoman Turks in opposing the Habsburg Empire.[1] The simple point is that such a grouping cooperates to maintain a regional balance of power sufficient to deny an aspirant's effort to establish hegemony.

Such balances of power involve, in the common phrase, "all elements of national power," including economic leverage and soft power.[2] Yet because most states naturally do not want to be subject to such hegemony and are willing to fight for their independence and autonomy, efforts by a state like China to gain such ascendancy create deep tension and thus potential for conflict. In other words, an aspirant's demand that other states submit to its hegemony, if pushed hard enough, will likely ultimately result in a fight. And because force is the foundational form of power and the ultimate arbiter of disputes in the anarchic international arena, the regional balance of power is at its core a question of military power. Matters of less profound interest to states may be solved with less grave forms of power, but whether states will bow to another's hegemony will ultimately be determined by the balance of military power.

This means that the regional balance of power is ultimately about whose military power would prevail in a test of arms. The question of who is weightier in the power balance would be decided by whether, when the conflict concluded, the aspirant was able to establish predominance over the region. This crucial conflict is a *systemic regional war,* the decisive war to determine whether the aspirant can establish hegemony over the region.

Such a systemic regional war is defined not by its contours but by its effect; it is the *decisive* conflict over whether an aspiring regional hegemon can achieve its aims.[3] A systemic regional war could take a number of forms, involving different groupings of nations engaged at different times and at varying levels of intensity. Its critical aspect, though, is that it decides whether an aspiring hegemon achieves its goal; even if the aspirant has not actually or fully defeated all those that oppose it, if it can gain through that war enough power to secure regional predominance, then the conflict is a systemic regional war.

To be effective, then, an anti-hegemonic coalition must involve enough states to be able to win such a war. These states may contribute in different ways—directly or indirectly, collectively or individually—but together they must be able to prevail in that contest if the coalition is to fulfill its purpose.

Given the stakes, such a conflict would naturally engage much of the combatants' strength. But, critically, a systemic regional war would not be resolved simply by tabulating the absolute strength of the sides.

This is for several reasons. First, if a distant state is important to the coalition, geography and military particularities might limit the degree to which its absolute power can be translated into war-making ability in the region. The continental United States is very far from Asia, for example, and this could impose a substantial tax on America's ability to fight in a systemic regional war there.

Second, a war to resolve the question of whether an aspirant like China would dominate a region like Asia might very well not engage the full power of one or both sides. In other words, such a war, even if very large, might remain limited in terms of the commitment of one or both sides. This is for a simple but extremely important reason—one or both sides might judge the perceived benefits of prevailing in such a total war not to be worth the costs and risks, and thus elect to restrain itself in the hopes of inducing restraint by the other side as well.

Thus the outcome of a systemic regional war would not be determined simply by the absolute power balance of the two sides. Rather, it would be won by the side that, within such constraints, had the will and way to employ its military forces to meet its objective. Because of this, situations may arise in which a state with much greater aggregate military power may not be willing or able to deny another state's bid for regional hegemony. Thus the United States might be more powerful than China in global terms, but if China were better able to project its power in Asia, or willing to fight harder and risk more to attain its goal than Washington was willing to commit to deny it, it could establish predominance over the region. This is why the *regional* balance of power is so critical.

It is important to understand how the prospect of this systemic regional war functions. The threat of such a conflict is normally latent and largely obscured; in the vast majority of state interactions, it is not a conscious consideration. The influence of a potential systemic regional war is most commonly felt through *imagined* wars—calculations by states about how such a war would unfold if it were to happen. These imagined wars normally remain implicit or latent because their outcomes are often relatively clear. Few wonder, for instance, how an Algerian or Sri Lankan invasion of the United States would go.

The more important imagined wars are those that might actually happen and would matter. States determine their courses of action on fundamental matters of political, military, and economic import based on their assessment of how such wars would unfold and how they would fare in them, and these decisions provide the framework within which the rest of state action takes place. Cold War history is incomprehensible without understanding that both NATO and the Warsaw Pact continually evaluated how a war between them would resolve and that they adjusted both their defenses and their political and economic policies accordingly.[4]

The influence of a systemic regional war functions in the same way. Because of the unique importance of such a decisive war, states make judgments as to how to behave based on their assessments of how it would resolve. If an aspiring hegemon judges it would prevail in such a conflict, it has the incentive to push the region to accept its hegemony. Normally, its interest is not to provoke such a war, since that would be costly for itself and reduce the value of its gains; rather, it is normally better off inducing other states to adjust their behavior based on the judgment that it would prevail if such a war were fought. If those other states perceive that a systemic regional war would result in victory by the aspirant, they will be impelled toward accommodating the aspirant's demands in order to avoid the futile suffering such a war would entail.

The Challenges to Forming and Sustaining an Anti-Hegemonic Coalition

The goal of an anti-hegemonic coalition, then, is to prevent an aspiring hegemon like China from dominating a region like Asia by convincing important states that it would prevail in a systemic regional war. The aspirant's goal is positive: establishing predominance. The coalition's goal, by contrast, is negative: *denial.*

An aspirant's attainment of its goal would mean that the other states in the region would lose or suffer the decline of goods that are normally considered central to a state's interest, including autonomy in decisions regarding trade, economic activity, and the employment of military force. Once established, moreover, a hegemon like China would have the power to coerce and thus direct these states, leaving them vulnerable to diminishment of goods that are even more central to their interests, such as domestic political self-determination and even independence.

Regional states thus have extraordinarily powerful incentives to resist the imposition of hegemony on them and should therefore be keen to form an anti-hegemonic coalition. This coalition need only be bound together by its shared opposition to an aspiring hegemon's bid for predominance; it can be very ecumenical. These factors would seem to make the formation and maintenance of an effective anti-hegemonic coalition relatively easy and reliable, and indeed history is replete with examples of effective intraregional balancing efforts. The history of Europe in the second millennium AD is one long record of them. In this light, should we not expect such countries as Japan, India, and the Southeast Asian states to come together in an effective coalition to check China's aspirations?

We should not be so sanguine. Such coalitions do not always form or always work if they do form. Sometimes aspiring hegemons get their way. This is because, despite regional states' shared interest in preserving their autonomy, their incentives do not always align in the ways needed to deny hegemony to an aspirant like China. The other states have varying degrees of vulnerability to a strong state's power, and the aspiring hegemon can exploit this divergence to undermine, divide, and fracture an anti-hegemonic coalition.

When regional states face an aspiring regional hegemon like China, their basic decision is whether to join the anti-hegemonic coalition and thereby seek to check the aspirant or to endorse or at least not resist its bid for predominance. This dilemma is commonly referred to as *balancing* or *bandwagoning*.[5]

The advantages of balancing for a state involved are that it fortifies the coalition, increasing its chances of checking the aspirant's bid for hegemony and wrapping the state in the coalition's broader defensive power. The risk is that, by placing itself in the aspirant's way, the balancing state exposes itself to the aspirant's power. Because Beijing has a powerful incentive to prevent such balancing, it has a great interest in deterring such behavior, including by punishing those that do balance. The choice to balance could thus lead to extensive damage to a balancing state at China's hands.

The advantage of bandwagoning or accommodating an aspirant like China, by contrast, is that it avoids such risks. By joining with the aspirant or merely not contesting it, the bandwagoning state removes itself from the aspirant's sights. Bandwagoning may also lead to rewards and preferential treatment. China, having such a large economy, has the ability to provide material inducements to bandwagoning states. It can also offer them a special place in the regional pecking order it seeks to establish. The cost of bandwagoning is that it can amount to a preemptive surrender of at least a portion of national autonomy, with no assurance that there will not be further loss if the aspirant achieves its goal. Moreover, it may expose the bandwagoning state to punishment by the anti-hegemonic coalition, which may also use violence as well as inducements to pursue its strategic aim of denial.

This choice between balancing and bandwagoning is not binary but rather falls along a spectrum. States can aggressively balance or fully kowtow, but they can also soft balance, attempt to be neutral, and pursue a range of other policies between the poles of full resistance and submission. A state's ideal policy is often to free ride—to stay out of the conflict and hope that the balancing coalition succeeds in checking the aspirant's bid for hegemony.

Asian states face just this kind of dilemma. Smaller, less developed states in Southeast Asia, for instance, worry about the compromise of their autonomy and the deference to Beijing entailed in a Chinese-dominated region, but they also fear being exposed to China's ire if they seek to balance. Even larger Japan and India wrestle with these trade-offs.

So, too, does the United States. The fundamental interest of the United States is in ensuring favorable regional balances of power so that it can deny any other state the ability to achieve hegemony over a key region. Critically, this does not necessarily dictate American involvement. America requires only that there be sufficient power and resolve whereby *some* state or coalition can defeat an aspiring hegemon such as China in a systemic regional war. Because of the enormous costs and risks of such a war, the United States has a very great interest in minimizing its involvement in such an effort—or avoiding it entirely.

Indeed, for the first century and more of the American Republic, the United States effectively free rode on European states'—above all Great Britain's—willingness and ability to check the emergence of a hegemonic European state that could project power into the Western Hemisphere. The United States' primary goals of security, freedom, and prosperity were served by a foreign policy—typified by the Monroe Doctrine—that sought to deny the intervention of outside powers into the Western Hemisphere that could threaten these goals. Yet given the very small effort and resources the United States dedicated to national defense during the nineteenth century, this policy's successful implementation relied largely on anti-hegemonic coalitions in Europe and on the British ability to prevent continental European states from projecting power into the Americas.[6] Behind this protective shield, the United States could focus on internal development and expansion while establishing strategic dominance in North America and eventually Central America and the Caribbean.

This basic US interest in denying another state hegemony over a key region, however, requires that enough individual states make decisions to balance together, despite their competing interests and the temptations to bandwagon or free ride. On what basis, and under what conditions, will enough states choose to do this? Naturally, many factors would enter into any state's decision on this point. At its core, however, a state is likely to choose to balance if it judges that the benefits of doing so outweigh its costs and risks. Put more concretely, enough states necessary to besting an aspiring hegemon in a systemic regional war need to see not only the appeal of preventing another state's hegemony but also that participating in balancing is prudent.

Most fundamentally, this requires that enough states judge that the balancing coalition is likely to work. They have to believe that the coalition stands a strong enough chance of prevailing in the ultimate court of appeal, the systemic regional war. If a state's leaders think the coalition would lose such a war, they will very likely conclude that joining the effort not only would be futile but would eventually expose the state to the victorious aspirant's chastisement. China, for one, is clearly not afraid to punish states that buck its will. It attacked Vietnam in 1979 and more recently has clashed with India along their disputed border and imposed punitive sanctions against Japan, South Korea, the Philippines, Taiwan, Vietnam, and others.[7] Thus the perception that the coalition would lose makes bandwagoning more attractive and would drive potential balancer states' incentives toward early accommodation. If, however, enough states join together that they would be able to win a systemic regional war, then this concern should be addressed.

But how a systemic regional war would play out is not the only factor for a deciding state. It needs to make its decision based on how *it individually* would fare in light of the aspirant's strategy, considering the balance of the costs *it* would endure against the benefits *it* would gain. Foreign policy is not missionary work, and national leaders think about such matters largely through the prism of their states' self-interest. Because of this, even a state that strongly values independence and autonomy could judge accommodation the more reasonable course if it believes the costs and risks it will incur by fighting the aspirant in a systemic regional war are too great.

This is for several reasons. First, while in principle regional states all share a powerful interest in resistance because they should all gain by protecting their independence and autonomy, in reality some states may value independence or sovereign integrity more highly than others. This means that some may find the hegemon's likely rule less objectionable than others. In addition, some states may have cultural, ethnic, ideological, or religious reasons for being less averse to an aspirant's achieving its goal; they may even prefer it. A state with a Communist government might welcome hegemony by another Communist state, just as some Christian states in the Middle East historically welcomed Christian European intervention in the region.

Then there is the more crucial factor of costs. What would a given state have to suffer to achieve the benefits of autonomy? Even if all states highly value independence, they might face different cost-benefit equations because their costs of resistance may vary. Anti-hegemonic coalitions are not formed or sustained in a vacuum. They take place in a given geography, among states with different characteristics, strengths, and weaknesses. In the case of Asia, this means most pointedly that potential members of such a coalition would be exposed to Beijing's military force and other forms of coercion to greater or lesser degrees depending on their location, strength, economy, and skill. Since violence is the ultimate and most effective form of coercion, at root this means that different states have different levels of vulnerability to an aspirant's ability to damage, assault, or conquer them. Simply because of distance, Australia is far less vulnerable to Chinese military attack than, for instance, Vietnam. Even if both states have the same level of resolve to protect their independence, Australia's risks in doing so are less severe than Vietnam's.

These differing assessments of both the value and the costs of resistance mean that there is no strictly rational compulsion for states to perceive the situation in exactly the same way and thus no reason to expect them to form common judgments as to how to respond to given moves or provocations by an aspirant such as China. This generates coordination problems, and the more states that must be involved in the coalition and the more those states' strategic situations differ, the more difficult those problems will be.[8]

The Focused and Sequential Strategy

This coordination problem is made especially acute because an aspirant like China is a strategic actor that can employ its coercive power and inducements specifically to prevent the potential coalition members from coalescing against it. Most essentially, it can focus its imposition of costs, or threats thereof, on one or a few potential coalition members while threatening great harm against the other members only if they defend the targeted class. China might, for instance, try to isolate Taiwan or Vietnam by offering to spare other members of such a coalition unless they come to its aid. Beijing can also use inducements to sweeten the bitter pill of compromise both for the directly targeted and for those considering defending them. The more powerful the aspirant is relative to the states in the coalition, the more daunting its threats and the more alluring its inducements. It can thus exacerbate the differences among coalition members and make it harder for the coalition to form or be sustained.

An aspirant like China can pursue this most pointedly through the threat or execution of focused wars against isolated coalition members, coupled with other coercive measures and inducements that together would be unlikely to result in a systemic regional war with the coalition that China would be too likely to lose.[9] Crucially, an aspirant like China can do this *sequentially*, deliberately not provoking or catalyzing a systemic regional war as it progressively shifts the balance of power against the coalition by selectively picking off its members, removing them from the coalition and possibly bringing them into its own pro-hegemonic coalition. The aspirant's optimal strategy is to avoid threatening or provoking a systemic regional war until it is confident that it can prevail in such a conflict.[10] By definition, then, when a state such as China assesses that the regional balance of power is not in its favor, its incentives are to avoid risking the systemic regional war until it has shifted the balance. Once it has attained the preponderance of power in the region, it can then advantageously threaten or, if need be, provoke the systemic regional war in order to definitively establish its predominance.

An aspirant like China can also create its own (possibly informal) coalition, composed of states that it has subordinated to the degree that they would dedicate resources to furthering its aims. The group might also include states that, for structural or other reasons, welcome the hegemony of a state such as China. These states could be motivated by cultural, ethnic, ideological, or religious reasons, but they also could include what we might call tertiary regional states— states that look to the aspiring *regional* hegemon to defend them against a potentially domineering *subregional* state. These smaller or weaker states might prefer a more distant, perhaps more detached regional hegemon over a nearer, secondary state whose dominance would be more painful or humiliating. Cambodia, for instance, has traditionally feared Vietnamese dominance and looked to China to restrain Hanoi; Pakistan looks to China to restrain India. Nor would the aspirant benefit only from affiliated states: states that chose not to affiliate with it overtly could also contribute to its efforts by, for instance, supplying crucial resources, as Sweden did for Germany and Thailand for Japan in the Second World War.

We can call this comprehensive approach the aspirant's *focused and sequential strategy*. If a state such as China can pick off or neutralize enough coalition members or potential members, it can eventually marshal enough combined power to win a systemic regional war against the anti-hegemonic coalition and thus establish its own hegemony. The effect of this is that, *even if* most states in a region prefer independence or autonomy, an aspirant like China could still attain hegemony if not enough states were willing to suffer the costs required to resist the aspirant when the balance of power was still in the coalition's favor. This is particularly relevant because, even though China is exceptionally strong, it is still not as strong as the rest of Asia, the United States, and other engaged actors in the region combined. If Beijing provoked a systemic war against such a broad coalition, it would likely lose. Hence the great appeal to Beijing of the focused and sequential strategy.

The upshot of this is that the fundamental calculus for any state deciding between balancing and bandwagoning would include not only whether the anti-hegemonic coalition would prevail in a systemic regional war at any given time. It would also need to include whether that coalition could operate effectively in the face of an aspiring hegemon's focused and sequential strategy, because left unaddressed, such a salami-slicing approach would ultimately enable Beijing to prevail.

It is crucial to stress here that although military force need not be the only component of a focused and sequential strategy, it is essential. It is often said that China poses primarily an economic and political challenge, not a military one.[11] But an aspirant like China cannot expect to establish regional hegemony with inducements and political and economic coercion alone, especially because it would need to recruit to its side major states with long records of independence, such as Japan, South Korea, India, Australia, and Vietnam. These states have the most potent incentives to act to preserve their autonomy, and Chinese inducements and promises can only go so far; if too generous, they would compromise Beijing's ability to secure predominance. Conversely, these states can work with each other and with other extraregional states to mitigate losses due to Beijing's political and economic coercion. For Beijing to achieve regional predominance, then, these states would need to see a much more potent disincentive to bucking China's aims, and although costs can be imposed in many ways, nothing is more effective leverage than the threat of physical violence. Thus even though China would presumably prefer to establish its hegemony peacefully, it must be able to wield a compelling threat of military force in order to persuade strong independent states to accept its predominance. This does not mean that Beijing must always emphasize the military instrument, certainly not on a day-to-day basis; rather, it means that China's military power must cast a sufficiently dark shadow over these states to persuade them to accept Chinese hegemony.[12]

Unsurprisingly, the growth of China's military maps very closely to this logic. Beijing has developed armed forces that are highly suited to attacking nearby states while being able to strike effectively at more distant potential coalition members, including the United States.[13] This will increasingly enable China to wage focused, sequential wars and thus to cow enough regional states to eventually gain the edge in the regional balance of power against the antihegemonic coalition.

The Importance of a Coalition Cornerstone

How can a sufficiently strong anti-hegemonic coalition be assembled and maintained in the face of this strategy? In particular, how can enough states that fear or might come to fear Chinese hegemony—states such as Japan, India, Australia, Vietnam, the Philippines, South Korea, Indonesia, Malaysia, and Taiwan—be convinced that by joining or aiding such a coalition, they will not be left standing alone should mighty China target them?

What they need is confidence. And what is therefore highly useful—even necessary—in such a context is a *cornerstone balancer:* a very powerful state to anchor the coalition.[14] Such a cornerstone state is so important because a very powerful aspirant like China has abundant means to pursue a focused and sequential strategy against any other regional state. Thus any potential coalition state, even stronger ones, could be subjected to the aspirant's painful attempt to isolate it. If even the strongest members of such a coalition are weak compared to the aspirant, as all states in Asia are to China, then they will likely buckle in the face of its concentrated power, and the coalition will eventually fail.

In such circumstances, the margin of error is simply too narrow for a coalition to function effectively. Any coalition state could be subjected to China's focused pressure, and in that position, it would have to rely heavily on multiple other coalition members, each of them also weak compared to Beijing, coming to its aid. Such a defense could ill afford to lose any significant coalition partners. Many things, therefore, would need to go right in coordinating such a grouping. This lack of resilience would tend to make regional states cautious about joining the coalition.

The involvement of a very strong state comparable in power to China is thus highly valuable for several reasons. First, the involvement of such a state by definition makes the coalition more powerful and improves the likelihood of its success. Second, a powerful state's involvement makes forming and sustaining the coalition less complicated. If simply getting the coalition off the ground requires assembling myriad smaller entities, each with its own calculus, the task is much more complex and uncertain. The involvement of a very powerful state makes each smaller state's involvement less necessary, widening the coalition's margin of error and increasing the reasonableness of affiliating with it.

Third, such a powerful state is likely to be less susceptible to the aspirant's coercive influence. Such a state is therefore more likely to remain in the coalition, stand firm in its role, and help defend other coalition members. Together, these factors make affiliating with the coalition a more attractive and prudent option for the weaker states, thereby further improving the coalition's prospects.

These dynamics are familiar from everyday life. Anyone who has raised money for a company or an initiative knows the value of a cornerstone investor or donor, just as anyone who has put together a conference or event knows the value of engaging a big-name speaker early. Money, time, and effort are scarce, so people look to see who has already given their money or time to ensure that they are not wasting their own. When a big mover is involved, one can feel more confident that one's money or time will not be wasted. The international arena is little different: having a cornerstone state in a coalition makes other states more confident that they will not be left exposed and helpless before the aspiring hegemon.

Such a cornerstone state can be located within the key region, but it need not be. It may instead be an *external* cornerstone balancer. It merely needs to have the ability to project power into the region sufficient for the coalition's purposes. This concept is particularly relevant to the United States.

The United States as an External Cornerstone Balancer

The United States cannot, then, simply assume that effective anti-hegemonic coalitions will always form and cohere in the key regions of the world. And the more fragmented a potential coalition is and the weaker its potential members are relative to the aspiring hegemon, the harder it will be for such a coalition to form and operate. But although the United States has a great interest in preventing another state's hegemony over any key region, it also has a potent interest in avoiding unnecessary entanglement. Accordingly, the United States should become heavily engaged only if such a coalition is unlikely to form and sustain itself without such US involvement.

This is crucial because, again, the United States does not *need* to be directly engaged in generating or sustaining favorable balances of power in the key regions of the world. Indeed, all things being equal, it is better to avoid such engagement, which carries substantial costs and risks. As a general principle, then, the United States should look upon heavy, risky intervention in key regions with distinct skepticism. If a favorable balance of power denying an aspirant regional hegemony can be maintained without US involvement, so much the better. The United States should become directly and substantially engaged only if a favorable balance of power is unlikely to be maintained in a key region without it.

Historically, deep strategic US engagement abroad has been driven by just such an assessment. The United States resisted deep engagement in Europe for most of its history, even after the First World War, but committed to sustained involvement after the Second World War when it became clear that Great Britain and France could not, by themselves, hold off a Soviet bid for hegemony over the continent. The United States became heavily involved in Asia much earlier, largely because Asia had no stable anti-hegemonic coalition; the United States took a leading role in denying Japan regional hegemony beginning in the 1930s. The United States became more heavily involved in the Persian Gulf in the 1970s after Britain's withdrawal, when it appeared the Soviet Union might seek predominance over the region's oil fields.[15]

This focused approach to engagement in other key regions has meant that countries in Europe and Asia have had less reason to fear the United States. Moreover, because so many states in these key regions have a strong interest in a sufficiently powerful external cornerstone balancer to protect them from hegemony by their neighbors, many countries actually have an interest in the United States sustaining a hegemonic position in its own region. Whatever interest Japan, India, Australia, or Vietnam has in diminishing US hegemony in North and Central America is outweighed by their interest in having a strong and capable state to help deny China hegemony over them, which is greatly eased by America's hegemonic position in its own sphere. In other words, many states have an interest in US hegemony in its own region because this increases America's ability to project power to help deny other states hegemony in distant regions.[16]

This criterion for US strategy also helps explain a puzzle left by the conventional narrative of American strategic history, which identifies the nation's entry into the Second World War and its international leadership afterward as embodying a national shift from isolationism to internationalism. This account overlooks the United States' long history of active engagement in Asia, which dates back at least to the occupation of the Philippines and the Open Door Policy, and even to the opening of Japan in the 1850s. A more parsimonious account explains US behavior as resulting from the increasing importance of its role in ensuring that no other state could dominate a region key to American interests, not from a wholesale transformation in the United States' conception of its role in the world.

In other words, although history does not follow straight lines, US behavior over the long course of the Republic fits the proposition that America has become deeply engaged in other key regions when its intervention was necessary to avert another state's establishment of hegemony there. So long as the United States did not need to become actively involved in denying other states' regional hegemony, it largely did not, since free riding was, and if tenable remains, a more attractive course. When intervention became necessary, America's behavior changed—not its fundamental strategic goals.

My approach in this book—arguing that America's key foreign policy goal is to prevent another state from gaining hegemony over a key region of the world—is, then, consistent with how the country has behaved over its history as an independent republic. Hewing to it does not involve a fundamental change in Americans' conception of how their nation should behave in the world.

The Prospects for Anti-Hegemonic Coalitions Today

American strategy, then, should be based on whether effective anti-hegemonic coalitions are likely to form and sustain themselves in key regions without significant US involvement. What are the prospects for such coalitions?

Asia

The United States is already deeply embedded in East Asia and the Western Pacific through a network of bilateral alliances. Leaving aside for now the difficulties that would attend to withdrawing from these positions, it is very unlikely that an effective anti-hegemonic coalition would form and operate in the region if America did pull out from the region. Given China's enormous power, comprising roughly half of Asia's total, any coalition in Asia to check Chinese pretensions for hegemony that did not include the United States would need to include the great bulk of the other important states: not only Japan and India but also South Korea, the major Southeast Asian states, Australia, and probably even Russia. No such purely Asian grouping exists today; links among the Asian states are relatively attenuated compared to those within Europe, and thinly tied multilateral institutions such as the Association of Southeast Asian Nations (ASEAN) are ill suited for this role.

There are two states in the region that could plausibly try to serve as cornerstones to address these issues: Japan and India. The rest of the states in the region are completely dwarfed by Chinese power, rendering them implausible for such a role. Other than the United States, no outside state is strong enough to project enough power into the region to serve as a cornerstone.

One of the regional candidates, Japan, was one of the two primary regional states during most of the modern period (China being the other). Japan is today the largest advanced economy in the region outside of China. But it is doubtful that other regional states would view Japan as a workable cornerstone. Most important, Japan is simply not powerful enough; it is estimated to have less than one-fifth China's overall power.[17] Although its economy is more sophisticated, it is a quarter the size of China's and likely to keep shrinking in relative terms; the technological gap between the two nations is also narrowing. Even if Tokyo were to develop its military power, the power imbalance between China and Japan would remain vast. Moreover, given Japan's reach for regional hegemony in the 1930s and 1940s, any effort to take the leading part in regional political and military affairs might well face strong opposition from neighboring states.

India, by contrast, is a very large economy that could at some point rival China in total power. The Indian economy is over 40 percent the size of China's, and India is estimated to have over one-third of China's overall power. For the coming decades, however, India's economy will be much smaller and less developed than China's.[18] Moreover, India is located in South Asia and has very little ability to project substantial power into East Asia and the Western Pacific in the face of Chinese opposition. India would therefore face great difficulty putting up meaningful resistance to a focused and sequential coercive strategy directed by China against Asia's other leading economies, such as Japan, South Korea, or Taiwan.

Japan and India could couple as joint cornerstones of an anti-hegemonic coalition. This could form the basis for a strong coalition, which would need also to include such states as South Korea, Vietnam, and Indonesia. But such a coalition would be at best comparable in power and quite likely inferior—perhaps substantially so—to a Chinese coalition that might include states such as Pakistan and Cambodia.[19] Even if such an anti-hegemonic coalition could stand up to China, given the power differential the defection of any important state would be a significant and possibly decisive loss. Beijing's power advantages as well as the great distances among the key players would make a Chinese focused and sequential strategy very difficult to resist.

Forming and sustaining a coalition in Asia is thus quite likely impossible without the United States playing a significant role. Even if some states did band together to seek to block Beijing's pursuit of regional hegemony, the resulting league would likely be weaker than China and its confederates, as well as disjointed. It therefore highly behooves the United States to act as an external cornerstone balancer in Asia.

Importantly, such an anti-hegemonic coalition appears to be forming in Asia, although its precise contours and nature remain unclear. Indeed, the coalition could take a variety of political forms. It might build on existing mechanisms such as "the Quad" (composed of the United States, Japan, India, and Australia) to create a formal body and add additional members.[20] Or it could incorporate or integrate with other political arrangements, including less formal ones. Or it could involve both, in a web of formal and less formal arrangements.[21]

Regardless of how precisely an anti-hegemonic coalition forms, the United States is already deeply engaged in Asia in ways that give such a coalition a very solid grounding.[22] Washington is allied with many of the region's key states—including leading economies Japan, South Korea, and Australia—and has a deepening partnership with India. Although these alliances are bilateral rather than multilateral, this is by no means incompatible with an effective anti-hegemonic coalition, as I will discuss later.

Europe

Europe already has an established, integrated anti-hegemonic coalition—indeed, a full-fledged alliance, the North Atlantic Treaty Organization (NATO), which provides a baseline for any anti-hegemonic efforts on the continent. In addition to being established, the anti-hegemonic coalition in Europe faces much less

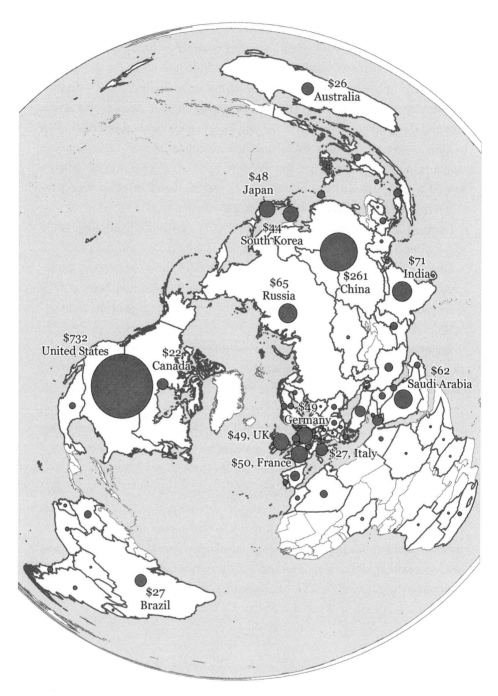

Global defense spending. Proportional circles depict 2019 defense spending, per SIPRI database. Values listed in billions for countries with defense spending over $20 billion. SIPRI does not report data for some countries, including Vietnam and North Korea. Lambert Equal Area Projection. Original map by Andrew Rhodes.

pointed difficulties than in Asia. No state in Europe has anything like the power advantage that China enjoys in Asia. Although the United States plays an important role in Europe as an external cornerstone balancer, this role is much less demanding than in Asia.

Russia once aspired to predominance in Europe, but today it is almost certainly incapable of mounting a serious bid for regional hegemony. Even though Russia has historically been adept at turning a relatively constrained economic base into military power, it is still at such a power disadvantage to the rest of Europe that no amount of efficiency in translating wealth into armed might could realistically compensate for its deficiencies. Moreover, the other powerful European states' geographic and military positions are tightly coupled, unlike those of Japan and India. For Russia to pose a military threat to Germany, it would also thereby threaten France and Italy, and if Moscow secured hegemony over Germany, it would directly intensify that threat to Paris and Rome. This alignment makes a coalition in Europe easier to coordinate.

This is not to say that Russia does not pose a threat. Russia threatens Eastern Europe in ways that could jeopardize the effectiveness of NATO and stability in Europe. This is an important issue I will discuss later, but it is not in the same category as a threat of regional hegemony.

It is possible that an aspirant to regional hegemony other than Russia could materialize in Europe, but it appears unlikely at least through the medium term. Moreover, the United States would likely have substantial strategic warning and would enjoy a distinct power advantage over whatever plausible aspirant state emerged.

The actual most powerful state in Europe is Germany. Even leaving aside Berlin's membership in NATO, Germany appears highly unlikely to make a bid for hegemony in Europe in the foreseeable future, and it would very likely be manageable if it tried. This is for at least three reasons. First, Germany does not enjoy a particularly large power advantage over the other principal European states, such as the United Kingdom, France, and Russia. It is somewhat more powerful than each of the others, but not more powerful than a plausible coalition of European states. Second, it is far weaker than the United States, meaning that the United States could readily work with other European states to check any German ambition for regional hegemony and undermine its attempt to assemble any pro-hegemonic coalition. Last, because of its history, there are significant constraints on how Germany can employ its power. These factors might change, of course, but such an evolution would likely generate ample warning.

The most plausible alternative to Russia as an aspiring hegemon in Europe is likely the European Union or a more cohesive entity emerging from it. Although a loose coalition of states is unlikely to be able to seize and hold hegemony because of its inherent fractiousness, a unifying superstate could. The United States itself, initially a loose confederation, evolved into a highly unified strategic actor. In the 1860s, Great Britain and France considered intervening in the American Civil War in part to prevent the rise of such a powerful superstate.[23]

Considered solely in the transatlantic context, then, the United States is therefore better off if Europe is not a highly unified superstate for the same reasons that it should oppose establishment of a cohesive hegemony over any key region of the world. This does not mean that the United States should oppose *any* degree of European integration. It has an interest in a Europe that is reasonably stable and can act coherently on matters of mutual concern. A Europe with the ability to ease collective action challenges and help resolve disputes is in the interests of the United States. A confederated Europe can ameliorate instability and stave off conflicts within the continent that otherwise might draw in the United States; it can also act effectively in ways beneficial to American interests. But this does not mean the United States would benefit if the European Union or a successor became a truly unified entity capable of establishing regional hegemony and unduly burdening or even excluding US trade and engagement.

The prime variable that could modify this US interest is China. Because Asia is the world's largest economic zone and China is the most serious potential regional hegemon, the US interest in Europe must be shaped by the requirements for ensuring that China does not establish predominance in Asia. If a disunified or even confederated Europe proves incapable of supporting or even indirectly enabling efforts to deny China hegemony in Asia, the US interest will tilt toward fostering a more cohesive Europe that aligns with the United States in checking China's aspirations, even if it means some loss of leverage with respect to dealing with a unified Europe. Some of Great Britain's interests suffered when the United States rose to dominance in North America, but these losses ultimately paled in comparison to the benefits of having a cohesive superpower that could help prevent Germany and then the Soviet Union from achieving hegemony over what was, for London, the more important theater—Europe.

A comparable logic holds for US relations with Russia. The stronger China is, the more the United States and other states have an interest in Russia's participation in, or even just tacit support for, an anti-hegemonic coalition against China. Given Russia's significant power and its geographical position astride China's northern border as well as regions where China could increase its power base, such as Central Asia and Northeast Asia, Moscow is a natural potential collaborator with or even member of an anti-hegemonic coalition against China. Moreover, Moscow shares this interest. Russia would find its autonomy and even its territorial integrity at substantial risk were China to establish hegemony over Asia. Because Russia is far weaker than China and likely to become more so given their respective growth trajectories, an unchecked China would mean that Russia's autonomy and integrity would increasingly become a matter of China's sufferance. This vulnerability will be all the greater the more isolated Russia is from any anti-hegemonic coalition against China in Asia, since any such coalition will be less likely to try to protect Russia if Moscow refused to cooperate with it. The United States and Russia thus share an interest in preventing China's regional hegemony in Asia, and this shared interest points toward increasing collaboration over time.

The Persian Gulf

There is at present no regional power that could plausibly establish hegemony over the Gulf States in the face of regional opposition, not to mention even minimal opposition by the United States. The state most frequently mentioned, Iran, comprises less than one-fifth of the region's economic power. Saudi Arabia, Egypt, and Turkey all rival it in strength, and Israel and the United Arab Emirates are also significant players.[24] There therefore exist ready ingredients for intraregional balancing to prevent Iran from establishing hegemony over the Persian Gulf. Moreover, with relatively little effort, given its enormous advantage in power, the United States can encourage and help sustain such a coalition.

It is more plausible that an external state could establish hegemony over the Gulf. During the latter part of the Cold War, the United States was especially concerned that the Soviet Union would be able to do this. Today, however, Russia cannot project sufficient force into the area to pretend to regional hegemony. It can work with local forces and conduct focused operations to advance its regional position, but it has no significant deployable fleet or air forces that could dominate the Gulf in the face of US opposition.[25]

China will eventually be a more serious potential hegemon. But if China is unable to establish regional hegemony over Asia, it will by definition be unlikely to be able to project sufficient power to establish predominance over the Gulf. To do so it would likely need to project power at least in part by sea, and if the United States and other states successfully check China in the Western Pacific, they would be able to check its maritime power projection outside Asia as well.

It is possible that China could seek to achieve hegemony through a combination of sea and land power projection, for instance, by leveraging the strategic advantages from its One Belt, One Road initiative and other efforts. To do so, however, it would have to directly impinge on the zones of several significant states, including India. If China has not already established predominance over Asia, it is very likely that such states will be able to contribute to curbing Beijing's ambitions in the Gulf.

Ensuring no state other than China establishes hegemony over the Persian Gulf is therefore likely to be relatively undemanding for the United States, and its success in denying China predominance there will depend on the strategic contest in the Indo-Pacific.

The Rest of the World

The rest of the world is less important in terms of military-economic power. Moreover, there are no serious pretenders to regional hegemony in the world's remaining regions. These two factors are not always coupled; North America was a much less important theater than Europe in the eighteenth and nineteenth centuries, but the United States was a serious potential hegemon. In theory, regions that are not important now could become so later. This appears unlikely, however, for the foreseeable future.

No state in Latin America could plausibly pretend to regional hegemony. In part due to slow economic growth, the largest Latin American states, Brazil and Mexico, are incapable of mounting hegemonic challenges under foreseeable conditions.[26] It is also implausible that a state from outside of the Western Hemisphere could establish hegemony over Latin America, given US proximity and stringent opposition to such an outcome.

Likewise, no state in sub-Saharan Africa could plausibly pretend to predominance over the region, as there are a number of large states with comparable amounts of power, including Nigeria, South Africa, and Kenya.[27] More plausible would be the establishment of hegemony over Africa by a state outside the region, especially given the continent's abundant natural resources. Like the Persian Gulf, however, Africa's fate will be determined by how the contest in other regions played out. If a state such as China were able to establish hegemony over Asia, it would have the power and favorable position to do the same in Africa. Without Chinese hegemony in Asia, however, the United States and others would by definition have the strength and positioning to frustrate any attempt by China to gain hegemony over Africa. They could exploit China's distance from Africa and the resistance of states in between the two to prevent such an outcome.

If a state could establish hegemony over Central Asia, as czarist Russia and the USSR did, this would add to its power but only to a modest degree. All things being equal, the United States therefore has an interest, but a limited one, in keeping Central Asia from falling under the sway of a state such as China or Russia that could then pretend to hegemony in Asia or Europe. Unlike Latin America and Africa, however, Central Asia's fate would not necessarily be a by-product of the competition in the decisive theaters of Asia or Europe, because it does not lie on the other side of these decisive theaters from the most plausible aspiring hegemons, China and Russia. It is the United States that would most likely have to project power across their territories, or areas where they wield influence, to contest Chinese or Russian bids for hegemony in Central Asia. There is thus relatively little that the United States can do there; it can support regional parties, but its direct options are limited.

The fate of the rest of the world's regions, such as Oceania and the poles, is essentially completely determined elsewhere.

Accordingly, the prospects for anti-hegemonic coalitions in the world's key regions should lead the United States to focus on acting as an external cornerstone balancer in Asia to ensure the formation and maintenance of a coalition against any Chinese bid for regional predominance. The United States should remain engaged in Europe to ensure a favorable regional balance of power, but in a considerably narrower and more concentrated way than in Asia, because of the absence of a plausible regional hegemon in Europe. In the Persian Gulf, the United States should focus on ensuring that the wealthy Gulf states do not fall under another state's predominance, but this should not be difficult given the absence of any plausible regional hegemon. The rest of the world does not demand significant focus.

3

Alliances and Their Effective, Credible Defense

THE TOP STRATEGIC PRIORITY FOR THE United States, therefore, is to be the external cornerstone balancer for a coalition designed to frustrate Chinese pretensions to hegemony in Asia. What, then, should such a coalition look like, and which states should be part of it?

From the American perspective, the ideal way to perform this role would be in a manner that minimizes US risk, commitment, and expense. Even as the external cornerstone balancer, the United States benefits from doing and risking the least amount needed to deny China regional hegemony over Asia. This is simply prudent—the United States is better off jeopardizing as little as possible to protect its interests. Intuitively, the natural way to do this is to keep its relationship with any such coalition loose and discretionary. By keeping such links elective rather than compulsory, the United States may avoid entanglement in costly, unnecessary, or risky wars and crises that might arise if it were more enmeshed in the region.[1]

But such a loose commitment is unlikely to foster a sufficiently cohesive and powerful coalition. A very large power such as China poses an acute threat to weaker and more vulnerable neighbors, and a loose, discretionary relationship with the United States is unlikely to alleviate their anxieties. Precisely because such an American commitment would be loose and uncertain, such states would be less inclined to join in a coalition balancing effort.

These states' reluctance would be rooted in the fact that while a strong external cornerstone balancer like the United States has a very powerful interest in preventing an aspiring hegemon like China from dominating a key region, that interest is still inherently partial—but the costs of vindicating it could be extraordinarily grave. Denying an aspirant the attainment of regional hegemony is important for fundamental American national purposes. But whether China dominates Asia is not likely to be a question of survival for the United States. The stakes, though exceedingly high, would not be truly existential. The costs of going to war with China, conversely, *could* well be existential. China could inflict a great deal of harm on the United States; in a world of nuclear weapons, China can with high confidence and enormous effect impose the most grievous costs on America—even threaten its very survival.[2]

This means that the United States might decide that the struggle in Asia is not worth these costs, leaving China to attain regional hegemony there while the United States retires to the Western Hemisphere, where it can stoutly defend itself. Moreover, America can disengage from the region at any time—including during a crisis or war—leaving its confederates in the lurch. Great Britain's liberal use of this advantage as an offshore state is one reason many continental Europeans deplored "Perfidious Albion."[3] Indeed, the allure of a bluffing strategy is that such a moment of crisis or conflict may be the most appealing time for such an offshore state to withdraw.

For states more vulnerable to the aspiring hegemon, though, how the coalition fares is not a partial but *the* central interest. The stakes for them are truly existential. They cannot withdraw; if they resist an aspirant like China but it still secures dominance, it could very well mean the end of those states as independent entities. Like medieval cities falling after compelling the attacker to mount a siege, they will have nothing to protect them from its wrath. An aspirant like China would have both reason to punish them, to make an example for others, and possibly inflamed passion.

This divergence between the United States and regional states in Asia creates the possibility of starkly different perspectives. Moreover, the potential for this divergence does not change over time frames meaningful to strategic decision-making, because it is a product of long-term economic trends, demography, and geography.

When judging whether and to what degree to participate in an anti-hegemonic coalition, a vulnerable state needs to account carefully for this possibility of abandonment. For an external cornerstone balancer like the United States to keep its relations with other coalition members loose and discretionary would merely exacerbate such a state's concern, since the purpose of keeping the links loose and discretionary could only be to make it easier for the external balancer to extricate itself. It would be a tell that the external balancer was *not* actually willing to bear the costs and risks entailed in frustrating the aspirant's pursuit of regional hegemony.

The Role of Alliances within an Anti-Hegemonic Coalition

The key for the United States—and, as necessary, other coalition members—is, then, to provide other states important to the coalition's success with enough confidence that they join or stay with it. Unless conquered outright and subjected directly to the occupier's compulsion, the regional states are the ones that decide where to allocate their power—with the coalition, with the aspirant, or somewhere in between. This means that the coalition's center of gravity is the confidence of its potential member states that the benefit of joining or staying in the coalition will exceed the benefit of remaining outside or withdrawing.

Such decisions are, of course, shaped by the political and economic incentives and consequences of affiliating with such a coalition as opposed to staying out. Given China's wealth and political influence, these will be significant. Yet given the fundamental incompatibility between China's appetite for hegemony and regional states' high valuation of their autonomy, the issue will ultimately boil down to a question of force.

A coalition will therefore be effective only if enough of its members judge that they will be provided a sufficient defense. The natural way to provide this is to bring to bear the full power of the coalition in response to the threat China poses to a member. In other words, if the aspirant's strategy is to divide and conquer, the coalition's natural strategy is to bind together to prevent its members being picked off singly. If vulnerable coalition members anticipate that they will be sufficiently defended in this way, that expectation should lead them to join and stand strong in a coalition—and an aspirant like China to use caution in attempting to apply its focused and sequential strategy against them. Undermining Beijing's theory of victory in this way would strengthen the coalition and, by making it less advantageous for China, make war less likely.

For the anti-hegemonic coalition, this approach is likely to entail alliances. The core concern of vulnerable coalition members is whether a strong enough part of the coalition will *actually* use its power to defend them sufficiently against China. Alliances are especially relevant in this context because they are, in essence, promises to fight with or on behalf of others, especially *when a state's rationale for defending another state is not self-evident.*[4] The term *alliance* here refers to any relationship in which a state has committed to come to another's defense; this commitment may be made and communicated through any number of methods, including formal treaties, but also other government statements, legislation, and patterns of behavior.

Alliances, in other words, are strong and usually costly signals of intent to fight for interests that are not manifestly compelling.[5] They therefore deter the potential opponent by increasing the likelihood of an effective collective response if the adversary challenges an alliance member, including through the kind of focused wars that do not, on their face, seem to call for a large response. And alliances encourage balancing over bandwagoning among coalition members by fortifying the confidence of vulnerable states that, if they participate, they will not suffer more than they are prepared to endure. Largely for these reasons, the United States retains a web of alliances, including with Japan, South Korea, Australia, and the Philippines in Asia, as well as a quasi-alliance with Taiwan, and with the North Atlantic Treaty Organization in Europe (and Canada).[6] Washington also has less formal but nonetheless deep relationships in the Middle East with the key Gulf states, Israel, and Jordan.

Thus, although the presence of an aspiring hegemon like China creates a strong impetus toward formation of an anti-hegemonic coalition, this impetus is coupled with doubts among vulnerable regional states over whether the United States, which is very distant and can formidably defend itself in the Western Hemisphere, is truly committed to denying China hegemony in Asia should the costs rise too high.[7] Indeed, some leaders of states important to checking China's aspirations have already begun to question whether the United States is prepared to endure what China can inflict on it. The Philippines' Rodrigo Duterte has been the most blunt, but such questions are also heard in Australia, Japan, South Korea, and beyond.[8]

The formation or sustainment of alliances between the United States on the one hand and regional states on the other is a natural method of addressing this problem. This tendency may lead to the formation or sustainment of multiple alliances, including interconnected ones and even a single, fully integrated alliance. But it need not result in a single, interconnected alliance for an anti-hegemonic coalition to succeed. Not all members of the coalition need to be allies for it to be effective. Nor do all members of the coalition that are allies need to be allied with one another. These points are particularly important with regard to Asia for several reasons.

First, an effective anti-hegemonic coalition may contain allies (including quasi-allies, those that are also recipients of US security commitments), nonallies—hereafter termed *partners*—or both. It is vital to emphasize the difference between the anti-hegemonic coalition and alliances. Such a coalition is a broad network of states actively pooling their power to deny an aspirant like China regional pre-dominance. Members of this coalition *may* elect to come to each other's defense if subjected to China's focused and sequential strategy, but they have not specifi-cally and formally committed to do so just by being members.

With that said, some coalition members may choose to form alliances, thereby committing to come to one another's defense. Doing so reassures nerv-ous coalition members that they will be protected in the face of the aspirant's focused and sequential strategy. Alternatively, however, coalition members might choose not to make such a commitment and yet remain partners within the coalition. Partners may still come to other coalition members' aid in the event of a Chinese assault, but they have made no formal pledge to do so.

Ultimately, then, it is the coalition that denies China regional hegemony. An effective coalition accomplishes this goal by bringing enough states together to prevail in a systemic regional war. Alliances, meanwhile, promote the coali-tion's ability to operate effectively. Thus, whereas alliances may improve the efficacy and reliability of a coalition, they are not strictly necessary. If a state does not want or need an alliance commitment from other states in order to par-ticipate in the coalition, then there is no strict need for it to receive one so long as it reliably participates in the anti-hegemonic coalition. Many states partici-pated in what was effectively an anti-hegemonic coalition against the Soviet Union in the 1970s and 1980s, including not only such US allies as Japan and NATO but such informal partners as China. This is not to say that alliances are not useful or even sometimes critical, only that they are not always necessary.

Second, even coalition nations that are in alliances need not be allied *with each other* to act against a common foe. A multilateral alliance has the advan-tage of bringing to bear the full power of a network of states, whereas a disag-gregated network of bilateral or smaller multilateral alliances does not. Nonetheless, a more disaggregated model can still provide the confidence re-quired for vulnerable states to remain on side. After the Second World War, the United States developed a hub-and-spoke alliance network in Asia, in which

Washington allied with multiple states but those states were not generally allied with each other. This network proved sufficient during the Cold War. Japan and South Korea were both part of the US coalition but were not allied with each other; each was separately allied with Washington.[9]

These points are critically important because there may be considerable reluctance to make new alliances within any anti-hegemonic coalition against China. For one, the United States may be reluctant to add alliance commitments. But regional coalition members may also balk at adding newly formed alliances to existing ones. This disinclination, even among states already opposed to Chinese hegemony, stems from several sources.

First, some coalition members may believe that they do not need alliances for their own security. They may think themselves sufficiently secure in the face of China's focused and sequential strategy that alliances with other coalition members are not worth the potential compromise of autonomy and entanglement that they might impose. India, for instance, because of its growing strength, may judge that it can resist Chinese employment of its focused strategy and that an alliance with Washington carries more risk than potential gain. From a different vantage point, New Zealand may believe that its small size and distance from China make it an unlikely target for Beijing and that joining an alliance would expose it to more, not less, risk of attack. In each case, these states might contribute to an anti-hegemonic coalition but keep clear of alliance relationships.

Second, some coalition states, including those already in alliances, may be reluctant to extend commitments to additional coalition members, especially the more vulnerable ones. US allies such as South Korea, Japan, and Australia may resist formally committing to the defense of Taiwan or the Philippines. They may judge that a US guarantee should be enough to keep such nervous states on side and that they can always choose to become involved later, for instance, through a coalition of the willing formed to deal with a particular contingency. This route preserves their flexibility and, they may hope, diminishes their exposure to Chinese ire.

Last, political factors may inhibit the formation of new alliances or the linkage of existing ones, and such currents are very much alive in Asia. Japan and South Korea, for instance, are often at loggerheads and have had difficulty sustaining even a modest strategic partnership.[10] India and Vietnam have strong traditions of nonalignment and opposition to the United States.[11] Political reluctance can, however, often be overcome by compelling strategic necessity;

France and Germany were able to come together in postwar Europe, as Great Britain and France did before the First World War. But overcoming such resistance may impose other costs and alienate key constituencies in these countries.

A fully integrated, completely reliable multilateral alliance network can make an ideal coalition. An Asian NATO is certainly conceivable, even if it has not existed in the past; given China's rise and its increasingly assertive behavior, the prospects for forming such a tightly integrated, multilateral alliance are improving as its value grows more apparent. During the Cold War and until recently, the United States was overwhelmingly powerful in maritime Asia; individual US allies, moreover, could not contribute very much to the defense of others. Hence the hub-and-spoke model made sense; US allies could focus primarily on defending themselves in concert with the United States. With the rise of China, however, the United States is no longer dominant, whereas such US allies as Japan, South Korea, and Australia can contribute to collective defense. Further, during the Cold War, lingering resentment against Japan for its conduct during the Second World War was a major hindrance to a multilateral alliance with its neighbors. Today, that legacy is receding from living memory.

In light of this, the United States and others ready to participate in an anti-hegemonic coalition in Asia would in principle benefit from a tighter, multilateral framework such as an Asian NATO. Moreover, the perfect need not be the enemy of the good; even if the members of the coalition could not come together in a full NATO-like structure, they might profitably form additional alliances, including smaller multilateral alliances. Japan and Australia might ally, for instance, in addition to or integrated with their pacts with the United States. It is likely in the US interest to encourage such arrangements.[12]

But while a more developed and integrated alliance network might be beneficial, achieving it could be difficult and present some risks. Some obstacles are largely political: trying to form such a fully cohesive alliance network might alienate some coalition states or important constituencies within them, jeopardizing these states' participation in the coalition. Such an effort also might consume political capital that could be better used to support the coalition in other ways, such as raising military spending or permitting military access by other coalition members.

Deeper strategic reasons for caution also exist. These reasons are rooted in the reality that adding new and sustaining legacy alliances to face a determined adversary is not without costs or risks. An alliance defense must be *effective* and *credible,* and failing to tend to these requirements risks undermining not only an individual alliance but related ones, and even the broader anti-hegemonic effort. Stretched too far, an alliance network can weaken and even break. This was a problem with the Pactomania of the 1950s, which helped lead the United States into the agonizing Vietnam War and threatened to impair, if not collapse, its whole Cold War effort.[13] Thus before determining how the United States and the coalition should adjust the contours of their alliance networks in Asia—if at all—we must first understand what such alliances require.

An Effective Defense

The key element of a meaningful alliance facing an aspiring regional hegemon is that the alliance promises an *effective* defense of its members. The goal of the alliance is to defend a member state enough to keep it onside and contributing its part to the coalition. *Effective* in this context therefore simply means the *denial* of the conditions that would cause the targeted state to leave or stop contributing to the alliance and thus withdraw its strength from the coalition. These conditions, of course, depend on the nature and terms of a given alliance. But because it is about the will of the vulnerable state to continue to dedicate its power to the alliance's—and thus the coalition's—efforts, effectiveness is largely a *relative and contingent,* rather than an absolute, standard.

This is crucial because it means that a great deal rests on how much a vulnerable state is willing to endure and do in the face of what an aspirant like China can do to it. The only truly necessary part of this criterion is defense against outright and lasting conquest, particularly of its key territory, since that by definition entails the state's enduring submission to the aspirant's will and ultimately the cessation of any resistance the ally could offer. Beyond that, how much is needed for an effective defense is a product of how much the vulnerable state is willing to suffer, risk, and do to gain the benefits the alliance (and the coalition) offers.

This is of such elemental importance because the more a vulnerable state is willing to resist and suffer, the less demanding the standard of an effective defense will be. The less willing such a state is, conversely, the more demanding the standard will be. If a state is willing to bear great harm or be patient in waiting for its deliverance, defending it will put less stress on its allies; such a state could endure awful barrage, blockade, or even temporary conquest and still contribute to the allied effort so long as it expects to be delivered or freed. Meanwhile, a state that would buckle and renege on its contributions should it suffer even modest damage requires a very robust defense, stressing the ability and will of its allies to help protect it. A stout and resilient state, such as the Finland of 1940, demands less from an alliance than a fragile one, such as the Belgium of the same year.

For this reason, what an ally demands for its defense has the most significant implications when choosing which states to take on or keep as allies. And how much an ally demands for its defense is a product of how it balances the gains of affiliation against the suffering and sacrifice expected of it: if it sees the benefits as high, it is likely to be prepared to suffer and do more, and vice versa. The benefits include the state's independence and autonomy, along with whatever other inducements an alliance can offer; the costs are, most prominently, the damage an aspirant like China can impose as well as forfeiture of the inducements it can offer.

What is asked of the vulnerable ally will also vary. One state might be expected to stoutly defend itself and seek to deny to the aspirant the use of its territory and resources, such as West Germany in NATO. Another might be expected simply to bear up under attack and provide access, such as Iceland in the Cold War.[14] Moreover, an ally could perform its alliance duties even if it is occupied, so long as this is consistent with the alliance's strategy for defeating the aspirant. Such a conquered ally could, such as the Philippines in the Second World War, be liberated or regained at the peace table.

How vulnerable states balance between these costs and benefits cannot be generalized as a rule. This is particularly because survival of a state as an independent entity does not obviously or universally supersede other goods. History is replete with examples of states that have compromised their autonomy and even their very existence as independent entities, such as Scotland in the early eighteenth century.[15] How much a state is willing to sacrifice to protect such high goods is a preference that is shaped by many factors but is finally a reflection of how much the state's people, and especially its decision-makers, value their freedom and autonomy. Some may see purple as the noblest winding sheet, others that survival is preferable to liberty.

This is particularly important because the more powerful the aspirant and the weaker the targeted state, the more the question of how much the targeted state truly values its independence will come to the fore. With a strong aspirant like

China, inducements by allies tend to be canceled out because both sides can offer significant carrots. At the same time, a powerful state like China can likely hold at risk whatever inducements the targeted state's allies can offer, jeopardizing their value.

In principle, however, *the standard of an effective defense demands nothing from the adversary,* though such concessions may be instrumentally useful or advantageous. This makes it quite unlike some other approaches to US defense strategy. A grand strategy posited on ensuring the ascendancy of democracy or liberalism might demand a defense strategy that can produce changes in China's form of government, since under this logic, only after China is a liberal democracy can the United States be truly safe.[16] A strategy, meanwhile, that demands actual US hegemony in Asia—as opposed to the denial of China's hegemony—might require a defense strategy that actively weakens or hobbles China. The standard presented here, conversely, can coexist with a very powerful China led by different types of government. But it does require effective defense of allies.

The Challenges to Mounting an Effective Defense

Such a defense must be more than theoretically effective. It must also be *credible.*

Whether another state will fulfill its alliance commitments is inherently uncertain. Alliances are created because a vulnerable state fears that it will be left isolated without such assurance; an alliance is a resulting promise by other states not to leave their vulnerable confederate alone, and especially to fight effectively on its behalf when tested. But like all promises, such a pledge can be broken or implemented only half-heartedly. Bluffing can be an alluring strategy for more distant alliance members because it holds out the possibility of gaining the deterrent benefits of alliance while avoiding its most grievous costs if the deterrent fails. Knowing this, vulnerable allied states that rely on such a pledge as well as the aspirant itself have the strongest incentive to look closely at how likely the committers are to follow through on their promises—in other words, to determine just how credible those promises are. This is all the more true when it is not manifestly clear that it is in the committers' own interests to follow through on their pledges—precisely the conditions in which an alliance is most relevant.

Credibility is especially important when facing a mighty aspirant like China, because Beijing's employment of a focused and sequential strategy can play on the fundamental misalignment of interests and perspectives among the states in the anti-hegemonic coalition, particularly between an external cornerstone balancer like the United States and its regional confederates. A very powerful aspirant such as China can try to frame a conflict as largely about local issues—about disputed claims, for instance, or matters of internal sovereignty—so that the stakes appear remote to Americans and other Asian states. Many Americans regularly remark that they do not want a war with China over "rocks in the South China Sea" or even about "an internal matter" such as the status of Taiwan. At the same time, China can impose great harm not only on smaller states but on larger ones such as Japan, India, and the United States. If Beijing can frame a conflict in this light, some coalition members' resolve may be insufficient to surmount the fear of these risks.

The result of this is that, in the face of a focused war strategy pursued by an aspirant like China, an alliance demands of its members a readiness to contemplate a great deal of loss for an apparently narrow issue—more than, on its face, it may appear to warrant. An alliance rests on the logic that it is better to risk hanging together rather than hanging separately, because the aspirant will only continue salami-slicing until it can gain the predominance it seeks—that states may not be dominoes, in the phrase made infamous by Vietnam, but that their fates are surely interconnected.[17]

But this tension invites an aspirant like China to test whether and how much the other members of an alliance are *truly* ready to sacrifice so much for their vulnerable ally. Beijing can do this by playing on the other allies' uncertainty as to whether Beijing is *really* seeking hegemony or whether such hegemony would be so intolerable as to be worth the suffering entailed in defending the targeted member state.

This gets at a very real and indeed foundational issue. An alliance designed to deal with a powerful state like China seeks to help forestall a hegemony that its members fear but can rarely be sure is inevitable or, if it does arise, will be so intolerable. Yet the costs of forestalling that potentiality are real, concrete, and substantial. Put another way, alliances may promise to help block a large regional state's bid for local hegemony by guaranteeing aid to vulnerable members—but they also risk the entanglement of their member states in unnecessary or disproportionately destructive and costly wars. This is rooted in three quandaries that call into question how real, and, if real, how significant, the gains of fighting an aspirant like China over a focused war actually are.

First, it is possible that a rising potential aspirant like China may not actually end up pursuing full-fledged hegemony or pursuing it fully enough to succeed. Even very powerful states may become satisfied with their gains. This means that wars fought to frustrate what looks like an aspirant's focused and sequential strategy may not be necessary. And waiting a bit longer to see if the potential aspirant is *actually* intent on hegemony will seem a very attractive option compared to the high costs of confronting it. Many will ask: Could not those bound to come to the ally's aid wait to see if the *potential* aspirant, whose hunger for hegemony is likely to be consistently denied and thus appear speculative, might not be sated by its gains? US territorial expansion in North America effectively ended with the Mexican-American War, leaving Canada and Mexico independent. The Soviets never used military force against Western Europe and effectively stopped directly testing the boundaries of the postwar European settlement after the Berlin and Cuban Missile Crises of 1961–1962. Indeed, it is still a matter of historical debate whether the USSR sought regional hegemony or merely a sufficient buffer for itself.[18] Even proverbially imperial Rome stopped expanding and even withdrew from portions of its conquests in the second and third centuries. Examples like these are likely to be front of mind for those deciding whether to follow through on an alliance commitment and fight what could be an immensely damaging war.

The questioning will be especially pointed when the aspirant has plausible historical, cultural, linguistic, or other reasons for its particular war aims to which it can point as evidence of the limits of its ambitions, since such reasons can appear to provide a natural terminus for its goals. A state that argues that it merely wants to unify with its coethnics, fellow language speakers, or common confessors may persuade others in the region that its goals are limited to this end.

Nor must such reasonableness be confined to nonstrategic factors. Straightforward strategic or security factors can seem or be made to seem reasonable and defensive to allied states considering whether it is truly necessary to bear the painful costs of war. To those wondering whether great suffering is worth the cost, an aspirant's contention that it simply wants a more resilient or buffered defensive position, and has no plans to use any gains as a prelude to further assertion, may have a comforting allure. Was the Soviet imperium over Eastern

Europe a buffer it had earned after absorbing and defeating Nazi Germany's assault, or was it a stepping stone to mastery over Europe? These topics were hotly debated in Western Europe and the United States throughout the Cold War.[19]

Second, there is always a tendency to wonder whether there are not better grounds on which to draw the red line. Even if one agrees that the aspirant's bid for regional hegemony must be checked, is it necessary to fight the war in *this* way and on *these* grounds? This is often an especially difficult question because, for every rued historical example of a failure to stand firm against an ambitious aspirant, there is an example of a costly and agonizing war that might not have been necessary or that might have been less costly if fought elsewhere, under different conditions. For every Munich 1938 there is a Sarajevo 1914, and for American lack of clarity about whether it would defend South Korea, there is Vietnam. The First World War and Vietnam now seem, if not unnecessary, at least out of proportion to the benefits of checking imperial Germany and Communism in Indochina, respectively. Britain, France, and Russia fought the First World War to check German ambitions, but the spark that lit the conflagration was defending Serbia from Austrian domination. Was it necessary to fight there and then? Might not a war—if necessary at all—have been better fought elsewhere at another time, or avoided entirely while still preventing German hegemony over Europe? Even a century later, debate on this question continues. The closest the world has come to the brink of general nuclear war was the Cuban Missile Crisis, which was intimately linked to the Berlin Crisis and in particular the fate of West Berlin. Would protecting a free West Berlin as a symbol of US and NATO resolve have been worth a thermonuclear war?

The quandary is that there is always a case for waiting until the aspirant has presented clearer and more brazen evidence of its ambitions and aggressiveness, and for more advantageous political and military conditions before venturing to directly confront it. Yet a wily aspirant, conscious of this, will have every incentive to present its focused wars in ways that exacerbate rather than relieve this predicament, never presenting unambiguous evidence of its intentions until there is an advantage in doing so. And for the anti-hegemonic coalition, the danger is finding out that the best time to check the aspirant's ambitions was two years ago, or five, or earlier, when things were not so clear.

Third, states may wonder whether the aspirant's predominance, if realized, will really be so bad as to justify the costs needed to resist it. All states have some substantial interest in the independence and autonomy afforded by being free of a hegemon. But not all empires or ascendancies are intolerable. Rome was brutal and oppressive in many respects, but it also created the Pax Romana, facilitated trade and exchange, and was generally lenient if its provinces did not rebel. There is a reason Gibbon judged the second-century empire under the Antonines to be the happiest period in human history.[20] More recently, Canada might have preferred to avoid American hegemony over North America, but has it been so bad? Many have not unreasonably wondered whether a German ascendancy resulting from a victory by the Central Powers in the First World War would have been as awful as the losses in the trenches. Thus, to a state facing a modernized People's Liberation Army (PLA), would Chinese predominance be as awful as the costs of resisting it?

Yet to each of these arguments there is a compelling counterargument. An aspirant like China has the most powerful incentive to hide the extent of its ambitions in order to dampen other states' willingness to run such risks and bear such costs to stop it. And if a large state's current leadership is genuinely focused on nationalistic and revanchist rationales and not primarily or deliberately seeking hegemony, that may still be the upshot of its policies. Even apparently limited demands may advance the aspirant's ability to establish hegemony, whether that is an intentional result or not. Acquired territory may be strategically valuable, and appetite often grows with eating. The next set of leaders may be more ambitious than today's. Prussia had nationalist reasons to fight Denmark, Austria, and France in order to unify Germany, but these victories made Prussia (and then Germany) a much more powerful state capable of pursuing European mastery, which it subsequently sought to grasp. Nazi Germany's desire to unify the German-speaking populations in Central and Eastern Europe was *both* grounded in nationalist arguments that appealed to the spirit of the age *and* strategically threatening to other states because it resulted in a state of such power in Central Europe as to pose a hegemonic threat.

This dynamic is especially relevant to contemporary China. Although some still argue that China's true ambition is only to settle its foreign disputes and take its rightful place at the high table of international affairs, the increasing weight of evidence indicates that China has either shifted its approach toward pursuit of regional hegemony or has pursued this aspiration for a long time, the only change being that it has recently become more obvious about it.[21] Thus China may have long-standing political claims to Taiwan as an internal province based on its having been part of the Qing Empire; cultural and ethnic reasons for ensuring the so-called protection of Chinese-speaking populations in Southeast Asia; and historical claims on parts of the South China Sea, Japan, India, Russia, and other states. Yet even if, in the minds of Beijing's leaders, China's pursuit of these interests is not solely or even primarily intended to advance it toward predominance over Asia, fulfilling these aims would nonetheless make it much more capable of attaining this goal. Innocent intentions do not necessarily make for innocent policies.

Further, there are reasons not to draw back the defensive line in search of putatively better battlegrounds. Doing so is riskier the more powerful the aspirant is; it is safe to wait and see against a weaker rival, but an anti-hegemonic coalition cannot afford to lose much margin against a very powerful aspirant like China. Second World War examples tend to be overused, yet it is nonetheless true that interwar diplomacy shows the great peril of waiting too long to counteract an aspiring hegemon. Germany *would* have been better confronted in 1936 or 1938 by well-prepared Western powers. And although the war in Korea was painful and costly, it played an important role in cohering the anti-Soviet coalition in both Asia and Europe by signaling the lengths the Communist Bloc was prepared to go to advance toward its aims.

And the argument that regional hegemony will not be so bad can be met by the indisputable counterargument that, once an aspirant establishes such predominance, states under its sway will be essentially entirely at its mercy. That places an enormous trust in the hegemon's good will and self-restraint. It is worth remembering that Rome's history was largely written by the Romans or by those seeking their favor or fearing their disfavor. The many peoples who rebelled against Roman rule clearly did not consider their rule so benign, and it seems reasonable to wonder whether the subject peoples who did not rise up were more content than those who did. More to the point, submission to a great state's regional hegemony might be better than *some* alternatives: Roman imperium may have been better than exposure to Hunnic deprivations, and rule by imperial Germany better than by Soviet Russia. But it is presumably, as a general rule, not better than a state's autonomy in peace.

But the fundamental point is that these questions are real—the risks and costs of fighting such wars are likely to be high, while the gains invariably will appear speculative, especially if the challenge is met earlier and thus normally more effectively. It is not impossible that a rising power might become satisfied; nor is it unreasonable to think that it might be better checked on some more advantageous battlefield; nor even to conclude that its hegemony, if it comes to pass, may not be so terrible. At the same time, the costs of resistance are immediate and potentially of the gravest sort.

The basic problem, then, is that an alliance asks its member states—especially a state distant from Asia like the United States—to commit to fighting a costly and potentially very damaging war that is by no means self-evidently worth the suffering and jeopardy it entails. If a war for an embattled ally raises questions along these lines that are powerful and well-grounded enough, they may lead alliance members, including most prominently the United States, either to balk at defending a victim of the aspirant's focused strategy or to defend it half-heartedly and ineffectively. Yet a failure by important allies to effectively defend a member of an alliance cannot but have serious and possibly the most far-reaching consequences, not only for that alliance but for the anti-hegemonic coalition as a whole.

The Importance of Credibility

This is because of the fundamental role of credibility in alliances. Credibility is a fraught topic, and its role has often been exaggerated, sometimes grossly, including particularly in this context of alliances. One of America's most searing experiences, the war in Vietnam, was in key respects a result of overestimating the importance of credibility to American foreign policy.[22] Partly in reaction to that experience, some maintain that credibility makes little difference in international life.[23]

That argument is impossible to sustain. Credibility is a universal factor in human life. It is an essential part of social interaction whenever a party pledges future action, especially when that promise entails exposing itself or its resources to harm or loss. This is as true in the international arena as it is in private life.

The simple reason is that one cannot know with certainty how another will act. No state can have perfect confidence when trying to anticipate another state's future decisions. Even decision-makers within a state cannot know exactly how their state will behave, just as individuals cannot know with certainty what decisions they will make in the future. Because of this uncertainty, states seek formal commitments from other states so that the risking state can avoid having to rely, when they are putting a great deal on the line, solely on speculative assessments of another state's interests.

But states do not normally take such commitments at face value. Those who expose themselves and their assets by relying on another's promise cannot simply presume the counterparty's good faith. They must therefore look to the best evidence available to judge how reliable the other party is. And a firm basis for this is the pledger's reputation for reliability based on its prior behavior. In this, credibility is like an individual's or firm's credit rating. Just as a company that has a history of reneging on agreements or loans will find it harder to secure such a loan in the future, so a state that has been willing to default on certain kinds of commitments will encourage others to believe that it may act similarly in the future.

Credibility is especially salient in the environment created by China's aspirations for hegemony. Credibility makes one believed even if it is not clearly in one's immediate interests to honor one's pledge; thus, credibility matters most precisely when the benefits of acting do not clearly outweigh the costs. When the costs of fulfilling a promise are high or the benefits unclear, credibility is more relevant because there will be more pain or less to gain from honoring these commitments than from not fulfilling them, increasing the allure of balking. And China can impose very serious costs.

Moreover, credibility is valuable because, while states can take measures to reduce its salience, it cannot be eliminated without incurring other, frequently insuperable, costs. For instance, a state can offer hostages or collateral to its performance, but in an international environment lacking a common sovereign, enforcement is difficult if not impossible. A bank may accept a borrower's house as collateral because it can be sure that the government will enforce the contract. But a weaker state cannot enforce the terms of an alliance agreement against a reluctant stronger state; it lacks the power to do so. If the stronger state is willing to walk away from its commitment to the vulnerable state, it is surely ready to live with any suspended bonds and confiscated investments it offered as collateral. And although states can and historically did exchange hostages, those hostages were by definition costly tokens; they were not as valuable as the equities of independence and autonomy or immunity from great cost. History is full of states violating pledges underwritten by hostages.[24] Last, an endangered or attacked ally can threaten its confederates if they do not honor their pledges, but such a threat is likely not only to be ineffective given the power asymmetry but also risks alienating rather than inspiring its potential aider.

The limitations of these other measures are why credibility is especially important to an external cornerstone balancer, such as the United States, that has interests in multiple parts of the world. Credibility lessens—and its absence increases—the resources and entanglement required to underwrite a given commitment. A firm with a good credit rating can borrow more money with less collateral, and at more favorable interest rates, than one with a poor rating, which must risk more of its assets and pay higher interest rates to borrow. Similarly, nervous allies and possible attackers will demand less of a state with good credibility and more from one with a poor record.

A deficit of credibility causes several difficult problems for a committing state. First, a state that must put more down to convince others that it will uphold alliance commitments in one place will be unable to employ those resources elsewhere. This will reduce the state's flexibility.

Second, because these forces or resources cannot be employed more flexibly, the committing state will need to spend more to cover the same set of commitments than if it could employ its forces more flexibly. A committing state with high credibility, meanwhile, can use the same set of forces to reassure partners in multiple places. This reduces the requirement for forces overall and thus the costs of national defense, making the committing state's economy more competitive and imbuing it with more of the economic vitality necessary for military strength.

Third, because there is normally a ceiling on military spending, a committing state with poor credibility is more likely to have to prune its commitments, reducing its potential influence. To be clear, pruning may be advisable for other reasons, but it is better for a state not to have to abandon or forswear useful commitments because it lacks the resources to make them credible, given its reputation for unreliability.

Last, down payments to compensate for a lack of credibility could make it difficult or impossible for the committing state to back down or extricate itself if it ultimately decides that that is the best—or least bad—option. Such down payments, in other words, may work, forcing the committing state to fight a war it does not believe necessary or in a way it does not want. For instance, a committing state with credibility problems may have to predelegate decisions to local commanders or place its forces under allied command. This is the essence of entanglement. Thus a lack of credibility may make entanglement more rather than less likely.

For these reasons, credibility—and especially a state's credibility with respect to something as fundamental as its alliance relationships and willingness to go to war—is a precious commodity.

Differentiated Credibility

Credibility is therefore highly important in alliance relationships, especially for an external cornerstone balancer like the United States. But it is important to specify what *kind* of credibility matters. That is, credibility's primary influence is not felt through generalized assessments of behavior. An undifferentiated picture of credibility, taking in all of a state's actions and considering how it will behave under any and all circumstances, is unlikely to be as useful for predicting whether and to what degree it will do something specific, such as incur great costs to defend other members of an alliance.

And *that* is the question. Vulnerable members of an alliance do not care so much whether committing states follow through on other obligations. They care whether and to what degree the committing states follow through on their pledge to defend *them,* just as a lender cares about a borrower's likelihood of paying back its loan, not about the borrower's overall moral repute.[25]

Of course, the logic of a generalized assessment is that there tends to be a connection between how a state regards fidelity across different domains—and this is often true. A person or firm that is willing to cut corners in one area is usually thought more likely to do so in others. Thus a reputation for general credibility is valuable, and a perfect record would be a great asset. In the ideal, a person or a state is best off if it matches its actions fully and completely with its pledges.

The salience of differentiated over generalized assessments of credibility derives, then, from two sources. First, a state may be more reliable on some matters than others. It may be fickle on living up to its pledges on, say, human rights but take its core security commitments much more seriously. Second and more fundamentally, the appeal of this perfect standard must reckon with reality. States will leave a great deal of money on the table—they will miss important opportunities—if they take as their highest goal ensuring that they can fulfill every pledge. Gainful commitments often involve reaching beyond what one is absolutely sure one will be able to do or want to bear.[26] A state that is too conservative risks being overtaken by those willing to run greater risks. Thus, to best serve its interests in the world, a state, especially an important state like the United States, may need to make commitments it cannot be absolutely sure it can sustain. Indeed, the United States officially acknowledges that it consciously "takes risk" in its defense planning; it is not fully prepared or equipped all the time, everywhere.[27]

Moreover, states must make such commitments in conditions of profound uncertainty. Shifts in power, as well as in a state's own or other states' willingness to run risks and bear costs, are difficult to anticipate. Yet such shifts can mean that the logic that once justified or enabled a commitment may no longer obtain. Commitments that appeared feasible or advisable in one set of circumstances may appear imprudent if trends do not unfold as anticipated, just as many companies and local governments made pension guarantees based on growth expectations that did not pan out and now cannot fully honor their commitments.[28]

More mundanely, states may make mistaken or simply foolish commitments. While they tend toward cost-benefit decision-making on the whole, and especially on what they perceive as important issues, governments are not perfectly rational. They are composed of collections of individuals who sometimes make poor judgments, or at least judgments that subsequent governments think are too costly for the benefits. They do this even on issues of great consequence. For example, most Americans, including many involved in the decision itself, now agree that the US decision to invade and occupy Iraq was a major error, even given the information available at the time.[29] The need to revise previous commitments, moreover, is often particularly pronounced because governments have powerful incentives to make promises that bring immediate benefits and leave it to future governments (often of different parties or factions) to deal with reducing or even reneging on them. Those pension commitments now viewed as well beyond what any reasonable growth projections could sustain were often loudly applauded when earlier governments made them—leaving it to their successors to reckon with the consequences.

Critically, these realities often lead to situations in which a state has to make choices among past commitments—it simply may not have the power or wealth or fortitude to fulfill all the pledges it made in an earlier set of circumstances. This is especially so if a state believes that it needs to make new commitments or needs to allocate greater resources to substantiate certain existing commitments than it had forecast. In such circumstances, a state trying to fulfill every

commitment and earn a spotless record can very well find that it lacks the resources or popular support to uphold some of them and, perhaps as ominously,
is unable to assume important new commitments.

For the United States, following such a perfectionist course would be antithetical to its core purposes. Upholding unwise promises, especially for a state
that is supposed to promote the interests of its citizenry, is not the ultimate
measure of merit; looking out for its citizens' security, freedom, and prosperity
is, even if that involves walking back some pledges. A company that goes bank-
rupt by fulfilling every obligation is serving neither its shareholders nor its
workers. Likewise, a state that exhausts its strength or its citizens' will following through on every pledge, however peripheral to its interests, is not serving
its own fundamental aims. No state, despite John F. Kennedy's stirring words,
is actually likely to "bear any burden" to follow through on a pledge if the benefits are too modest in relation to the pain—as demonstrated by the eventual
American withdrawal from Vietnam.[30]

This is especially important because demanding unerring fidelity to past
pledges risks bringing down the whole edifice of commitment, as the consequences of exhaustion and failure may spread beyond one commitment to others. A nation will bear only so much; if it spends too much of its resources in
one struggle, it may not be available in another or may give up on the whole enterprise, as the United States flirted with following Vietnam.

When a state is not able to fully follow through on all its commitments, it has
to husband its strength and resolve and make hard choices. Under these conditions, sacrificing lesser commitments on behalf of more important ones actually
tends to *increase* the state's credibility with respect to the more important ones.
This is only logical: if a state needs to preserve its strength and will, then it must
reduce its less important obligations. Doing so, in turn, is an indication of its
resolve to follow through on its most important, taxing commitments. Thus a
lack of follow-through in some directions can lead to greater credibility in others. In some conditions, then, failing to follow through on certain pledges is actually *evidence* of a state's commitment to other, higher-priority commitments.

These difficult circumstances are likely to obtain for the United States when
it comes to countering China's bid for hegemony over Asia. A powerful aspiring hegemon like China is a rising power, whose emergence on the international stage must change other states' calculations. If other states, such as the
United States, correctly anticipated, fully internalized, and adapted to the con-

sequences of its rise, how it will behave, and the pace at which it is rising, they should hardly need to change their policies. But this is unlikely. The implications of such a state's rise, which upsets the international order in ways that demand that other countries fundamentally adapt their policies and commitments, are rarely well anticipated, and the corresponding adjustments are seldom implemented in a timely fashion.

And indeed, America is almost certainly overburdened with pledges that it made without accurately anticipating the full scale of China's rise. The United States has made an enormous number of commitments in the past seventy-five years; by one count, some fifty countries are the recipients of US security pledges.[31] During most of the Cold War, these commitments were largely limited to the core industrialized areas of Western Europe and East Asia, but since the 1990s they have grown significantly.[32] The United States led in expanding NATO to encompass almost all of Europe; Washington also made far-reaching pledges in the Middle East. Some of the more ambitious elements of these policies may charitably be ascribed to the difficulties of charting an uncertain future; but some seem to demonstrate, if not hubris, then a confidence in the endurance of America's primacy, the end of power politics, or both that China's rise has discredited. The collapse of the Soviet Union appeared to many American policy-makers and those who influence them to augur a lasting unipolarity and even "end of history."[33] Later, the attacks of September 11, 2001, indicated to many that the primary challenges to US security were transnational, nonstate threats and that addressing them demanded aggressive efforts to fundamentally reshape societies in the Middle East.[34]

It seems fair to say that US decision-making with respect to its international commitments did not fully internalize China's rise as an enormously powerful state that would aspire to predominance in its region. Rather, to the extent that it was seriously considered, this period largely reflected an expectation that China's rise would *not* be transformational.[35]

Looked at from the present moment, some of Washington's recent international commitments may be justified even in light of China's rise, but others appear less so. Some suited the structural environment when they were made but now fit poorly in a world shadowed by such a mighty China. Others were overambitious or unwise even at the time, based on the need for the United States to maintain unipolarity, to ensure the ascendancy of liberal democracy or the observance of ambitious conceptions of international norms, or to transform the Middle East.

The United States will very likely find it impossible to uphold fully all of these legacy commitments and also act as external cornerstone balancer in an anti-hegemonic coalition in Asia. Trying to uphold them all would be highly taxing, consuming substantial resources and political will. For instance, trying to implement Washington's open-ended commitments to stabilize Afghanistan and Iraq would devour both direct resources—money, time, the attention of US armed forces, and lives—and more indirect but vital assets, particularly the domestic political support needed to fight and sustain distant wars.[36] What is used for the Middle East will not be available for Asia.

This was not such an issue in a unipolar world; when it was preeminent, the United States could afford to cover down everywhere and have resources to spare. In today's world, however, this is a real problem. The American war effort in Vietnam drew strength away from the US defensive position in Europe and sapped American political support; the former led, by the 1970s, to a serious deficit in the military balance in Europe, and the latter to much reduced support for a firm stance against the Soviet Union.[37] There is already deep opposition among Americans to the "forever wars" in the Middle East, sentiment that could lead to a weakening of the US position in Asia if these wars drag on and especially if the latter is not distinguished from the former.[38] Americans' wealth, suffering, and willpower must be jealously safeguarded, not liberally spent.

Fully upholding such less important commitments would thus be *more rather than less* likely to call into question the US ability and resolve to serve as an effective external cornerstone balancer in Asia, since it would raise doubts about America's ability to dedicate enough power to what is now the main challenge in the primary theater. Asian states evaluating the firmness of American pledges would have to reckon that unerring fidelity by the United States to all of its past commitments could vitiate its ability or resolve to uphold its pledges to the anti-hegemonic coalition in Asia.

How, then, would states distinguish Washington's backing off from some commitments from its willingness to fulfill others? And how would they interpret these decisions in trying to anticipate future US behavior? As I noted, the best that states can do to predict how another state will behave is to look at its patterns of behavior. And the most reliable bases for prediction are patterns of behavior relating to the commitment in question.[39] That is, other states must look at the most relevant information available.[40]

Any such assessment would partly be based on a judgment of the stakes at issue and the power available to the committing state.[41] Surely the United States would fight harder for California than for Afghanistan, but that does not say much about how it will act on more finely balanced issues. The questions states must grapple with are more like: How far will the United States go to defend Japan, the Philippines, or Taiwan? The answers to such questions are far from clear for the simple reason that these states' importance to the United States is relational and subject to interpretation. Americans' willingness to defend them would depend on the anticipated costs, risks, and benefits involved. Indeed, this holds true even for Americans' willingness to defend different parts of the United States itself. Massachusetts is likely to be willing to do more to defend Connecticut than California, and this relativity might become an issue if the risks and costs are high enough.

In short, interests are not fixed, Platonic forms that can be deduced in the abstract and used to predict a state's behavior. A state's interests can be broadly delineated, but how and how resolutely it will pursue them depends on context. Decisions in which the benefits clearly outweigh the costs and risks can usually be anticipated reasonably well; tough decisions about an uncertain balance are harder to predict. And it is precisely these hard, painful choices that Beijing is incentivized to present to the United States.

This is particularly important because, although America has long been willing to fight wars and endure costs to ensure that no other power dominates maritime Asia, this history is unlikely, on its own, to reassure regional states deliberating how to respond to China's focused and sequential strategy. This consistent willingness to risk and suffer to vindicate the US interest in Asia is important because it shows that any commitment relating to it is likely to be founded on solid ground. But vulnerable states are likely to look for something more, some greater assurance that *they specifically* will be effectively defended against an opponent as powerful as China. They will want a concrete, credible pledge from the United States (and potentially others) not to leave them in the cold but rather to effectively defend them in *these* circumstances.

Such states will therefore look at the United States' *differentiated credibility.* They will look at how it has treated that particular commitment or those similarly situated in the past. If America has sacrificed and risked much to uphold this or similar commitments in the past, this suggests that it judges upholding *this kind* of commitment worth a great deal of sacrifice and risk. The converse also holds—if the United States has been unwilling to sacrifice and take much risk on behalf of *this* commitment or those much like it, then this suggests that it does not really value the stakes enough to uphold it in the face of a tough and painful contest.

In an alliance, then, what matters most in ascertaining an ally's reliability is how it has behaved in circumstances that tell directly on how much it is willing to do and bear for that particular alliance. For Asia under the shadow of Chinese power, then, the United States is most credible to its regional allies—and to China itself—if it upholds its compacts in Asia, particularly against Beijing. In simpler terms, to sustain the credibility of alliances designed to help deny China hegemony in Asia, the United States should first and foremost ensure that it upholds its commitments to *those* alliances.

This means that a state can have a high degree of differentiated credibility with respect to one set of commitments and a lower level for others. This may cost it with the latter but help with the former. So the United States can be highly credible in Asia against China even as it downplays, shakes off, or ignores commitments in less important areas and for less important purposes, such as in the Middle East, especially beyond the Persian Gulf. The United States is a signatory to both the North Atlantic Treaty and the Rio Pact, but everyone knows it takes the former more seriously.[42] The United States withdrew from Vietnam but upheld its alliances in Europe and even strengthened them in the late 1970s and 1980s.[43] Washington can, then, withdraw from commitments made for Afghanistan, Iraq, and Syria without hollowing out its compacts in Asia.

If, that is, it follows through on its commitments in Asia. The less relevant are the instances of following through on ancillary pledges, the more important is its behavior in relevant circumstances. If the United States can back off commitments in secondary theaters such as the Middle East and not damage (or even help) its differentiated credibility in Asia, the same reasoning makes the consequences of *not* upholding its commitments in Asia all the graver. This is especially important because, although commitments are not necessarily interconnected, some are more interconnected than others—and *some are very tightly coupled.* If a committing state such as the United States decides it is too costly and risky to fight China for one ally in Asia, other similarly situated states will have to ask: How does this logic apply to us? Will the United States make the same cost-benefit calculation toward us, especially when conditions resemble those facing the state it abandoned?

Much, then, depends on what states see as similar situations or circumstances. This is of course a matter of judgment, but that does not mean it is entirely subjective. Human social life is built around systematizing just such judgments; indeed, much of what the courts do is to categorize, regularize, and apply such distinctions through "fact patterns," precedent, "reasonable man" standards, and the like.[44] States apply the same kinds of practical judgment. They weigh such considerations as whether they are part of the same alliance, located in the same region, face the same opponent or a similar military predicament, or provide a similar benefit to the guaranteeing state.

It may help to be more concrete. If the United States were to withdraw from Afghanistan, that decision would almost certainly be clearly distinguishable to Japan, Taiwan, Indonesia, or India as to how the United States would treat them vis-à-vis China. Afghanistan is distant from the wealthiest parts of Asia and has negligible impact on the balance of power in that region. But if the United States allowed Taiwan to fall to Chinese attack or coercion, that would present a very different picture to these states. As I will discuss later, the United States has a commitment to Taiwan's defense that is not a formal alliance but is widely viewed in Asia as real and highly significant. If the United States failed to uphold its commitment to defend Taiwan against attack by the People's Liberation Army because it judged—openly or not—the costs to be not worth the benefits, this would present a clear fact pattern. How would that pattern of action be distinguished from, say, how the United States would regard the Philippines—let alone nonallies such as Vietnam or Indonesia—as those states' vulnerability to Chinese military power increasingly resembled that of Taiwan? Why would the United States calculate its cost-benefit assessment differently for the Philippines, Vietnam, or Indonesia when the PLA threat to them became comparably fearsome? Why should they expect the United States to suffer enough and take sufficient risks for their defense if it was not willing to do so for Taiwan?

Thus if the United States, under the shadow of China's focused and sequential strategy, were to balk at defending a state in Asia to which it had provided a security commitment against Beijing, this decision would have profound implications not only for other allies in the region but for the anti-hegemonic coalition as a whole. It would provide direct evidence of America's unwillingness to defend a confederate in the Western Pacific under the darkening shadow of

Chinese military power—evidence that could not but be pointedly relevant to governments in Seoul, Manila, Hanoi, Jakarta, Kuala Lumpur, Bangkok, and even Canberra, Tokyo, and New Delhi. This action would speak far louder about the United States' cost-benefit calculus regarding China and Asia than its behavior in a clearly distinguishable situation such as the conflicts in Afghanistan or Syria.

Differentiated credibility is therefore of enormous importance in the context of the anti-hegemonic coalition. The Asian states at most risk from China's focused and sequential strategy—such as South Korea, the Philippines, Vietnam, Indonesia, Malaysia, Thailand, Australia, and even Japan and India—must wager a great deal if they are to affiliate with an anti-hegemonic coalition, whether in an informal partnership, legacy hub-and-spoke model, or multilateral alliance. Because the consequences of getting it wrong are so severe, their judgments about whether to so affiliate or continue to do so will be sensitive.

The United States therefore has the highest incentives to preserve its differentiated credibility related to denying China regional hegemony. If that repute is forfeited or compromised, states critical to the anti-hegemonic coalition are much more likely to balk at helping to check China's aspirations to regional predominance, with baleful consequences. Thus the United States should strive to follow through on its pledges to defend these states, even if doing so is costly, risky, or distasteful. At the same time, it should jealously guard its ability to make good on those pledges, including by pruning commitments elsewhere.

4

Defining the Defense Perimeter

EVEN DIFFERENTIATED CREDIBILITY, HOWEVER, IS AN instrumental good. Maintaining its own repute is not the ultimate goal of state action for the United States. The ultimate goal is serving its citizens' security, freedom, and prosperity. High credibility is a benefit, but it pales in comparison to avoiding great damage—let alone to national survival. When the protection of its credibility conflicts with these core national goods, the latter should prevail, as it would be foolhardy for a state to honor pledges in ways that result in costs far out of proportion to the gains. This is true even in the context of an anti-hegemonic coalition for the most important area of the world.

The United States should therefore try to avoid allowing these goods to come into conflict. It should seek to make and retain commitments that can be attended to in ways that reflect a reasonable correlation between benefits and costs. This is particularly important for the United States; it must make sufficient commitments to give the anti-hegemonic coalition enough substance and strength, but because of the consequences that would follow from its exhaustion or withdrawal, it must be judicious in its pledges.

Calibrating America's Commitments to Support Its Differentiated Credibility

There are three primary ways a state like the United States can ensure that it strikes the right balance between the burden of its commitments and what it is prepared to sacrifice to uphold them. First, it can maximize the power it has available for its alliances in Asia by ensuring the growth of its economy and limiting its engagements in peripheral theaters. Greater capacity reduces the pain of trade-offs in the primary theater.

Second, it can prepare to fight to uphold its commitments in ways that better correlate the benefits with the costs and risks it incurs; this will be my focus for most of the remainder of this book.

Third, it can carefully select which states should be included and excluded from its alliances. This brings us to the classic strategic question of drawing a defense perimeter, a subject that sounds archaic but is more contemporary than many realize. A defense perimeter defines the area for which one is committed to fight; it encompasses a state's own territory and the states to which one has made alliance commitments, whether by treaty or other, less formal methods.[1]

To repeat, alliances exist to provide the reassurance needed for anxious states to contribute effectively to the success of the anti-hegemonic coalition. In the case of the anti-hegemonic coalition against China, not all members need to be formal allies of the United States. Nor must all alliances include the United States—Australia and New Zealand are closely tied, and India and Vietnam might also form a pact. But because the United States is the crucial powerful state anchoring the coalition, the American alliance network—its defense perimeter—is uniquely significant for the coalition.

In setting its defensive line, the United States faces polar risks of undercommitting and overcommitting—of bringing on too few allies and bringing on too many, especially too many of the wrong kind.

Undercommitting risks leaving out states that, if sufficiently reassured by this bond, could add material strength to a coalition but that, if left exposed without an alliance guarantee, might elect to bandwagon rather than balance. If such states are acquired or subordinated by the aspirant, they could add to its power, thereby increasing China's power advantage relative to the coalition. Thus if the United States is too selective in choosing its allies, the coalition risks being too weak to check Beijing. In a vacuum, then, having more allies renders the coalition more powerful.

But overcommitting also carries great risks. By including a state within its perimeter, the United States ties its differentiated credibility directly to that ally's fate. Yet a vulnerable state can offer an aspirant like China an advantageous target for fighting a focused war. If the United States fights such a war, it could be weakened by the losses it has sustained, leading others to begin to question its ability to uphold its pledges to them. Conversely, if the United States balks at fighting, or fighting effectively, on the vulnerable ally's behalf, its differentiated credibility will be sorely wounded. More broadly, overcommitting carries the risk that the American people will be so sapped and dispirited by painful entanglement in distant conflicts that disengagement, however costly, seems the better option.

For the United States, and for the anti-hegemonic coalition as a whole, the question of who is in and out of the US defense perimeter is therefore essential. Those within the perimeter are the states for which the United States commits to go to war—and not just go to war but wage war to such a degree that the vulnerable state opts to stay with the alliance and, by extension, the broader coalition. Washington offers its differentiated credibility as mortgage to that pledge. Critically, then, to justifiably include or keep a state in an alliance, the United States should have a *plausible way to fight and prevail in such a conflict consistent with its level of resolve.*

This may be extraordinarily difficult in the face of an aspirant as powerful as China. The key, then, is for the United States to include enough states in its defense perimeter such that together these alliances enable a coalition strong enough to deny China hegemony in Asia—particularly by being strong enough to prevail in a systemic regional war—but also be discriminating enough not to overextend itself.

Crucially, the United States' choice is essentially binary—states are either in or out of its perimeter. It is tempting to hedge by making partial or ambiguous commitments, but this is imprudent in the face of a very strong aspirant like China. Ambiguity is tenable when a potential attacker is weak. When such an opponent can be effectively resisted at relatively low cost, ambiguity about a defense perimeter is tolerable and even attractive, because the aspirant cannot do anything too consequential and the ambiguity preserves leverage over the vulnerable states' behavior. This is the case in the Middle East versus Iran. The United States could readily defeat an Iranian invasion of Saudi Arabia or the United Arab Emirates.[2] Iran has little ability to mount such an assault, and Riyadh and Abu Dhabi have little reason to bandwagon toward the Islamic Republic to prevent it. Meanwhile, ambiguity over the precise extent and nature of the United States' pledge to them gives Washington leverage. The United States has long practiced this policy toward Taiwan as well.[3]

Ambiguity becomes more problematic, however, as the costs and risks of effectively defending allies rise and the consequences of failing to do so become more grave. In these circumstances, vulnerable states will naturally seek more credible assurance that they will be effectively defended and will naturally tend to regard ambiguity as evidence of lack of resolve—as will the aspirant. This is reasonable; the costs of backing down from an ambiguous pledge are lower than from a clear one. Thus a desire to keep the costs of backing out low is a fair indicator that a vulnerable state should be skeptical of a pledger's commitment, which will increase the appeal of bandwagoning. For the same reasons, ambiguity heightens the allure to an aspirant like China of challenging the commitment.

Half-hearted commitments are therefore ill-advised in the face of an aspirant like China. The United States can certainly aid and support states that are not allies; there is no barrier to its even fighting wars alongside them. But ambiguity is ill-advised because it implicates the quasi-guarantor's credibility. A defense perimeter is ultimately a declaration of the states and territories the committing state will effectively defend—will do, suffer, and risk what is necessary to keep them onside. Because ambiguity muddies this message, it raises the risk that the pledge will be discounted precisely when it is most needed: when the aspirant is strong and the vulnerable state is anxious. Ambiguity may provide leverage when there is little peril, but when there is a serious threat it makes the pledge seem shaky, even as it implicates and thus places at risk the guarantor's differentiated credibility. Effective, prudent alliances in such circumstances involve picking clear lines and sticking to them.

This is particularly important for an anti-hegemonic coalition in Asia, especially as it relates to the US commitment to Taiwan. The scale of China's power may make halfway commitments seem attractive, but this is a siren song. The United States should not try to be half-pregnant: it should thus either commit to Taiwan's effective defense or withdraw its pledge and separate its differentiated credibility from the island's fate. Importantly, the former does not require a formal treaty; a clearly communicated commitment to defend the island from China would be sufficient.

In general, the United States should be willing to include states as allies if, on balance, they add to the anti-hegemonic coalition's effectiveness in denying China's pursuit of regional hegemony. In other words, if the benefits of adding a given state outweigh the risks and costs imposed by its vulnerability, then it should be incorporated in the US defense perimeter.

This means first that prospective allies should help defeat China in a large war for mastery of the region *or* help defeat China's focused and sequential strategy. The "or" is important. A state might, for instance, offer advantageous geography within the likely bounds of a focused war but little in a large one. Alternatively, it might offer much in a major war but little in a plausible limited one, for example, because it has a high threshold for becoming actively involved. A state might bring great power, such as India or Japan today in Asia or West Germany or the United Kingdom in the Cold War. But a state might also bring attractive geography or other relevant advantages for a plausible limited war, even though it contributes little to the alliance's overall economic and military power, as Iceland did for NATO during the Cold War or the Philippines does in the contemporary context.

But whether including a state as an ally improves, on balance, the coalition's ability to deny China's pursuit of regional hegemony is not just about the benefits that that state would bring to the coalition. It is also about the costs and risks associated with bringing that state into an alliance with the United States. If those costs and risks exceed the benefits associated with forming an alliance with that state, then the United States should not do so.

The primary limiting factor for including a state, then, should be its *defensibility.* At its core, the criterion of defensibility means that no ally's effective defense should so deplete the guarantor's power or resolve that it becomes unable or unwilling to uphold its commitments and responsibilities to the anti-hegemonic coalition, let alone vitiate its ability to defend its primary interests. Put simply, adding a state as an ally should not require the United States to break or exhaust itself trying to defend it.[4]

This means the United States must be able to effectively defend its vulnerable allies in ways that it judges sufficiently correlate the costs and risks with the benefits of doing so. The costs of the fight and its results must be compatible with American resolve. This is what it means for a state to be "defensible." A weak state that is highly defensible, such as Palau in the Pacific or Ireland for NATO, may be at worst a distraction, but it will not threaten the alliance's viability. Even a strong state that is indefensible, however, could be a disastrous addition if its inclusion leads to defeat of or balking by the United States.

Washington can balance these competing factors by applying the principle of marginal utility: if the benefits of adding a given state outweigh the risks and costs imposed by its vulnerability, then it should be incorporated in the US defense perimeter.[5] If a state is powerful or otherwise important enough, then it should be included even if it is hard to defend. West Germany was vulnerable during the Cold War but very powerful, and so the United States and its allies strove to keep it in NATO. Likewise, if a state brings little to the alliance but is easily defended, it may still merit inclusion. Portugal brought little to NATO during the Cold War but was easy to defend. Yet if a state is hard to defend but adds little—such as Georgia with regard to NATO or Mongolia in Asia—it should be excluded.

Defensibility is in part subjective, because how much a state is willing to venture and bear is not a matter of fixed and geometric constants. Such willingness depends on many factors, and making this variability a conscious part of American defense strategy is at the heart of this book's argument. The main point is that the defensibility of its members is a central factor in assessing the advisability of forming an alliance. There are limits to how much a committing state is willing to risk and bear, and these limits become more constraining and pressing the stronger the opponent is.

There is an important proviso to add. Commitments, once made, take on a different complexion from commitments that have not been issued. In the abstract, it might seem that the same formula should apply to decisions to retain commitments as to making them in the first place. But just as firing a worker is a weightier matter than not hiring one, so decisions to abandon an alliance are more fraught than decisions not to enter them in the first place. Alliance commitments are designed to be sticky.[6] The intent is to bind; therefore extrication, even if it follows established procedures, calls into question the firmness of cognate commitments. This may be true even if the withdrawing state claims that it did not act out of fear. Nervous allied states may not believe such protestations, given that the balking state has an incentive to dissemble in order to quarantine the consequences. Thus even if a withdrawal is not actually founded on fear, it may still reverberate among those similarly situated.

Such fear will emerge especially in situations in which surety is particularly sought, such as among anxiously vulnerable states in the shadow of a powerful aspirant. The United States' willingness to abandon South Vietnam in the 1970s, for instance, and to shift recognition from the Republic of China on Taiwan to Communist China—even though done with warning and through diplomatic channels—nonetheless caused serious disquiet in South Korea, which judged itself similarly situated. If the United States was willing to walk away from South Vietnam and Taiwan, what did that say about its commitment to Seoul?[7] An unwillingness to make commitments may suggest fear or concern, but it does not directly call into question other commitments—if anything, it may signal the contrary, by demonstrating one's unwillingness to make them lightly.

It is also important to emphasize that the anti-hegemonic coalition, and the alliances that are fundamental to it, need to be bound together only by shared opposition to the aspirant's pursuit of regional predominance. This is crucial because it indicates that, within the limiting factor of defensibility, the coalition benefits from taking an ecumenical approach—all the more when the aspirant is very powerful. This means that the United States and any anti-hegemonic coalition should not weight heavily factors unrelated to the core criteria of power and defensibility, such as ideology, religion, or ethnicity. States that are fundamentally different and may even detest each other can still make highly effective allies in an anti-hegemonic coalition, as evidenced by the strange but successful partnership among Catholic France, the Protestant powers, and the Ottoman Turks against the Habsburgs in the Reformation era or the effective coalition of the rebellious Americans with absolutist France and imperial Spain during the American Revolution.

It is important to recall here that although the purposes of American politics include the promotion of Americans' own republican government, the way US policy in Asia can best accomplish this purpose is to check China's bid for hegemony by agglomerating sufficient power within the region to do so—*not by focusing on affiliating with other democracies,* let alone by affiliating only with such states. In other words, achieving republican ends for the United States does not mean associating only with other republicans. It may be advantageous or even necessary for an anti-hegemonic coalition to associate with nonrepublican governments. This is especially important in Asia, where many states are not democracies or are only inconsistently or imperfectly democratic.[8]

The most important nongeopolitical reason to exclude states from an alliance, or even from an anti-hegemonic coalition, is how their inclusion would affect the resolve of Americans or other key populaces to uphold the alliance. If a state's behavior or orientation is so repugnant that Americans or other allies would not defend it or would do so only half-heartedly, or its inclusion would diminish the alliance's standing and thus Americans' willingness to uphold it, then it is likely unwise to include it unless it is very strong or its behavior can be moderated.

Moreover, perspectives on whether a disliked or discordant state should be included are not fixed. The more dire the circumstances, the more lenient the United

States is likely to be in affiliating with unpalatable states. The United States fought alongside the Soviet Union in the Second World War even though many Americans had vehemently opposed it before the war and the United States would wage a long Cold War against it afterward. The United States and the Western Alliance brought in and rearmed the Federal Republic of Germany just a decade after they had fought the largest war in human history against the Third Reich. The United States sided with authoritarian South Korea in the Korean War and stood with the dictatorial Nationalist government on Taiwan in the crises of the 1950s. Republican states, including the United States, can and often do sustain alliances with states of quite differing political orientation, sometimes while encouraging those states to move toward more republican forms of government.[9]

Implications

For the United States, whose vast legacy network of pledges is increasingly in tension with its crucial role in Asia as the external cornerstone balancer, this problem of which commitments to make and uphold and which to forbear or withdraw from is especially acute. How should it resolve this tension?

As I have noted, America's core interest is in preventing the hegemony of any other state over a key region of the world, and the main threat to that interest is China in Asia. China poses by far the greatest potential for gaining regional hegemony anywhere, and Asia is by a considerable margin the world's most important region. Russia ranks as a significant but distant second because of its ability to threaten comparable US interests in Europe. The scale of China's power and the gravity of the stakes mean that the United States must be sure it can allocate enough of its power and its willingness to bear risk and cost to denying China hegemony in Asia. All alliances and other defense commitments should be made, retained, deferred, or exited in light of this priority.

Because the United States can singlehandedly or with impromptu coalitions defeat any plausible challenger to regional hegemony anywhere outside Asia and Europe, it should seek to avoid, reduce, or eliminate costly or demanding commitments in other parts of the world, including the Middle East, so that it can concentrate on the most demanding theater. It should therefore scale down its commitments in Afghanistan, Iraq, and Syria. That said, the United States can still seek to form or sustain more limited partnerships in these secondary regions, in part to reduce its own exposure and demands on Americans.

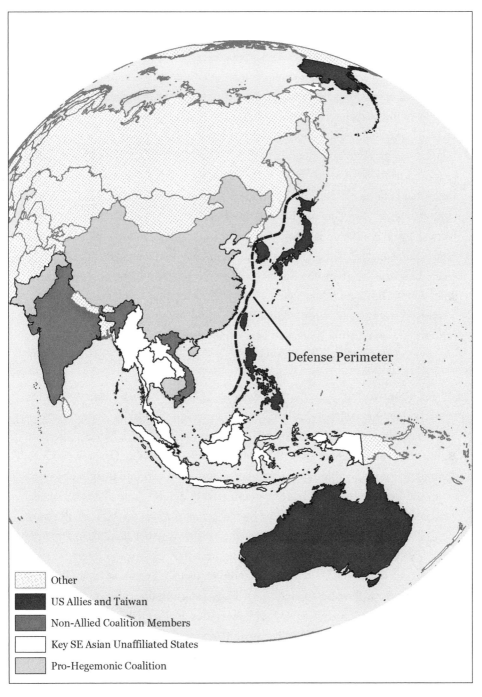

Defense Perimeter

Other

US Allies and Taiwan

Non-Allied Coalition Members

Key SE Asian Unaffiliated States

Pro-Hegemonic Coalition

Anti-hegemonic coalition. Original map by Andrew Rhodes.

The question, then, is what America's defense perimeter in Asia and Europe should be.

In Europe, the North Atlantic Alliance greatly outmatches Russia and any unaffiliated states that Russia could align with in seeking to reverse the regional balance. There is thus no strategic need to add new states to the alliance. Washington could reasonably support adding easily defensible states such as Switzerland or Ireland, since doing so would incur no meaningful added cost. But it should not agree to add Georgia or Ukraine to NATO because both are highly exposed to Russian attack while offering no meaningful advantage to the alliance that is remotely comparable to the costs and risks that their defense would impose on it.[10] Sweden and Finland are a closer call. Both have capable militaries, and the alliance is already exposed in Northern Europe with the Baltic states and Norway. Although Sweden and Finland would provide rather modest added capability, given the alliance's massive power advantage over Russia, they would bring an advantageous geographic position and capable, forward-deployed forces; moreover, adding them would involve bringing forward and solidifying an existing defensive line rather than creating an entirely new defensive position. Thus, although the United States should be cautious, their inclusion in NATO might be worthwhile.

The more pertinent question is whether NATO should withdraw from the more vulnerable states in Eastern Europe, especially the Baltic states, that create demands on the US military while adding little to the alliance's strength. Given the consequences of withdrawing alliance commitments, however, expelling these vulnerable NATO member states could be more than trouble than it would be worth if the alliance can effectively defend them at a level of risk and cost consistent with the United States' primary focus on Asia. I will return to this issue after I have examined the question of whether there is an effective military strategy for upholding such commitments.

It is Asia where the United States should focus its will and power and seek to maximize its differentiated credibility. I will return to this issue as well, but in the interim, it is enough to say that the states fearing China's hegemony—including not only the United States but many others—benefit from an anti-hegemonic coalition that is as strong as possible, because a potent coalition is more likely to deter and check Beijing. Given how potent China will be, the United States should seek to encourage as many states to participate in this coalition as feasible. Some strong states that are better able to resist China's attempt to isolate them, such as India and possibly Vietnam, might participate in such a coalition without an alliance guarantee from the United States. Given the costs and risks of extending such a guarantee, Washington should not seek to compel or even urge such states to become allies if such a bond is not necessary for them to become effective coalition members.

Vulnerable states considering whether to join or remain in such a coalition, however, will likely seek reassurance they will not be left exposed. It is these states on which US alliance formation and sustainment should focus. Because it is critically important that the coalition contain enough strong and well-positioned states to outweigh such a mighty China, the United States should be willing to retain and take on as many of these as allies as are defensible. By the same token, it should exclude and, if their vulnerability is significant enough, prune as allies any states that are not defensible.

With some countries, the issue is straightforward. Japan is the world's third largest economy, occupies important territory directly east of China, and is a long-standing US ally. There is no hope of forming an effective anti-hegemonic coalition without Japan, and reneging on the alliance with it would sabotage any attempt to persuade other states of America's resolve to uphold its commitments in Asia. Accordingly, Washington should clearly retain its alliance with Tokyo.

Australia is far from China and a long-standing and capable US ally. If the United States cannot effectively defend Australia, what hope do China's closer neighbors have for effective US aid? Washington should therefore maintain its alliance with Canberra.

Last, Washington has quasi-alliances with many very small Pacific island nations that are critical for power projection from the United States to the Western Pacific. Given that these are highly defensible if the United States is at all capable of operating effectively in the Western Pacific, maintaining and strengthening these guarantees makes sense.

India is critical for any anti-hegemonic coalition in Asia. Its strength means that its participation is critical, and its opposition to Chinese domination of the region means that it is likely to be a reliable coalition member. Its long-standing emphasis on autonomy and the ability to defend itself, moreover, mean that it may not need an American alliance commitment to participate in the coalition. I will return to this issue later.

States such as Mongolia and Kyrgyzstan, on the other side of China, might oppose Beijing's hegemony over them, but they have little power and any effort to defend them would be costly and almost certainly futile. Washington should not extend alliance guarantees to them.

The United States, Japan, India, and Australia by themselves, however, are probably not enough to prevent China from establishing regional hegemony. If China can subordinate or entice the remaining states in the Indo-Pacific area, it might be able to isolate Japan, India, and Australia and then induce their agreement to its predominance. Adding the remainder of the region to China's power could give Beijing a large power advantage over an anti-hegemonic coalition composed only of these states and the United States.[11] Such a strong pro-hegemonic grouping would also have enormous geographical and other advantages that would enable it to employ the focused and sequential strategy against these few remaining coalition members. The anti-hegemonic coalition will thus almost certainly need other states in the region to affiliate or collaborate with it. And because many of these states would be highly vulnerable if isolated by China, the United States will need to maintain or extend alliance or alliance-like guarantees to some of these states to give them sufficient confidence to associate with the coalition.

Because heartland Eurasia is much less defensible, given China's location, these states almost certainly need to come from the East Asian littoral and Southeast Asia. Some states in these areas have substantial and growing wealth and thus power and are, to varying degrees, at least potentially defensible against Chinese military power.[12] South Asia could also provide candidates, though the area is farther from most of developed Asia and, with the exception of India and to a far lesser degree Pakistan, its states are less wealthy and powerful.

The defense perimeter question is particularly important in the cases of South Korea and the Philippines, both of which are US allies, as well as Taiwan, which has a special quasi-alliance with the United States. Withdrawing commitments from these states would have tremendous consequences for America's differentiated credibility, and they would need to become essentially indefensible before Washington could take such a drastic step. Moreover, they are (not coincidentally) arrayed along the first island chain, providing a critical geographical position and forming a natural military boundary. Excluding Taiwan or the Philippines from the American defense perimeter would open a major gap in the first island chain and enable China to project military power into the broader Pacific and Southeast Asia. Abandoning South Korea, meanwhile, would mean excluding from the coalition one of the world's largest and most advanced economies. It would also heavily expose Japan, the linchpin of the American defensive position in Asia. Washington should therefore want to retain Taiwan, the Philippines, and South Korea in its defense perimeter if at all possible. The question is whether it can develop a military strategy for defending them that does not demand too much from Americans.

Washington must also determine whether it should be willing to extend its defense perimeter to include any of the other significant states in the region, particularly Vietnam, Thailand, Indonesia, Malaysia, Singapore, and Myanmar. As I will discuss later, this is important not only because of the power these growing economies would bring but because of their geography. US alliances in the Western Pacific trace the first island chain from Japan through the Philippines, hampering China's ability to project military power by sea—except to the south, through the South China Sea. Consequently, the first island chain states and the parts of Southeast Asia around the South China Sea are likely to be the locus of strategic competition between the US-led anti-hegemonic coalition on one side and China and its pro-hegemonic affiliates on the other. This is where the struggle for the advantage in Asia is likely to be most hotly contested.

Other states in the region, such as New Zealand, Sri Lanka, and Bangladesh, are less powerful and geographically remote from this locus of competition; their affiliation one way or the other is unlikely to make a major difference. Still others, especially those which fear one of the members of the anti-hegemonic coalition, appear to be moving into Beijing's pro-hegemonic camp, particularly Cambodia, which worries about Vietnam, and Pakistan, which fears India.[13]

To conclude, then, the United States should lead in developing and sustaining an effective anti-hegemonic coalition that must be strong enough to prevail in a systemic regional war as well as be resilient to China's focused and sequential strategy. This will require maintaining and possibly forming new alliances with important states in the region. The leading criterion for whether a state should be included in the US defense perimeter is its defensibility.

As I have noted, however, defensibility is not merely the sum of measurements of national power. Rather, it is supremely a matter of strategy. How, and thus how well, the United States and others could defend vulnerable allies against China is a central factor in whether a given state is defensible. Before determining what America's right defense perimeter is, then, we must first determine the best US strategy for defending vulnerable states against China in ways that correlate the risks and costs Americans are willing and able to assume with the benefits of such a defense. This will give us a clearer sense of the limits of what can be done. Once we know what can be defended, we will better know what should be.

5

Military Strategy in Limited Wars

THE UNITED STATES' ABILITY TO DENY China's bid for regional hegemony rests on its ability to muster and sustain an anti-hegemonic coalition strong enough to outweigh the power of China and its coalition, particularly in a systemic regional war. If such a coalition is to succeed, however, the United States must design and implement a defense strategy capable of effectively defending those coalition members bound to the United States by an alliance or quasi-alliance relationship from a Chinese effort to subordinate them. The victory mechanism of such a strategy is to provide enough confidence in American protection to enough regional states that they believe they can safely affiliate with the anti-hegemonic coalition, thereby making the coalition strong enough to prevent China from attaining regional predominance.

This is difficult to achieve, however, because a coalition consisting only of more secure states such as the United States, Japan, India, and Australia is unlikely to be powerful enough to deny China's bid for hegemony. Beijing would likely be able to assemble a stronger pro-hegemonic coalition from the rest of Asia through a combination of coercion, inducement, and outright force. An effective anti-hegemonic coalition must therefore include at least some nations that are more vulnerable to Chinese action, such as Taiwan, the Philippines, or Vietnam. If insufficiently protected, these states would be exposed to Beijing's ability to draw them under its dominion, weakening the anti-hegemonic coalition and eventually enabling China to establish hegemony over Asia.

The task before the United States, then, is to put into effect a defense strategy that enables the anti-hegemonic coalition to defend those nations without whose participation the mission of denying China's bid for regional hegemony will fail. This goal requires not only that such a strategy work in an abstract sense but that it can work at tolerable cost and risk to the coalition's members—that is, in a manner that keeps the costs and risks of defending those vulnerable nations proportional to the benefits the coalition members stand to gain from doing so. This is especially critical for the United States, given its essential role as external cornerstone balancer. If a war with China is seen to bring costs and risks that exceed Americans' tolerances, US policy-makers could find themselves on the cusp or in the midst of a necessary war only to realize that the American public does not want to fight or to fight hard enough.

And because no country can be expected to engage in total war on another country's behalf when its own vital interests are not immediately threatened, such a defense strategy must prepare the United States and its allies and partners to fight and achieve their aims in a *limited war* against China.

Military Strategy in a Limited War

Critical to such preparation is adopting the right *military strategy*.

As defined earlier, a *defense strategy* is a way of employing, posturing, and developing military assets, forces, and relationships to attain a set of goals or requirements that are themselves derived from and designed to serve a set of broader political aims.[1] A military strategy is a subcomponent of a defense strategy; it is specifically about how to fight a war. That is, it is about employing the military forces that the broader defense strategy has developed, trained, postured, and allied with to attain a nation's objectives in an actual conflict. Like the overall defense strategy, a nation's military strategy cannot sensibly be divorced from its political circumstances and goals; rather, it, too, should serve and conform to political ends.

In light of this, the United States must find a military strategy that enables it to defend vulnerable Asian allies within the anti-hegemonic coalition. Absent a credible ability to do so, the United States will be unable to raise and sustain a coalition capable of denying China's bid for regional hegemony.

The fundamental problem facing the United States is that it has only so much power and resolve to use in pursuit of that objective. Given China's strength and location in Asia, the United States cannot simply overwhelm it. The United States must therefore pay special attention to how to deploy American power and resolve, especially given that they are interdependent. The more resolute Americans are, the more power they will be willing to allocate, and the more powerful the United States and its allies are, the more resolute they are likely to be in applying some fraction of it.

The right military strategy will therefore use America's power and resolve favorably relative to China's. This means identifying the most effective ways in which the United States can employ its military power while reducing Beijing's ability to do the same. It also means finding ways in which the United States can use its power to bolster its own resolve while weakening China's ability to do the same.

Military strategy, though elemental in all conflicts, is less important when one combatant is much more powerful than the other. In such conflicts, so long as both sides are reasonably resolute, the stronger side typically prevails. Sitting Bull may have outsmarted George Custer at Little Bighorn, but the Americans were ultimately far too powerful for the Sioux to withstand, no matter how effective their military strategy was. But when combatants are more evenly matched, how a side develops and employs its power can be the difference between victory and defeat. Napoleon was able to overrun multiple powerful foes through effective employment of France's military forces. Germany was able to decisively defeat the Anglo-French forces in 1940 because its blitzkrieg was a better military strategy.[2]

Military strategy tends to be especially important in limited wars, in which the constraints on the use of force affect how much power a combatant brings to bear. These constraints can reduce or neutralize even great inequalities between combatants. The mighty United States sharply circumscribed the use of its military in Vietnam, for instance, making strategy far more relevant than if the United States had waged on North Vietnam and the Vietcong the total war it fought against imperial Japan. A similar dynamic has obtained for the United States in Afghanistan in this century.

The military balance in the Asian theater between the United States and China is highly competitive. Moreover, any war between the United States and China would, for reasons I will discuss later, almost certainly be limited. As a consequence, the outcome of such a war would very likely hinge on each side's military strategy—in particular, on how the constraints of the limited war evolved and which side was better able to employ its power and resolve within those constraints. America's success in Asia, and thus its interests in the world, depend on its ability to design and execute the right military strategy for a limited war.

Thinking about Limited War

Many see *limited war* as a contradiction in terms. Yet the limitation of war is deeply rooted in human behavior and history. Fundamentally this is because, even with the passions a war brings forth, human societies in conflict still have the strongest incentives to survive and preserve some of what they have, and thus to rationally correlate what they venture with what they can gain. In other words, while a state of war impels human beings to do things they might not otherwise do, it does not automatically transform human societies into clans of berserkers. The limitation of war is an expression of the desire or need to fight for something important but not truly existential without risking too much on the combat.

In the long period of civilized life before the advent of nuclear weapons, the vast majority of wars were limited.[3] This was not least because of the difficulty in the preindustrial era of mounting a war of total destruction; wars were often limited as much by incapacity as by choice. Industrialized warfare in the twentieth century, however, permitted destruction on an unprecedented scale. And the advent of nuclear weapons introduced the ability to wreak annihilating damage on societies quickly, surely, and at a dramatically lower cost than with conventional weapons. These two factors radically altered states' assessments about how readily wars could become total.

They also shifted expectations from a presumption that war would not be total to a concern that it very well might be—and quickly—especially in conflicts between nuclear-armed states. No longer were there material or technical barriers to imposing widespread destruction on an adversary's home territory. A nuclear-armed state now had a choice whether to impose that swift devastation—the "big stick in the closet" or "atomic queen" ready to be used.[4] In the Cold War, the United States and to some extent the Soviet Union increasingly recognized that the limitation of war could not be assumed but had to be actively sought and shaped.

This same dynamic would be central in any Sino-US conflict. The United States and China each possess survivable nuclear arsenals, meaning that each can inflict the most grievous harm on the other no matter what the other side does.[5] For each side, then, engaging in—or even seriously risking—a total war against the other would be tantamount to courting a most devastating response.

For any state, the only good that might plausibly justify enduring such cata-strophic suffering would be national survival itself. Yet America's survival as a na-tion would not be at issue in a systemic regional war with China, let alone a smaller war resulting from Beijing's focused and sequential strategy. To make sense, there-fore, any war the United States could plausibly contemplate against China *would have to be limited;* it would be utterly irrational and foolish to adopt an unrestrained approach to fighting China over stakes short of America's national survival because doing so would invite damage well beyond what the stakes were worth.

For the United States, this rules out strategies of preventive war. This is im-portant because even though preventive war sounds repugnant, it has a long his-tory and can seem attractive for established powers dealing with rising ones. Indeed, preventing another state's rise has been a fundamental driver of major war in the past. One of Germany's primary reasons for plunging into war in the summer of 1914 was to confront and degrade Russian power before it became too great; Russia in 1914 was the rising power of Europe. American decision-makers considered launching a preventive war against the Soviet Union early in the Cold War.[6] Yet the steps that the United States would have to take to pre-vent China's further rise—dismemberment, occupation, even destruction—would not only be exceptionally difficult and morally reprehensible but would unquestionably call forth a cataclysmic riposte.

But China, too, would also have the strongest possible incentives to limit any war it fought with the United States. National survival is not only the highest good for China but is of course the sine qua non for the attainment of all its other goals. Just as for the United States, then, the only scenario that could plausibly justify Beijing triggering a devastating American nuclear attack would be if China's national survival were in jeopardy. So long as the United States refrains from pursuing China's national destruction or collapse, then, Be-ijing, too, would face the most potent incentives to avoid impelling the United States to resort to devastating nuclear use.[7]

In sum, *both* sides in any plausible conflict between the United States and China would have the strongest possible incentive to keep a war limited. At the same time, however, it is still possible that such a war would become a contest of unfettered violence. It therefore is critical for the United States to actively plan and prepare to keep such a war limited.

Yet some might dismiss the case for preparing for limited war against China by arguing that there has never been a limited war between nuclear-armed great

powers, that such a war is an impossibility, or that it is too dangerous to contemplate. But even though nuclear-armed great powers have never fought a major limited war, human nature, history, and logic all strongly suggest that the
combatants would—and should—seek somehow to meaningfully limit any war
between them. Moreover, the history of the Cold War testifies that states seeking to defend their interests under the threat of nuclear devastation can not only
contemplate limited war but also plan for it. Fears of total war dominated the
minds of US and Soviet leaders throughout the early years of the struggle, for
instance, but as both sides' nuclear arsenals grew more survivable and reliable,
both camps grew progressively more focused on the potential for a limited war.
Moreover, as they came to recognize that such a limited war could be enormously consequential—it might, for instance, have determined the fate of
Western Europe—both sides devoted serious attention to ways of limiting war
on terms favorable to themselves.[8]

Thinking about limited war may even be more important today because the
likelihood that war between the United States and China would remain limited
is probably higher than it was between the Western Alliance and the Soviet
Bloc. This is due, first, to the perceived stakes. Throughout the Cold War but
especially in its earlier years, the stakes in a US-Soviet war appeared to be
total—hence the often-heard, if impolitic, refrain, "Better dead than red." And
because apocalypse seemed a plausible outcome of any US-Soviet war—even,
to many, the probable outcome—both sides felt compelled to avoid anything
that might meaningfully risk it, including a limited war.

That is not say fear of total war produced stasis. Indeed, the United States
and Soviet Union both conducted brinkmanship under the nuclear shadow during the Cold War. But both parties limited how far they went because an apocalyptic war seemed a highly credible result if war broke out.[9] Compared with the
prospect of losing everything to Soviet Communism, the American stakes in
preventing China's hegemony in Asia may not seem so high. Few are likely to
countenance a cataclysmic war over it. As a result, strategies of uncontrolled
warfare are even less appealing or credible in today's Sino-American competition than they were in the Cold War. This makes limited war more plausible,
which in turn makes limited war strategies more necessary.

Second, during the Cold War, both the United States and the Soviet Union
relied heavily on nuclear forces. They deployed thousands of nuclear weapons,
including with their forward forces in Europe. The United States, for example,

so thoroughly integrated nuclear weapons into its tactical aviation and naval forces during the early Cold War that it was essentially incapable of defending Taiwan with conventional weapons during the Taiwan Strait Crises of the 1950s.[10] Consequently, a war between the blocs, particularly in Europe, seemed very difficult, if not impossible, to prevent from escalating into a total thermonuclear exchange.

But nuclear weapons play a much less prominent role in the Sino-US competition today. Although both the United States and China possess survivable nuclear forces, neither relies on them for their military operations to anywhere near the degree that the United States and Soviet Union did for much of the Cold War. This means that it is more plausible for a war between the United States and China to remain short of a large-scale nuclear exchange.

These apparently soothing realities may, however, actually make brinkmanship, crisis, and war between the United States and China more likely. The sense that the stakes might be lower in Sino-American relations than they were between the Cold War superpowers may cause leaders to discount the potential for catastrophic escalation if they do go to war, thereby increasing their propensity to countenance risking or entering a conflict. Likewise, the fact that nuclear weapons are less central to the sides' force postures makes a conventional or limited nuclear war more feasible. However distasteful it might be, then, the United States will have to prepare for such a conflict in order to effectively deter or, if necessary, attain its objectives in one.

How Nations Limit Wars

The task for the United States, then, is to figure out how to prepare to fight and achieve its objectives in a limited war with China arising from Beijing's attempt to apply its focused and sequential strategy against a US ally in Asia. This requires a clear understanding of how exactly a war can be limited.

A limited war is fundamentally about *rules*. It may be thought of as a war in which the combatants establish, recognize, and agree to rules within and regarding the ends of the conflict and acknowledge or seek to have acknowledged that transgressing those rules will constitute an escalation that is likely to incur retaliation or counterescalation.[11]

Rules governing combatants' behavior in a limited war can take two forms. The first is limitations on the means employed. These limitations are akin to the rules in wrestling, in which the combatants hurt and try to dominate the other, but scratching and punching are barred. In the military context, the *means* restricted refer not just to the weapons deployed but also to how they are used. For instance, one or more combatants might seek to limit the geographic scope of military operations by designating certain areas off-limits. They might designate certain types of targets off-limits as well, such as national leadership, political symbols, civilian populations, critical infrastructure, or forces that are not directly involved in the conflict. Combatants may likewise seek to restrict the pace, intensity, or other aspects of force employment. Means can also go beyond strictly military instruments of war. For instance, combatants may seek to restrain provocative rhetoric or the use of economic or other nonmilitary forms of national power.

The second form of rule in a limited war constrains the ends sought by the combatants. These limitations might involve not seeking to overthrow an enemy's government, dismember its territory, disarm its military, compel it to pay war reparations, or otherwise confiscate its valued possessions. Such limitations might also include more symbolic aspects; one or both sides might not demand that the adversary make a formal surrender, issue an admission of guilt, or undertake other humiliating actions.

Restrictions on the ends sought during a war matter because, in the simplest terms, a limited war must leave the defeated with something, or else the losing side will have little reason to end the conflict.[12] The adversary must see itself as better off settling than continuing to fight; a nation is much less likely to agree to end a war if it believes its adversary is intent on overthrowing its government, annexing a large chunk of its territory, or threatening its very existence. In such circumstances, even a battered nation might judge that continuing to fight is better than conceding. Germany, for instance, faced near-certain defeat by 1944, but it fought on until it was wholly defeated because Hitler and his government saw no compelling reason to capitulate.[13]

Rules in a war can arise directly, through the efforts of the combatants themselves or from external sources, and they can arise either before or during a conflict. Combatants can set explicit rules by, for example, privately or publicly communicating to an adversary that a particular area or target is off-limits, as the United States announced constraints on its bombing campaign against North Vietnam.[14] Combatants can also set rules implicitly, for example, by forbearing certain action when one's preferred rules are observed and carrying out those actions when they are violated. During the Korean War, the United States limited its airstrikes north of the Yalu River while Beijing, for similar reasons, limited its use of airpower by not targeting US forces at sea and in Japan. The two sides carefully watched and calibrated these limitations, as did the Soviet Union—but they were never formally agreed to.[15]

Combatants need not, however, set the rules themselves. The formal laws of war that bind compliant states are the product of a long history involving multiple states. Third parties can also set rules for conflicts more directly. During the Korean War, the United States considered using nuclear weapons but ultimately decided against it, in substantial part because of international opposition, including a forceful intervention by British prime minister Clement Attlee.[16] A similar dynamic played out during the Vietnam War, as US considerations of expanding the war and intensifying bombing against the North were constrained by concerns about strong international blowback.[17]

Regardless of who sets them, the rules in a limited war do not enforce themselves, and their enforcement cannot be assumed. Action—or the credible threat of it—is required on the part of the combatants or third parties to ensure that a particular set of rules will be observed. Such rules are effective only when those intent on seeing them upheld can convince one or more of the combatants that the costs or risks of violating those rules will be too high to justify doing so.

This is an especially pointed problem in a war between two exceptionally powerful states such as the United States and China. There is no omnipotent umpire standing above these states able to adjudicate the application of the rules in a war between them. This makes enforcement both critical and especially knotty, not least because the rules limiting a war can change as the conflict evolves.

Indeed, any rule governing the means employed or ends sought in a war is subject to modification during the war. A combatant might violate a rule, for instance, if it realizes that doing so will help its cause enough to justify absorbing the other side's retaliation. Or it might seek to change a rule if it determines that observing that rule in its original formulation is no longer in its interests. Combatants may also create rules in response to emergent circumstances or updated strategic evaluations. The United States and North Vietnam, for example, both adjusted the bounds of the war in Indochina as the conflict evolved. The United States for many years heavily restricted its and Saigon's activities in Cambodia, but the two allies conducted a major intervention into that country in 1970 when they judged it sufficiently beneficial to do so. Hanoi, meanwhile, initially observed the dictates of the Paris Peace Agreement but determined it was worth the risk to launch the major invasion of the south in late 1974 that led to the Republic of Vietnam's downfall.[18]

Last, the rules in a limited war need not be symmetrical. One side could agree not to attack certain things or seek lesser war aims without expecting reciprocity. That said, the more generalizable and readily explicable a formula is, the more likely it is to be respected, especially between combatants of comparable power. Formulas for limitation that seem highly individualized are more likely to be seen as discriminatory and thus less likely to receive either the opponent's consent or important third-party support.[19] The potential for asymmetry only underscores the value of identifying and enforcing an advantageous set of rules.

How a war will be limited, then, is not fixed. The rules are inherently malleable and subject to influence by both sides and by third parties. War limitation is thus itself a product of negotiation, a matter, in Thomas Schelling's famous formulation, of violent bargaining.[20] The process of war limitation therefore provides latitude—often great latitude—for establishing and amending its formulas for constraint. It thus opens the field for the deliberate shaping and exploitation of these formulas for one's purposes. This makes the rules of a limited war a front of their own.

The Battle for Advantageous Rules

Determining how a war will be limited—and how well prepared one is to exploit those limitations—may therefore very well determine the war's outcome. Wars are resolved by how much of what the combatants have they are willing to apply to and lose in the struggle, how they employ what they are prepared to dedicate, and the bounds they are prepared to establish or accept—and how these factors interact with the same on the part of the adversary. Hence wars can be won by the weaker side, even the much weaker side, as in the cases of the American rebels against the British Empire, the Vietcong against the United States, or the Afghan mujahideen against the Soviets.[21]

But this dynamic is especially important in the Sino-American context because the power balance between the United States and China is not lopsided but highly competitive, especially in Asia. How constraints would limit the two combatants in a war would be highly significant in determining the result. How well the military strategy of the United States and its allies and partners exploits those constraints to achieve advantages in a conflict would therefore be critical, and possibly decisive.

These considerations are important in shaping American, Chinese, and other states' behavior not only in war but also in peacetime. As discussed earlier, states do not assess how the "imagined wars" that shape international politics would unfold through simple comparison of potential combatants' GDPs or their abstracted level of resolve over a potential controversy. Rather, states evaluate how such imagined wars would be resolved by judging how the two sides' strategies for using their power and resolve would fare against each other within the likely rules that would confine such a war.

Effectiveness at limited war, then, is equivalent to strategic advantage in war and peace—and vice versa. Thus, the side that prepares itself in accord with the better strategy for limited war will have an advantage, quite possibly a decisive one. That is because, although a limited war is by definition limited, it is also by definition a war. The fact of being limited does not mean that the war will end in a draw; limitation does not preclude one side coming out better than the other. That the war is limited means that one or both sides want to limit the damage they incur; that there is a war at all, however, means that they are willing to fight and take risk to gain or protect something. Thus a limited war remains a contest for, if not total victory—since a limited war means that objectives must be more modest—then at least for one side to achieve its aims more fully. Within the potentially fragile and elastic confines of a limited war, then, both sides can and indeed likely must fight, coerce, jockey, and bluff to gain advantage.

Prevailing in Limited War

For the United States and any engaged allies and partners to prevail in a limited war with China, three conditions must be met: (1) the war must remain limited in both means and ends; (2) the United States must be able to achieve its political ends by operating within those limitations; and (3) Beijing must agree to de-escalate or end the conflict on terms acceptable to the United States.

Crucially, then, America's prevailing in a limited war with China does not mean a full defeat of China. Rather, as I will discuss in later chapters, it means that the United States achieves its political objectives through a constrained war.

The United States will prevail in this sense so long as it does better than China within the set of rules that govern the war. The rub is that, between such capable opponents, each side has the option of escalating in response to the other's attempt to impose rules that put it at a disadvantage. In other words, if a side that is losing within one set of rules believes that a different rule set would give it an advantage, it has a very powerful incentive to try to change the rules to that rule set.

Prevailing in a limited war therefore requires not only superior performance within a given set of rules but *persuading* the other side not to continue the conflict or escalate and instead to accept a limited but meaningful defeat. Since neither the United States nor China would be able simply to impose its will on the other, succeeding in such a limited war ultimately requires convincing the adversary that the costs and risks of continuing to fight or of escalating the war would outweigh the benefits.

Limited wars end when both parties—particularly the loser—find settlement less distasteful than continuing to fight. Because the war is limited, both sides must come away with something. But because it is a war, what they come away with need not be equal. Fundamentally, then, a side will *choose* to settle—to lose—if it regards the alternatives as worse. That choice does not mean that the losing side is incapable of continuing or escalating, only that the loser does not think that persisting or escalating out of its defeat within the existing rule set, or escalating to try to find a new, more advantageous rule set, promises enough gains to outweigh the prospective costs and risks. These costs can include outright physical damage to its military or other valued things, as well as the toll on its reputation, political instability, and other, softer costs and risks. The more painful and more likely a combatant anticipates these costs will be, the more likely it will judge the risk of triggering them too great to continue fighting or escalating.

Thus the winning combatant in a limited war is the side able to employ a military strategy to achieve a decisive advantage relevant to the attainment of its political objectives within a given rule set and is then able to persuade the adversary that continuing or trying to escalate further is too costly or risky for the prospective gains. The loser is the one that fails within the rules observed and cannot find a sufficiently palatable way to exploit or change the rules to its advantage.

The Burden of Escalation

For a capable combatant, the alternative to a limited defeat within a given set of rules is to try to escalate its way out of failure. Escalating out of a failing bid is not unique to warfare. In any bargaining interaction between sufficiently powerful parties, a side that is unsatisfied can raise the pressure on the other side to come to its terms. At an auction, one can escalate by outbidding a rival; when buying a car, one can do so by threatening to go to another dealer. A state at war can escalate by intensifying or expanding its use of force.

Escalation does not take place in a vacuum, though. It is always easier or harder, safer or riskier, depending on what the other party can and is willing to do. In an everyday negotiation, a lowball offer can be met by the counterparty with a calm willingness to continue bargaining—or by walking away. If the first side thinks that the counterparty will react by calmly continuing to negotiate, the burden of lowballing is light and there is little risk in trying. But if the first side thinks that the counterparty may react negatively, breaking off negotiations and leading others to be disinclined to do business with the first party, then the risk of escalation is heavier, and the first side will be much more cautious about trying a lowball offer.

Accordingly, in any bargaining scenario, the winning side is the one who can make further escalation by the other side so costly and risky that the other side would rather accept defeat than up the ante. We can call these costs and risks *the burden of escalation.* The heavier this burden, the less likely one is to escalate. In the military context, then, for a side to prevail in a limited war, it must persuade its opponent that the opponent cannot win within the existing rule set *and* that the burden of escalation associated with trying to move the conflict to a more favorable rule set is too heavy to bear.

This requires, of course, that the winning side prevail within the existing rule set. Doing so is not difficult when one side is vastly stronger than the other and can use its advantage within the given rule set. For instance, in the First Gulf War, the United States and its coalition partners could readily identify and exploit such a rule set, expelling Iraq from Kuwait and presenting Baghdad with the choice of accepting its expulsion or risking occupation or unseating of the government. Iraq could not stop the coalition's recapture of Kuwait, and although it had options to hurt coalition members, such as by launching Scud missiles, these could not change the fundamental dynamic and, carried too far, risked bringing American and allied military power more fully down upon Iraq itself.

Prevailing is considerably tougher, however, when a combatant is better positioned to prevent its opponent—even a stronger opponent—from achieving its objectives within a given set of rules. During the Vietnam War, for instance, the United States was orders of magnitude more powerful than North Vietnam, but the Communists north and south were far better positioned to contest America's ability to defend the Republic of Vietnam than Iraq was to hold Kuwait. At the same time, domestic and international opposition, among other factors, limited the lengths to which Washington was prepared to go to support South Vietnam. Even though the United States had some success suppressing the Vietcong insurgency, eventually expanded the war to Cambodia and Laos, and launched fierce bombing campaigns against North Vietnam, the Communists were ultimately able to endure and escalate in ways that the United States was unwilling to match.

Competitions in Resolve

This problem is most acute in a more evenly matched contest, such as a war between the United States and China would be. The United States would not only have to defeat China within a given rule set but would have to persuade China, a nation with plenty of options for escalating, to instead agree to war termination on terms favorable to the United States. How could the United States persuade Beijing to concede, especially in a war that impinged on interests China might consider vital?

This question is particularly pointed when a powerful losing side like China might appear to care more than the United States about the stakes at issue, for instance, Taiwan. China might be willing to bear much more suffering and risk to achieve its goals, and even if it were defeated within a given rule set, it might prefer to escalate to a more favorable rule set despite the attendant risks.

This quandary is especially salient when survivable nuclear arsenals overhang the contest. In such circumstances, a side losing within a given rule set can always resort to nuclear employment in a bid for escalation advantage. At that point, if the other side is resolute enough to respond with nuclear strikes of its own, the conflict would tend toward becoming a pure contest of who can better and longer bear the pain each can inflict on the other. Thus, if taken to its logical extreme where the parties cannot stop each other from inflicting great pain on the other, such a war would tend to become a pure contest of resolve—a battle of knife cuts and ultimately sharp and deep stabs.[22]

At first glance, this would seem to mean that the side with more resolve would always win such a contest. Taken to the extreme, if one side is more willing to risk large-scale nuclear escalation, then it should have a decisive bargaining advantage. If one party is willing to countenance everybody losing out while the other is not, it might appear to have a determinative bargaining edge.

But this is not necessarily true. That a side is more resolute over a given issue does not mean that it is actually prepared to commit suicide over it, even if it wants the other side to think so. It is one thing to threaten suicide and another thing to mean it, let alone follow through. China, for instance, may care more about the disposition of Taiwan than the United States does, and Beijing certainly benefits if Washington believes that China would pull down the temple over its head rather than accept a limited loss over Taiwan. But China is exceedingly unlikely to invite its own destruction, given that this would mean the loss of everything it values—and the United States can see that.

Further, in war as much as in peace, a nation's resolve can change, especially as the population's perception of what is at stake changes. Beijing might at first appear more willing than the United States to tolerate nuclear escalation in a conflict over Taiwan, but whether that remained the case would depend heavily on how such a war unfolded and what appeared to be at issue. A state's willingness to suffer in a conflict depends not only on the reasons why the sides began fighting or bargaining—and thus not on abstracted, isolated questions of resolve over a given issue—but also on factors that can emerge during a conflict and may even overshadow the original controversy. Accordingly, a state's willingness to suffer and risk in pursuit of an objective depends heavily on how a war evolves.

The factors affecting a nation's resolve include its understanding of its adversary's intentions and ambitions, its beliefs about the adversary's openness to de-escalation and conciliation, its assessment of its adversary's strength and resolve, how much that nation has already suffered, and political opinion at home and abroad. These and other elements inform an instrumental calculation of whether further fighting or escalation would be profitable. Moreover, to the degree that nations go to war and fight not only based on strategic calculation but also for reasons of honor, prestige, and vengeance, these factors can also bear heavily on a nation's resolve to fight. During the Second World War, for instance, few Americans could detail the actual disputes that led to the outbreak of war with Japan. But all remembered Pearl Harbor, the Bataan Death March, and the behavior of Japanese forces on their rampage through the Asia-Pacific, and it was those events that really hardened Americans' resolve to fight and ultimately dominate Japan in the Pacific theater, despite the fearsome costs.[23]

Moreover—and critically—many of the factors affecting a nation's resolve to fight *can be deliberately shaped.* A state can induce its adversary to act in ways that strengthen its own commitment, thus mitigating or even neutralizing its adversary's original advantage in resolve. A nation can also behave in ways that undermine its adversary's resolve, even in situations in which the adversary originally seemed more committed to fight. In other words, actions taken before or during a conflict can affect both combatants' will to fight and prevail. Abraham Lincoln maneuvered such that it was the South that at Fort Sumter fired the first shot, catalyzing northern resolve to a degree that would almost certainly not have been the case if the North had taken the first violent step.[24] This means that each side can take actions that increase its own resolve and diminish its adversary's.

For the United States and any engaged allies and partners, this would entail causing China to act in a manner that validates the perception of Beijing as a grave threat not just to the state it is currently targeting but to other members as well. Although it would be patently irrational for the coalition, including the United States as the external cornerstone balancer, to suffer the grave damage of a major war, let alone nuclear attack, just for the sake of a single vulnerable ally, its members could countenance such loss and risk if China had demonstrated that it posed a severe threat to their vital interests and that the best way to head off the threat was to defend the vulnerable state.

The upshot is that a limited war is not determined by two fixed, abstracted levels of resolve engaged in a brinkmanship competition. Rather, the two sides' will to fight evolves through the contest, and their respective abilities to influence each other's resolve also changes as the war progresses. Thus, how the war resolves is as much about how the fight unfolds and what it impels each side to do as it is about how much each side originally cared about the issue that prompted the war in the first place.

Passing the Burden of Escalation

This is why the burden of escalation is so important in a contest between two powerful nations like the United States and China. Because each is armed with survivable nuclear forces, neither can truly take away the other side's ability to escalate. Therefore resolve is crucial. Ultimately each nation decides whether it will escalate or not. But the more unpalatable the path of escalation can be made to appear, the more it will tax the resolve of the combatant considering whether to escalate, and thus the less likely that combatant will be to choose that course. The United States did not want to abandon South Vietnam, but it finally determined that escalating to prevent Saigon's fall would be too costly relative to the stakes at hand and that, even though withdrawal would be embarrassing, it would also be tolerable. In the 1980s, the Soviet Union could have tried to escalate its way out of its losing war in Afghanistan; yet Moscow ultimately concluded that doing so would be both difficult and prohibitively costly and thus less tolerable than a painful retreat.

A combatant can weigh down its opponent's burden of escalation in two basic ways. First, it can simply deny or degrade the opponent's ability to escalate *effectively.* For instance, even if neither side can realistically preempt the other's nuclear forces before they can be used, that does not mean that both sides have equally good options for incremental escalation below the apocalyptic level. This is crucial because, for any interest below the existential, states will not want to be left with the choice between "suicide and surrender."[25] A state that can escalate only to the level of mutual thermonuclear cataclysm has little leverage, since the other side is unlikely to believe that it will commit suicide over anything short of a truly existential interest. Thus the side that can reduce the other's ability to escalate incrementally gains a major advantage.

Second, a combatant can cause its adversary to escalate in ways that catalyze the former's own resolve. This was what Lincoln did with Fort Sumter. On the other side of the coin, Japan launched a surprise attack on Pearl Harbor and massacred civilians and prisoners in a rampage across Asia; these actions contributed greatly to the United States' willingness to enter the war and prosecute it with great resolution. If Japan had attacked only the European colonial possessions in Asia and conducted itself in keeping with civilized norms of military behavior, the American people might not have supported the kind of war needed to defeat it.

Resolve over what initially seemed the stakes at issue can only do so much against these two measures. One side may be more resolute about the controversy in some detached or abstract sense. But this will not gain the side very much if the only way that it can try to vindicate its interests is either to unleash a full nuclear war that results in its own as well as its adversary's destruction or to make the conflict about something more than those initial stakes and thus catalyze its adversary's will to fight. Japan surely cared more about its own political independence before the Second World War than Americans did, but by

1945 Americans' resolve had become so hardened by the Japanese conduct of the war that the United States was willing to insist on unconditional surrender from Japan, despite the fearsome costs Americans bore to impose it.[26]

Wars are almost always limited, then, and any war between the United States and any participating members of the anti-hegemonic coalition and China would almost certainly be limited. In a limited war between two nuclear-armed states of roughly comparable power, the upper hand will go to the combatant best able to limit the conflict using rules within which it can gain a meaningful advantage, exploit those boundaries to achieve its objectives, and place its opponent in a situation from which escalation out of defeat will seem prohibitively costly or risky. Thus, how well prepared and suited the United States and the anti-hegemonic coalition are to frame and fight such a war will be crucial, not only in determining which side would prevail in a war, but also in the peacetime political influence that will derive from judgments as to how such a war would resolve.

The United States and the anti-hegemonic coalition therefore need to be able to frame and fight a limited war against China over interests that are important but still partial. They must employ a military strategy that enables them to fight such a war more effectively than Beijing and place China in a situation in which settlement appears less distasteful than continuing to fight or escalating further. This means limiting the scope and violence of the war sufficiently to correlate it to the interests at stake while inducing China to bear the burden of escalation.

6

The Importance of Focusing on an Opponent's Best Strategies

THE WARS THAT WOULD ACTUALLY TAKE place between China and the United States and the anti-hegemonic coalition, or as imagined wars shape states' choices and behavior, would almost certainly be limited, because both sides would have the most powerful interests in keeping them so. The nature of those limits would, though, be subject to manipulation by both sides, meaning that each side's military strategy would be crucial in determining which side prevailed.

What military strategy would best enable the United States and its allies and partners to deny China's efforts to undermine the anti-hegemonic coalition? The answer depends first on our understanding the strategies that would best enable Beijing to achieve its strategic objectives.[1]

Why It Is Important to Understand China's Best Military Strategies

From both geostrategic and military vantage points, US interests in the Asian theater are fundamentally defensive. The United States has no inherent interest in harming China or in imposing its own hegemony over the region. US goals are limited to preventing Beijing from achieving regional hegemony, since this would imperil America's critical interests. In other words, the United States seeks to establish and hold a line behind which enough states can gather to outweigh China and whatever confederates it might rally to help Beijing achieve hegemony in Asia. Once that balance has been achieved, America's priority will be to maintain it.

As America pursues these objectives, however, China will remain an independent actor with an exceptional degree of power. Beijing therefore has a critical vote in how any geopolitical interaction—and ultimately any war—with the United States unfolds. It is up to China what to do with the US defensive line. Beijing can accept it or challenge it, and it can challenge it here or there, in this way or that. This leaves China much leeway in shaping how the United States will react. Any American strategy must therefore be resistant and resilient to China's efforts. Ignoring what China will or could do is tantamount to hoping for the best against a state of immense power—an unwise course.

To adopt an effective military strategy, then, the United States must develop some estimation of how China might act. This is especially important because the power and resolve available to the United States and its allies and partners for defending against China's bid for regional hegemony are at a premium. Against a powerful aspirant like China, those resources are likely to be scarce at the margin because of the closeness of the balance of power.

This scarcity matters because different military strategies work better in different situations and against different opposing strategies. One side may be stronger militarily, for instance, but if it disperses its forces along a long defensive line, it may be defeated by an opponent that concentrates its forces and rolls up the defender's scattered units. On the other hand, a state that holds its forces back may fail to mount a timely defense against an enemy incursion, allowing the adversary to harden its gains and establish a strong defensive position. An actor is best positioned if it has a sense of what military strategies the other side might pursue and then allocates its own scarce resources as efficiently as possible to counteract them.

The Trouble with Predicting How an Opponent Will Act

Anticipating how China will behave is, however, an inherently imperfect and uncertain task. Human beings have difficulty predicting how they themselves will behave; forecasting what others will do is all the harder. Even when human decisions proceed largely from cost-benefit rationality, it can be difficult to anticipate how circumstances will evolve and how actors will assess the balance of costs and benefits. And human decisions are influenced by emotion and sentiment, which are even harder to anticipate.

State decision-making, though generally more deliberate and rationalistic than that of individuals, has its own eccentricities, such as bureaucratic and organizational dynamics. There is still debate, for instance, about why some of history's most studied and important decisions went as they did, such as those leading to the First World War and Washington's and Moscow's during the Cuban Missile Crisis.[2] Other choices remain puzzling, if not baffling, such as Japan's decision to attack the United States in December 1941 and Germany's decision to follow suit and declare war on the United States.[3] If we have such trouble explaining why states behaved as they did in the past, how can we hope to predict what they will do in the future?

Beyond this is another difficulty: it is difficult to gain material information when others seek to protect it, and it is rare to have grounds to be entirely sure that the information gleaned is valid. For instance, the Central Intelligence Agency's operations against the Soviet Bloc were infamously tied in knots in the later 1960s by doubts over whether the revelations of KGB defector Yuri Nosenko were genuine; debate about whether Nosenko was a genuine defector or a Soviet plant continues to this day.[4] Such uncertainties are especially acute in the case of military and sensitive political information, which is what is at issue here. Such information is usually closely guarded, and China is even more secretive than most major powers in part due to the particular characteristics of the Chinese Communist Party, which places a special priority on secrecy, deception, and other ways to frustrate foreigners'—especially Americans'—ability to understand what it is planning.[5]

Further still, states are adaptive. If a state fears that important information has been compromised, it may change course, rendering formerly accurate information invalid. Take, for example, the Mechelen incident in early 1940, in which the Belgians famously came upon Germany's original, more conventional plan to invade the West. The compromise of this plan ultimately helped lead the Germans to adopt the daring—and tremendously successful—Manstein Plan, focusing their attack through the Ardennes Forest.[6] But even this kind of discovery does not always have straightforward results. Robert E. Lee's detailed battle plan for invading the North fell into the hands of the Federal Army in 1862, yet Generals George McClellan and Henry Halleck feared that the captured document was a ruse and failed to capitalize fully on their advance knowledge. Likewise, even though the Soviet Union came into possession of the actual Fall Blau plans for Germany's 1942 Eastern Front offensive, the Soviet leadership ignored the find, believing it to be a trick. They remained convinced that, contrary to what the plan said, Germany would continue its advance on Moscow rather than shift its attention to the south—which is where the Germans actually did allocate their main effort that year.[7]

This is why markets put such high prices on credible, material information about how others will behave—it is scarce and often fleeting, and even more so in a war. As Clausewitz put it, "Many intelligence reports in war are contradictory; even more are false, and most are uncertain." He thus defined war as "the realm of uncertainty."[8] Accordingly, any concrete and detailed assessment of China's military strategy will almost certainly be highly qualified and filled with caveats. Empirical information allows the United States only to see as through a glass, darkly.

Dealing with Strategic Uncertainty

Fortunately for the United States, achieving its geopolitical aims does not require perfect or even very precise information to deter and, if necessary, prevail over China to the degree needed. The United States' core concern is not to fully understand China or predict its every move—it is to keep Beijing from doing things that run contrary to important American interests. Washington's core interest is thus fundamentally defensive: it wants to deny any other state hegemony over a key region of the world. America's concern, in essence, is whether China jeopardizes this interest. The United States thus needs to understand China only to the degree required to serve this goal. While deeper and broader understanding of Chinese thinking can help—as long as it does not create false confidence or expectations that only on such basis can effective action be taken—it is not necessary.

Indeed, the United States could satisfy this interest with a modest understanding of China's intentions and military strategic planning. States never have perfect—and rarely even very good—information about their rivals' detailed plans. Yet effective deterrence and defense are common. During the Cold War, the United States was routinely perplexed, when not wholly in the dark, about the plans and activities of the Soviet leadership, military, and intelligence apparatus, but the Soviet Union never mounted an assault or large-scale coercion against NATO. In fact, it appears that the Soviet Union had a considerably better intelligence picture of the West than the other way around, yet the West eventually prevailed in their long struggle.[9]

The United States was able to protect Western Europe in the Cold War despite this uncertainty because it could account for that uncertainty while still guarding its interests. Homeowners can buy insurance, and investors and gamblers can spread their bets. States, meanwhile, can design and develop military forces and postures, alliances, and economic arrangements to deal with uncertainty. This is not to laud ignorance; the less one knows, the higher the premium one will to have to pay or the wider one's spread will have to be. It is only to say that uncertainty and a degree of ignorance are not fatal for military strategy. They are a part of what a strategy must be designed to deal with.

Focus on the Adversary's Best Military Strategies

A state like the United States should deal with this inherent uncertainty about what China will do by identifying China's best military strategies and planning its defense around them.

What does it mean to say that a military strategy is better than another, though? And how does one identify what such strategies are? The United States' fundamental concern is that China could attain regional predominance by agglomerating more power than the anti-hegemonic coalition could array against it. The best military strategies for China are, therefore, those that most effectively advance its progress toward this goal of regional hegemony. These are what the United States should focus on.

We can qualify the *best* in *best strategies* by two factors. First, it describes strategies that would rationally advance China's interests—meaning that they would result in gains that outweigh the costs. Second, they would advance China toward its goal of regional hegemony. These factors define the set of strategies that should occupy American and coalition strategists. The first focuses them on the strategies that could actually pay off for Beijing. The second narrows their attention to strategies that matter to the United States' core aim of preventing another state from achieving predominance in any region.

If regional hegemony is indeed its goal, China must become stronger than the United States and its partners in the region, meaning that it must be able to defeat them in a systemic regional war. To do so, Beijing must prevent the formation of, hollow out, or break apart any coalition designed to frustrate its bid for regional hegemony. This means that, as far as the United States is concerned, China's best military strategies are those that, consistent with the focused and sequential strategy, defeat the anti-hegemonic coalition or prevent it from forming, consolidating, or holding together.

Alternative Models for Strategy

Many argue, though, that it is not actually prudent to focus on China's best military strategies and that it is more appropriately humble and wise for American planners to concede that they cannot know the future. They should, in this view, be as ready as possible for anything that might come. Others contend that the United States should look to the most likely strategies an opponent might pursue. A third camp argues that the United States should concentrate on those approaches a state like China could employ that would be most destructive.

Before unpacking China's best military strategies, then, we need first to look at these alternative ways of conceiving the challenge China poses to the antihegemonic coalition. This is especially important because these alternative approaches have implications for how the United States and its allies and partners should allocate their resources and efforts that are dramatically different from the approach I advocate.

Preparing for Any Eventuality

The first camp argues that we simply cannot know the future, and thus the United States must be equally prepared for any eventuality. This approach would lead military planners to distribute resources as evenly as possible; because one does not know the future, one must spread one's bets widely.[10]

The problem is that, by allocating scarce resources equally to the perilous and the picayune, the plausible and the fanciful, this approach makes one vulnerable to the strategies that matter. Some threats are more dangerous and substantial than others and require greater effort to counteract; allocating resources without concern for the significance of the threat leads to the frittering away of those resources as more important areas receive insufficient attention.

In the search for flexibility and balance, then, this viewpoint risks inadequately preparing for the most important and consequential threats. France in 1912, for instance, had historical rivalries with England and Italy as well as broad imperial interests. Paris could have decided to spread its bets by prioritizing preparations for possible conflicts with Great Britain in Africa and with Italy in the Mediterranean. But placing its resources there would have left France inadequately prepared for war with Germany in 1914; it would have been swiftly defeated, rendering its more distant interests effectively moot. Likewise, if the United States in the late 1930s and early 1940s had paid as much attention to its history of banana wars in Central America as to the far greater threats from Germany and Japan, it might not have initiated the prewar buildup that ultimately made victory possible.

An important flaw in this viewpoint is its tendency to exaggerate the significance of surprise. Surprise can, of course, be important and consequential. Moscow was surprised by Operation Barbarossa, American leaders were surprised by the Chinese intervention in Korea and the Tet Offensive in Vietnam, and the Soviets and Americans suffered as a result. But absent more fundamental factors, surprise is not typically decisive. Although it may give the attacker an advantage as the defender recovers its composure and balance, surprise generally cannot make up for a bad military strategy. Foolish moves by an opponent may be surprising but not threatening—indeed, they may be surprising because it is clear they will not work. The Russians were probably surprised by the Charge of the Light Brigade, but they massacred the assaulting cavalrymen anyway. The United States does not currently expect Russia to invade Spain. If Moscow tried, the United States and its NATO allies would be surprised—but would have plenty of time and power to decisively defeat the Russians.

Thus, surprise is ultimately not the problem: being gravely damaged or conquered is. What matters, then, is if surprise is coupled with a good military strategy—*that* is dangerous. Surprise about an opponent's implementation of such a strategy is normally caused not by a lack of understanding what that strategy might be but rather by misapprehension, delusion, or an unwillingness to consider that the other side might put such a strategy into effect. The Soviet Union's military and intelligence leadership in 1941 knew that Germany might attack, but the USSR failed to act on the warnings.[11] The United States received indications that China might intervene in Korea in 1950 but discounted them.[12]

Indeed, it is rare to find instances of genuine *strategic* surprise in the modern world. Although there are many examples of operational or tactical surprise, it is hard to find an example of a state wholly unexpectedly attacking another or attacking in an entirely unanticipated way as, for instance, the Eastern Romans appear to have been surprised by the severity and potency of the Arab invasions in the seventh century and the out-of-the-blue attack by Kievan Rus on Constantinople in 860.[13] There is no longer any terra incognita from which invaders can emerge without report. The Allies in 1940 knew that Germany could invade France and the Low Countries but were surprised by *where* Germany attacked.[14] The Americans were surprised at Pearl Harbor on December 7, 1941, but they knew before then that Japan was a threat and Hawaii a vulnerable target.[15] US intelligence agencies knew that al-Qaeda was a menace but were surprised by exactly how, when, and where the group struck on 9/11.[16] A nation may conceal the movement of its armies and fleets, but it is nearly impossible to conceal their existence and basic orientation.

A prudent state can and therefore should identify the principal threats to its important interests, not the least because its adversaries—at least the savvier ones—will most likely do the same and optimize their efforts in those directions. A state that does not allocate its efforts and resources efficiently weakens itself against more judicious states, quite likely decisively when dealing with one as powerful as China. For these reasons, American and coalition strategic planners should not be content simply to plead ignorance of the future. In the face of a serious potential opponent, it is necessary to make choices about what is more and less important; that is one of strategy's central functions. Failing to do so is not humility but bewilderment and an invitation to disaster.

The Most Likely Scenarios

Another line of argument posits that, while the United States may be able to identify the sources of its principal threats, it should focus on the most likely military strategies of these potential opponents rather than their best ones. Many observers maintain, for instance, that the United States should not over-invest in preparing for high-end conflict against China because Beijing is more likely to pursue strategies below the level of armed conflict, advancing its cause while minimizing the risk of large-scale war. This is important because much contemporary defense discussion concentrates on the gray zone, contending that Chinese actions below the level of armed conflict are more probable than its outright use of military force. Adherents of this approach argue that US defense planning should focus on presence activities, nonmilitary missions, and flexibility rather than on preparing for major war.[17]

But focusing on this likelihood criterion fails on two fronts. First, common events are not always or even normally the most consequential, and consequential events are what the United States should particularly care about. Common but insignificant events require some attention, but it is significant events that demand special focus. A person may buy an umbrella and galoshes for rain showers and not give it much more thought. Floods, meanwhile, are much rarer, yet people spend time and money buying flood insurance and proofing their basements against the risk of being inundated. Similarly, whole cities are de-signed in Japan to survive a serious earthquake, a relatively rare but enormously consequential event if a city is unprepared. This does not mean that one should not take precautions against minor everyday occurrences: one should shut the windows during a rainstorm. The point is that these common events are not what should most shape one's planning for insurance and security—which is what defense planning is.

This is as true in international politics as in everyday life. Wars tend to be rare, but they can be immensely consequential, implicating the very shape and sur-vival of states. Indeed, they are the most significant events in international poli-tics. There has not been a major war in Europe since 1945—and its map is still defined by the First and Second World Wars, just as the map of the Near East was dramatically reset by the Six-Day War of 1967 and that of North America by the Seven Years' War, American Revolution, and the Mexican-American War.

This does not mean that international politics is not also shaped in more mod-est increments. But these, like rain showers, can be managed with smaller and less demanding steps. A major war between the United States and China—even a limited and focused conflict—would almost certainly have much greater sig-nificance for Asian geopolitics than anything that happens in the gray zone, which is, after all, a euphemism for actions that do not cross the threshold of major significance. Further, there are fundamental limitations on what any na-tion can achieve in the gray zone alone. China might be able to use gray zone tactics to assert control over small, peripheral portions of territory claimed by its neighbors, for instance, by seizing disputed uninhabited features in the South China Sea. But it is highly unlikely to be able to seize enough of an adversary's territory to assert domineering influence over that nation—which is, as I will discuss later, a prerequisite for achieving regional hegemony—without escalat-ing above the gray zone. Unsurprisingly, then, China's best exploitation of the gray zone so far has been of unoccupied territory, chiefly geographic features that were not territory at all until China created them.

The second reason likelihood is a poor criterion on which to premise one's military strategy is that likelihood is a dynamic property. Events that seem un-likely today may become more probable if key circumstances change. Strategic actors tend to behave based on their judgments of an action's costs and benefits. If the perceived benefits of an action are high and the costs low, an actor is more likely to take that action; if the reverse, less so.

Thus, what is plausible is contingent on the costs and benefits actors face. Actors adapt to each other's behavior. In strategic engagements, they can deliberately change the incentives that they and others face in ways that shift the plausibility of events. In most human interactions, costs and benefits depend largely on what the actors involved do or indicate they may do—their behaviors are products not merely of forces of nature or acts of God but of human action. If a jurisdiction that rigorously enforced speed limits now judges that speeding, because uncommon, is no longer likely, it may reduce enforcement—and thereby invite more speeding. If a more lenient jurisdiction tightens enforcement, speeding is likely to decline. In the market, this is the law of supply and demand—demand by some will trigger others to increase supply.

Indeed, focusing on the most likely events may well increase the likelihood of grave events once considered implausible. The perception that something is unlikely can lead to actions presuming its implausibility, which in turn can strain the rationale for its being unlikely in the first place. By the early 2000s, for instance, it was widely believed in economic policy circles that market management had reached such a level of sophistication that depressions were no longer plausible. This in turn led to policy changes that enabled riskier behavior, making economic catastrophe more probable and contributing to the 2008 financial crisis.[18] In the 1930s, the belief among many in Western Europe that war was no longer thinkable opened opportunities for German rearmament and aggression, thereby contributing to the outbreak of the Second World War.[19]

If a state believes it will suffer too much to justify the gains it may accrue by precipitating a war, it is unlikely to do so. But if it thinks it can gain more than it stands to lose, its incentives to risk or start a war will rise, making belligerent behavior more likely. Arguments that China would not risk a large-scale war with the United States generally (often implicitly) rely on the assessment that Beijing could not gain more than it could lose by doing so, which is in turn based on the assumption that the United States maintains a meaningful military advantage over China.

Yet if the military balance of relevance to a given type of conflict were to shift in China's favor—because, for instance, decision-makers believed that such a conflict was implausible and therefore not worth serious preparation—this assumption would no longer hold, and events that once seemed implausible could become entirely plausible—including China's starting a war to advance its interests. Focusing on the most likely occurrences to the detriment of maintaining a relevant military advantage would, like the financial policies in the 1990s and 2000s, make catastrophe more likely.

The United States should therefore not base its strategy on how plausible a given opposing strategy seems at any given moment. Probability in this context is largely a function of how the potential attacker perceives the balance of cost and benefit. If it can develop an advantageous way to put an improbable or even shocking strategy into effect, that strategy will become plausible—perhaps faster than an unprepared opponent anticipates or even can adapt.[20]

This has direct relevance in Asia today. For more than a half century following the Second World War, the United States enjoyed essentially unfettered military dominance in maritime Asia and the Western Pacific. Since the 1990s, however, the People's Liberation Army has been assiduously developing forces intended to prevent the United States from effectively defending its Asian allies and partners from Chinese action. So long as the United States maintains a military edge over China in plausible scenarios, Beijing will face an unfavorable cost-benefit equation in resorting to military force. But this will change if Beijing is able to shift the military balance enough in its favor that it could reasonably judge the use of military force to be to its advantage. In this case, it will become rational for Beijing to risk or provoke a war to advance its aims.

The Most Destructive Scenarios

A third camp argues that military planning should focus on the most destructive strategies that a potential adversary like China—or Russia, given its large nuclear arsenal—could wield, such as their ability to strike the US homeland with nuclear weapons.[21] According to this argument, the United States should first eliminate any vulnerability to the most destructive forms of attack before allocating resources to other goals; America should therefore invest the great bulk of its resources in developing the capability to eliminate or at least reduce the damage the worst forms of attack could wreak. This would represent a sharp change from the past half-century, during which the United States has essentially accepted vulnerability to attack from nuclear-armed great powers.[22]

There are two problems with the pursuit of true invulnerability. First, it is exceedingly unlikely that this goal is attainable. In an age of extraordinarily destructive technologies, even a small number of penetrating weapons can mean absolute disaster. It is thus unrealistic to expect to attain anything approaching invulnerability against a capable, adaptive, and sufficiently re-sourced adversary.

Moreover, the pursuit of invulnerability would consume the United States' ability to pursue its other geopolitical goals, even though these are crucial for Americans' security, freedom, and prosperity. A perfect defense would require enormous outlays while requiring far less from an attacker to breach it. The United States would need to ensure a perfect shield, but the adversary would need only to penetrate it with a few highly destructive weapons to have an im-mensely destructive impact. The expense of seeking such perfection would leave the United States hobbled in or even incapable of pursuing any broader interests. Meanwhile, an opponent like China could use its resources to pursue other goals, such as regional hegemony in Asia, and the United States would have far less ability to stop it.

Giving up on perfection does not mean leaving the United States unpro-tected, however. Rather, the way to defend against a truly catastrophic attack when perfect defense is impossible has long been and remains deterrence. A perfect defense is not necessary to protect oneself from severe attack. Rather, one can defend oneself by presenting the potential attacker with the credible prospect of retaliation that is more costly than the gains of attacking. This is not to say that deterrence is easy; it can be difficult and uncertain. But it is certainly possible. The history of international relations since the advent of the atomic bomb is a long example of the feasibility of deterrence.[23]

The United States has for many years not felt compelled to pursue total in-vulnerability because it has judged that it can effectively deter Chinese or Rus-sian nuclear attack through a combination of deterrence and limiting its own threats to those countries. Although each could inflict grievous harm on the United States, the United States has the undeniable ability to repay such an at-tack in turn. Incurring such a riposte would outweigh the benefits to Russia or China of an attack in any imaginable contingency save the truly existential. Even though either country could launch an enormously damaging nuclear at-tack on the United States, what gains could they garner that would justify the devastating retaliation they would suffer in reply?

The most damaging strategy an adversary can pursue, in other words, is not likely to be its most gainful one—indeed, in most cases, pursuing it is likely to be foolhardy in the extreme, if not simply insane. And insanity is vanishingly rare in state decision-making. Trying to obtain a perfect defense is therefore not only unwise but unnecessary. And since the United States cannot afford to be profligate in competition with a state of the potency and wealth of China, what is unnecessary is ill-advised.

In sum, if the United States is to defeat China's bid for hegemony, Washington must not become distracted by every potential path Beijing might take. Nor can it afford to sink scarce resources into the most apparently likely or most destructive ways in which Beijing might pursue this goal. Rather, the United States must identify and plan against China's *best* strategies for achieving regional hegemony in Asia.

7

Beijing's Best Strategy

IN ORDER TO ATTAIN REGIONAL HEGEMONY, then, China's best strategies are
those that enable it to become stronger than the anti-hegemonic coalition such that
it could win a systemic regional war. Beijing can then establish its hegemony either by threatening such a war or by actually precipitating and winning it.

Importantly, understanding what China's best strategies might be does not require us to uncover some hidden Chinese plan or capabilities. That is because
what is actually a state's best strategy does not ultimately depend on what the
state's leaders think it is. It is, rather, an objective reality that is a product of how
such a state might optimally achieve its strategic aims. But that state does not have
a monopoly on judging which strategy would work most effectively, since the efficacy of military strategies is a product not only of a particular state's actions but
of the interplay of multiple factors, including how the opposing side acts, third-
party reactions, and nonhuman factors such as geography and weather. A state's
hidden capabilities may give it an edge in executing a strategy, but that advantage
will be availing only if the strategy itself can lead to a successful outcome.

This means that, if the strategy China's leaders are following is actually not
its best, the United States should not entirely change its focus. Defeating a bad
strategy is easier and less costly than defeating a good one. Meanwhile, Beijing
might at any time realize that it has a bad strategy and try to correct to a better
one. Thus, although the United States must of course retain some flexibility in
its defense planning to deal with the unanticipated, it is better off developing its
forces, capabilities, posture, and plans to address its opponent's most effective
strategies.

So what are the best—the most gainful—strategies for China? How can Beijing advance toward its goal without incurring more cost and risk than is tenable?

One approach to doing so is to outgrow and, once sufficiently strong, overpower any potential coalition. Before moving on to more aggressive strategies, I will discuss this option to show why it is not workable for Beijing.

Hide and Bide—and Its Limitations

The least risky and thus most attractive way for China to become Asia's hegemon is simply to grow stronger and eventually, through the sheer weight of its power, overwhelm any realistic coalition that could form to check its ambitions. Since this strategy relies on continued growth, a rising power like China has an incentive to avoid a major conflict with the established powers because such a war would imperil its favorable trajectory. Left undisturbed, it will only grow stronger and thus better positioned to fight in the future. With the exception of small conflicts like the War of 1812, the war against Mexico in the 1840s, and the Indian Wars, this is effectively what the United States did in North America throughout the eighteenth and nineteenth centuries. The nation grew more and more powerful, until eventually all had to recognize American predominance in its region and deal with its ability to project power abroad.

This logic appears to have informed the approach Beijing followed from the era of Deng Xiaoping until more recent years. Deng recognized that China needed to develop economically before it could productively assert its power. In the famous phrase, he therefore advised Chinese officials to "hide our capabilities and bide our time." Beijing appears since to have shifted from this approach, presumably in part because it determined that China has become powerful enough to warrant a more assertive foreign policy.[1]

Beijing might, nevertheless, try to return to a quieter, outgrowing strategy to achieve regional predominance. Yet this would likely fail to gain China its goal. The United States and other nations have now seen that Beijing is willing to throw its weight around and abandon commitments that were meant to demonstrate the limits of its ambitions, such as Beijing's pledges not to militarize disputed islands in the South China Sea and to respect Hong Kong's autonomy.[2] Now that countries in the region know that China could once more pursue such an assertive strategy and that it is only growing stronger, they are more likely to coalesce in an anti-hegemonic coalition even if Beijing were to revert to a more measured approach.

Even more fundamentally, though, the problem with the hide-and-bide strategy is that it does not provide a way to overcome other states' very strong incentive to balance China. The United States as well as most states in the region share a profound interest in checking a Chinese bid for predominance. No matter how strong China is, if those states fear no sufficiently serious penalty for affiliating in order to balance Beijing, then they are likely to do so.

And there are enough states available to form a plausible coalition. There was no plausible combination of states that could outweigh the mammoth power of the growing United States in North and Central America in the nineteenth century. But in Asia, states such as Japan, India, Australia, Vietnam, South Korea, the Philippines, Indonesia, Malaysia, and Thailand could join an anti-hegemonic coalition with the United States. Such a coalition might also include extraregional players, such as America's European allies and even Russia. The stronger China grows, the more states will see the benefits of balancing it. And if Beijing gives them no sufficient disincentive, balancing would give them goods of enormous value—freedom from Chinese hegemony—at little risk.

China thus requires a strategy that discourages other nations from joining or remaining in the anti-hegemonic coalition. Beijing must be able to penalize other nations so that they judge that the costs and risks of joining outweigh the benefits. It can draw on diplomatic, economic, and other nonmilitary instruments of national power to fashion these penalties. But, crucially, China is very unlikely to succeed in attaining regional hegemony if the penalties do not include a core military component, given the unique coercive efficacy of force and the exceedingly high stakes for states seeking to avoid forfeiting their autonomy to Beijing. These military elements need not be the most visible, but Beijing must have recourse to them—and others must know of its ability—for the strategy to be effective.

This is not easy for Beijing because whatever penalties it threatens or imposes against other states must outweigh the goods that these nations anticipate from balancing—and because China would be seeking regional hegemony, those goods, particularly those nations' retention of their autonomy, would be the most significant conceivable. The goods China would demand would thus be of the highest order, and it would therefore need to impose penalties of equivalent or greater weight to convince its targets to give them up. Since violence is the most effective form of coercion, were China to threaten solely non-military punishments, it would severely limit and likely vitiate its ability to inflict the necessary harm on its targets.

States on the receiving end of Chinese attempts to isolate them diplomatically, for instance, could seek closer ties with the anti-hegemonic coalition. Those subject to China's attempts at economic coercion, meanwhile, could adapt their supply and consumption patterns to minimize exposure to Beijing's pressure. The United States' own record of economic coercion against much weaker states counsels us to be skeptical that Beijing could use such coercion alone to compel states to forfeit their most dearly held goods.[3] Nor are these speculative points: there is substantial evidence that both of these balancing reactions are already happening in response to China's diplomatic and economic pressure on an array of countries, including Japan, Taiwan, the Philippines, Vietnam, Australia, Canada, several European states, and the United States itself.[4]

Given that political and economic measures on their own will be insufficient, China's strategy for achieving regional hegemony thus requires an effective military component. At the same time, however, China must be able to employ military force in a way that does not precipitate the large war against the coalition that it is too likely to lose. This is the fundamental problem Beijing must solve if it is to make good on its bid for hegemony—and the solution, as I have discussed, is the focused and sequential strategy.

Implemented effectively, the focused and sequential strategy would allow China to deter states from joining the coalition, persuade them to break from it, or induce them to renege on their commitments to it. In the resulting circumstances, the anti-hegemonic coalition would be unable to agglomerate and effectively employ the strength needed to check China's pursuit of regional predominance. At the same time, Beijing could continue to increase its own power and translate that waxing power into military strength. If events unfolded in this way, China could ultimately attain sufficient power in the region to prevail in a systemic regional war. It would then have the strength to become the hegemon in Asia.

Implementing the Focused and Sequential Strategy

China could employ such a focused and sequential strategy in many ways. But if the United States is to defeat China's bid for hegemony, Washington must not become distracted by every potential path Beijing might take. Nor can the

United States afford to sink scarce resources into the most apparently likely or most destructive ways in which Beijing might pursue this goal. Rather, the United States must identify and plan against China's *best* options for implementing its strategy.

These best options must address Beijing's fundamental quandary. Given that the entire anti-hegemonic coalition, once coalesced, would be more powerful than China and its plausible allies, if Beijing precipitated a war that engaged the coalition's fuller exertions, China would very likely lose. Beijing must therefore execute the focused and sequential strategy in such a fashion that the coalition *elects* not to employ its greater strength to counter China's moves. The most logical way for Beijing to deal with this quandary is to fracture or sufficiently weaken the coalition by sequentially isolating and subjugating enough vulnerable members while convincing the rest to let them go. This would not only weaken the coalition outright but also, if used against US allies within the coalition, demonstrate to all that the coalition, especially its external cornerstone balancer, is unable or unwilling to protect its own members and that they are better off keeping their distance from or leaving it.

The most logical way for Beijing to try to fracture the coalition is by exploiting the differences in members' willingness to tolerate the costs and risks required to adequately defend the member states Beijing targets. Although all members have an interest in ensuring the effective defense of fellow members from Chinese assault, that interest is inherently partial because each nation will naturally look above all to its own security. Given the costs and risks China could impose on states more removed from the immediate threat, under some circumstances that partial interest might not seem compelling enough to motivate these states to come to the victims' defense with enough vigor. Using this isolating approach, China could then pick off coalition members in sequence, systematically weakening the coalition until it collapsed.

Targeting a US Ally

In putting this strategy into effect, Beijing would have to decide whether to target a US ally or just a US partner, given that any anti-hegemonic coalition will likely include states both with and without a security commitment from Washington.

Attacking a state allied with the United States would be more likely to trigger a formidable reaction from the United States because of its implications for

Washington's differentiated credibility. But at the same time, successfully subordinating the recipient of a US security guarantee would undermine that credibility and could strongly indicate—and even conclusively demonstrate—Washington's unreliability. Given the importance of US differentiated credibility for the functioning of the anti-hegemonic coalition, this could show the fundamental hollowness of the coalition, just as, in the 1930s, Italy's invasion of Abyssinia and Japan's invasion of China revealed the emptiness of the League of Nations' pledge to treat an attack against one as an attack against all. Thus, while attacking a US ally would be more risky, it would also, if successful, materially advance China's interest in weakening the anti-hegemonic coalition or preventing it from forming.

Attacking a coalition member not formally tied to the United States, conversely, would be less immediately risky for China but also less beneficial, since doing so would not implicate the United States' differentiated credibility. Even worse for Beijing, attacking a coalition partner that is not the beneficiary of a US security commitment could backfire for China by incentivizing more states to join the coalition and imbuing it with greater cohesion, including through the formation of more alliance relationships with the United States. This is because China's neighbors would see that it was willing to use its focused and sequential strategy against states not allied to the United States but was apparently sufficiently intimidated by American security guarantees to avoid attacking US allies directly. This implicit endorsement of the potency of those guarantees would likely increase the cohesion and strength of the coalition as a whole. This was the result in NATO following the Russian seizure of Crimea and incursion into Ukraine, as well as in the North Atlantic Alliance following the outbreak of the Korean War in 1950.[5]

Taiwan as the Initial Target

Taiwan is the most attractive target for China's focused and sequential strategy for several reasons. The first is related to China's own interest in it. For decades, the Chinese Communist Party has made clear that "reunification" with Taiwan is a national imperative.[6] Xi Jinping himself has described this goal as "essential to realizing national rejuvenation."[7]

But Taiwan is also an attractive target because of its importance to Washington's differentiated credibility. That is, even though Taiwan is not a full-fledged US ally, nervous regional states are unlikely to see its fate as materially different from that which would befall full-fledged US allies in similar circumstances. Indeed, these actors, wondering about US differentiated credibility, are more likely to regard Taiwan as a canary in the coal mine than as a bird of a different feather.

As noted previously, the United States does have formalized commitments relating to Taiwan, especially the Taiwan Relations Act, and it has made a number of less formal commitments and statements, such as the Six Assurances.[8] Perhaps as tellingly, Washington has demonstrated by its behavior that it is prepared to help defend Taiwan, as when the United States used its fleet to deter Chinese assertiveness during the Taiwan Strait Crisis of 1995–1996. And the defense of Taiwan has long been a point of concentration for American military planning.[9] As a result, the practical, quiet understanding in Asia—an understanding that Washington itself has cultivated—has long been that the United States would come to Taiwan's defense.[10] As a consequence, even if Taiwan is not a full-fledged ally of the United States, America's refusal to defend it would markedly undermine its differentiated credibility in Asia vis-à-vis China.[11]

Taiwan is an appealing target for military reasons as well. Taiwan is located close to China's centers of military power. At the same time, China dwarfs Taiwan in military strength and has deliberately developed its military to be able to attack the island.[12] Beijing has also specifically developed its military to be able to ideally block and at least markedly raise the costs and risks to the United States of intervening to defend Taiwan.[13] In addition, Taiwan tends to act as a cork in China's ability to project military power beyond it. If China left Taiwan alone and sought to attack states farther into the Western Pacific, it would leave its military power projection efforts exposed should Taiwan oppose it or enable other states to use its territory or air and sea space to do so. Subordinating Taiwan would remove this threat; it would also provide Beijing with additional bases both for denying other states access into the Western Pacific and East Asia and projecting power beyond the first island chain.

After Taiwan

If China could subjugate Taiwan, it could then lift its gaze to targets farther afield. The PLA is already moving well beyond a strict focus on Taiwan to develop the ability to project military power using aircraft carriers and more advanced surface forces, nuclear-powered submarines with land-attack and antiship capabilities, long-range bombers, a large and sophisticated space architecture, and amphibious and air assault forces, as well as the training and doctrine to employ all these effectively.[14]

Once it had subordinated Taiwan, China could use these capabilities to progressively weaken the anti-hegemonic coalition by subjugating and breaking off other states from it, and especially from alliance relationships with Washington. Though these more distant assaults would present more difficulties to Beijing than an attack on Taiwan, China itself, once it subjugated Taiwan, would be in a more advantageous position. Taiwan itself would no longer threaten China's ability to project military power, and doubts about the integrity of the anti-hegemonic coalition and especially the value of Washington's assurances would be graver in the wake of Taiwan's fall.

After Taiwan, China's best strategy would probably be to focus on Southeast Asia. These states are considerably less developed and weaker than Japan, for instance, which is likely too strong and resolute for China to readily subdue, absent a significant shift in the political-military balance. Wealthy and well-armed South Korea, though smaller than Japan, would also present a formidable target; moreover, given its geographical position, a Chinese attack on South Korea would very likely be seen to imperil Japan directly, thus likely bringing Tokyo into the conflict in addition to the United States.

In light of this, a natural next target for Beijing would be the Philippines. It is a long-established US ally, access to which is important for US military operations in Southeast Asia and the Western Pacific.[15] At the same time, it is a relatively weak state, and there are significant voices within it favoring accommodation toward China. Manila's willingness to defend itself might, then, not be as high as necessary to enable an effective defense by the United States and other allies and partners.

Vietnam, though not a US ally, might also make a good target. Hanoi is likely to be at least an informal member of the anti-hegemonic coalition, given its opposition to domination by China.[16] If Hanoi becomes a formal ally of the United States, conversely, it could present an even more lucrative target for Beijing. There would also be military advantages for Beijing to attack Vietnam. Vietnam directly abuts China, considerably easing the difficulties of moving forces against it. Moreover, although US forces hold particular advantages in the aerospace, maritime, and information domains, these are less useful in defending Vietnam, particularly the northern part of the country where Hanoi is located. There is a reason for the old American adage never to get involved in a land war in Asia: the

US military's strengths apply far less there.[17] This explains why America's lasting alliances in Asia have historically been with island nations—and one peninsula, South Korea, which is connected to mainland Asia by a single state, North Korea.

That said, attacking Vietnam would also present significant risks for China. Vietnam is a more capable state than the Philippines, with a formidable military. It also boasts a reputation for deep reservoirs of will to defend itself and its national sovereignty, earned through perseverance in rebellion against France, the war by North Vietnam and its affiliates in the South against the United States and its South Vietnamese ally, and the Sino-Vietnam War of 1979.

Still, China could seek to use its new military might to compel or force the Philippines, Vietnam, or both to disaffiliate from any alliance with Washington and the anti-hegemonic coalition and to adopt a policy supportive of—or at least accommodating of—China's bid for regional hegemony. And if its attacks against the Philippines, Vietnam, or both were successful but still not enough to demonstrate the hollowness of US alliance assurances and the anti-hegemonic coalition, Beijing could follow them with similar attacks against one or more other Asian states.

At some point, however, once China had demonstrated sufficiently that the United States and the anti-hegemonic coalition could not effectively defend member states in Southeast Asia, Washington's and thus the coalition's differentiated credibility would collapse, and China would become the area's hegemon. Critically, Beijing would almost certainly not have to fight a war against every Southeast Asian state to establish its hegemony there if it could successfully apply this strategy against enough states to undermine sufficiently the United States' differentiated credibility. Local states would very likely begin to accommodate Beijing's demands. Indeed, China might not have to fight many wars at all if it could demonstrate its ability and resolve to pursue this strategy effectively. In fact, if its power and will were manifest enough, and Washington's sufficiently lacking, Beijing might have to fight none at all.

If China could split states like the Philippines and Vietnam from the anti-hegemonic coalition while bringing other important Southeast Asian states under its sway, it might ultimately grow strong enough to defeat a coalition composed solely of Japan and India alongside the United States and more distant states like Australia. At that point China would already be able to channel the economic and other policies of Southeast Asia states in ways that would meaningfully undermine Americans' prosperity and ultimately their freedom. A China that held sway over Southeast Asia, which is projected to have approximately a ten-trillion-dollar regional economy by 2030, would be immensely powerful in its ability to shape global trade and project its influence into American life.[18] Nor would this power be limited to Southeast Asia. A China that could establish hegemony over Southeast Asia in the face of US resistance would almost certainly also be able to establish predominance over Central Asia. Such a powerful China could begin to project much greater power into additional regions, such as the Middle East and even the Western Hemisphere.

If Tokyo and New Delhi managed to hold out against Chinese predominance under these conditions, China's next rational step would be to seek to isolate and dishearten both of them (as well as Australia, which is much smaller). If Japan and India saw the rest of the region affiliating with China, they might not sustain the resolve needed to adequately defend themselves from China's focused and sequential strategy. Beijing could try to arouse internal opposition to strengthening coalition defense, as the Soviets attempted to weaken Western European support for the deployment of the Euromissiles in the 1980s. And a much wealthier and more powerful China would have far more leverage to do so than the Soviets did.

If Tokyo and New Delhi still did not fall into line, China would be well positioned to employ a focused war strategy against either of them. Its best course would still be to concentrate the war on just one of these states while seeking to diminish the US willingness and ability to come vigorously enough to the target state's aid. At this point, however, China would likely be so powerful that it might rely much more on its threat to escalate against the United States and any other remaining coalition members rather than trying to appear nonthreatening. Such a powerful China, in other words, would likely be able to make a US defense of the attacked state so difficult and costly, and to do so much damage to the United States in such a controlled and discriminate fashion, that it would need to worry less about appearing restrained.

If Beijing could compel either Japan or India to disaffiliate from such a rump anti-hegemonic coalition, the effort to deny China predominance over Asia would have failed. It is highly unlikely that the United States along with only Japan or India could resist China's establishment of hegemony in the region.

Punishment and Conquest

Beijing's best limited war strategy, then, would allow it to subordinate a vulnerable coalition member, starting with Taiwan, in a way that is sufficiently intimidating to deter effective coalition intervention but not menacing enough to convince other coalition states that China is so dangerous that they must effectively intervene despite the costs and risks. Most essentially, it would convince those nations that, though they are together more powerful than China, they are better off withholding a sufficient defense of its vulnerable counterpart. China's ultimate objective would be to demonstrate the hollowness of the anti-hegemonic coalition, especially by prioritizing targeting US allies, until regional actors no longer viewed the coalition as a viable vehicle for balancing against Beijing. At that point, they will be incentivized to bandwagon, thereby clearing the path toward Chinese regional hegemony.

As Beijing sought to isolate and subordinate a vulnerable coalition member while convincing its fellows to remain out of the fight, it could play on both ends of the cost-benefit equation. On the one hand, it could diminish the threat that its actions against the vulnerable coalition member seem to pose to other members. On the other hand, Beijing could raise the anticipated costs and risks to other coalition member states of effectively defending the targeted state.

Beijing has two broad ways of subordinating a coalition member in this manner without provoking too great a response by its allies and partners. We may call the first way the *punishment approach*. Under this approach, Beijing would use limited violence to impose costs on the vulnerable state until it capitulates of its own accord. In doing so, Beijing would likely seek to avoid provoking the target's allies and partners to the greatest degree possible, thereby minimizing their incentives to intervene.

The second way might be labeled the *conquest approach*. Under this approach, Beijing would use what Thomas Schelling termed "brute force" to impose its will on the target state—especially by seizing control of that state's territory—and thus present the target's allies and partners with new facts on the ground that, Beijing would reckon, they would consider some combination of too difficult, costly, and risky to reverse.[19] Although this approach would try to reduce the incentives for coalition intervention, it would primarily deter effective coalition intervention by raising the difficulty, costs, and risks such engagement would face. As I will discuss below, for an aspiring hegemon confronting an anti-hegemonic coalition whose combined strength is greater than the aspirant's, the fait accompli is the most effective variant of the conquest approach.

The Punishment Approach

The punishment (or cost imposition) approach works by inducing a vulnerable state to capitulate by imposing costs: pain and loss. It succeeds when the attacker is able to impose more costs than the target is able or willing to bear in order to protect whatever the attacker is demanding. Crucially, the target's ability to defy the attacker includes not only its indigenous capacity for resistance, important as that is, but its ability to secure relief from third parties. When the target is subject to intolerable costs and lacks foreign support—or believes that any such support will prove insufficient—it is more likely to accede to the attacker's demands.

Beijing might use an array of tools to punish a vulnerable state into submission. Nonmilitary forms of cost imposition might include travel bans, asset freezes, restrictions on capital, withholding of essential supplies, or other sanctions designed to harm, sap wealth from, and diminish the freedom of a targeted state. Military forms of punishment range from cyber or electronic attacks to blockade or bombardment. Given the especially coercive power of lethal force, I focus here on military forms of cost imposition.

However it is implemented, the central and distinctive quality of the punishment approach is that it does not involve a military assault designed to seize territory and force its target to submit. Instead, it relies on the attacker's ability to convince the target state to surrender rather than continue to suffer pain.

Perceived Advantages to the Punishment Approach

Why would China choose punishment over conquest in the first place? All things being equal, if an aspiring hegemon can use brute force to get its way, it would seem to be better off doing that rather than relying on an approach that turns on persuasion and is thus inherently less subject to the attacker's control. Just as carrying an obstinate child to the bath is typically easier than persuading the child to go, simply seizing an enemy's territory is usually more effective than persuading the enemy to give it up.

Brute force, in other words, makes the defender's will essentially irrelevant, thus eliminating a crucial variable that is otherwise beyond the attacker's control and greatly simplifying the problem confronting the attacker. This can be immensely valuable, particularly when an aspiring hegemon seeks to take away something the target state values greatly, such as its national autonomy or territorial integrity. Given that a targeted state is unlikely to want to sacrifice such a core good, the attacker may seem better off taking it by force than trying to induce its forfeiture.

Yet the punishment approach may seem to have its own advantages. For one, conquest may appear harder or more costly to implement even if it ultimately succeeds. Under some conditions, punishment might seem a less demanding option for advancing an attacker's objectives. For instance, after the First World War, shocked by the terrible costs of brute force victory on the Western Front, B. H. Liddell Hart famously developed the "indirect approach," a strategy premised on cost imposition that he hoped would allow Great Britain to defeat a continental army at a fraction of the bloodshed the war had demanded.[20] Giulio Douhet, similarly sobered by the war's horrors, argued that nations could use airpower to punish enemy societies into submission while avoiding bloody ground campaigns.[21]

Another appeal of the punishment approach is that, at least in its more cabined variants, it may appear less likely to trigger effective intervention by third parties. Any military action risks being seen as aggressive and therefore as justifying or demanding a response, particularly by a victim's allies and partners. The risk of provoking an intervention, however, tends to grow in relation to the scope, scale, intensity, efficacy, and replicability of the force employed. Thus the more expansive, ferocious, effective, or replicable an attacker's military strategy, the more plausibly the attacker will be seen as a menace to key onlookers' own security. Germany's employment of blitzkrieg in Poland, for example, struck fear in capitals throughout Europe. Tokyo, Canberra, and Hanoi would likely view an overwhelming, decisive Chinese invasion of Taiwan as a more pressing indicator of China's threat to their own vital interests than a narrowly focused Chinese blockade designed to persuade Taiwan to relent. China might therefore judge that using brute force to subordinate a target state would be more likely to trigger the coalition response it seeks to avoid.

China might then see the punishment approach as more feasible to implement in ways that avoid provoking effective third-party intervention.[22] In particular, Beijing might believe that it could achieve its objectives through blockade, bombardment, or other military actions that, while violent, might seem more limited and reasonable than outright invasion and so less likely to trigger intervention by an anti-hegemonic coalition whose members are, in sum, stronger than China.

"A Great Deal of Ruin in a Nation"

The punishment approach has significant limitations, however, for several reasons. The first stems from the reality that, as Thomas Schelling put it, "It is easier to deter than to compel."[23] In Schelling's logic, it is to easier to persuade someone not to do something at all—including by accepting things as they are or have evolved—than it is to persuade that person to take an action he or she does not want to take.[24] The party seeking to compel positive action must force some change to the status quo. This tends to be a heavier burden than deterring action.

As Schelling wrote, "I can block your car in the road by placing my car in your way; my deterrent threat is passive, the decision to collide is up to you. If you, however, find me in your way and threaten to collide unless I move, you enjoy no such advantage; the decision to collide is yours, and I enjoy deterrence. You have to arrange to *have* to collide unless I move, and that is a degree more complicated." The compeller must apply force "*until* the other acts, rather than *if* he acts."[25] The compeller, to succeed, must induce some positive action, while the deterrer achieves his goal if nothing happens.

Compelling states to cede something—like their territory or national autonomy—is all the more difficult because they are more likely to go to great lengths—even at great risk to themselves—to protect what they have than they are to try to gain what they do not already have. This argument builds on a very old insight. Demosthenes observed in the fourth century BC: "For no one would go to war as readily for aggrandizement as for the defense of his own possessions; but while all men fight desperately to keep what they are in danger of losing, it is not so with aggrandizement; men make it, indeed, their aim, but if prevented, they do not feel that they have suffered any injustice from their opponents."[26] Much modern scholarship supports this proposition.[27]

Not only is compellence more difficult than deterrence, however. Compellence by *punishment*—by imposing costs—is also particularly hard to make work. While states may compel another's action through cost imposition or denial, compellence by cost imposition tends to be considerably harder.[28] Most prominently, Robert Pape has examined strategies of coercive airpower and found that compellence by punishment rarely succeeds, for several reasons. First, the target of coercion often has great interest in the territory at stake and is willing to absorb high costs to protect it. Second, nationalism magnifies a target state's valuation of the territory the attacker means to seize. Third, societies are often willing to bear greater suffering in wartime than in peacetime, and as the conflict goes on, the sunk costs incurred make them less inclined to accept settlement. Fourth, if the attacker chooses to target civilian populations, conventional weapons used in such campaigns are often less destructive than anticipated and considerably less destructive than nuclear weapons. Fifth, states can minimize civilian vulnerability through defenses, evacuation, and other countermeasures. Last, a punitive campaign is more likely to encourage the targeted society's hostility toward the compeller rather than opposition to its own government.[29]

These difficulties are especially pronounced for compellence strategies that are purely punitive—that make no attempt to achieve their objectives directly, as with brute force—because if the target does not acquiesce, the strategy necessarily fails. And when strategies relying on cost imposition threats are themselves unlikely to work or costly to execute, threatening them is unlikely to be effective.[30] Thus, while compellence by cost imposition can work against an opponent with low resolve, limited resilience, or little hope of eventual respite, compellence by cost imposition is especially difficult to make work against opponents that do not fall into these categories.[31] In sum, compellence is hard, and compellence by punishment is especially difficult.

There is thus much reason to doubt a state's ability to use punishment to compel outright surrender, especially when the target both judges that its vital interests are at stake and thinks that it might outlast the attacker's punishment campaign, whether by defending itself, absorbing the punishment, or obtaining relief from third-party intervention.[32] A state so targeted often proves willing to endure tremendous punishment, under the logic that doing so, though painful, will be less distasteful than surrendering vital interests and that continuing to fight might yet prove availing.

The record of the twentieth century testifies to this point. The British withstood the Blitz and the privations of the U-boat campaign in the Second World War, just as a few years later the Germans withstood heavy bombardment. The Japanese ultimately surrendered in that war, but only following the American use of atomic weapons and under imminent threat of Soviet and US invasion; the vicious firebombing that took such a severe toll on Japanese society was apparently not enough, on its own, to persuade Tokyo to surrender.[33] The North Koreans and North Vietnamese similarly refused to capitulate during their respective wars with the United States despite intense US bombardment.[34]

One lonely exception to this tendency is the NATO bombing campaign against Serbia in 1999, which appears to have swayed Slobodan Milošević to accede to Kosovo's separation from Serbia. Yet even in this instance, NATO was not demanding Belgrade's full surrender, only a partial amputation. Furthermore, it appears that Belgrade gave in partly out of fear of a NATO invasion. Last, unlike North Korea and North Vietnam, Serbia found itself diplomatically isolated, with little hope of relief from abroad.[35]

In other words, there is "a great deal of ruin in a nation" when its national autonomy, territorial integrity, or other vital interests are on the line.[36] All things being equal, the higher the demands levied against a targeted state, the harsher the punishment required if compellence is to succeed. For the punishment approach to persuade a target to concede core goods, the attacker must be able and willing to do harsh, cruel, even terrible things, until the targeted state's resolve breaks.

An extreme punishment campaign might work against nations that are politically isolated. Such a state may have a high bar before it concedes on its core goods, but if it has no hope of getting relief from allies or other nations, it may decide that capitulation is the more prudent course. With a weakened Russia unwilling to protect it, Serbia eventually decided that it had to let Kosovo go.[37]

But a punishment campaign is less likely to work against states with allies and partners prepared to help their defense. Subjected to such punishment, states with strong support from abroad are more likely to hold on, hoping that they might yet be relieved by a coalition's intervention, as the British were after the Blitz. The attacker, faced with such resistance, must resort to even harsher and crueler forms of cost imposition to try to force capitulation. Doing so, however, increases the risk that other nations will view the attacker as malignant and dangerous enough to warrant precisely the effective intervention the attacker sought to avoid in the first place.

Furthermore, if the coalition does come to the targeted state's aid, the attacker will have limited recourse to deal with such intervention under the punishment approach. One option would be to further intensify its use of punishment to offset whatever relief the coalition provides. Doing so, however, would likely make other states see the attacker as malevolent enough to justify counteraction and thus to redouble their efforts to relieve the beleaguered nation.

Alternatively, the attacker could try to interdict the relief itself, for instance by attacking transport vessels, aircraft, or ground vehicles providing resupply.

Doing so, however, would necessitate expanding the scope of its military operations in ways that would risk triggering unwanted counterescalation from
the broader coalition, again setting the attacker on a path toward the larger conflict that it had sought to avoid. The risk of counterescalation would only grow
further if the attacker's actions were seen as disproportionate to the coalition's
relief efforts. This would be highly plausible, if not probable, given that military operations required to provide sufficient relief of the targeted state, which
could be credibly presented as defensive and humanitarian, would likely appear
much less escalatory than the measures required to interdict them.

The Demerits of Punishment

The punishment approach, in sum, is less likely to work when the object is to
persuade a state to give up its core goods. Yet that is precisely what China
would be demanding from its targets. The whole point of China's focused and
sequential strategy is to break members off from the anti-hegemonic coalition
and subordinate them to China's ambitions—and this, by definition, requires a
fundamental compromise of those nations' autonomy. The level of harshness
China would need to bring to bear to persuade a target to subordinate itself to
Beijing is probably very high, assuming that the target state has even moderate
fortitude to preserve its autonomy.

Moreover, potential anti-hegemonic coalition members in Asia would likely
exhibit at least this level of interest in preserving their autonomy. Indeed, those
states with strong traditions of independence, such as Japan, Korea, Vietnam,
and India, could be expected to require an exceptionally high level of punishment to subordinate.

The punishment approach is also less likely to work against a nation that is
not politically isolated. Yet by definition the targets for China's focused and sequential strategy would not be so disconnected but would be part of a coalition—either formed or in the process of forming—oriented on countering
Beijing's hegemonic ambitions, and Beijing's optimal targets would be recipients of security commitments from the mighty United States.

Taiwan is the most propitious target for a Chinese punishment campaign.[38] It
is close to the Chinese mainland, has ethnic and historical ties to China, and has
a fraught, ambiguous political status that entangles it with China. Yet even Taiwan, backed by its quasi-ally the United States and potentially others, is likely
to be able to resist such a campaign. Taiwan's populace appears sufficiently res-

olute to hold out under even a very tough Chinese punishment campaign, given its consistent opposition to forced subjugation to Beijing; overwhelming majorities of people on Taiwan oppose allowing their nation to fall under the control of the mainland.[39] This means that China would likely have to use a high level of violence to exceed Taiwan's threshold for giving up.

At the same time, the United States is likely to come to Taiwan's aid because of Taiwan's importance to Washington's differentiated credibility and its military significance in the first island chain. Because Washington would suffer a significant blow, both perceptually and in practical military terms, were Taiwan to fall, it is unlikely to willingly cede Taiwan. Given that, and so long as Taiwan and the United States were sufficiently resolute and the United States was capable of ensuring that enough supplies reached Taiwan that it could defend itself to the degree needed to sustain its resolve, the island could likely hold out indefinitely, if painfully, against a punishment campaign by China.

In these circumstances, Beijing might escalate to try to erode US and others' support for Taiwan. If Beijing sought to do so, however, rather than resigning themselves to fighting a war on terms most beneficial to China, the United States and any other defending states could propose a revised set of war limitations under which they would be able to strike Chinese assets involved in blockading or bombarding Taiwan or materially supporting those forces, while simultaneously seeking to deter effective Chinese counterescalation. Such an approach would not be easy or without cost. Indeed, a campaign designed to weaken China's ability to interdict the resupply of Taiwan would almost certainly require substantial attacks against Chinese forces and facilities, including those on mainland Chinese territory. Any campaign targeting Chinese assets beyond those immediately involved in interdicting blockade runners would inevitably mean a widening and intensification of the conflict.

Yet even this escalation by the United States and other coalition members could be readily limited, since the standard for what they would need to achieve by escalating would be relatively low. The purpose of such attacks would not be to generally suppress or even necessarily lessen China's overall military power but only to erode the PLA's interdiction ability enough to allow sufficient supplies to reach Taiwan to keep it resisting in the face of Chinese blockade and bombardment. So long as the United States, Taiwan, and any other participating states had adapted or could adapt their capabilities and plans to perform this task, they would be well positioned to defend Taiwan. If Beijing did not want to relent, it could then strike more directly and broadly at the forces and assets of the United States and other coalition nations. But this would greatly increase the chances of precipitating the larger war that China would have a most powerful interest in averting.

The burden of escalation in this situation would thus fall on Beijing's shoulders. China might be able to sink ships, shoot down aircraft, and strike at the island. But as long as Chinese forces could not destroy, damage, or turn away enough ships and aircraft to undermine the resupply effort; Chinese bombardment did not break the will of the people on Taiwan; and the situation appeared sustainable, the defenders would have the upper hand.

Critically, such a result would be a major setback for China, since Beijing would appear malign without being coercively effective: aggressive and cruel but resistible. Its menacing behavior would impress on other states the importance of balancing against it, but its failure to subordinate Taiwan would show that it was not so formidable that bandwagoning was the only prudent choice. Thus, a stalemate would very likely strengthen the anti-hegemonic coalition—a low bar for success.

The upshot of this is that, with neighboring countries so resistant to cost imposition, China will find it very challenging to thread the needle between using enough force to compel its target and not using so much force that it triggers effective coalition intervention. The high level and scale of violence required to subordinate its plausible targets and cut off aid to them, in other words, is precisely the kind of assault that would seem so provocative and aggressive as to impel the United States and other coalition members to intervene. It would also elicit sympathy and support from other countries, for instance in Europe, which could provide economic relief, important raw materials and goods, and transit rights while also pressuring China, such as through sanctions. During the Vietnam War, for instance, North Vietnam could resist American pressure not only because of its own fortitude and resilience but also because the United States feared that escalating too much might trigger painful consequences from China or the Soviet Union, and perhaps even direct intervention by China, as well as politically damaging international opprobrium.[40]

Moreover, even if Beijing did thread this needle—even if it found a way to use enough force to coerce its target but stay below the coalition's threshold for intervention—the other coalition members would still need to be willing to settle for losing a vulnerable counterpart, rather than escalating to try to relieve it.

That is, other coalition members might not object strenuously enough to the *way* the aspirant attacked their fellow coalition member—but they might still object sternly to the result. On that basis alone, they might choose to intervene or escalate regardless of the means Beijing employed.

A punishment approach would, in other words, require that other coalition members accept both China's preferred parameters of the campaign and its result, rather than escalate themselves to relieve the imperiled member. To deter them from doing so, Beijing would have to convince them that the difficulty, costs, and risks of escalating to prevent or reverse the capitulation of their fellow coalition member outweighed the benefits. Yet it would be very difficult for China to pose such a formidable threat without making those same states see it as such a compelling threat that they were better off counteracting it straight away.

This, then, is the predicament that would confront Chinese decision-makers as they weighed whether to pursue the punishment approach: the amount of punishment required to persuade a targeted state to forfeit its national autonomy and persuade its fellow coalition members to let it fall might very well exceed the floor for effective intervention by these other coalition partners, thereby invalidating the punishment approach's very premise. Indeed, if the target is even moderately resolute, the punishment approach, with all its cruelties, might even make the attacker look more malign and aggressive than if it undertook a direct conquest approach, which might resolve the matter quickly and cleanly.

An Alternative to Punishment

In summary, then, the punishment approach is likely to fail for China, even against a target as favorable as Taiwan. Although such a conflict over Taiwan could well culminate without a decisive victory for either side, with a high but reasonable degree of US engagement it could very likely stabilize with Taiwan resisting, thereby demonstrating both the United States' differentiated credibility and the strength of the anti-hegemonic coalition. This would represent a major defeat for China and a success for the coalition.

The basic problem with the punishment approach is that it forfeits China's ability simply to seize a target state like Taiwan. It is harder to induce submission through persuasion than it is simply to force submission through direct action. The former leaves the target with a decisive vote whereas the latter removes that variable. Conquering another state is a much more efficient and reliable method of subordination than trying to persuade it to give up its freedom. Why bother with persuasion if you can get what you want more reliably and decisively by direct assault? As Napoleon put it, if you want to take Vienna, take Vienna.[41]

Moreover, relying on punishment as opposed to conquest deprives an attacker like China of crucial leverage against a coalition choosing to escalate to relieve the target state. So long as China relies on cost imposition to bring Taiwan into its orbit, the coalition need only reach the relatively low bar of a tolerable stalemate to achieve its goals; Taiwan just has to keep resisting. That could be very hard on the people of Taiwan, but it is, by definition, enough for them to remain autonomous, which they would likely view as preferable to submission to the kind of opponent that would blockade and bombard them so harshly. But if China could seize Taiwan, the coalition would have to recapture it, which is almost always harder than defending. In Schelling's formulation, it then would be the coalition, not China, that would have to precipitate the collision.

These defects explain why blockade and bombardment strategies designed to force capitulation are rare in history. Plenty of stronger states could have blockaded their targets into submission, but such attackers almost always choose conquest because it is so much more effective; rather than wait for their victims to surrender of their own accord, the attackers simply conquer the defenders. By the same token, there are few examples of purely or even primarily cost imposition campaigns, and even fewer successful ones.[42] A state in China's situation is thus very likely to prefer the conquest approach.

More commonly, cost imposition is a support to a main effort to conquer and subordinate a target state directly. In the American Civil War, the federal government conducted a comprehensive blockade of the rebellious South but had to conquer it and defeat the Confederate armies to subordinate the southern rebellion. The United States in the Second World War subjected Japan to perhaps history's most fearsome cost imposition campaign—what Robert Pape called "the most harrowing terror campaign in history"—but that campaign occurred alongside the destruction of Japan's military forces and preparations to invade the Home Islands.[43] North Vietnam waged a long cost imposition campaign in South Vietnam, in large part designed to erode the will of Saigon's American backer to help defend it. Ultimately, though, Hanoi subjugated the south not through cost imposition but through invasion.

States usually resort to blockade and bombardment as their primary strategy when they fail at or cannot mount an invasion. Napoleon and Hitler both contemplated invading Great Britain before resorting to the punishment approach, in France's case the Continental System and in Nazi Germany's the U-boat campaign and the Blitz.[44] The punishment approach is generally a fallback—by definition less attractive than the preferred alternative.

Indeed, were China to choose to rely on the punishment approach in its bid to achieve predominance in Asia, the choice might actually communicate to Washington that Beijing had no better options and lacked attractive recourses for escalation. Germany's terror campaign in the Blitz was actually an admission that the German armed forces lacked a practical option for an invasion. Similarly, a Chinese attempt to subordinate Taiwan by blockade and bombardment without an invasion should probably be seen as an admission that China does not have an option to—or lacks confidence in its ability to—force the island's capitulation. This could only fortify the American sense that it could effectively defend the island, strengthening its—and other coalition members'—willingness to escalate to do so.

The fundamental problem with the punishment approach, then, is that its success rests on two factors: first, the willingness of the target state to surrender at a level of violence below that which would provoke the state's allies and partners to intervene effectively; and second, the unwillingness of those allies and partners to escalate—even moderately—to relieve the target state so as to keep it going. If the target state is willing and able to endure, the attacker must escalate, and that, in turn, is likely to provoke a more formidable response by its allies and partners and possibly others.

This is the paradox of the punishment approach under the shadow of coalition intervention—the things the attacker must do to a resolute target and its defenders are the kinds of actions that will cast doubt on its protestations of not being threatening to the broader coalition. These very actions will tend to increase the coalition members' resolve to intervene effectively on the target state's behalf, leaving the attacker with the options to escalate and risk the wider war it has been trying to avoid, accept a stalemate that is tantamount to defeat, or fold.

It is unlikely, then, that a state strong enough to pursue a conquest approach would settle for the demerits of the punishment approach. Meanwhile, a state that is too weak to try the conquest approach probably could not make the punishment approach work. Although a powerful state would likely include cost imposition in its overall strategy, it is unlikely to rely on it fully or primarily, given that approach's limitations. Weakening a victim through steps like blockade and bombardment can make a difference, but on their own they are unlikely to be decisive against a resolute defender with sufficiently powerful and committed allies and partners.

It is therefore hard to see why China would resort to the punishment approach. If it had the ability to invade and subordinate a target like Taiwan, that would be its better option.

The Conquest Approach

The fatal limitation of the punishment approach is that its success depends too heavily on persuasion. The conquest approach corrects for this deficiency by relying much less on persuasion and more on brute force.

Brute Force, Coercion, and Conquest

States conquer—meaning to seize and hold part or all of another state's territory—through brute force, coercion, or some combination of the two.

In its purest form, without any element of coercion, conquest involves the killing or expulsion of all of the enemy. History offers many examples of combatants using brute force to simply kill or expel all of their enemies rather than relying on coercion to get them to accept their dominion. The Israelites, for instance, are described in the book of Joshua as massacring every inhabitant of Jericho.[45] The Romans famously sacked and razed Carthage at the end of the Third Punic War, killing the inhabitants or selling them into slavery. They treated the city of Jerusalem similarly at the end of the First Roman-Jewish War.[46] Nor was pure brute force confined to battles or sieges, especially before the emergence of civilization. Several thousand years ago, the Yamnaya invaders from the European steppe appear to have completely supplanted the male populations of parts of Europe, suggesting mass killing of men in particular.[47]

Unadulterated brute force is exceptionally rare, however, in the modern world. This is in large part because of the moral revulsion and opprobrium that would be directed at those committing mass murder that could amount to genocide. But it is also because wars fought to the bitter end can be extraordinarily costly for the victors as well as the vanquished. The Second World War in Europe, for instance, was largely decided by 1944, yet legions died on the Allied side to conquer Germany. Moreover, completely destroying or even too greatly weakening an enemy can lessen the value of any gains. A destroyed opponent is less valuable once occupied, and the costs of helping it rebuild may be great. Moreover, destroying an enemy can be dangerous if its resulting weakness causes postwar rivalries over the ensuing vacuum. Precisely in order to avoid this, Metternich in 1813–1814 sought to ensure that France was not too weakened at the Congress of Vienna.[48] Many accounts of the Cold War trace its origins in part to the vacuum left in Europe by the complete destruction of German power in the Second World War.[49]

Because of these factors, even an overwhelmingly powerful attacker that could get its way exclusively by brute force almost always seeks to persuade its opponent to stop resisting and accept its terms. It is more gainful and efficient and less risky to persuade the opponent to surrender without further fighting, or at least without fighting to the bitter end. A modest reliance on coercion is thus compatible with conquest.

And defeated parties almost always oblige. Even highly resolute combatants almost always give up well before full destruction, recognizing that at a certain point, further resistance only causes more suffering and loss without changing the outcome.[50] They are better off accepting defeat rather than futilely resisting further.

So the vast majority of southerners accepted total capitulation in the spring of 1865 rather than undertake guerrilla war against the victorious federal government.[51] Once the Germans defeated the bulk of the French army in 1940, most French citizens recognized Berlin's victory rather than risk punishment by the German juggernaut.[52] The victors did not have to kill every southerner or every Frenchman to convince them to give up and accept the conqueror's terms once the war's verdict was clear. Rather, the attackers used brute force to seize their victims' territory and show them that further resistance would be futile; coercion was reserved for persuading the defeated to accept this new reality instead of fighting to the bitter end.

Invaders sometimes triumph even before having seized and established their hold on much of the enemy's territory, if it is clear that they will irresistibly prevail. Imperial Germany gave up in 1918 before the Entente Powers could invade much of the Reich, reckoning that total defeat was inevitable and accepting it would be better than fighting on.[53]

Coercion becomes more important for an attacker, though, when it does not enjoy overall military superiority over the target state. In such instances, although it may be able to use brute force to seize part of a target's territory, it must rely on persuasion to convince the defender not to try to take back the lost territory. Egypt, for instance, seized the Suez Canal in 1973 and stopped there, leaving the bulk of Israel's forces largely untouched in the hope that Israel would accept the new situation.[54] Argentina tried a similar gambit in 1982 with respect to the Falklands, seizing the islands but not striking at British forces farther afield.[55]

Coercion is of especially great importance to an attacker when it faces an opposing coalition against which it lacks military superiority. In such conditions, the attacker might be able to use brute force to seize part or even all of a coalition member's territory, but since the attacker cannot defeat the rest of the coalition's forces—which may include the victim's remaining forces as well as those of its allies and partners—it must rely on some degree of coercion to convince those states not to try hard enough to take the territory back.

The Strategic Uses of Conquest

An attacker has several ways of translating conquest into lasting political gains. One way is by annexation, whereby the invader assumes permanent control of the seized territory. The defeated state is incorporated into the victor's territory, leaving it no real agency to resist. Poland, for instance, was simply dismembered in the partitions of the eighteenth century and by Germany and the Soviet Union in 1939. The appeal of annexation is that it gives an invader essentially uninhibited control over the victim state, allowing it to direct the state's resources and efforts basically at will. The downside is that such control may not be desirable, both because of the direct costs of administering a potentially restive territory and because of indirect ones, such as increasing the fear among other states that the attacker is a menacing imperialist.

Alternatively, the successful invader can establish supervisory control over its victim—something akin to a protectorate.[56] In this model, the victor leaves the defeated state with a degree of independence but maintains the ability to intervene more or less at will. Knowing that they are always subject to intervention by the conqueror, decision-makers in the target state generally have little choice but to hew to the conqueror's line. Often in these circumstances, a government emerges that is dependent on or vulnerable to the victorious power—in its weaker form, a puppet government. The protectorate approach allows the attacker to recede from direct control while retaining a high degree of influence. The defect is that it risks entangling the victor in the affairs of the victim state but without the degree of leverage that direct control entails.

Napoleon, for instance, created multiple kingdoms and other political forms that were dependent on France for their support and subject to intervention by Paris, which maintained standing armies ready to deploy to these territories.[57] Germany incorporated Northern France into the Reich and kept ample forces there but left much of France under the administration of the Vichy government, which was answerable to Berlin.[58] The United States conquered Japan in 1945 and Iraq in 2003; instead of annexing their territory, it established governments in Tokyo and Baghdad that were more in line with Washington's policies. This supervisory form gives the victor a high degree of power over the defeated, making it difficult if not impossible for the defeated state to pursue an independent policy. This approach is common for states seeking hegemony rather than direct imperial control, such as China.

Last, an invader may want to withdraw from its conquest more fully. In these circumstances, it can use the occupied territory and the commanding position its occupation provides as leverage to compel the target state to comply with other demands. This is important because conquest is very often the most efficient way for an attacker to force its victim to do what it wants, even if the attacker does not want to consume its victim. This approach generally involves a decisive defeat of part or all of the armed forces of the targeted state, and the use of the leverage afforded by that victory to achieve significant but still meaningfully limited political aims. The appeal of this approach is that it allows true withdrawal by an invader that wishes to limit its longer-term involvement. Its defect is that, precisely because the conqueror's power is withdrawn, the conqueror enjoys less sustained influence over the defeated power; this may allow the defeated party eventually to pursue a more adversarial course.

In the Mexican-American War, for instance, the United States roundly defeated the Mexican army, occupied Mexico City, and used the resulting advantage to annex vast parts of its southern neighbor, while leaving Mexico's core territory independent before withdrawing and demobilizing most of its army.[59] German forces occupied much of France in 1870 and 1871, but Berlin did not simply annex all of France to the new German Empire. Instead, Berlin primarily used the victory to extract Paris's concession to the unification of Germany under Prussian leadership, which France had strenuously opposed.[60] In the decades following the war, however, a France not subject to Berlin's hegemony adopted an adversarial, revanchist policy toward Germany, and it ultimately regained its lost territories after the First World War.

The latter two forms of translating conquest into lasting advantage—establishing a protectorate and using conquered territory for political leverage—are especially relevant today because they allow an attacker to use conquest to compel the opponent to comply with its demands, even if the invader has no desire to annex the territory it has taken. Conquest of a victim's territory is likely to be the most potent way of securing its compliance with demands on its core goods that it might not otherwise countenance—even if the attacker has no long-term designs on the victim's territory.

If the conqueror is to generate the leverage required to get the victim state to forfeit its core goods, though, each of these approaches—annexation, establishment of a protectorate, or the use of conquered territory as leverage—requires that the conqueror seize and hold not just any land but what might be called the victim state's key territory or, like the Entente Powers in 1918, be seen as irresistibly on its way to doing so. *Key territory* here means the territorial source of a state's political, economic, and military power; it typically includes the target state's capital city and a substantial fraction of its more populous and developed territory. Control of this area is what gives a government its strength and materiality.[61] A government can exist on paper and maintain a claim to legitimacy without controlling this key territory, but unless it sooner or later reestablishes control, it will eventually come to be seen as a fiction. Seizure of this key territory is ultimately what enables an invader to secure or impose its will over the target state's core goods. If an invader cannot take and hold this key territory, the victim state is likely to continue resisting.

The Fait Accompli

The advantages of conquest are therefore straightforward for a potential attacker that is stronger than its victim and any allies it has. The issue is more complicated, however, if the attacker does not enjoy such a commanding edge. In that case, the best way for an attacker to thread the needle between the advantages of the conquest approach and any limits in its military advantages relative to the victim and its partners is the fait accompli.

With a fait accompli, the attacker uses brute force to seize part or all of its victim's territory but tailors its use of force to convince the victim and the victim's allies and partners that trying to reverse its gains would be some combination of unavailing, too costly and risky, and unnecessary. The fait accompli can take several forms. As a military strategy, it can involve the seizure of more or less of its victim's territory and the defeat of more or less of its victim's military while also incorporating elements of cost-imposition, such as blockades and bombardment.[62]

Regardless of the form it takes, the basic theory of victory remains the same. A fait accompli requires the attacker to persuade its victim, that victim's allies and partners, or both to accept the new disposition after it has seized part or all of the victim's territory. The attacker can do this through a number of ways. It can seek to persuade them that reversing its gains would fail, including by hardening its defenses over the seized territory. It can also try to convince them that trying to regain the lost territory would be prohibitively costly and risky, not only by such hardening, but also by explicitly or implicitly threatening escalation if they do mount the kind of counterattack needed to succeed. Last, by using force in as focused a manner as possible, the attacker can try to persuade them that intervening is unnecessary because the attacker does not pose a sufficiently compelling threat to those parties' other important interests. The attacker can often achieve this last effect by halting its offensive advance somewhere short of what seems likely to trigger an effective intervention. The attacker can also employ these methods in combination.

The fait accompli thus unites brute force and coercion, avoiding the punishment approach's overreliance on persuasion. Under the fait accompli, the attacker no longer has to persuade the victim and its victim's allies and partners to concede on the victim's core goods but instead uses force majeure to seize them. If the victim is either wholly subordinated or unable to reverse the attacker's conquest, this leaves only the need to persuade any remaining coalition members not to react strongly enough to reverse the attacker's gains. If the victim retains the ability to mount a counteroffensive, however feeble, then the attacker needs to persuade the victim not do so. Either way, while the fait accompli involves persuasion, it requires significantly less than that demanded by the punishment approach, since it requires only the defenders' passivity in the face of new realities. In Schelling's phrasing, it uses brute force to seize the defenders' territory and then relies primarily on deterrence to persuade them to accept the new reality.

The fait accompli is thus a classic limited war strategy of a weaker power. Unlike a strategy that relies almost exclusively on force—which requires that the attacker enjoy military superiority over all its opponents—the fait accompli leaves at least some of the initiative with the defenders, wagering that enough of the attacker's opponents will elect concession as the more prudent course.

Conditions for the Success of a Fait Accompli

A successful fait accompli strategy depends on two conditions. First, the attacker must be able to seize the territory in question—meaning it must move into territory a defender has left unprotected or from which it has been ejected. If an attacker cannot do this, it gains nothing and therefore has nothing to defend. For instance, China could not seize Hawaii under any foreseeable circumstances. Given the distances involved, PLA forces would be detected and defeated well before they arrived, whether by standing and ready forces or by forces generated on receipt of warning. This illuminates the point that a successful fait accompli requires that the attacker enjoy a *local* superiority in military power against the targeted territory or state.

If an attacker faces capable defenders, this means that it must be able to seize the territory in question before its opponents can mount—or without their mounting—an effective defense. If the attacker can seize part or all of its victim's territory without the victim and any allied and partner forces being able or deciding to muster an effective defense, then the attacker can seek to fortify its position, making it that much harder for its opponents to reverse its gains and augmenting its ability to convince them that a counterattack will prove fruitless. At the same time, the attacker can supplement this with the threat to escalate if they do attempt to seize back the lost territory. Hence a fait accompli is most likely to be effective in situations in which it is difficult—that is, requiring more force and consequent escalation—to dislodge an entrenched force. Because a prepared defense often has a natural advantage, this is a common situation.

Importantly, this condition does not require that the fait accompli be quick, cheap, or easy, though these attributes naturally increase its allure. Executing a fait accompli can take time and be hard and costly. The essence of the fait accompli, rather, is the attacker's ability to persuade the victim and its allies and partners not to try to regain the seized territory. It is thus largely about the resolve of the defenders—it exploits the reality that the defender and its allies and partners will typically only go so far to retake the territory in question. Success simply requires that the attacker be able to seize the territory in question and that the victim and its allies and partners be unwilling to suffer the costs and run the risks needed to reverse the gains.

Second, the attacker must be able to hold the seized territory or consolidate its control over it. This requires preparing defenses adequate to resist a counter-assault by the victim state and its allies and partners. Due to this requirement, if a territory is very hard for the attacker to defend, the fait accompli is unlikely to be an attractive option because, even given the new facts on the ground, some combination of the victim and its allies and partners will be able to readily eject the attacker. In such situations, it will be hard for the attacker to convince the defenders that intervening will prove ineffective or too costly or risky. For instance, although China might be able to occupy the Senkaku Islands, it would find it exceptionally difficult to defend its occupation of the tiny islets, since its forces would be vulnerable to ejection by a capable Japan and its American ally. The fait accompli is therefore not likely to be an attractive strategy for China for the Senkakus. That said, the standard for defensibility is not absolute; the attacker must simply make the new position defensible enough that the victim and its allies and partners judge that ejecting the attacker will be too difficult, costly, or risky for the benefits to be gained.

Using the Fait Accompli against a Coalition

Although an attacker can use the fait accompli against an isolated target, the strategy tends to be especially attractive for use against coalitions, especially ones whose combined strength exceeds the attacker's. That is because, if the coalition is weaker, the attacker is likely better off simply defeating it outright.

In circumstances in which the attacker is weaker than the coalition it faces, a fait accompli can be effective for the attacker because, although the target state's resolve to defend itself may be very high, it may be unable to do so on its own and with whatever coalition forces are available in time.[63] Meanwhile, although the rest of the coalition may be stronger than the attacker, its members' resolve and readiness to come to the single member's aid may not be high enough to go the distance in light of the costs and risks the attacker can impose on them. As discussed earlier, this is not an uncommon situation because of the asymmetry of interests between the state that is directly threatened and the other coalition members, whose interests are implicated only more indirectly.

The fait accompli tends to be most alluring when applied toward the edge of a defender's or coalition's territory and nearer to the attacker's military center of gravity, particularly when the former has areas of vulnerability along its pe-rimeter. Such circumstances can give the attacker the local military superiority it needs to achieve gains and harden its defenses over them.

Instances of local military superiority against a coalition are common. This is because a coalition—especially an anti-hegemonic coalition—needs enough members to offset its adversary's strength and naturally tends to attract that ad-versary's close neighbors because they are the most threatened by it. More dis-tant and thus secure states are more likely to free ride, whether by staying out of the coalition entirely or by not contributing much to its defense. For instance, Eastern Europe is more keen for a militarily meaningful NATO today than Western Europe, just as Western Europe was keen for the alliance when the bor-der with the Soviet sphere ran through the middle of Germany.

Yet these imperiled neighboring states are the very ones most directly under the shadow of the opposing state's military power. Their vulnerability is pre-cisely what makes them want to league with others to check its aims. And yet they remain vulnerable to their powerful neighbor, as the Eastern members of NATO are today and as West Germany was during the Cold War. This dynamic is more intense the more powerful the opponent is, particularly in the case of an aspiring hegemon. Its power requires additional states to balance it, but this means that the coalition, in embracing more states, is likely to have to take in more states that are subject to the aspirant's local military superiority—and thus more likely to be attractive targets for a fait accompli.

Situations of a potential attacker's local military superiority are also common because perimeters are not always well defended. One reason perimeters are of-ten left underdefended is resource constraints. States rarely want to pay the costs of developing and deploying the maximum possible defense of their pe-rimeters. Often reasonably, they prefer civil investment and consumption to de-voting large portions of their economies to military expenditures.

A second reason is military. Distributing forces all along a perimeter is rarely a compelling idea because it violates the principle of concentration; units sprinkled along a line lack the potency of a more massed body and are more vulnerable to being penetrated by a larger force and then rolled up.[64] Thus it may seem more effective not to meet attacks at the border but, in the interests of economy and concentration of force, to wait until the attacker has made its move and spent its momentum before responding decisively to expel or destroy them.

Moreover, to minimize the burdens military forces place on society, states generally rely on warning to mobilize their full military potential. Indeed, the time and conditions required for warning and reinforcement to function effectively are important features attendant to fait accompli scenarios.[65] An attacker may seek to exploit temporary local advantages that stem from the difference between the standing or shorter-notice defenses of the targeted territory and a more fully generated mobilization by the defender or defending coalition. Thus a fait accompli is especially attractive when a significant gap exists between the level of a routine defense and that of a fully mobilized one. Israel in the early 1970s, for instance, relied heavily on warning and mobilization for its defense. Aware of this, Cairo deliberately employed a cry wolf approach designed to diminish Israel's propensity to call up and deploy its forces on receipt of warning, leaving the Israelis unprepared when Egypt seized the Suez Canal to start the Yom Kippur War.[66]

Last, political and diplomatic reasons can also result in an ill-defended perimeter. Some coalition member states may lack an effective perimeter defense because they do not wish to host foreign forces or because other member states object to deploying their own forces there. Norway during the Cold War refused to base foreign forces on its soil. Today, Taiwan is the most vulnerable part of the US security perimeter, but there are major international political barriers to basing US or other forces there.[67]

Thus defenses of peripheral territory are often inadequate, especially in far-flung coalition networks, making it not uncommon for a potential attacker to enjoy situations of local military advantage that enable a fait accompli strategy. Because the attacker can choose the location and timing of its assault, it can exploit these weaker or more poorly defended parts of the defending coalition's boundaries to seize territory.

But as noted earlier, to make the fait accompli strategy attractive, any gains that can be secured from such a local advantage must be defensible. If the attacker can be readily ejected, the fait accompli has little appeal. As a general rule, however, territory nearer to the attacker, and especially to areas where the attacker can concentrate its military power, is more likely to be more defensible once seized. Contiguity and proximity are advantages because military power is generally limited by distance, especially when that distance is contested.

This military reality is a product of physics. War is a matter of violence produced using material implements, and those implements are difficult and costly to project through space. Missiles, radars, aircraft, and air defense systems have finite ranges; deploying them forward allows them to threaten new targets, but the costs and difficulties of such movements increase with the distance the materials must be transported, especially when the movements demand new logistics networks and infrastructure. Then, too, terrain and culture are likely to be more familiar the closer they are. A bordering or nearby territory is therefore generally easier to incorporate into an attacker's existing defense architecture than a distant one.

Thus an attacker can more readily seize nearby territory and simply extend its existing defensive architecture outward, since a contiguous or proximate territory is unlikely to require dramatic changes to a state's military forces or posture. The ranges of existing weapons may already encompass the nearby target, mobile systems can be relatively easily moved forward, and extant logistics networks can be simply extended rather than created wholly anew. Of course there are limits: the point attenuates as one extends farther out. Trying to incorporate Soviet Russia into its sphere of military dominance, for instance, was a different matter for Germany in the Second World War than doing so to neighboring Holland or France. A nearby island is harder to incorporate because it involves crossing water, and a territory across a major mountain range or desert may also present difficulties. But in general, proximity is a proxy for ease of incorporation.

The weaker the defense perimeter and the greater the aspirant's ability to defend its gains, then, the more attractive the fait accompli will be. When the aspirant faces a coalition, the weaker the coalition's forward defense and the more readily its peripheral members can be defended by the invader once gained, the more alluring the fait accompli is for the attacker. Moreover, because the fait accompli is an especially attractive strategy for a state that, while facing a stronger coalition, can muster superiority over an individual member or members, it is an ideal strategy for exploiting the gap between the coalition's latent power and how much that coalition is realistically willing to dedicate to contesting a focused invasion that would be difficult, costly, and risky to reverse. The fait accompli is thus the optimal strategy for a weaker aspirant against a coalition that is stronger all told but may not be sufficiently resolute to apply its superior power.

Using the Fait Accompli to Fracture an Anti-Hegemonic Coalition

An aspiring hegemon can try to fracture a coalition arrayed against it by using the fait accompli to compel a victim state to disaffiliate from the coalition. This will weaken the coalition by removing the power of the victim state, but as if not more importantly, it will demonstrate the coalition's unwillingness or inability to effectively defend at least some vulnerable members, which will undermine other vulnerable states' confidence in the coalition, increasing the chances that these states will disaffiliate or distance themselves from it. This dynamic will be especially intense if the vulnerable member state is an ally of other coalition members, putting these allies' differentiated credibility at stake, since this result will show the hollowness of this alliance and those like it. And diminishing the differentiated credibility of such alliances, which are likely to be critical for the coalition's success, will be especially damaging to it.

Clearly, this strategy is especially relevant for an aspiring regional hegemon facing an anti-hegemonic coalition, especially one composed of constituent alliances designed to reassure vulnerable states—as the US-led coalition against China would be. As we have seen, such a coalition, to be effective, must provide enough reassurance to vulnerable member states that it keeps enough such states on its side to outweigh an aspiring hegemon like China in the regional balance of power. If the aspirant can force or induce enough such states to separate from the coalition, it can eventually gain more power in the regional balance and be able to establish its hegemony over the region. It can do this sequentially, isolating states one by one in order to separate them from the anti-hegemonic coalition while avoiding a larger war that it will too likely lose, until the balance shifts. This is the focused and sequential strategy.

The fait accompli is ideally suited to this strategy, since it is precisely a means to isolate a vulnerable part of a coalition in a manner designed to avoid initiating that larger conflict the aspirant will too likely lose. The aspirant can then repeat the fait accompli against other coalition members until the balance has shifted and it is ready to risk a systemic regional war to establish its predominance.

Making such a strategy work against an anti-hegemonic coalition, however, requires not just any form of fait accompli. Simply seizing and holding some arbitrary part of a victim state's territory is not enough. The goal is disaffiliation of the target from the coalition, and inducing a state to disaffiliate from an alliance or coalition will almost certainly impinge on its core goods. The whole point of membership in such an alliance—and in the coalition—is precisely to protect the state's core goods, especially its political autonomy. Getting the state to give up its core goods will therefore require a degree of leverage that can plausibly come only from holding its key territory. The fait accompli in this context must therefore involve seizing and holding the victim state's key territory. Once an invader has done this, it can force or compel the victim's disaffiliation from the coalition and any constituent alliances by annexing the victim, installing a friendly government over it, or using the captured territory as leverage to coerce the victim's government. If the attacker does not seize and hold its victim's key territory, conversely, that victim is likely to continue resisting. Indeed, the People's Republic took the Yijiangshan and Dachen Islands from the Republic of China during the First Taiwan Strait Crisis, yet Taipei retained its affiliation with the United States.

The Fait Accompli in China's Strategic Calculus

Because it is so well suited to fracturing an anti-hegemonic coalition that is stronger all told than the aspirant, the fait accompli is the ideal strategy for Beijing.[68] It is precisely designed to enable a locally strong state to pick off members of a stronger coalition by exploiting that group's internal divergences in threat perception and resolve. China is much stronger than any other state in Asia, and it can increasingly project major military force against neighbors like Taiwan, the Philippines, and Vietnam. Effectively applied, this strategy would allow Beijing to isolate and pick off members of the anti-hegemonic coalition, progressively weakening it until it hollowed out or collapsed.

The utility of the fait accompli—and by extension the importance to Beijing of having the ability to conquer its neighbors—is a critical point that is often confused in popular discussion. Many argue that Beijing does not want to create a territorial empire in Asia.[69] This very well may be true, but it misses the point from a military planning point of view. *Even if* it does not want to directly control or annex other states, China does aspire to be the predominant power in Asia, and that means overcoming any anti-hegemonic coalition or preventing one from forming. The best way for it to do so is by using a focused and sequential strategy to compel states to leave the coalition. Yet as we have seen, the punishment approach is unlikely to give China the leverage it needs to achieve this end. Rather, Beijing's better course is to use the fait accompli against coalition members, conquering their key territory in order to compel their disaffiliation from the coalition. Therefore, from a practical military point of view, China *will* want to be able to conquer substantial parts of Asia. This is because only the ability to seize and hold the territory of its neighbors will give Beijing the degree of power needed to force key regional states to disaffiliate from alliance with the United States and from the anti-hegemonic coalition more broadly.

Importantly, with the exception of Taiwan, which Beijing considers a rene-gade province, China's political aim in executing this strategy would very likely not be annexation of any occupied territory. China is already a very large state. There is little reason to think that Beijing judges extension of its borders as the best route to its goals. Moreover, territorial aggrandizement is especially likely to make a state appear menacing. Thus, although China may possibly pursue territorial expansion, it is not necessary for it to do so to gain regional hegemony and could well backfire, as Germany's taking of Alsace and Lorraine in the peace settlement following the Franco-Prussian War contributed to French hostility under the Third Republic.[70] Rather, Beijing's core demand of any targeted state would more probably be that it disaffiliate from an alliance with the United States, if applicable, and the anti-hegemonic coalition.

China's optimal way of employing the fait accompli would be to start with the states or territories against which it has the best ability to conduct such a strategy—in other words, states that are some combination of within or near the orbit of its military power and are inadequately defended. Nearby states are likely to be within the shadow of China's military power and are more likely to be readily defensible once conquered. If China could use the fait accompli to subordinate these states, it could then consolidate and extend its military reach, before replicating this strat-egy against other, more distant regional states until the coalition collapsed.

Given that Beijing would profit most from subordinating a US ally within the anti-hegemonic coalition, China's best, most consequential strategy for es-tablishing hegemony would be to employ the fait accompli to conquer the key territory of a contiguous or proximate state or entity that is part of the anti-hegemonic coalition, ideally one that has a security commitment from the United States. This would necessitate defeating the victim's military forces and conquering its key territory in order to compel its surrender.

Such an approach, if successful, would directly implicate the United States' differentiated credibility, sending the clearest possible signal of the distinct and perhaps fatal limitations of Washington's guarantees and thus of the po-tency of the coalition as a whole. If China could then execute the fait accompli against enough other targets, it could avert the formation, materially under-mine, or break apart such a coalition, allowing Beijing to establish itself as the region's hegemon.

China enjoys local military superiority over Taiwan to a greater extent than it does relative to any other member of the anti-hegemonic coalition.[71]

Consequently, and in addition to the reasons discussed previously for why Taiwan is China's most attractive initial target, China's most net gainful strategy is to attempt a fait accompli against Taiwan first. Beijing would very likely need to seize much of the main island of Taiwan itself, particularly Taipei and adjoining areas, to bring about Taiwan's government's capitulation. Seizing territory of lesser significance would not suffice. Taking Quemoy and Matsu, for instance, would be very unlikely to yield Taiwan's surrender.

Being nearby, Taiwan would be relatively defensible by China if seized. Once done, China could transport material across the Taiwan Strait and also protect its gains using its military power on the mainland. The bulk of the formidable assets that China has developed to interdict US military intervention would be readily usable to defend a Chinese-held Taiwan. Were Beijing to seize Taiwan, it could also make use of the island as a launching point for subsequent attacks on other members of the anti-hegemonial coalition—the Taiwan cork would have been removed.

The Philippines would be an attractive next target. Indeed, given the growth of Beijing's power projection capabilities, China could be able to launch expeditionary operations against the Philippines by the late 2020s.[72] As with Taiwan, Chinese forces would need to seize the Philippines' key territory—probably at least most or all of Luzon—to generate enough leverage to compel it to disaffiliate from its US alliance.

Following the Philippines, Beijing could turn its eyes toward Vietnam and other targets in Southeast Asia. If the United States and other potential defenders had not already established a powerful defensive architecture to negate this strategy, Beijing could seize the key territory of one or more of these states and then present the anti-hegemonic coalition with such a powerful defensive position that it would seem too difficult and risky to try to reverse Beijing's gains. Over time, the sequential application of the fait accompli could allow China to annex Taiwan and subordinate a sufficient number of other regional actors that any remaining actors—for instance, Japan, India, and Australia—no longer viewed the anti-hegemonic coalition as a reliable counterweight to Beijing. Those states' incentives to join or remain in the anti-hegemonic coalition would decline as a result, ceding to Beijing the mantle of regional hegemony.

8

A Denial Defense

HOW, THEN, SHOULD THE UNITED STATES respond to this, China's best strategy?
To repeat, the United States' orienting purpose is to maintain the effectiveness of the anti-hegemonic coalition. As long as the coalition is stronger than
China and functions effectively, Beijing cannot attain the regional predominance it seeks. Because of the central importance of US differentiated credibility to the coalition's proper functioning, the United States must ensure an
effective defense of each ally, including the most vulnerable states. An *effective
defense* means one sufficient to maintain the attacked ally's expected contributions to the coalition—in practical terms, to avoid its being conquered or subordinated into bandwagoning or neutralization—in the face of Beijing's best
strategy.

The Infeasibility of Restoring Dominance

The most attractive military strategy for the United States is dominance. In
such a model, the United States could readily, decisively, and at relatively low
cost defeat a Chinese assault on an ally, with no good way for Beijing to escalate.[1] This sort of dominance, because it allows one to defeat the adversary's attack directly and at relatively low cost, imposes very little burden on the
defender's resolve. If an action calls for minimal sacrifice or risk, one is much
more likely to do it, even if for a lower benefit.

The United States enjoyed this kind of dominance over China with respect to
US security partners until recently. In the 1990s and 2000s, China simply could

not project meaningful, let alone decisive, military power even against Taiwan. In such a world, had Beijing sought to invade Taiwan, Chinese vessels would have been sunk quickly, its aircraft shot down or destroyed on the ground, and its missiles intercepted or done little real damage.[2] Although Beijing had a nuclear arsenal, a strike against the United States in the context of a losing attack on Taiwan would have been the most certain way of eliciting a devastating US riposte. The burden of escalation thus lay exceptionally heavily on China.

But even though US military dominance over China is certainly desirable, it is simply no longer attainable, particularly with respect to Beijing's ability to apply the focused and sequential strategy against the anti-hegemonic coalition. The most important reason for this is simply the enormous size and sophistication of the Chinese economy. In purchasing power parity terms it is already larger than America's, and China has been vigorously turning this economic strength into military power. Moreover, its defense expenditures are considerably lower than they might be. Indeed, China spends a smaller share of its gross domestic product on defense than the United States does.[3] If the United States tried to spend its way to dominance, China could very likely negate such an effort. Moreover, given the enormous demands of attempting to attain dominance against a power like China, the economic costs could be crippling, seriously stressing the US economy, the ultimate source of America's military strength.

The second reason is geography. The coalition states that Beijing would most advantageously target are far from America but close to China. And as discussed, distance matters greatly in military affairs. China's wealth and Asia's distance from America mean that the United States will simply be unable to reestablish dominance over China.[4]

Moreover, a US attempt to reestablish dominance would likely be counterproductive. Straining after infeasible military missions is more likely to lead to waste than to graceful failure. For instance, trying to suppress or take down broad swathes of China's integrated air defense systems—rather than opening select parts of it on an as-needed basis—is likely to consume an enormous number of munitions that could be used for other purposes. Likewise, seeking to completely dominate the threat from Chinese mobile missile strike systems would consume an inordinate amount of intelligence, surveillance, and reconnaissance assets and bandwidth; missiles and other strike capabilities; defensive systems; and other capabilities, denuding the United States of critical assets for other key missions, for instance, striking at invading ships or aircraft. And such an effort would probably require far more time than US forces would have before any invasion force could successfully prosecute its assault.

For all of these reasons, the United States therefore should not seek to restore dominance over China with respect to defending vulnerable allies in the anti-hegemonic coalition.

The False Allure of Cost Imposition Strategies

An alluring alternative for the United States, rather than directly contest a fait accompli attempt, is to rely on the imposition of cost—especially through horizontal escalation, or widening the war and imposing costs on China beyond the immediate area of battle—in order to compel Beijing to disgorge its gains. This strategy, a variant of the punishment approach, has a superficial appeal because it may appear to leverage existing US advantages in global military power against China's local strength in the Western Pacific.[5] Horizontal escalation is, however, a losing strategy for the United States in the face of Beijing's use of the focused and sequential strategy.

This is fundamentally because horizontal escalation relies on attacking things that Beijing is likely to value less than the target of its focused and sequential strategy. Horizontal escalation would, for instance, seek to compel Beijing to give up on Taiwan or the Philippines by imposing costs on its interests farther afield, perhaps outside Asia. Yet China's best way to gain global preeminence is first to establish regional hegemony in Asia. It has every reason to select targets that would help it do so, and that it thus would value more than, for example, bases in Africa or energy facilities in the Middle East. In other words, from China's perspective, the gains from subordinating Taiwan, the Philippines, and other US allies in Asia would greatly outweigh the loss of access to Chinese bases or other interests farther afield, which in any case could be replaced once Beijing gained mastery of Asia.

Moreover, the strategy would almost certainly be a wasting one. Once China recognized that the United States was not seeking to directly defend its allies in the Western Pacific but was attacking China's assets farther afield, Beijing could adapt its military accordingly. It could adjust the PLA's force structure, posture, and operational concepts to shift away from the near battle, which was no longer being contested, to focus on protecting those more distant assets and on menacing America's own. Given that US interests are far more dispersed around the world than China's, it seems likely that the United States would suffer more than it gained by globalizing the competition.[6]

Last, because of these factors, such a strategy would almost certainly be poisonous to US efforts to form, sustain, and cohere an anti-hegemonic coalition in Asia. States near to China would recognize that the United States was not seeking to directly defend them but rather forlornly hoping to compel mighty China to give them up. This is almost sure to promote bandwagoning by states that were otherwise inclined to participate in the coalition.

Nor do vertical escalation strategies make sense for America. The United States needs a strategy that correlates the costs and risks of fighting over important but limited stakes with what Americans are prepared to bear; it accordingly needs to keep the burden of escalation on China. Vertical escalation strategies, such as relying on punishment strikes against China to get it to disgorge any gains, including with nuclear weapons, have limited effectiveness in compelling a resolute opponent. Thus seeking to compel China to give up Taiwan or the Philippines by escalating to harsh conventional or nuclear attacks would almost certainly bring about a hardening of Chinese resolve while giving China a legitimate excuse to respond in kind, all without reversing local defeat. This would result in grave devastation to America and very likely failure. Relying on horizontal or vertical escalation strategies is therefore exceptionally ill-advised for the United States.

The Best US Strategy: Denial Defense

The question, then, is whether there is an approach that will allow the United States to effectively defend its allies in the anti-hegemonic coalition against a very powerful China and its limited war strategy. There is, and we might call it *denial defense*. This approach focuses on denial rather than dominance—specifically, denial of China's ability to fulfill the crucial victory conditions required to make its best strategy work.[7]

A denial strategy relies on a fundamental aspect of the geopolitical situation: China is the power seeking to use military force to change things. Beijing would be seeking to force or persuade a vulnerable member state, particularly a US ally, to cease affiliating with the anti-hegemonic coalition. In practice, this is tantamount to an allied state altering its core strategic orientation. China's strategic goals are therefore offensive in the most basic sense—Beijing seeks to forcibly change the political status of states. The best way for it to achieve this is to seize and hold the target state's key territory.

If China failed to meet this threshold, then by definition the vulnerable state would still be resisting and adding its weight to the coalition. The differentiated credibility of the United States and any other implicated allies would be upheld. And the anti-hegemonic coalition would continue to function, preserving its own coherence and integrity and balancing Chinese power.

In simpler terms, success for China is to subordinate the targeted state; defeat is to fail to do so. Success for the alliance, and thus for the anti-hegemonic coalition, is to keep the targeted state in the fold. As long as the defense is strong enough to keep the ally on side and affiliated with the coalition, then it is succeeding in its core strategic purpose.

This, then, is an effective defense. Critically, meeting this standard does not require dominance, only the ability to prevent the adversary from achieving its objectives. China, the aspirant, is the one that requires dominance or at least a very high standard of local military advantage. The United States and other defending states do not; they merely need to deny China the degree of advantage it needs to consummate its invasion. As Air Chief Marshal Hugh Dowding said of the defense of Britain in 1940, "There was a distinct difference between the objectives of the opposing sides. The Germans were aimed to facilitate an amphibious landing across the Channel, to invade this country, and so to finish the war. Now, I wasn't trying with Fighter Command to win the war. I was trying desperately to prevent the Germans from succeeding in their preparations for an invasion. Mine was the purely defensive role of trying to stop the possibility of an invasion. . . . We might win or we might lose the war, or we might agree on a truce—anything might happen in the future. But it was Germany's objective to win the war by invasion, and it was my job to prevent an invasion from taking place."[8]

This is not to say that denial is the ideal standard for the defenders. Denial of invasion and nothing more might be enormously frustrating and painful, particularly for the targeted state. The point is only that this is the bar for success—more would be better, but the threshold for the defenders is relatively low. This also makes deterrence of war in the first place, though by no means easy, more feasible.

A denial standard is highly compatible with an effective coalition approach to limited war. This is because the United States and other engaged states can employ a denial approach in such a way as to make China bear the burden of escalation. This is especially important because the United States, as the cornerstone external balancer, is likely the decisive factor not only in the immediate conflict but for the success of the anti-hegemonic coalition as a whole. Sufficient American resolve is critical for that success—yet the resolve of Americans cannot be presumed in a focused war with China in Asia. But the more China is framed as the initiator of escalation, the more that will catalyze American and other states' resolve.

The United States and other defenders' preferred approach to negating China's best strategy should therefore aim at frustrating the opponent's ability to subordinate the targeted state in as direct and focused a way as possible. In other words, such a defense would meet the adversary's focused and sequential strategy on its own strategic terms by denying its efforts against the vulnerable state. It would seek to keep US and other defenders' actions as focused and constrained as possible so that China, not the United States and its allies and partners, would bear the burden of escalation. Effectively done, this approach would mean that China would need to expand or otherwise escalate the war in order to try to meet its threshold—but in doing so, it would strengthen the US and others' resolve to defeat it.

How would such a defense work? As we saw in the previous chapter, Beijing's best strategy against a vulnerable state is the fait accompli. If the defenders can deny the fait accompli, China will be forced into a punishment approach or a protracted war, since neither horizontal nor vertical escalation could save its failed bid at conquest. And neither a punishment approach nor a protracted war is likely to yield Beijing's desired outcome.

The focus of US defense planning should therefore be to deny China's ability to effectuate a fait accompli against its allies within the anti-hegemonic coalition. And because Taiwan is the most attractive target within the coalition, the United States and (to the extent that they are willing to contribute) other coalition states must focus on preparing to deny a Chinese fait accompli against Taiwan. If they can deny China the ability to invade and hold Taiwan, they can almost certainly do the same for the Philippines, Japan, or other coalition members. So long as they ensure that Beijing is not able to subordinate such allies within the anti-hegemonic coalition, that coalition will cohere and balance a rising China.

Denying the Fait Accompli

As discussed in the preceding chapter, the two conditions of success for the fait accompli are: (1) for the attacker to *seize* the victim's key territory; and (2) for the attacker to *hold* that key territory. If the defenders can deny either of these conditions, the fait accompli fails.

Denial Option 1: Denying the Attacker's Ability to Seize Key Territory

The first thing an attacker must do to consummate a fait accompli is seize the target state's key territory. As noted before, *seize* here means to move into territory a defender has left unprotected or from which it has been ejected. If the attacker fails to seize the key territory, then there is no fait accompli.

The first option for defeating a fait accompli, then, is to deny the attacker's ability to seize the target state's key territory in the first place. Defenders can meet this criterion by destroying or disabling all of the invader's forces before they arrive at its key territory. Or they can destroy or disable enough of the invader's forces that those that do reach the target state are insufficient to seize its key territory. *Enough,* in this usage, might refer either to a certain number of forces or to certain kinds of forces. If an invader's ability to seize key territory depends on its ability to deliver particular numbers or kinds of units to the target state, preventing those units' arrival should be sufficient to defeat the fait accompli.

The defenders do not necessarily have to eliminate the entire first wave of invasion forces in order to prevent the attacker from seizing key territory. Nor do they necessarily have to destroy fully all the waves that follow. This is because denying an attacker's ability to seize key territory is not an all-or-nothing proposition. Unless the first wave of the invasion has the numbers and types of forces required to seize the target state's key territory, the invasion's success will depend on the attacker's ability to deliver enough of the right types of forces in subsequent waves. If the defenders can prevent that from happening, they should be able to prevent the fait accompli.

The degree to which defenders are able to prevent an invasion force from reaching its territory depends on several factors. Of these, geography plays an especially important role. That geography is influential on military affairs is an ancient truism: the annals of military history are filled with discussions of the importance of geography on military strategies, from Hannibal's surprise crossing of the Alps

to the Allies' difficulties getting across the Rhine. Geography can have an especially influential—even determinative—effect on an invasion's outcome, especially when the war's belligerents are otherwise closely matched.[9] Where the
geography favors the offense, the defenders will have a harder time keeping invasion forces from reaching and penetrating their lines; the reverse will hold where
defenders have a geographic advantage.

Crucially, the geography of the area of potential military conflict between
China and the anti-hegemonic coalition is likely to favor the defenders.[10] Most
of the plausible coalition members are separated from China by geographical
features that would greatly complicate a Chinese invasion and would make defeating a Chinese fait accompli an attainable goal. India, for instance, is separated from China by the Himalayas, which are inhospitable to major military
operations. South Korea and Malaysia are accessible by land from China, but
both are situated on peninsulas, which serve to channel ground invasion forces
and thus aid the defense.[11] Of the plausible coalition members that are readily
accessible to Chinese forces by land, only Vietnam, whose key territory is
separated from China by relatively passable terrain, finds itself particularly
vulnerable to Chinese invasion.[12]

The other plausible members of the anti-hegemonic coalition—Japan, Australia, the Philippines, Taiwan, and Indonesia—are separated from China by
bodies of water. This list includes all of America's allies in the region except
South Korea. It also includes America's most important regional ally, Japan, as
well as the two most attractive targets for a Chinese fait accompli—Taiwan and
the Philippines. These states benefit from what John Mearsheimer termed "the
stopping power of water." As Mearsheimer argued, following in a long tradition
of military analysis, it is generally far more difficult to move an invasion force
across a large body of water than to move it across land. As a consequence, potential attackers have historically struggled to mount large-scale invasions involving the delivery of large numbers of ground forces across water, especially
when control of those waters is contested.[13]

This is not to say that invasions across water cannot be mounted. History testifies otherwise. During the Second World War, the United States delivered
forces across both the Atlantic and Pacific Oceans in the face of determined enemy opposition. The Japanese did likewise in Asia in 1941–1942. In earlier
eras, the British, Dutch, and Portuguese used the seas to mount invasions
around the world.

But in the face of a capable defender, an invasion's success across water depends heavily on the attacker's ability to achieve something approaching naval and air dominance in the areas through which the invasion force must pass.[14] Japan's conquest of Southeast Asia and the Pacific Islands at the outset of the Second World War was decisively enabled by the fact that American, Britain, and other allies had limited forces in the Western Pacific. The American military buildup was still under way in 1941, and the bulk of US naval power was located far distant in Hawaii and on the West Coast. Britain had minimal naval and air forces in East Asia because those forces were needed elsewhere. When Britain did send the battleship *Prince of Wales* and battle cruiser *Repulse* to the region without air cover, the Japanese swiftly sank them.[15]

The reasons an attacker confronted by a capable defender must establish naval and air superiority—if not dominance—in order to invade successfully by sea are several. First is that, unlike on land, the maritime domain offers little natural concealment.[16] With a few exceptions, such as the open desert or tundra, most landscapes include such features as forest, underbrush, and tall grass; hills, ravines, and other landforms; and waterways such as rivers or streams that ground forces can use to hide their presence and movements. Artificial features such as human settlements and buildings can also provide concealment.

With the notable exception of the undersea realm, the sea offers relatively few options for concealment. Although different seas provide opportunities for concealment due to climatic, oceanographic, geologic, and other factors, these factors tend to offer less for effective concealment than is available on land. The air offers even fewer.[17] Sea and air forces can seek to offset these limitations with countermeasures that include speed, decoys, electronic warfare, and other ways of disrupting or degrading the defender's battlefield situational awareness.[18] Even so, however, all things being equal, it remains easier for a defender to target invading forces as they transit over a body of water than over land.[19]

The maritime domain also offers less cover—or protection from enemy fire—than the land does. On land, the same natural and artificial features that enable concealment can also provide cover against attack. Trees, rocks, buildings, and bridges can to varying degrees absorb bullets, blast, and shrapnel.[20] Moreover, the land itself provides significant protection; for example, properly constructed earthworks can absorb or dissipate a remarkable amount of kinetic energy, meaning that prepared ground forces can be very difficult to destroy.[21] Naval and air forces, however, lack analogous options for cover. Although they can use defensive countermeasures such as decoys and missile defenses, their ability to exploit the environment itself for cover is much more limited.

The maritime domain's relative lack of concealment and cover matters because human beings are not, it hardly needs to be stressed, built to swim long distances, let alone fly. The same holds true for the critical components of modern ground warfare, such as armor, artillery, and air defenses, which can be designed for crossing water or flying only at significant cost or compromise to their efficacy. Practically speaking, almost all of these things therefore need to be carried across large bodies of water either in ships or in aircraft. The more personnel and equipment needing delivery, the greater the size or number of ships and aircraft required. Moreover, the invading ships and aircraft must put themselves into the area the enemy is trying to defend, exposing themselves to enemy action and forfeiting the opportunities for evading or frustrating enemy fires that are available to naval and air forces operating at standoff range.

These realities impose distinct limitations on a large invasion force crossing water. The transport ships and aircraft on which the force would rely must be able to carry enough forces for the invasion to succeed. As a result, these platforms are normally optimized for capacity—size and bulk—rather than evading enemy detection. They consequently tend to produce larger radar and other signatures that make them easier to target.[22] And all things being equal, the more observable these platforms are, the easier they are to strike and ultimately disable or destroy.

These challenges are compounded by the reality that attrition is generally a more manageable problem on land. Invaders who survive an attack on a ground formation can often leave their disabled or destroyed vehicles, gather whatever equipment survived the attack, and either forge ahead with their invasion by mounting undamaged or repaired vehicles, commandeering other transportation, or even proceeding on foot, or else dig in to enable other invaders. The same cannot so easily be done when invading by ship or aircraft. Invaders who survive a sinking ship will be cast into the water or put to sea essentially helplessly in lifeboats, while their equipment, especially heavy equipment, is likely to go down with the ship. Invaders and equipment aboard a struck aircraft are even less likely to survive, much less proceed with an invasion. Moreover, vehicles damaged or destroyed on land can be more readily repaired or replaced in the battle area, given the generally greater complexity of transport ships and aircraft.[23]

The high cost of developing the platforms required to move a large force across a large body of water also means that states have less margin for error when attempting an invasion by sea. Because the ships and aircraft required to deliver forces over water are more expensive than those required to mount a land invasion, states tend to possess shallower reserves and have a harder time replacing them when they are lost. The attacker therefore has a powerful incentive to be judicious with its precious naval and air transport capabilities. If too many transport ships or aircraft are lost, particularly early in an invasion, then the invasion itself will have to be aborted, and it may take a long time before similar assets can be mustered again for another attempt.

For all of these reasons, an invasion force is highly vulnerable when crossing water. And this is especially true for the transport ships and aircraft carrying soldiers, tanks, artillery, and other equipment critical for victory once the force has landed. These platforms must be very well defended. This is why, against a capable defender, the ability to partially defend these ships and aircraft is not enough. An attacker needs naval and air superiority, if not dominance, to deliver an invasion force to its destination.

This was true in earlier eras. During the Second World War, the Allies recognized that to invade Europe they first had to secure naval and air superiority over the English Channel so that the Allied flotilla could pass uninhibited across it. German naval forces played a negligible role in the Normandy invasion, and German air forces, flying a tiny fraction of the nearly fifteen thousand sorties that Allied air forces did, shot down no Allied aircraft on D-Day.[24]

But the need for an attacker to have something approaching naval and air dominance before undertaking an invasion by sea is even more acute today, under what has been termed the "mature precision strike regime."[25] This phrase refers to the great advances in modern militaries' ability to strike precisely at targets, including moving targets, at greater ranges and under more conditions. These trends further reduce the opportunities for concealment or cover available to sea and airborne forces, accentuating the defensive advantages against invasion afforded by the maritime domain.

For context, in the Second World War, it took roughly a thousand US bombers carrying nine thousand bombs—a payload of over two million pounds—to achieve high confidence of destroying a single major target in Germany. With the introduction of laser-guided munitions in the Vietnam War, that rate dramatically improved; destroying the Thanh Hoa Bridge in North Vietnam required only fourteen F-4 aircraft carrying nine three-thousand-pound and fifteen two-thousand-pound laser-guided bombs and forty-eight five-hundred-pound un-guided Mark-82 bombs—less than one-twentieth the payload needed in the Second World War. The rate improved even further in the 1980s and 1990s with the maturation of the so-called Second Offset technologies, and it has continued to do so since then. Today, an aircraft carrying dozens of bombs or cruise missiles can strike accurately at dozens of targets.[26] Militaries such as those of the United States and China can thus launch large numbers of extraordinarily precise guided projectiles carrying a wide range of devastatingly effective warheads. Moreover, these projectiles can be specifically designed to penetrate the opponent's air and missile defense systems through a range of techniques, such as stealth, electronic jamming, decoys, flight profile, and pack tactics.[27]

Against a ready and capable adversary, precision strike technologies are by no means perfectly effective. They rely on kill chains—the network of systems and associated procedures required to find, identify, track, and engage enemy targets—to deliver effects.[28] Those kill chains, in turn, can be disrupted, degraded, or destroyed by many means, ranging from the use of deception and concealment to confuse targeteers through kinetic or nonkinetic attacks on the satellites or aircraft used to cue a munition, through countermeasures directed at a missile's seeker, to kinetic missile-defeat options at a munition's final approach.[29]

But a force's ability to disrupt, degrade, or destroy its enemy's kill chain depends on a host of factors. Here again, geography plays a crucial role. For all the reasons discussed earlier, the land domain offers more options for frustrating an enemy's kill chain than does the maritime domain. Ground forces can use natural and artificial landscape features to reduce the enemy's ability to find them or to diminish enemy weapons' ability to engage them if they are found. Maritime forces lack the same options. These are some of the reasons why modern strike forces still face serious limitations in finding and striking mobile ground systems and in destroying entrenched ground forces.[30] There are certainly ways that naval and air forces can disable enemy kill chains, but the lengths to which they must go to protect themselves are much greater—and the risks and consequences of failing to do so effectively are graver.

The maritime domain's relative lack of concealment and cover, and the difficulties of replacing sea and air forces suitable for invasion, therefore make any invasion by sea a risky proposition. The mature precision strike regime only accentuates those risks by further restricting naval and air forces' already limited ability to find concealment and cover in the maritime domain, leaving them more vulnerable to capable and well-prepared defenders.

To execute a fait accompli against a US ally in the coalition, and assuming the United States and other defenders were well prepared, China would very likely need to invade with a large force in a commensurate number of transport ships and aircraft. To defeat the Chinese fait accompli, the United States and other defenders would need only to prevent enough of those forces from reaching their destination so that whatever forces did land could be prevented from seizing the defender's key territory. All of these factors weigh in favor of the defenders' ability to defeat a Chinese attempt to invade a member of the anti-hegemonic coalition across a large body of water, including the US allies that are most likely to be targets of such an invasion: Taiwan and the Philippines.

As noted, China's best target would be Taiwan. Even so, denying China's ability to seize key territory in Taiwan is a tractable—though by no means easy—problem that the United States and its allies and partners can solve. It is true that Taiwan is relatively accessible to PLA forces, separated from China only by the Taiwan Strait, which is eighty miles wide at its narrowest point. Yet Beijing would still need to deliver enough of the right kinds of ground forces across that strait to execute a fait accompli. And those forces—specifically the transport ships and aircraft in which they would travel—would still be vulnerable to interdiction by US, Taiwan, and other defending forces, which would have many options for frustrating and ultimately defeating a Chinese invasion.

Thus, from the outset of a conflict, defending forces operating from a distributed, resilient force posture and across all the war-fighting domains might use a variety of methods to blunt the Chinese invasion in the air and seas surrounding Taiwan. One set of options would be to engage Chinese invasion forces before they even got under way. The defenders might, for instance, seek to disable or destroy Chinese transport ships and aircraft before they left Chinese ports or airstrips. The defenders might also try to obstruct key ports; neutralize key elements of Chinese command and control and intelligence, surveillance, and reconnaissance networks; or attack other critical enablers, including other targets on the Chinese mainland, so that surviving assets were more vulnerable to interdiction when they entered the Taiwan Strait. And once Chinese forces entered the strait, US and other defending forces could use a variety of methods to disable or destroy Chinese transport ships and aircraft. These defenses could be expected to grow in number and density as Chinese forces neared the Taiwan littorals. The ultimate purpose of such a layered defense would be to ensure that no Chinese ground forces actually made it to Taiwan or that those that did survive the strait crossing were insufficient to seize Taiwan's key territory.

The United States and its allies and partners might employ a variety of operational concepts to achieve these results. Any such concept, however, will benefit from exploiting Taiwan's favorable maritime geography, which gives Chinese forces transiting the strait limited opportunities for concealment or cover. Although the Chinese would attempt to use countermeasures to offset those limitations, if the defenders were sufficiently able to monitor activity in the relevant areas of the strait and interpret and act on the resulting intelligence quickly enough, the Chinese forces should find themselves hard-pressed to avoid interdiction. Provided that US and other defending forces had enough of the required weapons and munitions and that those forces were postured, networked, and sustained appropriately, then they should be able to capitalize on these advantages to disable or destroy enough of the right kinds of Chinese sea and air transports and their enablers to defeat the invasion.

China would also find itself vulnerable to the attrition of the forces needed for invasion. Even as strong a state as China can afford to produce, deploy, and maintain only so many critical transport ships and aircraft.[31] Once enough of those assets were disabled or destroyed, China's ability to mount an invasion across the Taiwan Strait would be seriously degraded. Beijing might then revert to bombardment or blockade to try to bring Taiwan to its knees, pause in order to rebuild its invasion capability, or even give up its attempt to compel Taiwan's subordination.

In essence, then, the United States, Taiwan, and other defenders must be prepared to turn China's vaunted strategy to deny America's ability to project power into the Western Pacific around. Just as Beijing has sought the ability to deny US forces' ability to operate inside the first island chain, so the United States, Taiwan, and other allies should seek to be able to deny Chinese forces' ability to operate in the Taiwan Strait. They could do so by exploiting the natural advantages of the maritime geography separating Taiwan from the Chinese mainland and destroying or disabling enough Chinese transport ships and aircraft to render Beijing unable to deliver the forces required to seize Taiwan's key territory.[32] Moreover, American and allied forces able to meet this standard would be well situated to defend other coalition members, such as the Philippines and Japan.[33]

Denial Option 2: Denying the Attacker's Ability to Hold Seized Territory

There may, however, be instances in which an attacker is able to seize part or all of the target's key territory. In these cases, the first option no longer suffices to prevent the fait accompli—the invader has already succeeded in the first of its two objectives. Fortunately, the defenders may still have recourse in such circumstances. Even if they have failed (or judged it imprudent to try) to prevent the attacker from seizing some portion of the target state's key territory, they may still be able to deny the attacker's ability to hold whatever territory it has seized.

This is because it is one thing to seize territory, which only requires moving into territory a defender has left unprotected or been ejected from, and quite another to *hold* that territory in the face of counterattack, which requires preparing defenses adequate to resist such an assault. The history of conflict is full of assaults in which an attacker pushed defenders back but then could not consolidate its hold on the position; the famous Confederate assault on Seminary Ridge at Gettysburg, for instance, penetrated the Federals' line, but the Rebels were unable to secure their gains.

This is the second way to defeat a fait accompli attempt: if the defenders can eliminate the invading forces or expel them from the target state's key territory before those forces are able to consolidate their defenses over—and as a consequence, their hold on—the seized territory, the fait accompli will fail. Until the attacker, in other words, is able to seize the target's key territory *and* muster such defenses as required to convince the target state and its allies and partners that continuing to defend it would be in vain or prohibitively costly or risky, the attacker will not have consummated a fait accompli.

It is important to note a crucial distinction between an effort to deny the attacker's ability to establish its hold over seized territory and an effort to recapture territory the attacker already holds. To reiterate, the fait accompli strategy succeeds only if the attacker can seize and consolidate its hold on the target state's key territory before the defense can respond effectively. If the attacker achieves these two things, the fait accompli has been consummated. At this point, the task before the target state and its allies and partners is no longer to defeat an invasion but to retake what has been lost. In other words, once the fait accompli has been achieved, then the paradigm shifts from denying it to a recapture campaign, which I will address more fully in the next chapter.

To illustrate the difference between resisting a fait accompli and a true recapture campaign, it is useful to compare the Yom Kippur War and the Pacific Theater in the Second World War. In 1973, Egypt attempted to execute a fait accompli against Israel. In a surprise attack, Egyptian forces crossed the Suez Canal and advanced into the Sinai Peninsula. But Israel consistently resisted the invasion, initially without dislodging the Egyptians but then more successfully once Egyptian forces exposed themselves in order to relieve pressure against their ally Syria. Meanwhile, the Israelis' progress against Syria allowed them to shift forces from the northern to the southern front. Never having let Egypt consolidate its holds on its seized territory, Israel was able to launch an effective counterattack approximately a week after the outbreak of the war, defeating Egypt's armies and recapturing the Sinai and the Suez Canal.[34]

The Pacific Theater during the Second World War, by contrast, is an example of recapture. In 1941 and 1942, the Japanese made lightning gains throughout the Western Pacific, seizing and consolidating their hold on territory throughout that vast expanse. The inadequacy of American and Allied forces in the region left the Japanese time and space to consolidate their hold over these areas. The task then confronting the United States in the Pacific was not to deny Japan's ability to seize or hold territory but to retake what had already been lost. The ensuing recapture campaign against a well-prepared and committed Japanese opponent proved extraordinarily costly; the United States was eventually able to take much of what Japan had seized, but only at great cost over a three-year campaign.[35] This, then, is an example of a recapture campaign, and indeed, one of the most compelling aspects of a denial defense is to avoid such a difficult and costly effort.

Defending forces might deny the attacker's ability to hold seized territory in one of two ways.

The first is by holding the line: halting the invaders quickly after they arrive in the defenders' territory and then reversing their advances. Defenders might choose to hold the line out of necessity, or they might do so because they regard it as the most effective way to defeat or expel the invaders.

Defenders might feel it necessary to hold the line because a significant part or all of the target state's key territory is especially exposed to invasion, for instance, because it is near a border or coastline. In their efforts to prevent the invaders from consolidating their hold on such key territory, the defenders will have powerful incentives to destroy or expel the invaders before they can do this, using whatever force is available.

During the US Civil War, for example, the Confederacy judged that Richmond and the core areas of Virginia were key territory; their loss would have had, the Confederacy judged, an outsized impact on the southern rebellion's chances of success. So the Confederates dedicated themselves to holding the line in northern Virginia, rather than ceding that territory and fighting Union forces farther south, where the Rebels might have taken greater advantage of the South's strategic depth.[36] Importantly, however, such a strategy of forward defense does not require fixed or static operational or tactical approaches. The Army of Northern Virginia often pursued offensive and unorthodox operational and tactical approaches, including to great success at Chancellorsville, where Lee's division of his army—against traditional principles of war—resulted in a great Confederate victory.[37] Likewise, in the dire early months of America's war against Japan, the US Navy pursued a similarly aggressive, asymmetrical approach to holding the line in the Central Pacific.[38]

Necessity is not, however, the only reason defenders might seek to hold the line. Rather, there may be cases in which defenders do so because they believe it is simply the best way to defeat the fait accompli. That is, even if much of their key territory is located farther inland or is otherwise difficult to reach by the invaders, the defenders might still choose not to allow the invaders to penetrate their territory. They might, for instance, hope to exploit a military advantage or anticipated advantage around the invaders' areas of penetration. Most pertinently, they may have tried but failed to prevent the invaders from seizing territory but have readily available enough of the right kinds of forces to exploit a local military advantage at the points where the invaders have penetrated the defense's lines. Or they may expect to enjoy a local military advantage because critical reinforcements are due to reach the front lines shortly after the invaders arrive.

From a practical standpoint, defending forces might seek to hold the line in one of two ways. First, they might seek to close the gap in their lines quickly. This might take the form of a rapid counterassault, as at Seminary Ridge, in order to deny the invaders' ability to consolidate their hold by striking back before they can establish their defenses. This immediate response to the invaders' arrival on friendly territory is most appealing when simply allowing the invaders to stay on the territory at all—even without consolidating their hold—is likely to have outsized military or political effects. At Gettysburg, for instance, Federal commanders feared that a break in the lines would jeopardize the whole Union position, so they quickly counterattacked to drive back the Confederate attackers.[39]

Alternatively, the defenders might take a more delayed approach. Rather than launch an immediate counterattack, they might resort first to raids, bombardment, supply interdiction, and similar tactics. Such softening up can be used to prevent the attackers from consolidating their territorial hold, convince them to withdraw, or buy time for the defenders to generate the strength and maneuver into position to launch a decisive counterattack. This approach is likely to be more appealing when the invaders have gained a local military advantage but the defenders expect to be able to reverse it in relatively short order.[40]

Regardless of whether the defenders choose an immediate or delayed counterattack, they will succeed only if they can gather the strength to eject, destroy, or coerce the enemy into surrender. It is not, of course, a given that this will be the case. The defenders' attempt to execute the first denial option—denying an invader the ability to seize any key territory—might have failed because the invaders have overwhelmed the defenders, leaving them exhausted or otherwise incapable of redressing their defeat. When the Western allies finally penetrated German defenses in the Hundred Days' Offensive of 1918, the Germans had little left with which to mount serious counterattacks.[41] In these conditions, trying to hold the line is a futile enterprise.

In other cases, however, the first denial option might fail for reasons or in ways that do not compromise the defenders' strength so much that they cannot mount an effective counterattack. This might be because the defenders misjudged what was required to effectively implement the first denial option, failed to adequately resource such a defense, or simply had bad luck. In these circumstances, the defenders may still have much or even most of their strength intact. For instance, they might have committed a small fraction of their total forces and strength to attempting the first denial option; indeed, that paucity might be why it failed.

In these conditions, the defenders might still have a great deal of power to put into the struggle. But their remaining strength can be more or less readily available; prepared forces located nearby can be brought in quickly, for example, while unready reserves that have not yet been called up will take longer. If this still-intact strength can be brought to bear before the invaders consolidate their hold on the seized territory, it can be used to defeat the fait accompli. If it takes longer but is not compromised or destroyed by the invaders, it can be used in a recapture effort.

However quickly or slowly they respond, the defenders can either use brute force to seize back the lost territory or, alternatively, seek to batter the invaders into surrender. That is, the defenders can pursue this second denial option through a counterattack to retake the territory from the invaders or simply to destroy them all. They can also, however, seek to coerce the defenders into surrender or withdrawal, for instance, through bombardment, harassment, starving them out, or similar measures. Or they can use both brute force and coercion, as the Turks coupled direct assaults with artillery barrages and confinement of the Allied forces to their narrow strip of land at Gallipoli.[42] This can be especially pertinent in a larger campaign in which some invaders are more readily expelled and others more readily pressed into surrender.

In the event that China invaded Taiwan, there is ample reason to believe that the defenders would seek to hold the line against the Chinese forces that did make it to the island. This is first a product of necessity. If Chinese forces did land on Taiwan, they might be able to seize part or all of Taiwan's key territory relatively quickly, since much of it—including the coastal cities of Taipei and Kaohsiung—is relatively exposed to amphibious attack or airborne assaults. It thus will be very appealing, if not necessary, for the defenders to hold the line and prevent China from consolidating its hold on that seized key territory.

There is also reason to think that Taiwan, the United States, and other engaged partners might have the forces required to destroy or expel Chinese forces even if they do make a successful landing. The mere fact that Chinese forces had landed on Taiwan, whether amphibious assault forces coming ashore on Taiwan's beaches or airborne forces farther inland, would not necessarily mean the destruction of the defenders' ability to resist, especially given the vast reservoirs of US power that could still be made available for Taiwan's defense. Thus China's success in penetrating onto the island would not necessarily translate into an ability to consolidate its hold on the seized territory.

US, Taiwan, and other engaged partner forces could use their remaining strength—including ground forces not previously involved in the defense against the attackers' initial crossing of the Taiwan Strait as well as US and other engaged partners' forces from elsewhere that were not deployed in time to join in attempting the first denial option—to seek to eliminate, eject, or compel the surrender of these Chinese forces by rapidly counterattacking against them, maintaining pressure on them to weaken them before counterassaulting, or both. If the defenders could destroy, expel, or compel the surrender of these Chinese forces before they could consolidate their hold on the seized key territory, they would have denied China's attempt at a fait accompli, upheld the United States' differentiated credibility, and supported the anti-hegemonic coalition in its effort to frustrate Beijing's focused and sequential strategy for achieving regional predominance.

There is another way, however, that defenders can seek to deny invaders the ability to hold seized territory. Rather than halt and reverse the invaders' advances where they arrive, defenders might judge it more prudent to allow them to take some territory before confronting them on more favorable terrain. This is particularly advisable if some of the territory the attackers must invade to achieve their objectives is easier to seize than to hold. Attackers seizing such territory might expose themselves by invading it, presenting better opportunities for the defenders than if they had met the invaders at the border. In these conditions, the defenders might judge it wiser to concede the difficult-to-defend territory at first and turn their efforts to preventing the attacker from holding it.

Take as an example the North China and North European Plains. Wide plains like these certainly provide opportunity for defensive preparation. But they are also widely traversable, meaning that even robust defenses can readily be circumvented.[43] A fortress positioned in the middle of the North China Plain, for instance, might easily be bypassed by invading forces and left isolated rather than confronted. The same goes for steppes, grasslands, and desert. These topographies differ from terrain such as rivers, mountains, and coastlines that more severely restrict and channel combatants' movements, providing opportunities to situate defenses in such a way as to force a confrontation between attacking and defending forces while allowing the defenders to control advantageous ground.[44]

In terrain that is relatively easy to seize, trying to prevent invaders from seizing any territory at all can be a risky and even losing proposition. In such terrain, such as the plains of Continental Europe or Central Asia, those who concentrate their defenses or position them too far forward often leave themselves vulnerable to envelopment, penetration, infiltration, or other tactics used by mobile forces.[45] In 1940, for example, the Allies relied for the defense of

Western Europe on fixed fortifications along the Maginot Line on France's eastern border and on the deployment of Allied forces forward into Belgium. Germany, however, broke through in between these concentrations in the Ardennes, where the Allies had economized on deploying forces, resulting in the splitting, encirclement, and eventual defeat of the Allied armies and ultimately the fall of France and the Low Countries.[46]

In such cases, a better approach may be what is often termed a *defense in depth*.[47] A defense in depth does not depend on preventing invading forces from seizing any territory. Rather, the defender deliberately accepts that invading forces will seize at least some territory and seeks to gain advantage from the costs and risks an invader incurs by doing so. Indeed, in some cases, the defenders might allow the invaders to seize a large swath of territory with the expectation that the invading forces will make themselves vulnerable—for instance, by overextending their supply lines or moving into territory that is especially favorable to the defending forces—thereby leaving themselves vulnerable to a decisive counteroffensive.

On Okinawa, for instance, Japanese forces judged that they could mount a superior defense by allowing US forces to land and move deeper inland before attacking the overextended assaulting forces from stronger positions. Although this approach ultimately failed in the face of insuperable odds, it proved highly costly to the American attackers.[48] In a much earlier time, Homer reports that the Trojans conceded the beach to the invading Greeks, judging that they could make a better defense from their stout city walls.[49]

A defense in depth trades territory for advantage. The strategy's effectiveness is a product of the fact that, by definition, invaders trying to seize defenders' territory must expose themselves. Any invading force must leave its prepared positions and advance, expending energy and resources and creating potential openings for counterattack. Skilled attackers can certainly protect themselves as they advance, but their ability to do so depends heavily on the terrain and the strength and skill of the defenders. With territory that is easier to seize than to hold, capable defenders may judge that it is better to let the invaders advance, exposing themselves and drawing down their strength, momentum, knowledge of the terrain, and other initial advantages, while the defenders husband their own strength and advantages before striking at the most propitious moment. This approach can be especially attractive if the defending country has more favorable conditions farther into its interior.

Russia, for instance, has repeatedly employed this strategy over many centuries. Russian forces have often used their country's enormous expanse to defensive advantage. Confronted by such formidable invaders as Charles XII of Sweden and Napoleon, Russian forces allowed the aggressors to penetrate deep into their territory. Then, once the invaders were tired, their supply lines had been stretched, and the weather turned in their favor, Russian forces struck back under the more favorable conditions found deep within the Russian interior.[50] The effectiveness of defense in depth for Russia is testified to as well by the fact that postmedieval Russia's closest brush with total defeat was likely the Second World War, when Moscow kept a large chunk of Soviet forces forward. Huge numbers of these forces were encircled and destroyed in the early phases of Operation Barbarossa.[51]

The defense in depth thus offers a viable option for denying the fait accompli for defenders that either cannot or judge it more prudent not to attempt to hold the line against invading forces where they make landfall. Rather than attempt to mount a forward, immobile defense in the manner of the infamous Maginot Line or the unlamented 1970s-era Active Defense doctrine for NATO, defenders in these situations can trade territory for advantage, thereby defeating the attempted fait accompli on more favorable ground.[52] Indeed, this principle of using depth to the advantage of the defense lay at the heart of AirLand Battle and Follow-On Forces Attack, the two famous concepts that supplanted Active Defense and are widely regarded as having been well suited to dealing with the threat to NATO from the Warsaw Pact. Each of these concepts envisioned weathering significant Warsaw Pact penetration of NATO lines while still preventing just such a fait accompli over West Germany.[53]

A complicating factor for a defense in depth in the circumstances the United States and its allies in Asia face, however, is the location of the target country's key territory. If that territory is located along the border with a potential invader or near readily accessible coastlines or airways, a defense in depth tends to be less attractive, because the invader can achieve its goals without penetrating deeply into the defender's territory.

With this caution in mind, American allies and partners in Asia might still benefit from a defense in depth, especially states whose territory consists largely of terrain that is easier to seize than it is to hold or whose key territories are located farther from their borders or coastlines. Should China grow much stronger, India might fall into this category. Similarly, for Vietnam, which shares a long border with China, the PLA might be so powerful that holding the line at the border may simply be untenable. Even though Hanoi itself is not far from that border with China, much of the rest of the country's wealth, population, and associated key territory are located farther south. Vietnam might, then, be best served by a defense that uses the depth of the country to draw in invading Chinese forces and counterattack them farther from the Chinese border. Vietnam has in fact used such an approach to defeat Chinese invasions in the past.[54]

But a defense in depth might also be useful for Taiwan, even though its key territory is more exposed to Chinese invasion. In the event of Chinese assault, Taiwan's defenders might give up parts of Taiwan's key territory in places such as Taipei and Kaohsiung and seek to draw Chinese forces into costly and difficult battles in urban, mountainous, or heavily forested areas. The defenders could exploit the vulnerabilities such advances might open among the Chinese invaders and seek to destroy, expel, or force the capitulation of Chinese forces once they had been weakened but before they could consolidate their hold on the key territory they had more easily seized.

That said, a defense in depth would be much more likely to succeed for Taiwan if it were coupled with the first denial option and the defenders could weaken and reduce the invasion force before it reached Taiwan, disrupt and degrade cross-strait lines of communication for Chinese forces once they had landed, or both. But its success would ultimately depend on the defenders' ability to lure Chinese forces onto ground favorable to the defense. Urban areas might provide some such terrain. Given that Taiwan's key territory is largely located along the coast, however, a defense in depth would likely have to include a compelling strategy for inducing the invaders to expose themselves by venturing farther inland.

The defenders might do this by using the more defensible terrain—for instance, parts of Taiwan's mountainous or forested interior—to mobilize forces for a counteroffensive to reclaim Taipei, Kaohsiung, or other key territory seized by Chinese forces. Doing so might lure Chinese forces into the interior, for instance, by inducing them to think that they could defeat a counteroffensive before it starts. Alternatively, the defenders might seek to lure Chinese forces inland by physically relocating some of Taiwan's key territory, for instance, by moving its seat of government and critical industries that Chinese forces must claim if they are to consummate the fait accompli. The Soviets moved much of their industrial base east of the Urals during the Second World War, in effect shifting some of their key territory farther inland.

Neither of these approaches would be easy or a sure bet, though. Rather than venture into riskier terrain, Chinese forces might simply elect to strengthen their defenses around seized territory in anticipation of a counterattack, judging waiting to be the better course. Moving its key territory, meanwhile, would be immensely taxing for Taiwan; most likely it would require substantial, perhaps enormous investment before any Chinese attack. Moreover, it might not work, since unlike the Soviet Union of the Second World War, Taiwan has far less territorial depth to exploit.

Let us suppose, then, that a denial defense of some kind has succeeded—whether by stopping the invasion before it arrived on Taiwan or by preventing those Chinese forces that did land on the island from consolidating their hold. China's invasion would have been defeated, but its ability to wage war would not have been. The United States and its allies and partners would therefore need to be ready for the possibility of a longer, broader war and be prepared to end that war on favorable terms.

9

Limited War after an Effective Denial Defense

POSIT, THEN, THAT THE UNITED STATES, Taiwan, and other allies or partners have denied China's fait accompli. How might Beijing respond once it became clear that its initial attempt to invade Taiwan was failing? Although China could escalate horizontally, vertically, or both in an attempt to alter the war's boundaries, if the defenders' denial defense attempt were successful, the coalition would be well positioned to respond in ways that kept the burden of escalation on China's shoulders until Beijing determined that folding was the better course.

The Defenders' Preferred Rule Set

One of the major advantages of a denial defense is that operations under this strategy can be limited in ways that both favor the defender and are likely to seem relatively simple, intuitive, and communicable. Because the core purpose of a denial strategy is to defeat an invasion rather than destroy, dismember, or even broadly defeat China, the defenders can clearly focus their rule sets to serve this purpose. All that the defense requires from these rule sets is that the PLA invaders are either prevented from landing on Taiwan's key territory or, if they manage to do so, are evicted from that territory before they can consolidate their hold. Satisfying such requirements is by no means easy, and it would almost certainly necessitate military action beyond the immediate environs of Taiwan. But logically, a denial defense does not require anything approaching a total war.

These rule sets might take a number of forms. For instance, given that an effective denial defense would essentially be about the resolution of the battle for Taiwan, the defenders could limit full-scale military operations to a given distance around the main island of Taiwan itself. They could couple this bounding with proposals to enable attacks outside this zone against, for instance, forces directly or substantially engaged or implicated in the conflict and possibly on select key capabilities such as over-the-horizon radars and counterspace systems. They might seek to have these rules recognized through both explicit messaging and demonstrated behavior.

This approach would very likely necessitate at least some strikes on the Chinese mainland. But there is almost certainly no way the defenders could succeed without striking at the mainland, where the vast bulk of China's military power is located and from where its invasion would be launched and supported. If the United States forswore the ability to attack targets on the Chinese mainland that were materially involved in the war, it would gravely weaken its ability to defend Taiwan; treating them as off-limits would also only raise questions about US seriousness and resolve. This is not to say that these strikes need to be indiscriminate or even expansive. To the contrary, any strikes on the Chinese mainland should follow a clearly elucidated logic. For instance, the United States could make clear by both its official statements and the deeds of its forces that the defenders would strike mainland targets only if they were directly engaged in or supporting the campaign against Taiwan or were within a designated geographical area around the Taiwan battle area.[1]

Coupled with an effective denial defense, this approach is likely to leave a heavy burden of escalation on China's shoulders. In the face of such cabined strikes, China would have abundant reason not to dramatically escalate, as this would be likely to provoke a far more devastating counter-response than the US had already mounted. It seems clear that the Chinese themselves are prepared to conduct conventional military operations to defend the mainland from such attacks, instead of relying on dramatic escalation; this is almost certainly why China has developed the world's largest and most formidable air defense network over the mainland, something that would be unnecessary and wasteful if Beijing deemed even focused and limited mainland strikes intolerable provocations demanding dramatic—especially strategic nuclear—escalation.[2]

That said, what is good for the goose is good for the gander. If China has to accept the harder implications of such rule sets, so do the United States and the other defenders. If China agreed to a rule set permitting attacks on *directly engaged* forces, this definition would likely include at least some air and naval bases in the United States as well as cyber and space assets. The defenders should therefore propose and seek acceptance only of rule sets that are advantageous and whose implications they can live with.

The Limits of Chinese Horizontal Escalation

Were the Chinese invasion to falter, one option for Beijing would be to try to rescue victory from defeat through horizontal escalation. It could seek to broaden the conflict geographically or in terms of the interests engaged. For instance, it could attack the United States and other defenders outside the previous bounds of the conflict; it could also expand the war into the economic domain, for instance, with economic sanctions. At first glance, this approach might seem attractive to Beijing. The anti-hegemonic coalition would be composed of multiple states, each with far-flung equities. The United States is uniquely exposed in a global conflict because it has so many interests, including military forces, that could be targeted all over the world.

But horizontal escalation is unlikely to work for Beijing. First, if Chinese forces could not effectively project military power against nearby Taiwan, what hope would they have beyond the first island chain? With its fait accompli attempt blunted, China's direct military leverage, perhaps except in such places as Central Asia that it abuts and the coalition does not, would be minimal. It is therefore unlikely that China could directly threaten US or allied equities that are anywhere near as important to the anti-hegemonic coalition as Taiwan, especially once Taiwan has taken on an even greater, very bloody value as a test of US differentiated credibility. It is very likely, moreover, that China's military forces would be weaker beyond the immediate battle area than those of the United States, other defenders, and allies and partners farther afield, such as European nations that might be willing to support the United States and other engaged states outside of the Taiwan battle area, even if they do not enter the fray near Taiwan itself. Although China would no doubt trade victory over Taiwan for its more distant interests, this would not be its choice. Were it to escalate horizontally, it would more likely lose both.

China might also expand the conflict by using its enormous economic and other nonmilitary leverage to hurt the defenders, seeking to coerce them into giving up Taiwan. It could, for example, threaten to dump its US investments, withhold critical exports, or cease buying certain imports from the United States or other allied states. But this, too, would be unlikely to work for two reasons.

First, such an effort might not hurt the defenders, especially the United States, as much as some fear. The United States has already begun decoupling critical elements of its economy from China with the idea of reducing Beijing's economic leverage, and others appear to be following a similar course. China may not, then, have much practical ability to use economic leverage against the most important parts of the anti-hegemonic coalition.[3] It is also entirely possible that China would suffer more than the United States if it dumped its US Treasury bonds. Such a move might, by reducing Chinese capital flows to the United States, actually raise the US savings rate and possibly spur US economic growth. Moreover, Beijing could be hard-pressed to reallocate its investments productively.[4]

Second, Chinese economic coercion in this context would be more likely to catalyze the defenders' resolve than lead to their capitulation. Beijing would in effect be seeking to reverse a local military defeat by turning the conflict into a societal contest of wills, a competition in pain tolerance. It would thereby make the conflict about much more than the disposition of Taiwan. The war would become about the security of the allied societies themselves, and their fates would now be much more clearly tied to the solidity of the alliance and the coalition's ability to resist Chinese coercion. If China could escalate in this way and reverse local defeat, it would demonstrate not only the inefficacy of the alliance and thus the broader anti-hegemonic coalition but also China's ability to coerce at will in Asia, an ability it could then turn on others in the region. Thus, no longer could the war plausibly be seen as a local matter internal to China; instead, it would be about whether Beijing could coerce even the world's other most powerful states at will.

There is, of course, no way that the United States and its allies and supporters could tolerate this. Nor would they be likely to do so; by going to war to defend Taiwan they would almost certainly have anticipated that China might do something like this and resolved to resist it—otherwise they would never have exposed themselves to the fray in the first place. Moreover, the defenders would not be supine in the face of Chinese pressure. They could, for instance, align further among themselves to make up trade losses while collaborating to impose trade and other economic restrictions on China.

Crucially, this is especially likely because it would be China that was escalating the war into a contest of societal pain tolerance. The defenders would be *responding* to China's escalation, not initiating it. Fence-sitter states would see that it was China—not the defenders—that was jeopardizing the global economy and bringing the world closer to the precipice of catastrophe. This would increase these third-party states' incentives to press China for restraint and even to join with the defenders in actively seeking to restrain Beijing. Moreover, all the defenders would have to do is hold on; if things resolved by a halt in place—a natural focal point to end such a spiraling conflict—the coalition would prevail.

Together, these factors would constitute an exceedingly heavy burden if Beijing hoped to use horizontal escalation to escape defeat. Moderate forms of expanded pressure would almost certainly fail to convince the United States and its allies to back down from a successful defense, and more dramatic steps would be more likely to catalyze their resolve than depress it.

The Limits of Chinese Vertical Escalation

A similar logic explains why vertical escalation by China is also likely to fail. In the event of an impending or actual defeat of its invasion forces, China could use its strategic strike capabilities—including its nuclear weapons—to try to reverse that failure. Indeed, analysts frequently worry that China would go nuclear rather than lose a war over Taiwan.[5] But it is very hard to see how vertical escalation—whether to high nonnuclear or nuclear levels—would not, like horizontal escalation, fail.

China might, for instance, conduct nonnuclear attacks on the defenders' critical infrastructure or other sensitive targets to inflict pain on what it might judge or hope to be weak-willed populaces in the United States or other coalition countries. Such strikes, if they were not very harsh, would be unlikely to change the allies' calculations. But if the attacks were harsh, they could very well spur resistance rather than cow their targets. By definition, China's strikes would not be coupled with a plausible way of attacking and subjugating allied states, which would have already won the local battle. They would thus be cruel but feckless. The German V-1 and V-2 rockets in the Second World War inspired terror among Londoners but did not affect the war's outcome.

Moreover, the defenders would have significant options to impose severe costs on China in ways that, because China had struck first, would seem highly justifiable. The United States alone has multiple options for selective responses using its long-range strike, cyber, and other capabilities. Those options would allow the United States to hurt China, leave Beijing no closer to victory over the local battle, and promise only more such pain and frustration if China elected to continue. Beijing's striking at allied and partner civilian targets would legitimate and no doubt catalyze these responses, motivated by what Clausewitz called the "flashing sword of vengeance."[6]

China could also try to use its nuclear weapons to rescue victory from the jaws of defeat. This would constitute the first hostile use of nuclear weapons since 1945, an epochal crossing of perhaps the clearest threshold in international politics.[7] Given that China would be doing this not to defend itself from conquest or forcible change of its government but rather to subordinate a neighboring country—even if it considers Taiwan a renegade territory—this would certainly bring down immense moral castigation and pressure on Beijing and make it seem even more imperative that the United States and its allies defeat it.

Even more fundamentally, the United States at a minimum, and likely the anti-hegemonic coalition as a whole, would have enormous incentives to ensure that they were not seen as vulnerable to nuclear blackmail. If the United States folded in the face of such brinkmanship, everyone—China, US allies and other coalition members, and fence-sitter states—could not but conclude that Washington was shown, when faced with the ultimate trump card, to be a paper tiger. If China is willing to use nuclear weapons and the United States is not, Beijing will dominate over whatever interests are at stake—whether about Taiwan's fate, that of another US ally, or free American access to Asia more broadly. Moreover, given the repercussions of such a conflict for the anti-hegemonic coalition as a whole, the stakes at issue would likely be much broader and deeper than just about Taiwan. Conversely, a state willing and able to use its nuclear weapons effectively can show its opponent the inutility of or high costs associated with employing nuclear weapons against it, thereby almost certainly making such nuclear employment against it less likely in the future. This does not mean, of course, that a state must immediately resort to Armageddon in the face of any nuclear use by an adversary. But that state must have some way of responding effectively with its own nuclear forces—or it will be dominated.

Fortunately for the coalition, the United States has plausible options for a limited nuclear riposte. Although China has a survivable arsenal and is modernizing and (thus far) moderately expanding it, it is still far smaller and offers less opportunity for controlled, discriminate employment than the American arsenal.[8] If China used nuclear weapons against, say, a US base on Guam or in Japan, the United States has—and continues to develop—multiple options to respond with proportionate nuclear force, including in ways that would diminish China's ability to continue such a conflict. If China went further and struck a civilian target such as Honolulu, the United States would have not only multiple options for retaliation but also the tremendous resolve formed by a combination of vengeance and the need to demonstrate the inutility of such a maneuver—and quite possibly international backing from allies, partners, and fence-sitters.[9]

Faced with a United States resolute and prepared to this degree, the strategic logic behind China's employment would be at best questionable, supremely risky, and quite possibly enormously destructive and counterproductive for China itself. Such a strategy would be based on the idea that China cares more about Taiwan's disposition than the United States does and is thus more willing to bear pain in a brinkmanship contest. But things would not be so simple.

First, such a contest would surely be perceived by Americans and others as about more than just Taiwan. If Taiwan were the only thing at stake, then China might indeed care more. But a Chinese attempt to use nuclear weapons against the United States to turn Beijing's local defeat into victory would inevitably have wider implications.

Furthermore, a China that used nuclear weapons in such circumstances would very likely seem to be far more dangerous than other states had previously anticipated. Allowing it to triumph in these conditions could only augur worse things in the future.[10] If China could reverse a coalition victory in a war over what is effectively a US ally in Taiwan, why would it not do the same in a war over Vietnam or the Philippines or, ultimately, Japan and Australia? Such an effective limited nuclear strategy by China to reverse a conventional defeat would be dominating. China would consistently win wars over these kinds of stakes against an irresolute America that was ready to give up even what it had already successfully defended. Thus the victor in a nuclear brinkmanship contest over a blunted Chinese invasion of Taiwan would not just prevail in the local fight but very likely gain a dominating position in the overall question of whether China would establish hegemony in Asia. The recognition of this would very likely impel Americans to support dealing with China effectively at once rather than deferring until later, when conditions would likely be considerably worse.

In addition, a Chinese brinkmanship strategy would not be very credible, as it would almost certainly end in a bluff. A series of tailored nuclear strikes against select US targets—sharp knife thrusts—would be one thing, but actually resorting to large-scale nuclear use against the United States would be another. Following through on such a course to its end would be genuinely crazy, since China would then lose *everything* in a major nuclear war over Taiwan—a highly valued but still decidedly partial interest. This madman approach might work if the stakes were low for the United States, but as we have seen, they would not be low. China might want the United States to *think* that it is prepared to pull the temple down on everyone's heads over Taiwan, but the United States would be ill-advised to credit such threats since the Chinese campaign to seize Taiwan, however important the island is to Beijing, would not actually rise to the existential level.

Beyond this, Chinese nuclear employment would surely prompt key states in the region, such as Japan, to consider their own nuclear arsenals, especially if they found the US riposte lacking. Such proliferation, while risky for global stability and unfortunate for Washington, would almost certainly be far more damaging and dangerous to China than to the United States. Nuclear arsenals in the hands of other regional states would not, as I will discuss later, magically solve all the anti-hegemonic coalition's strategic problems. But they would surely make any Chinese effort to establish its hegemony over the region harder and riskier. Facing an anti-hegemonic coalition with additional nuclear-armed states, China would have to reckon far more carefully about applying its focused and sequential strategy against those states.

If Not Escalation

It is highly unlikely, then, that either horizontal or vertical escalation could avert defeat for China. In practice, brinkmanship strategies when neither side has a commanding advantage in resolve usually end by ratifying the existing state of play, since in a situation in which all will suffer the most grievous conceivable harm, the natural focal point for settlement is simply to stop.[11] But halting in place under these conditions would, of course, benefit the defenders. Accordingly, China's best course of action would very likely be to avoid such a brinkmanship contest in the first place.

Rather than escalating or giving up entirely, Beijing might revert to the punishment approach. But this might be difficult or even infeasible since much of the force required for a blockade and bombardment campaign might have been lost or damaged in the invasion attempt. More to the point, after the attempted invasion had demonstrated both the gravity of the threat from the mainland and the defenders' ability to defeat it, why would a cost-imposition campaign work? Taiwan, having already withstood a direct attack, would see the feasibility of holding out, and key members of the anti-hegemonic coalition would already be involved. Meanwhile, other coalition members as well as fence-sitters would see both that China was dangerous and that it could be successfully resisted. It is hard to see how a punishment approach in these circumstances could succeed.

Protracted War

Another alternative for China is a protracted war in which it could seek to re-generate the ability to mount another invasion attempt while improving the conditions for this subsequent effort. In this model, Beijing could work to re-build its invasion force while seeking to erode the ability and resolve of Tai-wan's allies and partners to effectively defend the island against the next assault. It could try to do this by selectively escalating or expanding the conflict in ways that played to its advantages, such as by using targeted strikes or economic lev-erage to pressure key defenders or supporters. The logic of such an approach would be for China to apply pressure on Taiwan and the other defenders by con-tinually degrading their defenses and resolve while regenerating its forces to prepare them to create or exploit a window of vulnerability in Taiwan's defense.[12]

Settling In for a Long War

If Beijing chose this course, the United States and other involved states could seek to terminate the war, but—it is important to emphasize—they would not need to. They could accept a protracted war as the new normal if they preferred to avoid the considerable risks of trying to coerce China's agreement to ending the war.[13]

In such circumstances, fighting might continue in places, but the defenders would likely have good responses to such attacks. Having defeated China's first attempt to invade Taiwan, they would likely be in a position to sink and destroy much of a regenerated Chinese invasion force, either preemptively or once it had sallied forth into the Taiwan Strait. If China attempted to blockade and har-ass coalition members' shipping, for instance, the United States and others could sink or otherwise degrade the Chinese platforms that were impeding trade. Meanwhile, the defenders could continue to improve the island's de-fenses while suppressing Chinese aircraft, missile forces, cyber assets, and tar-geting capabilities to thin out the strength of the Chinese bombardment.

Resolve would likely not be as pointed an issue for the United States and others at this stage. Support for a firm defense would likely be high among the participants and other friendly nations, as the conflict would have demonstrated both the need for a strong posture against an aggressive China and the efficacy of a properly supported effort. Meanwhile, the defending states and their supporters could adapt to Chinese attempts at economic or other nonmilitary coercion. And given the defenders' advantageous position, many third parties could be expected to incline more toward working with them than with Beijing, furthering China's isolation.

Such a protracted war has ample historical precedent, including the Peloponnesian, Punic, Hundred Years', and Napoleonic Wars. The last, for instance, continued for another ten years after Napoleon called off the planned invasion of Great Britain in 1805.[14] Such a protracted war can continue at a relatively high level of intensity if the sides direct their industrial bases toward sustaining such a conflict. Or it might become rather desultory. It is even plausible that trade and other nonbelligerent interactions between the defenders and China could resume amid such a protracted war. Alternatively, the war might persist at varying levels of intensity.

So long as China remained within bounds tolerable to the United States and the other engaged allies and partners, the defenders could seek to meet their denial goal by mowing the lawn—degrading or destroying any invading or potential invading forces. Although such a war would be far from optimal, the United States and other defenders would likely come out the better from it. Given the risks involved in trying to coerce China's agreement to end the war, this could be the least bad course of action for the United States and its allies and partners.

Compelling an End to the War

Rather than face a protracted war, the United States and the other defenders might decide that the costs and risks of such a conflict outweigh those of trying to end it and seek to compel China to stop fighting and accept defeat. At a minimum, a long war would be a lethal nuisance; at worst, it could escalate into something far graver. Or the defenders might do so out of concern that a change in government in an important allied or partner state could worsen the coalition's ability to prevail. Such shifts are far from unprecedented; the death of the empress Elizabeth and assumption of power by Czar Peter III during the Seven Years' War led Russia not only to withdraw from its alliance with Austria and

France but to intervene actively on Prussia's side, likely frustrating Vienna's ability to retake Silesia, which was its core war aim.[15]

It must be emphasized that, in attempting to coerce China to terminate the war, the defenders would need to demand no more of China than that Beijing accept its failure to subordinate Taiwan and cease hostile efforts to subordinate it or any other US ally within the coalition. They would not need to require that China do something more fundamental, like change its government or give up territory. Moreover, they would not need China to relent formally; Beijing might meet the defenders' demands informally. There has been no war on the Korean Peninsula since 1953, despite the two sides' only having concluded an armistice; nor did Japan and the Soviet Union ever conclude a peace treaty after the Second World War, yet they have not fought since 1945. Both have been tolerable situations for the United States and its allies.[16]

To persuade Beijing to end the conflict along these lines, however, the United States and other defenders would need to do more than simply continue their denial defense. Such a focused defense would, by definition, not have persuaded China to concede.

This is entirely plausible because, in order to keep the war limited, the coalition's preferred boundaries attendant to such a denial defense would have concentrated specifically on defeating China's invasion of Taiwan. While such a focused defense of Taiwan would very likely include strikes on mainland China, it would have to be bounded in ways consistent with the logic of limited war. For instance, the United States and its partners might only strike mainland targets directly engaged in or supporting the battle over Taiwan, or within a designated geographical area.

These boundaries would almost certainly leave a great proportion of China's military forces and industrial capacity untouched. Even if China threw a great deal of its military might into an attempted invasion, much of its armed forces would be ill suited to or simply incapable of contributing to such an assault; moreover, given Beijing's perceived requirements for internal security and potential threats on other borders, it would almost certainly keep back a significant fraction of its military power out of these boundaries in order to deal with these other contingencies. Thus the very attributes that would allow such a denial defense to be limited in such a compelling and effective way—by, for instance, leaving alone China's military forces not involved in or enabling the invasion of Taiwan—would necessarily leave a great deal of China's strength and valued assets unharmed. That so much of its power remained intact might help convince Beijing both that the costs and risks associated with conceding defeat over Taiwan—such as resultant internal political instability—would be greater than those of continuing the struggle and that fighting on and attempting another invasion when ready would be preferable to accepting defeat, humiliation, and all they would entail.

In these circumstances, the United States and any other engaged coalition members would then need to do more than continue their focused denial defense of Taiwan. But they would not want to do too much. Even after its invasion of Taiwan was defeated, China would possess not only enormous resources to continue and expand the war but also survivable nuclear forces that it could employ whenever it wished—and the United States would be unable to stop at least a substantial portion of their delivery, including against America itself. Accordingly, any strategy designed to compel Beijing to accept the end of the war would need not only to stand a good chance of succeeding but also to do so without triggering a cataclysm, especially significant nuclear use by China against the United States itself.

A strategy for war termination should thus enable careful escalation management yet also fail gracefully if it does not work. It should not only press China but offer China's decision-makers reason to avoid a cataclysmic course and provide opportunities for de-escalation if things start to get out of hand. In other words, it should push China toward concession while giving it incentives to act with restraint. At the same time, a war termination strategy should allow for iteration and the prospect of error while avoiding prompting China to respond with massively destructive nuclear attacks. Such an effort would be an inherently experimental activity. The United States simply cannot know in advance what China's thresholds for pain and concession would be. Indeed, China's leaders themselves might not know. The task for the United States, then, would be to use force in such a way as to identify and take advantage of China's thresholds for concession while avoiding triggering undesired escalation.[17]

These criteria rule out an attempt to decapitate the Chinese government or eliminate its nuclear forces. Such efforts would almost certainly fail, given China's strength and consequent abilities to protect against such attempts, and they would very probably seem a genuinely existential threat—an attempted prelude to China's subordination or destruction—driving China toward employing its nuclear forces against the United States and its allies and partners. Moreover, such courses would leave little room for iteration. Killing leadership or destroying nuclear forces that can be moved or hidden requires catching them before they are dispersed and thus relies on surprise and coordination. Such attempts must necessarily tend toward one-fell-swoop approaches that could push Chinese leaders into a use-it-or-lose-it situation, thereby increasing the chances of significant Chinese nuclear escalation.[18]

The better option for the United States and its engaged allies and partners would be to combine elements of denial with the selective and conditional application of cost imposition on China until Beijing relented or the United States determined that further pursuit was too risky or costly. This approach would build on the efforts to weaken or disable China's ability to assault Taiwan again and then seek to persuade Beijing to agree to end the war, not through total victory or the destruction of the Chinese military, but by convincing Chinese leaders that they would not achieve their objectives and that continuing to try would cost them much more than they would gain by persisting.

A strategy employing cost imposition selectively, conditionally, and as a complement to denial operations—rather than as the primary or exclusive victory mechanism—would be distinct from the kinds of cost imposition campaigns that have so often failed in the past. Such an approach would not be about city-busting. Rather, it would be focused on attacking those things and capacities whose loss would make the Chinese government most likely to relent while maintaining the support of Americans and other engaged populaces. It would be similar to the logic of US war termination strategy in the latter part of the Cold War, especially the so-called Schlesinger Doctrine and Countervailing Strategy. These strategies called for the United States, in the event of war with the Soviet Union, to use force (albeit relying much more on nuclear weapons than is called for here) in discriminate and targeted ways in order to influence Soviet decision-makers. Their methods and targeting, moreover, were based on the US government's best estimate of what the Soviet leadership valued and how it would respond to different US employment strategies.[19]

In the conflict over Taiwan, this strategy would build on Beijing's recognition of the futility of trying to invade Taiwan again by adding to the Chinese leadership's calculations a sense of increasing costs. The strategy would do so through selective strikes against targets Beijing valued that would be unlikely to provoke significant nuclear use, especially against coalition members' home territories, or shift international perceptions in China's favor. These targets might include nonnuclear military forces beyond those relevant to the Taiwan battle, as well as internal security assets or critical war-supporting economic infrastructure.

To emphasize once more, the targets of the cost imposition elements of this strategy might focus largely—perhaps exclusively—on military forces and assets. The strategic logic of such strikes, however, would not per se be to deny China's ability to do something against the coalition (although this might be an ancillary benefit). Rather, it would be to *coerce* China's leadership into accepting defeat by selectively inflicting damage on things that China's leadership valued. Accordingly, such focused escalation might include nonmilitary as well as military forms of threat and suasion. For instance, while the defenders could set their initial war aims as simply the defense of Taiwan's autonomy, if China refused to relent after the invasion force was defeated, they could move toward recognition of a new political status for Taiwan.

Cost imposition, in this model, would be conditional. The logic of such strikes would be to make clear to China and important onlookers that China was bringing this harm on itself through its unreasonable recalcitrance, that the United States was not inflicting pain without good reason, and that China could end the infliction of such pain by recognizing the evident reality of its defeat over Taiwan—a limited equity well below the existential level. China's leadership, in this model, would be the main driver of the harm brought on China, and they could turn off that suffering at any time by taking the limited, reasonable step of acknowledging a partial defeat.

This conditionality would be important not only for limiting the war but for maintaining the defenders' cohesion. Were key American allies or partners to believe that the United States was initiating a cost imposition campaign recklessly or for punitive reasons unrelated to terminating the war as quickly and painlessly as possible, they might withhold support for the campaign or the broader war effort. This, in turn, could undermine the defenders' ability to end the war and might leave Taiwan dangerously vulnerable to a later invasion.

This selective and conditional approach would, then, primarily rely on coercion, not brute force, to end the war on the defenders' terms. The goal would be to convince Beijing that it could not reverse its local defeat over Taiwan, that the costs and risks of continuing its struggle were too great, and that its interests would be best served by acceding to the defenders' limited demands. The strategy would thus selectively and conditionally layer pain on a perception of futility, thereby leveraging both denial and cost imposition to influence Beijing's calculus. Brute force would play a role, but it would be a supporting one. The plain reality is that China is too powerful for the United States simply to make it cease fighting; the United States and any engaged allies and partners would therefore need to persuade it to do so.

This would represent a frame shift from the purely denial-focused approach that the defenders would have taken thus far, one designed to defeat the Chinese invasion of Taiwan. In this original frame, the defenders were not seeking to *persuade* China to stop the invasion; their theory of victory rested on denying China's *ability* to consummate it. The defenders would have reserved coercion in the focused denial defense of Taiwan for persuading China to abide by the rule sets they proposed.

In seeking to persuade Beijing to end the war, however, the defenders would begin to rely more—but not exclusively—on cost imposition. The appeal in these circumstances of the cost imposition approach integrated with denial is that it is both feasible and better suited to keeping the war limited.

First, a cost imposition approach would be better suited to keeping the war limited, especially as the conflict neared or even crossed the nuclear threshold, as it very well might. A cost imposition approach is meant to hurt the opponent enough to persuade it to relent, whereas approaches emphasizing denial require neutralizing a military force's ability to do something. The problem with applying a purely denial approach is that it would raise the question of what the United States would seek to deny China's ability to do. A denial approach to forcing an end to the war could not simply be about seeking to defeat China's invasion of Taiwan, since this would not be enough to persuade China to terminate the conflict. It would have to do something more. But what? The logic of a denial approach is to neutralize the enemy's ability to harm one's interests, but denial falls on a spectrum. One can deny an enemy this ability by destroying its invading army, but this alone does not deny the enemy's ability to send another one, raise a third, or develop the capacity to field better armies in the future. Germany was overcome by a denial approach that prevailed over its fielded armies in the First World War, but this defeat did not stop it from rearming and starting another war two decades later. It was more thoroughly defeated in the Second World War, but even this was a limited form of denial. Indeed, Henry Morgenthau famously suggested an even more thoroughgoing denial of Germany's ability to reconstitute by forcibly transforming it into an agrarian society.[20]

The most intuitive way for the United States and its partners to employ a de-nial approach against China would be to reduce its ability to reconstitute a ca-pability to attack Taiwan or other members of the anti-hegemonic coalition. Up to a point, this would make sense as part of a war termination strategy. Dimin-ishing China's ability to reconstitute an invasion capability would only make Beijing more aware of the futility of continuing. This alone might even be enough to persuade Beijing to relent, particularly if it had previously thought that it could quickly regroup to mount another invasion. If the only thing pre-venting Beijing from conceding was that it thought it still had a relatively at-tainable invasion capability at hand, pure denial might still work.

Yet Chinese decision-makers might not judge futility as a sufficient reason to give up. And at a certain point, the effort to push China's ability to reconstitute an invasion capability further to the right would require destroying more and more Chinese military and industrial targets. Since China could always move military forces from one zone to another, produce arms in new or different fac-tories, or launch air or missile strikes at US allies from various locations across its vast territory, all of China could become the target of a thoroughgoing denial campaign.

True denial of China's ability to reconstitute its capability to attack Taiwan or another US ally in the coalition could therefore turn into an effort to destroy a much broader fraction—if not the entirety—of the Chinese military and in-dustrial base. If the United States sought to deny China the ability to regenerate its battle fleet, for example, it would have to attack not only the ships them-selves but factories, shipyards, naval installations, and other facilities through-out China. The natural end point of a pure denial approach could well, then, be the full-scale defeat of the Chinese military and state, just as denying Germa-ny's and Japan's ability to reconstitute their capacity for armed aggression was seen to require total Allied victory in the Second World War.[21] Fears of Iraq's ability to reconstitute its nuclear weapons program were likewise critical to the US decision to overthrow the Ba'ath government in Baghdad in 2003. At some point, denial is likely to shift from a narrow goal to a general weakening or even destruction of an opponent.

Thus, whether Beijing elected to grit through the US attacks and eventually strive to reconstitute its invasion capability—however long this might take—or simply refused to relent in the face of futility, a denial approach would at some point necessitate expanding the war dramatically. But as previously discussed, it is by no means clear that the United States and its partners would win this larger war. China could very well be strong enough to defeat such an attempt, since it would be defending its own vast territory rather than trying to invade another state. This is true even if Americans and other engaged populaces supported this much more expansive and aggressive war—but that support could by no means be assumed. Those populaces might judge the costs and risks of that larger war too great for the prospective gains and balk at pursuing it.

Even more fundamentally, a denial campaign along these expanded lines would incur enormous risks. A Chinese leadership and populace defending their own national territory would likely fight harder and with great strength— indeed, with their own flashing sword of vengeance. More pointedly, such an expansive war could prompt China to use its nuclear forces and other strategic capabilities at scale. Even if the United States and its allies intended only to destroy and degrade Chinese military power rather than conquer the country and forcibly change its government, Chinese leaders might fear the latter, making cataclysmic war more likely. Such an outcome would defeat the purpose of the defenders' strategy—to keep the costs and risks incurred in the war matched with the interests at stake. Any victory of this sort would be pyrrhic—ash in the victors' mouths.

By contrast, a strategy employing both denial and cost imposition would be more tailorable and controllable, and more likely to fail gracefully. Such a campaign would be less prone to spiral into a catastrophic conflict against a China possessed of survivable nuclear forces. Imposing costs would simply require the infliction of harm rather than eliminating China's ability to take action, although the former might sometimes entail the latter. Thus targets could be selected to mitigate Chinese fears that the defenders' attacks represented a prelude to invasion, forcible change of government, or conquest.

That said, at the highest levels of escalation, it would be difficult to avoid provoking these fears, since the things Chinese decision-makers most value are likely to include government leadership and China's strategic forces—precisely the targets most likely to trigger a large-scale nuclear response. But the United States would have many other options to choose from before having to determine whether to strike at these targets. It could, in a sense, experiment with the myriad of targets below this level of escalation in the hope that destroying such targets would prove enough to tip Beijing's decision-making toward concession. Only if those attempts did not suffice would the defenders need to address whether to attack Chinese government leaders and China's strategic forces directly. At that point, the United States might well decide that enduring a protracted war is preferable to pushing the envelope too far, and de-escalate. And this should be possible because the strategy would be conditional and flexible enough to allow for it.

Importantly, the same war termination logic would apply at the nuclear level just as it does at the conventional. If China escalated to nuclear strikes, the United States could pursue the same logic, seeking to limit the war but mixing nuclear and conventional strikes to selectively and discriminately degrade China's ability to invade US allies and attack the United States itself while imposing costs on China in ways calibrated to avoid precipitating a massive response.[22]

In addition, a war termination strategy that integrated denial and cost imposition would be not only more readily limitable but also more feasible. Cost imposition strategies have many limitations, but they are better suited for inducing an opponent to accept things as they are than for compelling some positive action that another party does not want to take. They are ill suited for forcing an opponent to relinquish something, especially a powerful opponent who can retaliate.[23] But in this scenario, the defenders would not be demanding that Beijing relinquish something in its possession; they would want nothing more from Beijing than inaction and passive acceptance. Denial would have done the hard work of ensuring China could not seize and hold Taiwan; cost imposition would only coerce Beijing to accept this reality.

In other words, the defenders would demand of China only that it accept things as they had developed—that it swallow the results of a successful denial strategy. They would not need to compel China to give up anything more, such as territory or political concessions, to achieve their goals. The defenders would rely for war termination on measured doses of denial, augmented by cost imposition, particularly as denial reached a point at which it might provoke significant Chinese nuclear use.

Such an approach would present China with the choice of either conceding or continuing to lose valued things with no good prospect of reversing the situation. Moreover, any attempt by Beijing to escape from this predicament through horizontal or vertical escalation would be more likely to worsen its situation than improve it, since it would likely catalyze the defenders' resolve and enlist other states' support. Beijing's situation would be like that of the victim of a boa constrictor, in which the victim's exertions only tighten the serpent's grip. The more China sought to escalate its way out of its quandary, the more it would worsen its predicament. In these circumstances, Beijing would face enormous pressure to end the war.

Ideally, China would not only agree to end the war but change its tune. It would see that attempting to secure regional hegemony by a focused and sequential strategy costs and risks more than hegemony is worth and that accommodating the anti-hegemonic coalition in a stable balance is less unpalatable than continuing its aggressive pursuit of regional predominance. This, again ideally, could lead to détente.

Alternatively, though, Beijing might decide to give up the war, but only for the time being, and, like so many frustrated great powers in the past, plan to rearm and try again in the hope that, in its second attempt against Taiwan, it would resemble Napoleon's successful defeats of the powers that had previously humbled France. In the face of those plans, Taiwan's defenders could then prepare to deter and, if necessary, defeat such an attempt, with the conviction that China's previous behavior established both the necessity of deterrence and the defenders' ability to prevail. If needed, the members of the anti-hegemonic coalition could also add to and tighten the coalition and the alliances within it in order to better defend themselves.

Or China could fight on, despite the increasing costs and evident futility of doing so. If it elected to do so, though, this war termination strategy would likely fail gracefully for the defenders, since they would have blocked China's focused limited war strategy and left Beijing without plausible options to reverse the defeat of its invasion. At the same time, they would likely be able to weather a protracted war better than China, since they would have demonstrated not only their strength and resolve but their willingness to stop the war on terms that fell far short of the dismemberment, forcible change of government, or destruction of China. This would strengthen the defense's hand in enlisting the support of third parties, such as European states, which would be particularly significant in a protracted war that could involve blockades, counterblockades, and other types of economic warfare.[24]

This kind of cost imposition approach layered on military victory has ample precedent, especially among great powers. When wars cease before the losing party has been totally defeated, their endings often combine military victory with the threat or imposition of pain—which may come from the other combatants or third parties. The British effectively lost the Revolutionary War at Yorktown, but it took the threatened loss of possessions in other theaters, unrelated to the American conflict, before Britain agreed to give up.[25] The Russians lost the Russo-Japanese War of 1904–1905 even though they could have kept fighting; the threat of social disorder and risks in other theaters, combined with the apparent futility of continuing the war, convinced Saint Petersburg to come to terms.[26]

In summary, then, the optimal strategy for the United States and other defenders of a threatened state in the anti-hegemonic coalition would be a combination of denial and cost imposition: denial defense against the fait accompli, with cost imposition layered on that effective denial to persuade China to accept the defenders' preferred rule sets for limited war and as an option for inducing China to accept local defeat and agree to terminate the war. Denial would defeat China's theory of victory against the vulnerable state; cost imposition layered atop denial would induce it to accept the defenders' preferred rule sets and accept local defeat.

But we must be clear: making a denial defense strategy work will not be easy or cheap. It is hard to overstate the scale and sophistication of the resources Beijing can bring to bear to subordinate Taiwan. Despite Taiwan's separation from the mainland by a significant body of water, taking it is far from an impossible military problem for a state of China's magnitude. And defeating such a mighty attacker within the focused boundaries that the United States and other defenders would prefer would be exceptionally challenging. Nor, if Taiwan had fallen, would the defense of the Philippines or Vietnam be anything like an easy matter.

This is so even if we assume that the United States adapts its military to better contest a Chinese attempt at subordinating Taiwan or a US ally in the Western Pacific.[27] Even with the substantial changes in US forces needed to optimize such a posture, it will be tremendously difficult to deny a determined assault by China while keeping such a war limited in ways that correlate the demands of a denial defense with the resolve of Americans and the populaces of other participating nations. And without such changes, it may be impossible.

10

The Binding Strategy

WHAT IF THE UNITED STATES AND its allies and partners cannot mount an effective denial defense or cannot do so within their desired bounds? As discussed, denial defense within tolerable boundaries is clearly the preferred course for the United States and its allies and partners. Its success relies, however, on defeating a Chinese attempt at a fait accompli *and* doing so within boundaries the United States and its allies and partners are prepared to countenance. What if this is not feasible?

Why a Denial Defense Might Fail

A denial defense might fail for two primary reasons, each having unique implications. First, the United States and its allies and partners might have the strength to mount an effective denial defense but be unable to implement it without substantially escalating the war in ways that put the burden of escalation on themselves rather than on China. This problem could arise because a relatively narrow, focused denial defense might not be sufficient. Chinese forces might be too strong, broadly dispersed, or arrayed or equipped in ways that would cause such a constrained defense to fail. In such conditions, the United States and possibly critical allies and partners might need to attack many more Chinese targets, a wider set of them, across a much wider expanse, or using more ferocious levels of violence in order to successfully defend Taiwan or another target. In such circumstances, a denial defense would fail if the United States or critical allies or partners were not prepared to initiate such daunting escalation. In essence, there might be a mismatch between the steps needed for effective denial and the resolve available. Critically, though, the United States and its allies and partners can recognize this deficit in advance and seek to correct for it so as to make the broader denial defense workable.

Second, it might simply be unworkable to conduct a denial defense to deny the fait accompli. It might simply become impossible to deny an extraordinarily powerful China that will enjoy the advantages of proximity to Taiwan the ability to seize and hold the island. Of note, it may be unworkable to defeat the fait accompli because the costs required to do so are prohibitive. That is, there might come a point at which a local defense could become so difficult and costly that it jeopardizes the anti-hegemonic coalition's ability to win a systemic regional war against China. This would happen if Beijing could, within the bounds of a localized war, inflict damage on the United States and its allies and partners at a significantly higher rate than vice versa; at some point, continuing to defend Taiwan could diminish the coalition's overall war-making capability enough to compromise its advantage in that larger war. Since victory in a systemic regional war is the ultimate determinant of whether an aspiring hegemon like China can establish its predominance, the coalition cannot allow this. Such a situation would be tantamount to a denial defense not being workable.

The difference between the first and second variants of infeasibility might be illuminated by historical analogies. The first is akin to the questions that NATO planners faced toward the end of the Cold War in Europe, when the United States and its allies hoped to develop and field a theater defense capable of defending Western Europe from a Soviet Bloc invasion. Had NATO achieved such a standard, the question then would have been whether the Allies would have, in the event of war to blunt a Communist assault into Western Europe, possessed the resolve needed to employ that power fully and broadly enough against the Soviet Bloc, given the enormous risks of escalation. The second variant resembles more the situation of the United States in the Western Pacific in the years before the Second World War. American military leaders in that period knew, given the constraints under which the US military was operating, that the United States simply would not be able to deny an effective Japanese assault on the Philippines. It was not a matter of whether the Americans had the resolve to fight; effective defense was simply impossible, given the assets and other resources available to the US military at the time.[1]

The failure of a focused denial defense might, moreover, extend beyond Taiwan. Although Taiwan is the most vulnerable plausible coalition member to Chinese military strength, China might simply grow powerful enough to punch through any attempt by the United States and others to defend the Philippines, South Korea, and even Japan.

This is not just doomsday prophesying. Taiwan and other potential coalition states *can* be effectively defended, but doing so demands strict focus on developing and preparing an effective defense posture. Developing such a posture is feasible but difficult; it requires that the United States, Taiwan, and potentially other states such as Japan and Australia promptly and resolutely adapt their strategies and forces to meet the requirements of the denial strategy.[2] But it is possible that some or all will fail to prepare sufficiently. This could result from a failure to appreciate the severity of the threat China poses, confusion about how to respond to it, fear of Beijing's wrath, distraction, or simple inertia.

Adapting to the Failure of a Denial Defense

The need for a serious, credible defense strategy would be all the more urgent if a focused denial defense was unworkable, since the absence of a fallback strategy would leave Beijing a clear path to regional hegemony. How, then, would the United States and the anti-hegemonic coalition adapt? This is a crucial issue not merely in theory but for defense planning today. The United States and other members of the coalition, even though they should seek to make a focused denial defense work, must also have a sense of what they would do if this approach proves inadequate.

At one level, such planning is simple prudence; preparing a fallback is always a good idea, especially in a domain like the development of military forces and posture, in which decisions can take decades to play out. The more specific reason, though, is that the United States, its allies, and other coalition members need to understand how preparations for a denial defense might contribute to or detract from a fallback defense and vice versa. This is important because they should favor actions that strengthen denial defense while at least not detracting from their ability to develop whatever fallback defense they would pursue if a focused denial defense no longer proved tenable. Conversely, they should be hesitant to take steps that would strengthen a focused denial defense but might compromise their ability to mount a fallback defense.

What, then, would a fallback to a focused denial defense look like? The optimal response to each contingency—denial being workable but requiring significant escalation, and denial being simply unworkable—is different.

In the case of the first contingency, the problem facing the United States and other defenders would be the need to escalate the war in order to deny China's ability to seize and hold allied territory. The recourse is to do precisely this—the United States and its allies and partners would need to shoulder that burden of escalation. The question is what would render them willing to do so.

The second contingency would require a more fundamental reassessment of US and coalition strategy. The attempt to deny China's ability to seize a US ally within the coalition would have failed, whether outright or because continuing to try to do so would lead to the compromise of the coalition's edge in a systemic regional war. In these circumstances, the United States and the coalition would need to fall back from defending the imperiled ally to recapturing their lost territory, an option that not only could work but would also satisfy the core political logic of the anti-hegemonic coalition and the critical role US alliances play within it.

A Recapture Approach

To repeat, the United States needs to ensure the *effective defense* of a targeted ally. US alliances—the states to which Washington has made security commitments—form the steel skeleton of the anti-hegemonic coalition; by placing its differentiated credibility on the line to these allies, Washington reassures them sufficiently that they are willing to participate in the coalition. So strengthened, the coalition is powerful enough to outweigh China. Upholding this commitment means ensuring the conditions the ally needs to continue contributing to the alliance. At the end of the day, this means that the ally's key territory must be free—or freed—from subordination to Beijing.

Denying Beijing a fait accompli is, once again, preferable. But it is not strictly necessary to meet this criterion. The key point is to ensure that, at the end of the war, the ally is free of the attacker's domination. If the United States and other states cannot block China from taking their allies in the first place, then they can later liberate the conquered allies—including at the peace table. To do this, the United States and its confederates can resort to a strategy that expels China from the targeted ally's territory.

Such a recapture approach differs from the second denial option, in which the defenders allow the attacker to seize part of the target state's territory before counterattacking without ever letting the invaders consolidate their hold on the seized territory. Recapture assumes that the invader has been able to consolidate its gains and establish its defenses. Because of this, it would almost invariably require drawing on a much larger fraction of the United States' strength as well as that of its allies and partners. If these states had already committed the full weight of their militaries to trying to defeat China's invasion of an ally and had been defeated, then their ability to liberate that ally would likely be negligible.

In reality, however, that is unlikely. In raw terms, the United States and its plausible allies and partners are collectively considerably more powerful than China and almost certainly will remain so for the foreseeable future. Yet for the reasons described earlier, including most fundamentally the asymmetries of interests between Beijing and the states considering coming to the aid of China's victim, it is unlikely that any of the states involved, besides the victim itself, would contribute the full measure of its strength to stopping an initial invasion attempt. Thus, even if China defeated the United States and its allies and partners in its bid to conquer a US ally, these states would still be able to draw on their untapped reservoirs of strength to try to liberate the victim state. The question is whether they would be *willing* to do so.[3]

History suggests that they might be willing to do so, since it offers abundant examples of successful recapture campaigns. The Crusaders seized Jerusalem and parts of the Holy Land, but over succeeding generations, these lands were eventually recaptured by Islamic powers. Conversely, the Spanish and Portuguese progressively recaptured the Iberian Peninsula from Islamic rule. In the Second World War, the Allies freed occupied Europe, and the United States and its Pacific allies liberated many of Japan's occupied territories in Asia. And allies or territory can also be regained at the peace table. The Allies never forcibly retook Malaya or the Dutch East Indies; Tokyo relinquished them at the end of the Pacific War.

In a recapture approach, the United States and any potentially participating confederates would face a choice analogous to Beijing's in its initial conquest: they could employ a punishment strategy to seek to make China give up the captured ally, or they could rely primarily on brute force to seize it back. A sufficient recapture approach does not necessarily require freeing every piece of seized territory; rather, it means liberating the captured state's key territory to ensure that the ally can be restored as an independent state contributing to the coalition. In the context of Taiwan, this would very likely require freeing the main island—but not, for instance, the offshore islands of Quemoy and Matsu. In the case of the Philippines, meanwhile, it would mean freeing the main islands such as Luzon, but not necessarily Scarborough Shoal or other features that Manila claims in opposition to Beijing in the South China Sea.

The Demerits of Relying on Horizontal or Vertical Escalation for Recapture

Although the punishment and conquest approaches would differ in critical respects, both would almost certainly require the United States and its confederates to expand the war.

A punishment approach would mean a larger and more violent war because the engaged allies and partners would have to impose sufficient costs on China to induce it to give up the subordinated state. Given that Beijing would have manifold reasons to resist disgorging such a prized gain, and with so much riding on the resolution of the conflict, these costs would have to be very high even to prompt Beijing to consider giving up the held state.

Such a punishment approach would be very unlikely to work, however, for the same reasons that it would very likely not work to deny China's acquisition of the target in the first place. As in that instance, horizontal escalation alone would be unlikely to be effective because China is unlikely to possess anything beyond its borders that the coalition could threaten that is as important to it as prevailing in a war critical to its establishment of hegemony in Asia. Beijing would, for instance, almost certainly trade its bases in the South China Sea—let alone Indian Ocean or other outposts—for this goal, both on its own terms but also confident that it could rectify the threats to its more distant interests later if it could subordinate, for instance, Taiwan or the Philippines and thereby weaken the anti-hegemonic coalition.

Alternatively, the United States and its allies and partners could in theory seize other parts of Chinese territory and seek to trade them for the targeted ally. If for instance Taiwan were difficult to seize back, however, mainland territory would almost certainly be even harder, especially since China has no distant separated territories, as Hawaii is for the United States or Polynesia is for France. Moreover, such seizure could well provoke Chinese nuclear employment in defense of its territory, which in turn might seem legitimate both to its own people and to important third parties. Horizontal escalation in these circumstances is therefore likely to result in a Chinese victory.

Conversely, relying on vertical escalation alone to reverse defeat would generate these downsides perhaps even more acutely. Crossing the nuclear threshold would turn a recapture attempt of a Chinese-occupied ally into a nuclear brinkmanship contest while catalyzing China's flashing vengeance, hardening its people's resolve, and leading either to Chinese victory or to mutual devastation.

The United States and its allies and partners could also pursue a punishment strategy that mixed horizontal and vertical escalation. They could try, for instance, to expand the cost imposition campaign to include much or all of mainland China while also increasing the intensity of the attacks. Even were this possible—and there is abundant reason to doubt that they could mount such a campaign against a China strong enough to seize and hold Taiwan or the Philippines—this approach would rest on the highly dubious proposition that China would relent and disgorge its gains before the United States gave up. It would thus voluntarily turn the conflict into a contest of societal pain tolerance without a clear end point, hardly an attractive or promising recourse given the limits on Americans' interests in Asia discussed earlier.

Consequently, in the event of the failure of a denial defense, the United States and other involved states would very likely need to seize back the conquered territory directly. This would require an invasion of the seized state, and because of the location of US allies in Asia, this would almost certainly involve an amphibious assault. As previously laid out, a successful amphibious invasion in these circumstances requires air and maritime dominance or something approaching it. Obtaining this dominance—if feasible at all—would very likely require a much larger, riskier, and costlier war effort than the more localized and constrained war envisioned for a focused denial defense.

Recapturing Taiwan

Let us take the case of Taiwan. If Taiwan had been lost to China and Beijing had been able to consolidate its defenses over the island, recapture would almost certainly be a highly costly, risky, and arduous venture for the United States and any engaged allies and partners. Instead of benefiting from the advantages of defending their position on the island, the United States and any engaged confederates would be the inherently exposed attackers facing a prepared defender.

To enable an invasion to recapture Taiwan, the United States and its engaged allies and partners would probably first have to weaken the island's defenses. This would likely mean isolating Taiwan and the PLA forces on it from mainland China, which, in turn, would likely mean denying China the use of the maritime area and airspace in and around the Taiwan Strait. Because of the PLA's size and sophistication, this would almost certainly require a very large number of attacks against assets and facilities across a much greater expanse of territory. The United States and other engaged states would almost surely need to heavily degrade the PLA Navy and Air Force, both to isolate Chinese forces on Taiwan and ultimately to protect any invasion force from PLA interdiction.

If these efforts to sunder—or at least substantially degrade—the links between the mainland and PLA elements on Taiwan were successful, China's forces on Taiwan would still likely be powerful, not least because China would probably anticipate such a response. Over time, however, lacking reinforcements, relief, or critical military supplies that likely could not be replaced from the island such as replacement munitions, spare parts, and oil and gas, PLA forces on Taiwan would grow weaker and more vulnerable.

Assuming that China did not surrender the island—a very reasonable assumption given the tremendous stakes—this situation could last some time, largely because the military requirements for a counterassault would be very high. Given that Taiwan is well within range of forces on the Chinese mainland, obtaining the necessary aerial and maritime dominance would require an enormous effort against a military power that had exhibited the strength and skill to take the island in the first place.[4] Moreover, the range of modern munitions and platforms means that achieving this dominance would implicate a territorial expanse well beyond Taiwan. US and allied and partner forces would have to destroy or degrade not only the transport shipping and aircraft resupplying PLA forces on Taiwan but also China's fighter, attack, and bomber aircraft, warships, and land-based strike systems that could threaten US and other friendly forces off Taiwan and ultimately on it.[5] This would almost certainly constitute a much more far-reaching and violent campaign than either of the denial options would require, and it would impose a heavy burden of escalation on the United States and its allies and partners.

To make such an effort feasible, the United States and any other engaged states would need to redirect their economies to develop and sustain the forces needed for such a conflict, which would likely involve high rates of attrition.

This, too, would almost certainly take a long time. The largest Western Allied counteroffensives in the Second World War did not take place until 1944, almost three years after the United States entered the conflict—and even longer after the United States, then the world's largest industrial power, began to ramp up military production as the Arsenal of Democracy.[6] And modern military weaponry can take considerably longer to field than that of the Second World War. Producing individual missiles under current circumstances can take years; production could be accelerated, but it is not clear by how much, especially since the demand would vastly outstrip current production capacity.[7] Moreover, unlike in the Second World War, the United States would not enjoy a decisive advantage in industrial capacity; it is no longer unquestionably the world's premier industrial state—indeed, that moniker may go to China.[8]

If the United States and other engaged allies and partners were able, even despite these difficulties, to secure such dominance over and around Taiwan, they could launch an amphibious and air assault to retake the island from the weakened PLA forces still on the island. Given how the isolated and weakened Japanese forces during the Second World War were able to defend Iwo Jima and Okinawa, however, it could well be an extraordinarily ugly fight.

Alternatively, the United States and the other engaged allies and partners could take a less conventional approach. Once they had established some substantial degree of air and maritime superiority, rather than launching a massive invasion reminiscent of Normandy or Okinawa, they could seek to insert smaller, nimbler force packages onto Taiwan. For instance, special forces could be used to degrade Chinese forces on the island and build up internal resistance. These efforts could be designed to undermine the efficacy of PLA forces on Taiwan, preparing the way for a decisive conventional assault. These special forces could be delivered, albeit at some level of attrition, without the full degree of dominance a full-scale regular assault would require.[9] These insertions of forces could take place in contested zones where neither side has dominance, as US Marines were put ashore on Guadalcanal in 1942.[10]

This approach would stand essentially no chance of success if the PLA were reasonably supplied and reinforced on the island and in decent air and maritime communications with the mainland. But if the Chinese forces on Taiwan were effectively cut off, and if reasonably significant Taiwan resistance forces were operating on the island, this approach might work, especially if it culminated in a larger assault or series of assaults once conditions were favorable.

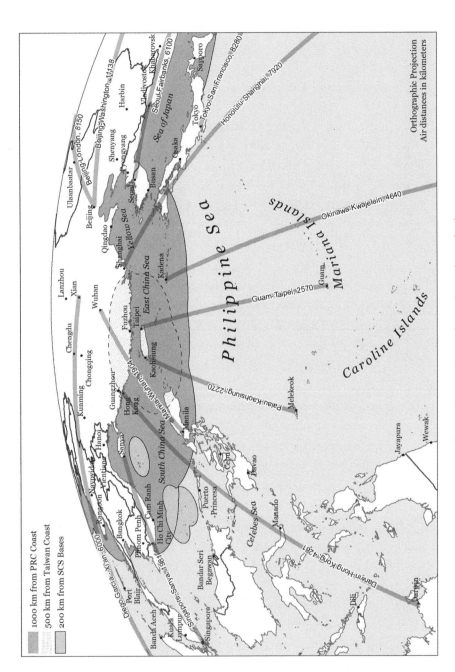

Approaches to Taiwan. Original map by Andrew Rhodes.

The Recapture Approach beyond Taiwan

Although Taiwan would present the most stressing case for a US recapture attempt, similar factors would apply to any effort to recapture another of Washington's Asian allies, especially if Taiwan had previously been subordinated. For instance, while the Philippines is farther from mainland China, and the shadow of China's military power currently falls more faintly on it, the subordination of Taiwan would allow China to focus its force development and posture on the Philippines, even as it faced a weakened anti-hegemonic coalition and a less credible Washington.

A PLA that could successfully invade and occupy the Philippines might be almost as difficult to eject from the archipelago as it would be to expel the PLA from Taiwan. This is for all the reasons explored earlier but also because, if China were able to subordinate the Philippines, the United States would lose its major potential base of operations in Southeast Asia. US and allied and partner forces might still be able to operate from Japan, Australia, and Pacific Islands bases, but these are far from the Philippines, and that distance would impose a significant tax on their military efficacy.

Washington might seek to replace its lost operating locations in the Philippines by looking to other Southeast Asian states, such as Indonesia, Vietnam, Malaysia, and Thailand. This strategy would face at least two problems, though. First, a China dominant over Taiwan, the Philippines, and the South China Sea could seriously hinder any such effort or even block it entirely, making it very difficult for the United States to access Vietnam, Thailand, and Malaysia. Second, Beijing could seek to persuade those states that the prudent course was to align with it or at least neutralize them, given its more imposing new position and the United States' failure to defend the Philippines and Taiwan. In such circumstances, those states might be considerably less willing to work with the United States, let alone ally with it. As a consequence of these diplomatic as well as operational challenges, an attempt by the United States and others to retake the Philippines would almost certainly require a much more expansive, violent, costly, and risky war compared to denying a successful Chinese invasion of the archipelago in the first place.

In summary, then, in either of the contingencies described earlier—either that the US and allied and partner effort to conduct a denial defense would fail without initiating burdensome escalation or that a denial defense would fail or had failed and thus that a recapture approach had become necessary—the

United States and its allies and partners would need to expand and intensify the war if they hoped to prevail, uphold the alliance in question and thus America's (and possibly others') differentiated credibility, and therefore maintain the cohesion of the anti-hegemonic coalition. They would have to assume a heavy burden of escalation in doing so.

China's burden for counterescalating, meanwhile, would be lightened. Although it would have immense incentives to avoid a general nuclear war even in the midst of a larger and more violent conflict, the broader and harsher campaign that the United States and its engaged allies and partners would have to wage would require attacking more Chinese targets and doing more damage to China and its interests. However the United States and its confederates might try to signal otherwise, this might be hard to distinguish from a military campaign with unlimited ends.[11] Even more, China would have a strong interest in not admitting that it did so distinguish. Rather, it would very likely seek to present such a campaign as an unreasonable, dangerous, and unjustified escalation and accordingly might well exploit this rationale to attempt to counterescalate itself—a move that might appear defensible, thereby increasing China's coercive leverage over its adversaries. Without some fundamental change in circumstance, this might well give China a commanding advantage over the United States and its engaged allies and partners in the critical combination of power and resolve.

This development would raise in the most pointed fashion the central quandary facing the United States in seeking to deny China hegemony over Asia: Americans' interests in a war in Asia are significant but not necessarily of the highest order. Yet mounting either a more expansive denial defense campaign or a recapture attempt would essentially demand that the United States risk great loss, certainly of large numbers of military personnel, platforms, and resources, but ultimately even devastation to the homeland, if the war escalated to the level of serious attacks on the two sides' home territories—all to defend or liberate a distant ally on behalf of an anti-hegemonic coalition.

On what basis would Americans—and others—see this as worth doing?

Generating the Resolve

Either an expanded denial defense or recapture would be feasible only if the United States and its allies and partners possessed both the strength and the resolve needed to make it a success. To repeat, an anti-hegemonic coalition stronger than China is unlikely in the foreseeable future to become a single, cohesive alliance. Alliances are likely to exist and new ones may form within the coalition, but it is unlikely that all states within the coalition will bind themselves to fight to defend the other members. In this context, it will fall to the United States, as the external cornerstone balancer, to play a central role as the hub of such a coalition, especially its military dimensions.

This does not mean, however, that only the United States can or would defend or recapture Taiwan, the Philippines, or other vulnerable states. Other coalition members, and even other states that are not members of the coalition, might help defend or retake these countries. States do not need to be formal allies in order to end up fighting alongside or for one another, just as the United States came to Britain's aid in two world wars even though the two had not been allied beforehand.

Strength and Determination

The success of an effort to defend a targeted ally from China, through either an escalated war or a recapture attempt, would come down to two factors: whether the engaged states were strong enough and whether they were sufficiently determined. As discussed before, the two are interrelated. Broadly speaking, the more states are involved, the less resolute each one needs to be since there would be more power available; the fewer involved, the more resolute those who are would need to be. Similarly, the more power they are willing to allocate, the less they would have to rely on resolve, and the more resolute they were, the less they would need to rely on overwhelming power.

In defending against Chinese ambitions, the United States would be the strongest state, but powerful states such as Japan, India, Vietnam, and Australia could make a material difference. More distant states such as Germany and other European countries, as well as the Gulf states, could affect the contest more indirectly, for instance, through economic assistance or pressure.

Resolve—the degree to which the states are prepared to dedicate their strength to the favorable outcome of the struggle—is critical because even an engaged state can assume a range of postures in a conflict, from fully committed to passive supporter. It thus matters greatly not only which states are engaged but also how much these states, especially the stronger and better positioned ones, are willing to allocate and risk for the venture's success. Naturally, the resolve of the United States would be crucial; but the willingness of other potential combatants and supporters to dedicate military effort, allow access, or apply economic pressure could be highly significant.

The key question would then be: How could enough states be enlisted, and the requisite degree of resolve generated among them, to successfully apply either of the much harder, costlier, and riskier approaches?

Choosing to Fight

Generally, a willingness to enter a war and the resolve to prevail in it proceed from a state's leaders and the populations they lead judging the benefits of doing so as worth the costs and risks. Any strategy guiding the defending coalition would thus need to appear to these audiences to link the costs and risks that it demanded they incur with the benefits that it would seek to gain or protect for them. A strategy that does not seem sufficiently reasonable and appropriate when it is seriously tested is unlikely to be followed and will thus likely be seen as a bluff. And a state like China, with the power and incentives to challenge such a strategy, is likely to call such a bluff.

Such strategies are not just impractical, however: they also do not deserve Americans' support. Asking citizens of the United States to suffer costs well out of proportion to the issues at stake violates the very heart of the proposition of the nation, which is to put the citizenry's interest first, consistent with a rational purpose. Strategies that demand too much sacrifice for what they promise are thus irrational in this most important sense. Even in war, as Clausewitz observed, the "noblest pride" is to behave "rationally at all times."[12] A similar logic would no doubt apply to citizens of other republics.

An effective expanded denial or recapture strategy would thus need to catalyze the resolve of enough powerful and well-positioned states that they would do what was required to prevail. In other words, if a focused denial defense failed or was expected to fail, the United States and its confederates would need to find ways that justified and impelled fighting a more expansive and intensive war than the one China preferred. But given that China would have tried to frame the war as limited in scope and consequence—for instance, as narrowly confined to Taiwan and its environs—why would the United States and other states see the situation as justifying such a costly and risky effort? If they allowed China to define the war's scope, they might well not.

Critically, then, the United States and other coalition states should not allow Beijing to be the one to determine the bounds of the war—they must set these bounds themselves. For although they would likely not be willing to fight the kind of war needed to prevail if the struggle seemed only narrowly to concern Taiwan or the Philippines, they might well be prepared to risk that larger war if it seemed necessary to stop China from dominating Asia.

The crucial presupposition for making this work is that the potentially participating states, above all the United States, would need to judge that China was indeed highly aggressive and dangerous and thus that letting it secure so much power would place their vital interests in too much peril. In other words, Americans and other relevant populations would have to find unpersuasive tempting rationalizations for not acting. In practice, this means that China would need to seem not merely a potential danger but an evident and manifest threat. Given the costs and risks entailed in defeating such a powerful foe, arguments for doing so would need to rest on more than speculation about how such a power *might* become more menacing once it gained more strength; they would need to point to clear, compelling evidence of how menacingly Beijing was already behaving and how unacceptably dangerous it would be to allow such a state to prevail in the conflict at hand and grow more powerful as a result.

China would of course have strong incentives to avoid arousing this much alarm. Accordingly, an effective strategy in these circumstances would require that China's *own* application of its focused and sequential limited war strategy would lead to a corresponding change in the potential participants' valuation of the stakes at hand.[13] That is, China's very use of its limited war strategy should lead members of the potential coalition to see how dangerous and aggressive Beijing is. This perception should lead more states to determine to deny Beijing the success of its strategy—even if that requires a very costly and risky effort.

At heart, this is a simple idea. If the costs and risks of fighting increase, then so, too, must the benefits if a combatant is rationally to keep going. In a limited war, the side will benefit that is more willing to invest a greater share of its total material power in the effort and that is able to make its opponent less willing to do so. Because the anti-hegemonic coalition must by definition be stronger than China, if enough members can be enlisted and sufficiently motivated to dedicate enough power, it should prevail, even if doing so requires a much costlier and riskier war. But for this to happen, enough coalition members must see some great and driving justification to enter or stay in the fight, fight harder, and commit more of their resources rather than back down.

The Inherent Subjectivity of Security

The crucial question, then, is: What would make states decide to fight and do so with the necessary vigor?

This gets at a deeper question of why states and people fight and why they decide to fight harder and more resolutely in the face of adversity rather than concede. From a rationalistic perspective, states fight primarily for their survival and their security interests—from "fear and interest."[14] The more a state perceives its security to be at risk, the more likely it is to fight and the harder it will fight.

But security is not a material thing that can be touched and precisely measured. It is an assessment inherently subject to judgment: the sense one has of whether one is threatened and to what degree. It therefore depends on factors that are not purely material, such as what one wants to defend and one's tolerance for risk. It also depends on judgments about others' future behavior that are inherently speculative, such as assessments of how likely others are to harm the interests one holds dear and how they might do so. The first two of these factors are preferences rather than tangible facts, while the third and fourth are about judgments of another's future behavior. None is amenable to precise measurement.

One person's definition of security can thus differ greatly from another's: one person may be willing to bear the risk of living in a dangerous neighborhood if it is lively or chic, while another might want a much lower crime rate; one person might tolerate living in a neighborhood of pickpockets and gangs, while another might want to live where the doors can be left unlocked. Similarly, one state might be content living within its existing boundaries, while another might insist on a buffer zone. One might be content to live under another's hegemony so long as its citizens' lives are protected; another might insist on freedom and independence, even at risk to its citizens' lives.

Yet, of course, security is not entirely constructed or subjective. The cardinal reality at the root of the idea of security is that humans are embodied beings who can be killed. But because subjectivity is present—because perceptions of security are not fixed and thus depend in considerable part on one's own judgments of what one needs and how threatening others are—people's and nations' judgments about security can be deliberately and strategically managed.[15]

Thus states, like individuals, do not determine whether and how hard to fight based only on strict considerations of the balance of power, as important as these are. They also try to assess other states' intentions and resolve. In other words, decisions to fight and how far to go are predicated not only on how powerful the other side is but also on how likely it is to use that power against one's self and what the consequences of that use would be.[16] The Germany-Japan Axis was very powerful, but it was not only their power that led to such a strong and resolute countercoalition. It was the *way* the Axis fought and behaved, and what that indicated about the consequences of an Axis victory, that spurred states to fight so hard to defeat it.[17]

This helps explain why states and individuals fight for reasons that do not appear purely rational—and why they sometimes fight harder than they might otherwise be expected to. For instance, states and individuals often fight and fight harder when they believe honor or justice is at stake. This of course has a *thumotic* component; human beings are thinking creatures, but they are also motivated and impelled by sensations such as pride, joy, sadness, anger, grief, revenge, and fear.[18] When strong passions are triggered and sustained, human behavior often changes with them. States are less passionate than individuals, but they are not immune to emotion and passion, since state action is a product of human decision.

But the influence of *thumos* also has a rational aspect. A state, like an individual, that is too unfailingly reasonable risks becoming a safe target because its reactions will incline toward the measured. A person, for instance, who always tries to calm an argument with business associates by trying to be reasonable and accommodating may well get run roughshod over by them. Thus the archaic-sounding honor of states stands as something of a proxy for how much they are respected and feared. States that allow themselves to be dishonored are states that can be bullied. This is of course an instrumental rather than a primary interest, and its overemphasis can lead to poor and even disastrous decisions, but it is far from irrational or unimportant.

When perceptions of injustice relate to how dangerous another state is and provide motivation to move against it before a too detached instrumental rationality might suggest doing so, then these perceptions can contribute to a rational conception of security. A state that is brutal and that disregards established moral norms is reasonably dreaded, just as a cruel and untrustworthy person is also reasonably to be feared. Dealing with such a state before it has accumulated enough power to become truly menacing may be wise. Indeed, it is not unreasonable to surmise that certain thumotic reactions became so strong among human beings for evolutionary reasons—because they help us survive.[19]

This all means that the fundamental way to ensure that more states intervene and invest more of their power is to make sure that their perception of threat and other sources of resolve are activated. This means that the war must unfold in a way that triggers this result.

The Binding Strategy

This is so important both because states may enter and leave a war at varying points and because how much they are willing to invest and risk in the contest may vary. Because these factors are at least partly subjective, they can be influenced and shaped. They therefore interact with strategy.

The way a war starts and is fought affects the perception of the stakes at issue—and thus it affects both who elects to intervene as well as the resolve of the combatants to prevail—including in ways that are much different from what appeared to be the stakes of and reasons for the war at its outset. The First World War was precipitated by a dispute over Austria's treatment of Serbia, but as the war ground on and expanded, it became about whether Germany would dominate Europe, freedom of the seas for the United States, and ultimately the survival of great empires. As it expanded, the war enlisted far more effort and sacrifice than the combatants had anticipated and drew in states that had planned to sit it out.[20]

But perception of a change in stakes can also happen more specifically because of the behavior of the enemy. Indeed, actions an opponent takes can trigger thumotic reactions on the other side that go beyond purely instrumental calculations. And this is not a phenomenon to which states must be passively subject. Indeed, generating this kind of thumotic effect has long been a core part of waging war—the history of warfare is full of actions designed to strike at an enemy's morale.[21] Bloodcurdling stories of what the Mongols or Tamerlane's armies had done undermined the confidence and thus the fighting strength of the victims these conquerors had yet to face.

By the same token, states can deliberately induce or even compel opponents or potential opponents to act in ways that change how they and others perceive those opponents and their goals. In 1861, Abraham Lincoln adroitly maneuvered the rebellious states into firing the first hostile shot at Fort Sumter, leading to a groundswell of support from the population of the loyal states and tens of thousands of volunteers—something it was by no means clear would have happened if the federal government had appeared to take the first hostile step.[22]

Likewise, lore has it that British troops fired first at Lexington Green on the civilian militia, leading to an outcry against the British and a groundswell of support for the Patriot cause. But some speculate that the first shot may have been deliberately fired by a Son of Liberty to goad the Redcoats into firing en masse. Whatever actually happened, what is clear is that the perception that the British had fired first helped turn the New England countryside into a beehive of Patriot activity and contributed to the appeal of the Patriot cause throughout the American colonies and beyond.[23]

This can also work at the state level. In the nineteenth century, Great Britain insisted that the European powers observe the neutrality of Belgium, located between the British Isles and French (and ultimately German) power. Belgium was so situated that an attacker had to violate the neutrality of an innocent third state in order to dominate the wealthy Low Countries, which also provided a natural jumping-off point for an invasion of the British Isles.[24] Berlin scoffed in 1914 that the 1839 Treaty of London, which guaranteed Belgian neutrality, was a "mere scrap of paper," but Germany's massive attack into Belgium in 1914 cost it dearly because it helped catalyze British and ultimately American resolve to stand with Belgium and France.[25] Similarly, during the Second Italian War of Independence, Cavour ensured that Austria attacked first, rightly judging that this would induce vital intervention by France on Sardinia's behalf.[26]

Japan's actions in the Second World War, especially its attack on Pearl Harbor and rampage through Asia in December 1941 and January 1942, serve as a textbook demonstration of how military actions can change the perception of threat by a state's opponents and heighten their resolve. Japan's basic need in late 1941 was to break out of the straitjacket imposed by the American oil embargo and free its hand to close out its war in China.[27] These objectives could arguably have been served by Tokyo's focusing its attacks on the European colonial possessions in Asia and specifically avoiding attacking the United States or its territories. With Britain occupied with the war in Europe and North Africa and France and the Netherlands under German control, the United States was the only power that could have taken Japan on over these European holdings. Seizing only the British territories in Malaya, Borneo, and Hong Kong as well as the Dutch East Indies—in addition to French Indochina, which Japan had occupied in 1940, on top of Tokyo's long-standing control of Formosa and Korea—would have given Japan something approaching ascendancy over the region and might have averted American intervention entirely.

Indeed, in late 1941, most Americans opposed entry into either theater of the war, and the cause of defending European colonial possessions in Asia would have provided about as limp a rallying cry as could be conceived. The United States might still have intervened against Japan for purely strategic reasons. Yet it is far from clear that the American people would have supported the enormous and ferocious war effort that proved necessary to defeat Japan in the Pacific, an effort that led not only to imperial Japan's defeat but to its near-total destruction and capitulation. Facing a more focused and restrained effort by Japan, the American people might have balked at going to these lengths and settled for something far short of total victory, leaving imperial Japan holding on to much more than it ultimately did.

Instead, Japan demonstrated beginning in December 1941 that it was far more directly dangerous to the United States than Americans had thought and, in so doing, catalyzed their "righteous anger," both through the perceived perfidy of its surprise attacks and by its conduct.[28] Reports of Japanese barbarities against US and Allied forces and civilians in the Philippines and elsewhere deepened and hardened the resolve of Americans to support and sacrifice for total victory.

In circumstances where a focused denial defense would too likely fail, then, the United States' strategic purpose should be to *force* China to have to do what Japan did voluntarily: to try to achieve its ambitions, China would have to behave in a way that will spur and harden the resolve of the peoples in the broader coalition to intervene and for those engaged to intensify and widen the war to a level at which they would win it. The question is how.

Making China Fight in a Way That Changes the Coalition's Threat Perception

The key is that Beijing itself must alter the potential coalition's perception of the stakes. China must not be allowed to precipitate and fight a war over Taiwan or the Philippines in a manner that makes it seem insufficiently threatening to other regional nations' vital interests. Instead it must be made to reveal the full extent and nature of the threat that it poses to their vital interests.

Since China's interest is precisely in avoiding being placed in this situation, however, ensuring Beijing would have to act in this way to try to attain its ambitions very likely needs to be the product of deliberate action. The United States in particular as well as its allies and partners must therefore prepare, posture, and act to compel China to have to conduct its campaign in ways that

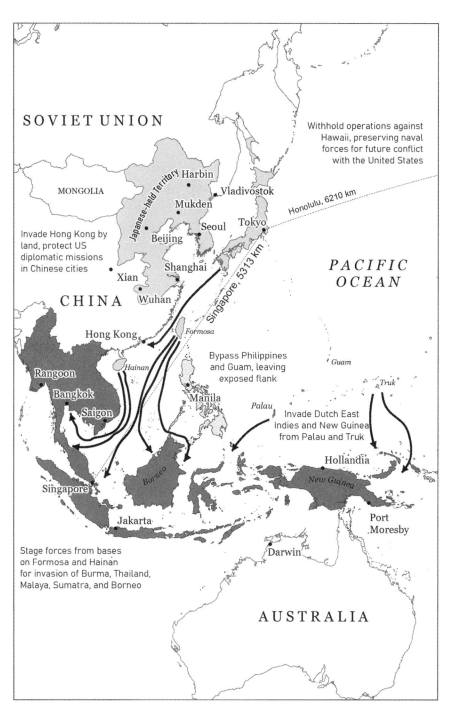

Japan's alternative strategy for 1941. Original map by Andrew Rhodes.

indicate it is a greater and more malign threat not only to the state it has targeted but to the security and dignity of the other states that might come to its defense.

We might call this approach *the binding strategy*. Successfully applied, it should lead even the more reluctant among the important members of the anti-hegemonic coalition to see the value of counteracting China presently rather than waiting and in confronting it through a larger and riskier war than the more confined one Beijing prefers to fight.

For the binding strategy to work, China's behavior is crucial because it is the factor that generates these changed perceptions. Although the coalition can take some positive steps, for instance, by revealing or amplifying previously hidden or underappreciated information about China's military investments or actions, ultimately this approach is about Beijing's behavior and what it signifies or reveals about the threat it poses.

Vitally, this means that China's actions must not be seen as defensive or reasonable responses to the coalition's provocation. The whole point of the binding strategy is to show that the attacker's true intent is not narrow and constrained but broader and more dangerous than had previously been supposed. The war must therefore not unfold in such a way that China's way of fighting appears to key audiences to be defensive, justified, or reasonable.

This is an instrumentally rational strategic point; behavior viewed as defensive will inherently seem more self-limiting and thus less threatening. But it is also a moral point that touches on intuitions and sensibilities that influence so much of human behavior. This is crucial because the moral sensibility is elemental for generating resolve—hence Napoleon's point that the moral is to the physical in war as three to one.[29] Defensive actions are likely to be seen as more reasonable and less threatening than offensive ones. Human beings and states alike tend to have a markedly different reaction to something being taken from them than to being inhibited from taking something they do not already have. Their resolve is generally greater to defend what they have than to seize what they do not.

This returns us to the crucial role of the burden of escalation. If a state has ways of fighting that are not only effective but also appear defensive and justified, then its burden of escalation will be lighter; if, by contrast, its ways of fighting appear offensive and unreasonable, then its burden will be that much heavier. The crucial task for the United States and the coalition is to present Beijing with a dilemma: to prevail in the focused war it seeks, Beijing must have to act in ways that will motivate coalition states to fight and fight hard and others to support them.

The Sources of Higher Resolve

The core idea of the binding strategy is to *deliberately* make China have to strengthen the coalition's resolve if it tries to attain its ambitions. Because states tend toward self-interest, especially in the painful crucible of war, the most important part of making the binding strategy work is to ensure that China clearly demonstrates the actual threat that it poses to the coalition states' security. But Beijing can also be induced to behave in ways that engage the thumotic aspects of coalition states' decision-making. Although these may be less reliable than pure self-interest, they may contribute to decisions both to fight and to fight harder.

An attacker like China may trigger other states' resolve by revealing or being made to reveal its aggressiveness, ambition, cruelty, unreliability, power, or disrespect for the honor of such states.

Aggressiveness

A China perceived as more aggressive will appear more likely to start wars, otherwise use violence, or threaten to use force to advance its interests. This is important because states might think that an aspiring hegemon like China will not use its massive military power to coerce them, even once it had subordinated Taiwan or the Philippines. If their perception of China's threshold for using violence changes, though, they might determine that checking Beijing earlier is the more prudent course, whether that means entering the war or expanding or intensifying it once engaged.

Perhaps the clearest and sometimes the most important way of making sure China is seen this way is simply by ensuring that it is the one to strike first. Few human moral intuitions are more deeply rooted than that the one who started it is the aggressor and accordingly the one who presumptively owns a greater share of moral responsibility. There is thus an enormous political-strategic benefit to being seen as defending or responding to an adversary's first move; a state or its allies reacting to such an attack may consider steps in response that they would not otherwise have contemplated. This is even more the case when such an attack is seen as perfidious or dastardly. For instance, after a century and a half of insisting on the rights of nonbelligerent shipping and having actually gone to war with Germany in 1917 in part to uphold neutral shipping rights, the United States declared unrestricted submarine warfare on Japan on December 8, 1941—but only *after* the attack on Pearl Harbor.[30]

In addition to striking first, another way that China could be perceived as dangerously aggressive is if it attacked more states. A country willing to do this gives other states great reason to fear, and to counter it promptly. Nazi Germany's willingness to attack so many states, even ones Berlin had left untouched in the First World War, such as the Netherlands, Denmark, and Norway, indicated a degree of aggressiveness that impelled its opponents to fight and fight hard enough to eventually overpower it.[31]

Based on this logic, the United States and its allies and partners could seek to ensure that China is not able to seize Taiwan or the Philippines without striking well beyond the vicinity of those states, for instance, at the forces, assets, or territory of the United States as well as other states both in the region and more distant. For this strategy to work, Beijing would need to see the military value of these attacks as too compelling to be ignored—for instance, because neglecting them would allow these other forces to do too much damage to any invasion force or blockade enforcers—just as Japan felt it necessary to attack US and British forces first and without warning in 1941. China should face a dilemma between striking at these important targets but in so doing catalyzing other states' resolve or withholding the strikes but compromising its military efficacy. Beijing could be made to face this dilemma not only at the outset but during a conflict, as Germany confronted such a dilemma about whether to expand submarine operations against a neutral United States in the two world wars.

The United States and its allies and partners could put this aspect of a binding strategy into effect in a number of ways. One is by enmeshing their military posture. Greater military integration would tempt China to attack a much broader set of states. If China needed only to attack Taiwan and its forces as well as perhaps those local US forces engaged in the island's defense in order to subordinate the island, such a campaign is unlikely to seem so aggressive. But if, to ensure that its attack on Taiwan succeeded, it also had to attack US forces, territory, and assets farther afield as well as those of Japan, the Philippines, Australia, South Korea, and perhaps others, that would clearly show Beijing to be far more aggressive than it would want potential opponents to believe.

In military terms, the most natural way to put an opponent in this position is by posturing and readying forces so that, if a state hopes to conduct a successful invasion or other coercive campaign, it must attack on a much grander scale, against more targets in more countries, than it might have preferred. During the later Cold War, for example, NATO's force posture meant that even if Moscow hoped only to subdue West Germany in an invasion, the Soviet Bloc would also have had to attack and likely invade a wide range of other NATO countries to prevail in such a contest.

Today, coalition states could posture or ready themselves to achieve this effect in a variety of ways, bearing in mind that not all participants need to pull the same weight or assume the same degree of exposure. Perfection is not the threshold for success, since even partial effects can have a significant impact on states' resolve. For instance, while the United States might prepare for direct, active combat against a focused Chinese assault on Taiwan or the Philippines, other states involved in the binding strategy might only host US and other states' forces. If China struck at these hosting states, that could provide the impetus for them to intervene more directly. Moreover, the more resilient, dispersed, and survivable these hosted forces and their facilities are, and the harder it is for China to ascertain how those forces and facilities would operate, the more targets it would need to attack and the more forcefully it would need to do so, making any such attack seem more aggressive.

To take one example, Japan hosts multiple US military bases, but it also has its own bases as well as commercial airfields and ports that US and Japanese forces could use.[32] China would face substantial risks by leaving those bases and facilities alone, but striking them would likely catalyze Japanese resolve. The same would apply to other states, including those not allied to the United States but which might provide support or access to US forces in a conflict.

As noted previously, a defensive or status quo set of political goals can be entirely consistent with an active, forward-leaning, even aggressive military or operational approach so long as it is kept within appropriate bounds. Likewise, the political goal of ensuring that the other side actually starts the war does not require making one's military posture passive or fragile. A military prepared for the opponent to strike first can be ready, resilient, and postured to launch quick counterattacks, as the US Navy undertook in the Central Pacific in the early months of 1942.

If China knew, then, that US and other engaged forces could operate from a large number of locations across the Asia-Pacific region, it would be tempted to strike at these targets to diminish those forces' efficacy. Moreover, it might be tempted to strike early and by surprise if it knew that those forces could, if al-lowed to escape, disperse and present an even more painful dilemma. Further-more, if China were unable to disable these airfields through strike operations, it might feel impelled to try even more aggressive and direct measures, such as assaulting them with ground forces. The concrete result would be to make China choose between allowing the United States and other engaged states to operate uncontested from these locations or striking widely at countries that might otherwise remain on the sidelines.

If China were compelled to act aggressively on this quandary, then even if Beijing were strong enough to compel the coalition to fight a larger war to de-fend or recapture Taiwan, it would still have likely prompted the formation of a broader, more resolute coalition of states prepared to wage that costlier and risker conflict. Of course, Beijing would prefer to avoid this outcome. But its preference would not be what mattered—it would be its revealed willingness to attack so broadly and with such violence.

This perception of the threat Beijing posed would be heightened further if the states engaged went beyond basing to interconnect their defense postures, mak-ing their defenses essentially interdependent. Although a truly interconnected approach would be politically difficult to arrange, it would be the most thor-ough and effective way of binding states together. If countries within the coali-tion simply could not defend themselves without relying on others, then their fates would truly be bound together.[33] For example, during the late Cold War, Japan's Self-Defense Forces planned in the event of war to hunt Soviet subma-rines and protect US airbases, providing safe passage to US naval assets and freeing up and enabling US strike operations against the Soviet Far East.[34] The effect was to bind together US and Japanese forces in the event of war around Japan—neither could accomplish the missions envisioned without the other's active participation.

Ambition

An opponent can also be made to seem more ambitious than was previously believed. If aggressiveness is how likely a state is to use violence to achieve its aims, ambition is the expansiveness of its goals. While aggressiveness tells on how likely potential states are to be attacked, ambition tells on how likely they are to have vital interests violated, be subordinated, or be consumed altogether. This of course touches directly on other states' most fundamental concerns:

how likely they are to become the object of another's acquisitiveness. Thus the more ambitious a powerful state like China appears to be, the more others have reason to fear that sooner or later they will become its prey.

A state's behavior makes a crucial difference in such assessments. In 1936, Western leaders might have credited Hitler's protestations that Berlin's goals were limited to returning Germany to equal status among the European states after the humiliation of the Treaty of Versailles; but German behavior toward Austria and Czechoslovakia in 1938 and 1939 and Berlin's attack on Poland in 1939 made it definitively clear that the Nazis hungered for far more and that the Western powers had better fight Germany even in a large war rather than be subjected to further salami-slicing.[35] European states thought that they could cut deals with Napoleon at first, but his many wars and the dramatically transformational settlements Paris imposed after them ultimately led them to conclude that he could not be dealt with.[36]

Moreover, how ambitious others believe a combatant to be can change during a war, since war aims are not fixed during a conflict. The federal government's demands from the Southern states dramatically rose over the course of the Civil War. The Triple Entente's demands from the Central Powers rose substantially during the First World War. Nor are a state's war aims always subject to cool deliberation. Bismarck was reluctant to annex Alsace-Lorraine but acceded to doing so in the face of a triumphant Prussian leadership that wanted more. The original war aims for United Nations forces in Korea in 1950 were the restoration of the status quo—two Koreas divided north and south—but victory at Incheon, momentum, and the personal influence of such individuals as Douglas MacArthur combined to widen those goals, at least for a time, to include unification of North with South Korea.[37]

Inducing China to behave in ways that make it appear more ambitious is not, however, as direct a matter as making it appear more aggressive; unlike aggressiveness, which turns on the means that a state will employ to attain its goals, ambition is about the goals themselves. For an attacker, leaving hostile military forces in otherwise uninvolved or minimally involved states presents a very pointed military problem; leaving them untouched could frustrate its achievement of its goals outright. The attacker does not strictly need to change its political goals to deal with this problem. That is because what matters in this context is not whether an attacker like China admits or even itself conceives that its aims have become more ambitious. It simply needs to *seem* more ambitious to other states—or even just likely to become more ambitious, given that others must make provision for a future in which such a formidable state might become so.

An aspiring hegemon like China therefore has a significant incentive to make its ambitions seem constrained and its war aims as modest and finite as possible. In the event of conflict with elements of the anti-hegemonic coalition over, for example, Taiwan, Beijing would likely want other states to believe that once it had fulfilled its desire to unify with Taiwan, it would be satisfied. But if enough states concluded that taking Taiwan was in fact only the first step toward grander ambitions on Beijing's part, they would have an incentive to try to frustrate those ambitions sooner rather than later, even at the price of a larger and more costly war.

Perhaps the clearest way to make an attacker like China seem more ambitious or likely to become so is to ensure that it cannot achieve an easy, clean victory. If Beijing had to face a frustrating and costly war to achieve even as focused a goal as Taiwan, it would be tempted or pressed to expand its aims to match the costs it incurred, just as the combatants' aims in the First World War grew with the suffering they endured. This requirement is likely to put a premium on the resilience of the military posture of the United States and its allies and partners. The more resilient US and other relevant forces are, the more they can hold out and inflict damage on Chinese forces, extending the conflict and raising the costs to China.

Another way to force Beijing to appear more ambitious is similar to the tactic of making it choose between aggressiveness and failure. The United States and other engaged states can force Beijing to choose between allowing hostile forces to take sanctuary in states that otherwise might be only minimally involved and striking at those forces. If Beijing strikes at forces in otherwise minimally involved states, that action is likely to trigger fears that Beijing's appetite might grow with the eating, especially if Beijing were facing a tough and protracted war. In such circumstances, regional states might fear that China will feel compelled to go so far as to seize some of their own territory to disable or deny US and other defenders' operations from their territory—and then insist on retaining any territories it seized to make the costs of such a war appear justified.

Beijing might, for instance, lash out at or seize territory from the Philippines to deny it to US forces—and then insist on holding that territory or extracting some other equity if it prevailed in the war. It is worth remembering that

Washington had no claims on most of the Pacific Islands before December 1941 but concluded the war in possession of or watching over the great bulk of them after having suffered mightily to extract them from Japanese control. Likewise, the United States made no claim on the Philippines at the beginning of the Spanish-American War, which was caused far more by matters in the Caribbean, but ended up with it at the war's conclusion.[38]

To take another example of how this approach can be implemented in practice, a Soviet assault on NATO designed primarily to subjugate West Germany would, because of the laydown and operating patterns of NATO forces, have almost certainly required an attack on much of Western Europe. Such an attack might not have proved Moscow's aspiration to subordinate all of Western Europe beyond the Federal Republic, but other Western NATO states would have had abundant reason to fear that it had that intention, especially in light of its semi-imperial control over Eastern Europe. In effect, NATO's military posture made it more likely that Western states would fear that any Soviet attack on the West would not lead to localized, incremental political demands by Moscow but to a Soviet effort to dominate all of Europe.[39]

Cruelty

States must also take account of how another state, especially an aspiring regional hegemon, would behave if it achieved its goals. If China appeared cruel in waging the war, states might fear that it would behave this way—or worse—once it had accumulated even more power. This concern could increase their willingness to prevent Beijing from amassing the power to subject other states to such treatment.

Such reactions are common in military history. Reports of the rapacity and oppressiveness of French rule powered popular support for the campaigns against Napoleon's armies. Asian populations that might otherwise have supported Japan's efforts to unseat widely resented European colonial supremacy were alienated by Japan's treatment of its occupied territories. Reports of the USSR's staggering cruelties drove fears of what Soviet domination would mean and undergirded the Allied defense posture in the Cold War, which ultimately rested on the threat to effectively obliterate the Soviet Union in what would have been the most destructive act in military history.[40]

The United States and its allies and partners could increase the likelihood that China would be perceived in this light by inducing Beijing to choose between, on the one hand, striking at military targets and risking also hitting nonmilitary targets and, on the other hand, forbearing from striking at those military targets in the first place. The defenders could do this by making their military fortifications and operations more resilient and difficult to precisely and efficiently attack. This simple counsel of military necessity could induce China to attack more cruelly than it would prefer. An unscrupulous defender might force this choice by deliberately commingling military facilities and assets with facilities sure to provoke anger if struck, such as places of worship, hospitals, and schools. But this would violate even the most basic conception of the laws of war and would likely vitiate any advantage in resolve that the coalition might obtain from such strikes.[41]

Fortunately, there are other ways to pursue this part of a binding strategy. The laws of war do not call for bankrupting or ensuring one's own defeat by completely divorcing anything military from anything civilian.[42] A combatant can only have so many ports, airfields, rail yards, ships, transport aircraft, and other facilities available to it, and these can reasonably be segregated from nonmilitary assets only to a certain extent. Consequently, any war effort against an opponent as powerful as China would have to use things that are dual use, close to civilian infrastructure, or hard to distinguish. San Diego, Honolulu, Yokohama-Yokosuka, and Busan are critical naval ports but also cities with commercial harbors. Commercial airports may not serve primarily as military airfields, but they might need to be called into such service, especially if primary airbases are destroyed. There are few dedicated military roads or railways outside of military bases, especially in the United States and its plausible fellow coalition members, so military convoys are likely to need to use civilian roads, railways, fuel depots, and marshaling yards.

If China could collect very good and current information and use it to strike precisely and promptly, it would not face much of a dilemma. But the United States and its allies and partners would have every reason to interfere, by every practical means, with China's ability to do this. China would thus likely face situations in which it would not know where opposing military forces were and would have only imperfect control over its ability to strike at them.

At a minimum, then, such an approach would tempt China to compensate for these challenges by launching larger and broader assaults. Yet these offensives would surely result in destruction well beyond purely military targets, including highly sensitive things. A barrage assault on a port that was supporting military operations could hit a cruise ship or ignite an oil tanker, and the fire could spread to adjoining neighborhoods. An attack on an airfield could destroy a passenger airliner instead of a transport aircraft or a terminal instead of a military hangar. The infamous Italo-German attack on Guernica during the Spanish Civil War was meant to hit military targets, but the civilian damage caused worldwide revulsion and contributed to anti-Fascist sentiment.[43]

Largely for this reason, it would be unwise for the United States and its allies and partners to allocate scarce resources such as air and missile defenses to defending purely civilian facilities. China has no right under the laws of war to strike at such facilities, and attacks on them are far more likely to generate anger and fear that would result in a strong response. Purely peaceful assets are guarded by outrage; attacks on them catalyze the senses of vengeance and justice. Meanwhile, military assets and those directly supporting the military would be fair game—and thus need defense.

This assumes that China would not deliberately attack civilian targets. But a sufficiently resilient defense could tempt Beijing to use terror tactics, which would deepen fears of what Chinese dominance might look like. The Germans initially tried to suppress the Royal Air Force to enable invasion of the United Kingdom, but when that failed, they turned to the terror tactics of the Blitz, which only hardened Britons' resolve to keep fighting and increased international sympathy for the British cause. Beijing, if it attacked Taiwan, might have expected a quick, decisive war; frustration that it was meeting stiff resistance and that a larger, longer, possibly indecisive or unfavorable war was in the offing might cause it to lash out for similar reasons. It might be tempted to try to gain victory by incorporating terror tactics, as the Germans did at Rotterdam in 1940.[44] Such a fearsome display would demonstrate how cruel China could be.

China might also act cruelly or rapaciously in its behavior in the parts of the coalition members' territory that it was able to occupy. Much of an occupying state's behavior is largely, when not entirely, within its control; it holds the area, after all. That said, an occupier may also respond to what those under its occupation or its remaining opponents do.

For instance, the defenders could promote peaceful political resistance movements that would operate within Chinese-occupied territory. Such movements could conduct workers' strikes and create blockages, detracting from the occupier's ability to consolidate its control and to use the new territory for military or other purposes important to its hegemonic ambitions. During the Second

World War, Germany relied heavily on industrial production from its occupied European territories; had the Nazis been more sensitive to views about their cruelty and therefore less willing to use exceptionally harsh methods to enforce compliance, as China likely would be, peaceful stoppages or citizen protests could have significantly hampered the German war effort. Such movements would stress the occupier's administration of the allied territory; it could either accept the decline in its ability to leverage the territory's wealth and services or crack down in the hope of compelling compliance. Cracking down, of course, would demonstrate exactly the kind of oppressiveness that would make other states fear falling under the attacker's sway.

More aggressively yet, the coalition could help willing resisters on Taiwan and elsewhere to prepare and back insurgencies, in the tradition of the independence and partisan movements of the Second World War. These would do more than merely withhold goods and services from the occupier. Such efforts attack the occupier's forces; if successful, they not only directly destroy or damage at least some of these forces and their supplies but also cause virtual attrition by compelling the occupier to reroute, provide greater protection, or otherwise adapt to such attacks. French forces in Napoleon's war with Spain, and US forces in South Vietnam in the 1960s and 1970s, had to expend great effort and resources to protect their supply lines, not knowing where the guerrillas might strike. The United States and others could deliberately seek to catalyze such movements, as the Allies did in the Second World War through the Office of Strategic Services and Special Operations Executive.[45]

Large-scale political movements and insurgencies may provoke cruelties, even by normally humane states. Even a restrained approach to dealing with this kind of problem demands that the occupier take a firmer hand. If military necessity requires that a road be cleared or oil be extracted, it must be done, and this requires coercion if people are resisting it. This alone would make the occupying power appear more oppressive, belying claims of its liberality.

And things could always get worse. Occupying forces that have to deal with a ghostly enemy that appears without warning and disappears into an apparently sympathetic population may become frustrated and lash out, if they do not deliberately perpetrate atrocities. Britain may have had a better record than other colonial occupiers, but its forces still perpetrated the massacre at Amritsar in India and Bloody Sunday in Ireland.[46] Likewise, it has consistently been US law and policy to deter and penalize war crimes by its own forces. Yet such atrocities became major news sensations during Vietnam, in part because US troops in the field were so frustrated in their efforts to root out the Vietcong insurgency. Even though they were relatively isolated examples, these reports undercut the American war effort. Moreover, states may try a more lenient approach but shift policy if they believe that it is not working. France tried a lighter touch in its attempt to hold on to Algeria before shifting to a much tougher approach, which brought down much opprobrium on France's head.[47]

Further, such efforts might make a practical military difference. In the event that China is able to seize Taiwan, any counterattack to free the island is likely to benefit from or even need irregular forces. The stronger and more effective such an insurgency is—for instance, operating out of Taiwan's mountains and its large cities to tie down and erode PLA forces on the island as the coalition struck at them and cut them off from the mainland—the more it is likely to prompt cruelties from China.

The idea of this approach is to compel China to choose between costs to its military effectiveness and costs to its reputation. If it appears cruel or oppressive, this would stiffen the resolve of those states already engaged and deepen the involvement of those on the sidelines. Needless to say, such an approach can impose significant suffering on occupied civilian populations and is not to be undertaken lightly. The United States should thus be loath to fabricate an insurrection where there is no support for one; it should seek only to help those who want to resist. But given the opposition of people throughout the region to falling under Chinese control and the risks and costs the United States and others would incur to liberate them, the former would be justified in aiding and abetting such efforts where they have real roots.

Unreliability

The way China wages the war could also show Beijing to be less trustworthy and more perfidious than it might have seemed. This matters because an aspirant's bid for hegemony relies substantially on other states believing its pledges as to how it will behave as it grows stronger. Because an aspirant like China cannot take on everyone at once, it must persuade the less immediately threatened members of the anti-hegemonic coalition that, once it is ascendant, it will be respectful of their interests and autonomy. But if it fails to keep its promises early on, this will undermine its assurances of future restraint and good behavior.

This, in turn, will make those states more likely to resist it, even before it poses a clear and immediate threat to their own vital interests.

This can be thought of as an aspiring hegemon's version of the credibility problem. China's own differentiated credibility is crucial if its focused and sequential strategy is to work. Beijing must be seen as willing to honor its pledges regarding the autonomy, political integrity, and security of other regional states. Bending or breaking such promises would make these states more afraid of how Beijing would behave in the future, increasing their incentives to deal with China earlier and more resolutely, rather than risk allowing it to agglomerate so much power that it can no longer be held to account.

Thus, just as Beijing has an incentive to undermine the United States' differentiated credibility, so, too, the reverse. If China can be induced to undermine its differentiated credibility with respect to its future restraint and good behavior, this should catalyze the resolve of the anti-hegemonic coalition and generate sympathy for its cause. For instance, if China has pledged to respect the autonomy of or political rights in a conquered territory but then cracks down and imposes an oppressive administration, that will undermine its assurances. Contemporary China's erosion of the guarantees it made for Hong Kong's autonomy has already had a significant impact on perceptions in Taiwan of what a one-country, two-systems approach would mean, further undermining support in Taiwan for unification with the mainland.[48]

Moreover, to try to quiet balancing concerns, Beijing would very likely need to make other assurances of its restraint, for instance, by promising that it would not attack noncombatant states. The US and allied defense posture could therefore be adapted to make China choose between violating these pledges and suffering militarily by sticking with them. The United States and others could, for example, develop operating locations across many states in the region. They might not need to use all of these locations—but if China feared that they might, it would face an incentive to attack them. Just as Germany judged the military advantages of plowing through Belgium in 1914 greater than the enormous opprobrium Berlin suffered by violating Belgian neutrality, a China that, for instance, wanted to subordinate a well-defended Vietnam might find it tempting to violate Laotian neutrality in order to flank Vietnam. Violating such a pledge would directly undercut the credibility of comparable assurances. Ultimately, this approach would seek to force China either to accept military disadvantage or to betray its pledges.

Power

How an aspirant like China fights can change more than judgments about its intent; it can also reveal insights about its power in ways that affect other states' calculus of whether and how much to risk and suffer to contest it. In particular, Beijing's conduct of the war could show it to be stronger than it had let on or presented itself. This would be particularly significant if China's case for inaction by the anti-hegemonic coalition and nonaligned fence-sitters rested on the idea that it was not in fact so powerful and thus its protestations that its ambitions were finite were credible.

Others are more likely to believe a weaker state that insists that its ambitions are limited; by definition, it cannot extend its influence very far in the face of resistance. Few think that South Korea's claims against Japan over Dak To or Ecuador's against Chile and Bolivia are a prelude to a bid for regional dominance. But when such claims are issued by a much stronger power, they are more likely to be seen as just that. The Bourbons' assertion of a hereditary right to Spain triggered balancing reactions by the other European powers because, whatever the dynastic merits of the Bourbons' claims, France was too strong to be allowed to grow so powerful.[49]

Beijing has played the modesty card heavily in recent decades. The strategy of "hide our capabilities and bide our time," made famous by Deng Xiaoping, counseled China's leaders to stay under the radar of the major powers while building China's "composite national power" in order to allow a more assertive policy at a more advantageous time. But China's increasingly assertive and self-confident approach over the past decade has put the lie to China's claims of modest capability.[50] Although Beijing has been able to secure other nations' cooperation with—or acquiescence to—its own international designs, such as with the One Belt, One Road initiative, its behavior has simultaneously strengthened balancing forces, as states increasingly recognize the danger China poses.

In the event of war, therefore, the United States and other engaged states could seek to expose divergences between China's claimed and real power. For instance, they could seek to make or induce Beijing to reveal military programs, technologies, or forces that it had concealed or downplayed, as well as sources of economic strength and resilience that had not to that point been appreciated or known. If China turned out to have considerably more sophisticated aircraft, missiles, or space capabilities, this might indicate that it was considerably stronger than others had understood. Even in peacetime, this can have a significant impact; the extent of Chinese control over medical supply chains revealed during the Covid-19 pandemic awakened serious concerns.[51]

At the most basic level, doing this in war simply requires the United States and other engaged allies and partners to fight more effectively and force China to draw on its greater reservoirs of power. But this dilemma can also be deliberately imposed; missions and even larger-scale operations can be formed and dispatched with a primary goal of inducing an opponent to reveal such capabilities. During the Second World War, Great Britain specifically framed operations to tease out the German Enigma code capability (though London then hid its mastery of it).[52]

Ultimately, this approach seeks to induce an opponent to show that it is stronger—and thus more capable of attaining regional predominance—than other states might have appreciated. An aspiring hegemon like China has potent incentives to play down its growing strength. Forcing it to show how powerful it truly is can change other states' calculus of how dangerous it is, strengthening their incentives to fight, fight harder, and deepen their collaboration with those fighting.

Revenge and Honor

The categories laid out thus far touch on instrumental reasons that China's way of waging a war could trigger a greater opposing effort by increasing states' perception of the threat it poses. China might also do things, however, that trigger a strong desire for revenge or for vindication of national or other forms of honor, as Hector's killing of Patroclus triggered Achilles's rage in ways that seriously hurt the Trojans. Thumotic impulses can be powerful drivers of state behavior.

This is partially because, as noted earlier, instrumental reasons and thumotic impulses often overlap. The attack on Pearl Harbor showed Americans how dangerous and dastardly Japan was and also awakened their righteous might. Germany's violation of Belgium's neutrality in 1914 demonstrated that its assurances could not be fully credited and threatened to place German military power just across the English Channel, but it also insulted many Britons' senses of justice and honor. But even when they do not overlap with instrumental reasons, thumotic impulses like revenge could impel states to counter China's efforts.

Willing members of the anti-hegemonic coalition could make efforts to increase the likelihood that Chinese action would stir feelings of offended honor and vengefulness. Although trip wires and purely symbolic measures are generally not well suited as primary strategies for the anti-hegemonic coalition, such measures may sometimes have a place as part of the preferred denial approach.

At the political level, the United States and other coalition states could give (even if subtle) indications of their commitment to exposed members of the anti-hegemonic coalition such as Taiwan. This would increase Taiwan's symbolic value and stake any committing states' honor on it.

At the military level, planning could place especially symbolic or valued assets in harm's way. In the past, for instance, when unit battle flags were highly valued symbols, commanders would sometimes place them in areas of the field where they wanted special effort made. In the case of Taiwan, at least some portion of US forces could operate nearby, be ready to deploy there on short notice, or even be located on Taiwan, compelling China to have to attack them at the outset of a conflict. This approach might be especially useful with states that are not immediately threatened by China, including some that might not even be members of the anti-hegemonic coalition or only rather anemic ones. For instance, including European contributions to an anti-hegemonic coalition's defense, even if modest, could be useful if attacks on those forces generated outrage among Europeans and a desire to support the coalition's efforts.

Winning the War

How, then, should the United States and its allies and partners seek to leverage these strategies to achieve their aims?

The Binding Strategy and Denial Defense

Principally they should do so by integrating the distinct but compatible approaches of a binding strategy and a denial defense. A denial defense is the use of American and other power to stop China from seizing and holding allied territory; the binding strategy is a deliberate effort to compel China to have to behave in ways that catalyze US, allied, and partner resolve if it pursues its hegemonic ambitions. These approaches can be either fully or partially integrated.

Fully integrating the strategies among all participating states would make an attack on one member of the US alliance architecture (and potentially the coalition as a whole) an attack on all. In this posture, China could not attack Taiwan or the Philippines without very likely precipitating a larger war with the rest of the US-led alliance system. The downside of this approach is that it is politically very demanding to establish; given the divergent threat perceptions among US allies and partners, such an effort might fail if an important partici- pating state balked at following through in the event of crisis or war. It might also be so politically stressing as to cause fissures in the coalition.

Alternatively, the strategies could be partially integrated. One way to do so would be for the United States and others to partially integrate their forces and efforts for all the scenarios they believe they would face, including the most stressing, such as an invasion of Taiwan or the Philippines. This approach would limit the degree to which a single member's balking would cause sys- temic failure. One partner's balking might hamper, for example, the antisubma- rine campaign or the menu of potential operating locations but not necessarily lead to failure.

The United States and any participating allies and partners could also par- tially integrate by binding their preparations for certain contingencies but not others. In this model, willing states could prepare to defend especially vulner- able allies like Taiwan without intertwining their postures, but they (and possi- bly others uninvolved in preparing for a defense of Taiwan) could prepare to defend the rest of the allies through a more fully integrated approach. In other words, during a war over Taiwan, though the United States might still seek to induce China to act in ways that clarified the threat it posed to other states, it would not seek to leverage those converging threat perceptions for military-op- erational effects in Taiwan's defense; rather, it would seek to deny a Chinese fait accompli through the focused efforts of American, Taiwan, and perhaps a few additional nations' forces. But other prospective victims of Chinese attack would be defended through more fully integrated denial and binding strategies. This approach would have the advantage of being less politically demanding and of optimizing defenses for all members of the coalition save Taiwan. It would, however, reduce the potency of the defense of Taiwan.

Some form of an integrated approach is likely to be the most advantageous for the anti-hegemonic coalition. Given the divergent threat perceptions and political sensitivities among coalition members, a fully integrated binding strategy may well be unfeasible. That said, excluding the most vulnerable allies from the binding strategy could leave them open to China's focused and sequential strategy if a narrowly focused denial defense for them proves unworkable.

The optimal strategy is likely to be one in which the United States and its allies and, likely to a lesser degree, its partners in the Western Pacific intertwine their posture and activities significantly but not fully. The degree of binding may differ according to the scenario: coalition members might, for instance, bind their efforts more fully in order to defend Australia than they would to defend Taiwan. The practical output of this is likely to be the development of operating locations across a wide range of participating states and a higher degree of integration among their military postures and activities. At the same time, the United States and its allies will have to prepare for the possibility that some participating states will balk and make sure that they can still execute effective operational plans even in such circumstances. Together, such a posture would be most likely to ensure that a Chinese attempt to apply the focused and sequential strategy would catalyze the resolve needed to mount the expanded denial defense or recapture approach.

Putting and Keeping the Burden of Escalation on China

If the binding strategy is applied effectively, China's behavior would catalyze the resolve needed either to escalate sufficiently to conduct an effective denial defense or to retake a lost ally. This would give the coalition an escalation advantage: at every plausible level, Beijing would be met by an effective strategy and coalition members resolved enough to implement it.[53] This means that the anti-hegemonic coalition would be able to fulfill its core purposes in the face of China's strategy: however China chose to escalate, the coalition would have the will and a way to effectively defend or relieve vulnerable member states while retaining the ability to prevail in a systemic regional war.

Successfully implemented, in other words, this strategy would keep the burden of escalation on China. It would be Beijing, not the United States and any participating confederates, that would have to escalate the conflict to avoid defeat. Yet taking this initiative would make China appear more offensive, aggressive, unreasonable, and menacing—catalyzing the resolve of those already fighting and encouraging unengaged nations to intervene. In so escalating, Beijing would find itself unable to confine the conflict within its preferred bounds. Meanwhile, in the larger conflict it would have to fight, it would face the choice between either settling or escalating in ways that would further catalyze the resolve of the engaged coalition while leading yet more states to oppose it. Its opponents would thus be able to prevail at whatever higher level of war China chose to take the conflict. This is the boa constrictor effect: the more Beijing sought to escalate its way out of its quandary, the more it would both widen its circle of opponents and strengthen these opponents' will to frustrate its aims.

Facing the prospect of a tightening boa constrictor and with much to lose, Beijing would have the most powerful incentives not to escalate but instead to settle the conflict—or, better, avoid it entirely in the first place. Escalating the war would only bring more damage and risk, without opening a path to gains that would justify them. Continuing the struggle would lead, at best, to protracted war with no reasonable prospect of success and, at worst, not only to frustration of its aims but to great loss at the hands of its opponents. In such circumstances, Beijing would face enormous incentives to terminate the conflict before it became too damaging.

China might want its adversaries to think that it is willing to escalate to mutual suicide to escape such a predicament, but this is unlikely to work. For reasons discussed before, China's opponents are likely to see a threat that would involve destroying itself as a bluff. China would be far more likely to resort to protraction or agree to settle a conflict over Taiwan in the hope of regenerating its power and trying again.

At the same time, the United States and any allies and partners participating in the conflict would have an interest in ensuring that their war aims were tolerable enough to satisfy China's threshold for settlement. Beijing would be less open to settlement if the terms were too onerous or humiliating, but the opposing coalition could set its demands relatively low. It would have no need to insist on a total or even a very satisfying victory over China. Upholding America's differentiated credibility at the heart of the anti-hegemonic coalition requires only that China's effort to subordinate a vulnerable US ally fail. This would be the sine qua non of the US and coalition position for war termination.

Logically nothing beyond this would be required. Thus nothing would *need* to be taken from what China possessed at the outset of hostilities. In fact, the United States and its confederates might sweeten the deal by offering to return things to Beijing; for instance, they might have judged it useful to seize Chinese equities such as financial holdings or overseas bases during the war in order to generate leverage at the peace table. These could be returned, as a triumphant Britain returned some of the territories it had seized from France during the Seven Years' War at the end of the conflict.[54]

Yet they might have reason to demand more. For instance, if something happened during the war to lastingly diminish the anti-hegemonic coalition's power or elevate China's, the United States and its confederates in the conflict might need to redress or compensate for this change as part of their terms for ending the war. This is important because they would need to ensure a sustainably favorable regional balance of power between the anti-hegemonic coalition on the one side and China and its pro-hegemonic coalition on the other following the conflict. If China had somehow jeopardized this even though the engaged part of the coalition had effectively defended or liberated a member state, they might well need to address this in the terms ending the war.

For instance, China might have added to its power by subordinating or seizing a state that is not a member of the anti-hegemonic coalition. China might have failed in its effort to take Taiwan but might have enlisted or coerced the support of Laos or Thailand. Relieving states that are not beneficiaries of an alliance guarantee from the United States is not necessary to uphold Washington's differentiated credibility, but Beijing's addition of such states to the pro-hegemony camp could alter the regional balance of power, which is relevant to the anti-hegemonic coalition's core goals. Their disposition, or compensation for such a shift, might therefore need to be addressed in the peace terms.

The Binding Strategy in Cold War Europe

This kind of binding strategy is not merely a theoretical conceit. Rather, it is similar to what NATO did in Europe during the latter part of the Cold War. Early in that long struggle, the United States relied first on its nuclear monopoly and then on its overwhelming nuclear superiority to deter a Soviet invasion of the Western Alliance. Until the mid-1960s, Washington could have launched a nuclear attack that would have not only devastated the Soviet Union but also largely blunted if not entirely denied its ability to strike back at the United States. Washington and NATO relied on this strategic dominance to dissuade the USSR from using its massive advantages in conventional forces within the European Theater.

As it became clear over the 1960s and 1970s that the Soviet Union would first develop a significant strategic nuclear retaliatory force and then approach, if not exceed, strategic parity with the United States, it also became increasingly clear that the strategic approach of threatening a massive nuclear response to a regional war in Europe was no longer tenable. If the United States launched a large-scale nuclear first strike, the Soviet Union would be able to do the gravest damage to the United States in retort. Courting such a response was no longer credible, let alone sensible, as US interests in Western Europe, while important, could not match the importance of avoiding devastation of the American homeland. The burden of escalation had grown too great for such a dramatically disproportionate strategy to make sense.

The United States and NATO therefore needed to find a way to deter the Soviet Union from using its theater military advantages in Europe to coerce Allied member states there despite the two sides' great mutual vulnerability—in the vernacular of the time, mutual assured destruction, or MAD.[55] In principle, the cleanest solution to this problem was for NATO to develop conventional forces capable of defeating a Warsaw Pact attack, making its traditional reliance on the threat to escalate first to the nuclear level unnecessary. In practice, this was an elusive goal, given lagging European efforts on conventional defense, American engagement in Indochina, and Moscow's heavy investments in its own forces. In the 1970s the question thus became urgent: In light of the Warsaw Pact's theater advantages, how could NATO effectively deter and, if possible, defeat an attack, thereby undermining the Soviets' ability to use those advantages for coercion?

The response in the 1970s and 1980s was essentially a defense posture designed to compel the Warsaw Pact to have to attack in such a way that it would have generated the resolve needed on the part of the United States and its NATO allies to resort to using nuclear weapons. NATO conventional forces postured and prepared to fight in such a way that the Warsaw Pact would have had to mount a massive, brazen, and manifestly aggressive attack that would have catalyzed the West's resolve to go nuclear. US nuclear forces, meanwhile, were increasingly pushed toward greater discrimination, providing options for a limited response that would have contributed to blunting a Soviet Bloc attack while also communicating restraint in order to persuade Moscow to halt the offensive.[56] Ultimately, the threat of total nuclear war hovered at the end of such a scenario, but that otherwise incredible threat became more credible as it would have followed a massive Soviet attack, an enormous conventional war, and several stages of nuclear escalation.

The basic strategic problem in later Cold War Europe is strikingly similar to what the United States faces with China today. NATO was fundamentally an anti-hegemonic coalition (albeit fully formalized as a multilateral alliance, which appears unlikely in Asia for the foreseeable future) designed to prevent the Soviet Union from securing hegemony first over Europe and then beyond.[57] The United States was the external cornerstone balancer of that coalition. Indeed, in key respects the military problem in the Cold War was worse than that facing an anti-hegemonic coalition in Asia today. NATO considered its conventional forces inferior to the Warsaw Pact's with respect to the strategically significant scenarios on which it had to focus, above all Central Europe and especially the Federal Republic of Germany. Few officials and experts believed that a denial defense for Continental NATO would really work (although there were hopes that the alliance was moving toward being able to mount one if the Cold War continued).[58] NATO therefore had to figure out how to make credible deliberate vertical escalation that would have profoundly risked the most grievous damage to itself—a harder problem than what the anti-hegemonic coalition in Asia should face, if it prepares well for a denial defense strategy.

And yet deterrence held in the Cold War. If nothing else, this suggests that it is possible to make deterrence work against a state as powerful as the Soviet Union even in situations of local conventional inferiority, if one has the right overall strategy and enough resolve. This suggests that an anti-hegemonic coalition in Asia could use a denial and binding strategy to blunt any Chinese aspirations for regional hegemony. China's true incentive in the face of such an effective strategy would be to avoid starting a war in the first place, which is also the highest goal for the anti-hegemonic coalition. Just as the Soviet Union never saw enough of an advantage to precipitating a war in Europe during the Cold War, true success would be for China to see how things would likely unfold and never risk war in the first place.

The crucial premise of the binding strategy is that military and other material power can be consciously employed to create political, perceptual effects that matter in the war. The key for this to work is to have the war unfold in such a way that key decision-makers in the coalition and in important fence-sitter countries increase their valuation of the stakes at hand. This means that strict military efficacy cannot always be the preeminent criterion for force planning. Military strategy must be designed to create or avoid specific, concrete political effects, which themselves shape the war.

Thus, to be truly effective in a limited war with China, US and other engaged states' military planning needs to serve political purposes, not only in an abstract sense of seeking to attain vague ends like regional stability or freedom of the seas, but in a much more immediate, instrumental sense. Planning must deliberately shape the war and how it is fought in order to influence the combatants' resolve. This simply follows Clausewitz's dictum that war is a continuation of politics by other means—but not only that war is a continuation of politics in some general sense or solely in its purposes but rather that "the political view is the object, war is the means, *and the means must always include the object in [their] conception.*"[59] Within these bounds, military necessity should naturally reign—since failing to give military requirements due primacy in appropriate bounds is to invite defeat—but defense planners must always be conscious of the political effect and circumstance of military operations.

This attention to political effect is not only for purely political goods. Properly done, orienting military ways and means to political objectives and within appropriate political bounds has concrete military-operational benefits. Greater resolve will result in more resources being allocated to a fight and fewer strictures on their employment. In the ideal, then, military and political actions should form a positive feedback loop, each strengthening the other.

11

Implications

WHAT DOES THIS BOOK'S ARGUMENT IMPLY for the United States?

Most fundamentally, the book describes how the United States can ensure an international environment conducive to its own security, freedom, and prosperity in a world where America is no longer as dominant as it once was. It charts a way for the United States to correlate the costs it would incur and the risks it would face to deny China, the world's most powerful other state, hegemony in the Indo-Pacific, the world's most important region. And it demonstrates that the United States can deny China its aim of regional predominance in a way that is feasible and responsible. This itself is tremendously important because it shows that conceding the Indo-Pacific is not, as some contend, the only way to avoid catastrophic loss.[1]

At the same time, this book also shows how the United States can satisfy its core national objectives of ensuring Americans' security, freedom, and prosperity without needing to pursue grandiose ambitions. Contrary to some arguments, the United States does not need to make the world democratic or liberal in order to flourish as a free republic, nor does it need to dominate the world in order to be secure. This, too, is enormously important because it shows that Americans do not have to reach too far or suffer too much in order to achieve what they reasonably want in the world.

But successfully pursuing this middle way will not be easy.

Military Implications

In this book I have sought to provide a framework, a conceptual structure, rather than a set of specific programmatic or operational recommendations. I hope that this conceptual structure will provide useful boundaries within which debates about the right force structure, force posture, operational concepts, technology, and other key aspects of military effectiveness can take place. Providing this framework is the core utility of a defense strategy, which is at best more a paradigm—a simplifying framework—to focus attention and effort rather than a detailed how-to manual.[2] Militaries and like institutions tend to function most effectively when they can work on a narrower and more focused problem or set of problems, such as this book has sought to provide.[3] Strategies that are vague or too broad fritter away limited attention, effort, and resources; by doing too little to distinguish between the important and the marginal, they leave those trying to implement them unsure of what to work on or toward or what the bounding constraints are for solutions. Strategies that are too specific or inflexible, meanwhile, increase the risks of error, overspecifying, and brittleness.

The cardinal implication of this book's argument is that the United States should focus on making denial defense a reality in the Indo-Pacific with respect to its allies, including Taiwan. Preventing China's regional hegemony there is the most important strategic objective of the United States; this goal should therefore receive strict priority in US defense planning and resourcing. Denial defense is the military strategy that most readily correlates the benefits of pursuing this aim with the costs and risks, and it is likely that a denial defense can work there *if* the United States and its allies and partners apply the needed level of effort and focus. Denial defense should therefore be the preferred standard for the United States and its allies with respect to China in the Indo-Pacific. Fortunately, the Defense Department's 2018 *National Defense Strategy* has already steered the US Joint Force in this direction.[4] Key regional allies such as Japan and Australia are also moving along similar lines.[5]

Denial defense is a reasonable criterion because, from a military planning perspective, if these most exposed allies can be effectively defended, other US allies to their rear are very likely to be effectively defensible as well. In such circumstances, China will find no good way to employ its focused and sequential strategy and will not be able to use military coercion to short-circuit or pry apart the anti-hegemonic coalition. Facing such an effective balancing coalition, China will have to negotiate the terms of its continued rise on equitable rather than dominant terms. This will open opportunities for détente and engagement with Beijing from a position of strength. Thus an effective denial defense posture will be the best way for the United States and its allies to ensure a desirable, stable peace in the Indo-Pacific.

In concrete terms, the United States should focus first on an effective defense of Taiwan, the natural first target of China's focused and sequential strategy. As outlined previously, Taiwan is militarily significant, given its location in the middle of the first island chain, and important for America's differentiated credibility. Walking away from its defense would therefore significantly reduce the United States' differentiated credibility as the external cornerstone balancer of an anti-hegemonic coalition. At the same time, Taiwan is likely defensible to the standard of an effective defense laid out in the book.[6] Taiwan cannot be immunized from Chinese attack, but it likely can be protected from conquest. Ensuring an effective denial defense of Taiwan should therefore be the primary scenario the US Department of Defense uses to prepare US forces for the future, with a fait accompli attempt by Beijing serving as the primary focus of such planning. US forces should first and foremost be sized and shaped to ensure they can defend Taiwan successfully to the standard laid out previously. At the same time, Taiwan itself must significantly augment and improve its defenses and make itself more resilient.[7]

Because it is possible that China might eventually seek to circumvent Taiwan or that an effort to defend Taiwan might fail, the United States and its allies should also prepare to ensure an effective denial defense of the Philippines against an increasingly powerful China. The Philippines is likely to be the second-best target among existing US allies for China's focused and sequential strategy. It is a US ally and so enmeshes US differentiated credibility; it also occupies a critical position along the first island chain. At the same time, it has limited capacity for self-defense and is reasonably close to China.

Concurrently, the United States must account for the possibility that a focused denial defense will fail. It and its allies should therefore make provision for an integrated denial defense-cum-binding strategy. This posture should ensure that even if China attempts to subjugate Taiwan or the Philippines, it will be forced to broaden and intensify the war in ways that would catalyze the resolve that the United States and other potentially engaged members of the anti-hegemonic coalition need to prevail, either through an expanded denial campaign or, if that fails or is judged infeasible, a recapture approach.

Because a focused denial defense is preferable, however, the United States and its allies and partners should seek to minimize the trade-offs generated by preparing this fallback posture. Whenever possible, their investments in a binding strategy should also contribute to a focused denial defense. This should be possible because investments in a binding strategy are largely about increasing the integration of allies and partners into a more cohesive defense posture, greater resilience, and adding basing and dispersal options. Many of these investments would add to or at least would not detract from the ability to conduct effective circumscribed denial campaigns on behalf of Taiwan or the Philippines.

These strategies form the bounding constraints within which American efforts should evolve and within which military-operational, technological, and diplomatic debate can take place. They have the benefit of being sufficiently narrow to concentrate attention but do not prescribe how they should be operationalized. Moreover, they are concrete and tractable—albeit still very challenging and complex—rather than merely aspirational or hortatory. This is far more likely to produce US military forces that are optimally developed, postured, and trained for the geopolitical interests of the American people. A similar logic holds true for how these strategies can productively frame the comparable efforts of US allies and partners in the anti-hegemonic coalition. Fortunately, much superb work is already being produced in this direction.[8] It is now a question of this work being developed, refined, and implemented to the purposes and standard laid out here.

The US Defense Perimeter

How far should this defense go? As indicated earlier, we cannot determine the optimal American defense perimeter without understanding the best military strategy for achieving US political aims in ways that correlate the costs and risks Americans assume to the interests at stake. To repeat, the American defense perimeter encompasses those states to which the United States has attached its differentiated credibility through a security guarantee, normally through a formal alliance but also, as in the case of Taiwan, through a quasi-alliance relationship. In the context of China's pursuit of regional hegemony in Asia, whether the United States sustains or eliminates its existing alliances, and whether and how it forms new ones, should be a function of the need to form and sustain an anti-hegemonic coalition that is stronger than China and its own pro-hegemonic coalition, especially in the context of a systemic regional war. US alliances should be designed to serve this goal by providing sufficient reassurance to nervous coalition members that they will be protected from China's focused and sequential strategy.

Now that we have a clear sense of what the optimal American military strategy is, we can determine more clearly the right defense perimeter for the United States. The best plausible outcome for the United States is an alliance architecture that achieves its purposes while presenting as limited a threat surface as possible. To ensure that China does not establish predominance over Asia, the anti-hegemonic coalition must be more powerful than China in the event of a systemic regional war. If the coalition is to entice and retain enough states to meet this standard, those states must feel sufficiently secure in the face of Beijing's best strategy, the focused and sequential strategy. The main purpose of the American defense perimeter is thus to provide enough reassurance to enough important states that might otherwise bandwagon with China that they can prudently work to balance it alongside the United States.

In simpler terms, Washington must not allow China to have such an open field that it can subordinate enough states to tip the regional balance of power in its favor. This, naturally, puts a premium on the United States adding states as allies. At the same time, however, the United States must take care to avoid adding allies that would be indefensible—meaning those that cannot be effectively defended without the United States losing, being so weakened as to compromise its ability to uphold other alliances in the coalition, or demanding so much from the American people that they elect to pull back from the coalition or the alliances within it.

As discussed previously, the current US alliance architecture in the region forms the baseline for any US decisions. Determinations about these alliances' futures do not take place in a vacuum, especially because of the fraught consequences of withdrawing from existing alliances as compared to adding new ones. Beyond this, that legacy alliance architecture presents important advantages. The states allied with the United States are some of Asia's most advanced and powerful nations, and they provide much of the strength needed to balance China. They also present a defensive logic, forming a largely uninterrupted perimeter along the first island chain of the Western Pacific. This is no accident but a product of US strategic decision-making after the Second World War.[9]

Primarily for these reasons, it makes sense for the United States to maintain its existing alliance relationships in the Asia-Pacific. Japan is absolutely critical; without it, the anti-hegemonic coalition would almost certainly fail. Australia is a highly advanced economy with a significant military; it is also distant from China and therefore highly defensible. Both of these US alliances should therefore be retained. I have already discussed at length the rationale for maintaining at least the legacy quasi-alliance with Taiwan.

It also makes sense for the United States to retain its alliances with the Philippines, the Pacific Island states, and South Korea. Although the Philippines lacks the ability to contribute significantly to its own defense, let alone that of other US allies, it forms the southern pillar of the first island chain and offers abundant locations for projection of military power throughout the southern part of the Western Pacific and the South China Sea. This is advantageous for the United States; by the same token, it would be highly beneficial for China if the United States abandoned Manila. The Philippines is also plausibly defensible. If the United States can defend Taiwan, it can almost certainly defend the Philippines.

The United States should also sustain its close linkages with many of the archipelagic and island states of the Central and South Pacific, including Palau, the Federated States of Micronesia, and the Marshall Islands. Together, these form what has been termed a second island cloud, affording geography critical for effective US power projection, strategic depth, and resilient support. They are also highly defensible since they lie to the rear of the first island chain.[10]

South Korea is the one legacy American alliance located on the Asian mainland, separated from China by North Korea and the Yellow Sea. Because of its proximity to China, South Korea is likely to grow increasingly challenging to defend from a determined Chinese assault, either with or through North Korea, by sea, or both. That said, including South Korea in the US defense perimeter is worth the challenges for several reasons. First, South Korea is one of the world's largest and most advanced economies; it would make a major contribution to an anti-hegemonic coalition, whereas its neutralization, let alone transfer to China's pro-hegemonic coalition, would be a great loss. Second, Korea is important to the effective defense of Japan; if China were able to use South Korea as a base of operations, it would greatly complicate the defense of Japan. Last, South Korea is plausibly defensible, located as it is on a peninsula next to Japan and especially given that it fields one of the most capable militaries in the

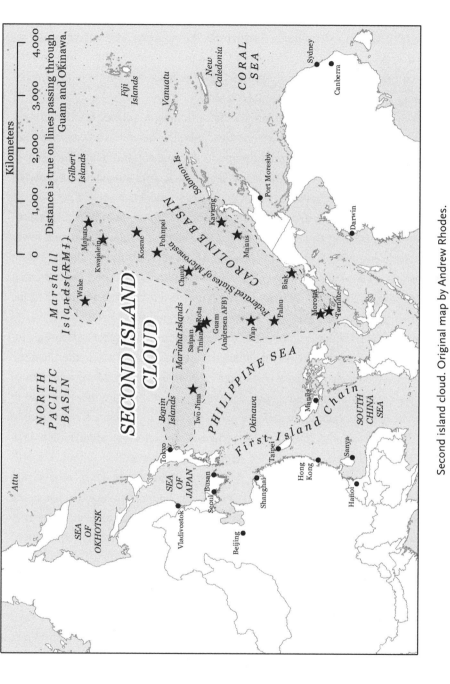

Second island cloud. Original map by Andrew Rhodes.

world, contributes significantly to its own defense, and is capable of contributing more, given the size and sophistication of its economy. Particularly given that the conventional military threat from North Korea has substantially receded in recent decades, if that from China grows, then South Korea and the United States can increasingly redirect their defense preparations toward defending against a potential assault by China.

Thus it makes sense for the United States to maintain its legacy defense perimeter in Asia. The main questions for American defense strategy, then, are whether the United States should expand its alliance commitments, and if so, to which states, and how much it should seek to orient its alliances more toward collective defense than the legacy hub-and-spoke model.

The first issue relates to the US defense perimeter. From the American perspective, all things being equal, an alliance architecture with more secure and fewer vulnerable members is better. This lessens American exposure to Chinese action by reducing the number of members susceptible to China's focused and sequential strategy while adding states that are readily defensible and can contribute to the common defense. The problem is that the states with the greatest incentives to form an alliance with the United States are those most vulnerable to Beijing's focused and sequential strategy; yet although these states might add to the alliance's total power, they also increase its exposure to Chinese action. More secure states that are fearful of Chinese regional hegemony, meanwhile, are more inclined to free ride; adding them to the defense perimeter may not add much in practice to the US ability to uphold the anti-hegemonic coalition and other alliances within it.

The second issue relates to the degree of interconnection among US alliances. Broadly, the more cohesive the United States can make its alliances in resisting China's bid for regional hegemony, the better. The problem lies in the difficulty and costs of making this a reality. It is hard to persuade states to truly align their strategic plans and postures given the self-help realities of the international environment. These difficulties are compounded in the case of US alliances in Asia by the far-flung and diverse geopolitical circumstances of America's various allies in the region. Given the widely differing strategic contexts of such countries as Japan, South Korea, the Philippines, and Australia, it will be difficult to bring them together in a collective alliance that intertwines their fates. The issue for the United States is how far to press the matter.

Any discussion of expanding the US defense perimeter must start with the fundamental criterion for the anti-hegemonic coalition, which is that it must be more powerful than China and its pro-hegemonic coalition with respect to a systemic regional war. US alliances should be retained and added with an eye to satisfying this condition. All things being equal, the more the military balance favors the coalition, the better. Moreover, the more the coalition can deny China the opportunity to apply the focused and sequential strategy, the better. The closer the military balance, and the more states to which China can apply its focused and sequential strategy, the more states must be included in the coalition and given US security guarantees, and the more tightly coupled these links will need to be.

In practical terms, this means that the farther forward in maritime Asia the coalition and US alliance guarantees go, the better, since this will leave fewer states susceptible to falling into China's pro-hegemonic coalition. At the same time, this interest must be balanced against the powerful US and coalition interest in avoiding including states that are not defensible.

The key determinant of the need to expand the US defense perimeter is, then, the relative power balance between China and its pro-hegemonic coalition on the one hand and the anti-hegemonic coalition on the other. Each coalition's side of the ledger could be augmented by internal growth on the part of existing members or the addition of states, and each could be weakened by internal stagnation or the withdrawal of members. For the United States, the primary dynamic on which to focus is that the stronger China itself grows and the more states it adds to its coalition, the more states Washington and its partners will need to add to their own coalition to compensate. This in turn is likely to impel Washington to add to its roster of allies and to make its alliances more tightly interconnected in order to reassure nervous coalition members.

Most directly, if China seizes a US ally from the anti-hegemonic coalition and brings it into its own, this would shift the balance in Beijing's favor, both through the direct transfer of the state's power and through the damage to Washington's differentiated credibility. Accordingly, the extent to which the United States and its engaged allies and partners can effectively defend existing US allies will be critical in determining whether and, if so, how much the United States needs to expand its defense perimeter and how much more cohesion is needed among these allies.

If, for instance, the United States and any other participating states fail to defend Taiwan effectively and China can subjugate it, this would remove a key blocking point in the first island chain, add Taiwan's wealth and power to the pro-hegemonic coalition while removing it from the anti-hegemonic coalition, and weaken US differentiated credibility. In these circumstances, because both the coalition's material power and American differentiated credibility would be weakened, the United States would have to pay a higher premium to ensure the coalition's effectiveness. The pressure on the anti-hegemonic coalition and the United States would only grow more pointed if China were then able to subordinate another US ally, such as the Philippines.

But if the United States and any other engaged allies and partners can effectively defend Taiwan, the pressure to expand the US defense perimeter will be more attenuated. Taiwan would still be affiliated with the coalition, and US differentiated credibility would be safeguarded. The anti-hegemonic coalition and thus the US alliance architecture would not be so pressed to add states, perhaps even none beyond those already participating. And the United States would be less pressed to push for greater cohesion among existing allies.

Changing the US Defense Perimeter?

Assuming, then, that the United States should at minimum hold to its existing allies in Asia, how should the United States consider altering its defense perimeter with respect to the region?

Outside Asia

As a general principle, it makes sense for the anti-hegemonic coalition to add as many affiliated states as possible. A plausible coalition in Asia is unlikely to be a fully multilateralized alliance; rather, it is more likely to be an informal or semiformal confederation that, while including some bilateral and possibly narrower multilateral alliances, does not bind the participating states to each other's defense in all cases. The benefit of this informality is that there is little downside to adding states; they increase the coalition's power without risking much. The trade-off is that such a loose confederation risks leaving exposed states out in the cold, subject to China's focused and sequential strategy, as more distant coalition members shy away from taking on Beijing's best strategy.

This means that the prime caution for the coalition lies in adding states that are exposed. Conversely, there is essentially only upside to adding states that are not so exposed. The United States and other coalition members should seek to add as many states as are willing to join the coalition that are to the rear vis-à-vis China of those states already in the coalition—and, because of the greater potency afforded by US security guarantees, especially to the rear of US allies. In practice, this is likely to mean east of the first island chain or west of India. Because these states are already effectively defended from China's best military strategy by the combination of distance and American and other allied and partner military power interposed between, there is little downside to including them in the coalition.

Still, these states are likely to add only limited value in the face of Beijing's focused and sequential strategy. Except for the United States, no state outside Asia can project significant military power into the region. (Russia is an Asian power, and even its ability to project military power in Asia is limited.) As a result, even those prepared to join the coalition are unlikely to be able to offer much. Moreover, many distant states will feel the threat posed by China less keenly and are likely to want to avoid the problem or even seek to collaborate with China. As a consequence, the United States and its allies and partners should not count too much on the contributions of states outside Asia.

That said, some states outside the Indo-Pacific area might be willing and able to contribute to the anti-hegemonic coalition in ways that, though not militarily significant to the struggle in the Pacific, are still meaningful. They might do so because they believe that their interests, for instance, in ensuring relatively free commerce with the region would be threatened by Chinese regional hegemony. Such states also might have enough power to make a difference in a war between the United States and the coalition against China, such as through economic leverage that could become relevant in a protracted war or war termination scenario. Further, such states might be able to backfill in handling security threats that, though secondary or tertiary in comparison to the resolution of a war in the Pacific, are still important.

These states might include France, with its far-flung island possessions and vast economic exclusion zones in the South Pacific, Canada, the United Kingdom, Germany, Saudi Arabia, and the United Arab Emirates. Their military efforts, however, are likely more efficiently allocated toward managing their own or nearby regions, thereby relieving the United States from the necessity of having to focus on Europe and the Middle East, rather than making what would almost certainly be marginal contributions in the Indo-Pacific.

India

India must be a critical member of any anti-hegemonic coalition. It is very powerful and therefore has reason to expect a high degree of influence in the region; Chinese hegemony would consequently cost India a great deal. Moreover, India and China share a long, disputed land border and naturally compete for influence in the Indian subcontinent and adjacent areas. With so much to lose, New Delhi has a most potent interest in denying China regional hegemony, and it appears to be in earnest about this goal and realistic about the scale of effort required.[11]

India can also defend itself. It is likely to become the world's third largest economy in short order (and possibly second before long), and it possesses a strong tradition of nationalism and self-reliance. It has built one of the world's most formidable militaries, including developing a nuclear arsenal that is likely to be capable of surviving an attempted disarming first strike by China.[12] Further, although India shares a long land border with China, its key territories, such as cities like Delhi and Mumbai, are located far from this border. Because of these factors, India is almost certainly capable of effectively defending its key territory against Beijing.

It is therefore unlikely that the United States will need to offer, or that India will seek, an alliance (at least of the kind focused on in this book) between Washington and New Delhi. India is likely to remain a resolute member of any anti-hegemonic coalition without requiring such a guarantee. And given these factors and America's interests in husbanding its strength and differentiated credibility, Washington has no reason to insist on one.

Moreover, there is a natural division of labor within the coalition between the United States, Japan, and Australia on one side and India on the other. Because Asia's most advanced economies are located in the Western Pacific and South China Sea and because many of them implicate Washington's differentiated credibility, this area will constitute the primary theater of competition between the anti-hegemonic coalition as a whole and China and its pro-hegemonic coalition. Given China's size, the United States and its allies in the Western Pacific will need to focus rigorously on preparing for a conflict in this area, particularly over Taiwan or the Philippines. This will indubitably consume a very great proportion of American resources and effort.

But China will also have the ability and interest to try to add to its coalition or otherwise enable its pursuit of regional hegemony in other important areas of the Indo-Pacific, particularly the Indian subcontinent and Indian Ocean area. Beijing might seek to add states in this area to its pro-hegemonic coalition or seek access agreements with local states to enable the employment of its military forces, including in ways that could affect a conflict over Taiwan or another state in the Western Pacific. Yet the United States, if it is primarily occupied with the Western Pacific, will almost certainly simply not have the spare power to simultaneously muster a leading effort in the Indian Ocean and South Asia.

India, however, has an even more powerful interest in limiting Chinese influence in this subregion than the United States does. Moreover, its military forces and other levers of power are more naturally suited for employment in its own region; India has a very large land force, along with air and maritime forces, that are readily employable in its own area but of distinctly limited utility beyond it.

Accordingly, the United States should encourage India to focus on its own area, both by directly balancing Chinese assertiveness and also by bolstering important neighboring states that might otherwise fall under Beijing's sway. New Delhi might even sensibly provide alliance guarantees to states such as Myanmar. The United States can seek to enable and empower India as much as possible in these directions.

A deeper alliance between the United States and India would become more advisable under two contingencies, neither of which appears pressing in the near term. First, a US guarantee would become advisable if India's resolve were faltering and such a commitment could meaningfully reinforce it. Conversely, an alliance would become attractive if the US and allied position in the Western Pacific deteriorated and a rising India could contribute to redressing it.

So long as China remains the primary and rising power in Asia, the United States and other coalition members to all practical purposes benefit unreservedly from a stronger India. They should therefore seek to increase India's economic and military power in order to provide as strong a counterweight as possible to China and to limit the pressure on the United States and other Western Pacific states.

Southeast Asia

The rubber meets the road for the United States in Southeast Asia, an area nearby China and much of which is not within the US defense perimeter but that includes countries that the United States and its allies and partners could plausibly defend. As a general principle, the coalition should encompass as many states in Southeast Asia as it can, since this both adds their power to the anti-hegemonic side and denies it to China's coalition. But these benefits must be weighed against the states' defensibility. Given that there is little prospect of effectively defending the landlocked states on China's northern and western borders—which are in any case small economies—this essentially means that the United States and other coalition members have an interest in an effective defense as far forward in maritime Asia as possible.

With a few exceptions, the countries of the region are not formally allied with either Washington or Beijing. The US defense perimeter peters out with the Philippines before picking up again far to the south in Australia, with Thailand as an ambiguous case. Cambodia, meanwhile, is usually thought of as within China's orbit.

Much of the area remains unaffiliated, however, not clearly in the anti-hegemonic coalition or in China's pro-hegemonic coalition. Southeast Asia therefore offers an open field within Asia for China to induce or subordinate states to back its bid for regional hegemony.[13] Moreover, many of these states have large and growing economies and occupy significant geographical positions, making their decisions important. For Beijing, dominance over this area would constitute a long stride toward regional predominance.

Accordingly, the United States and the anti-hegemonic coalition have an interest in bringing important Southeast Asian states into the coalition and perhaps in Washington's forming alliance relationships with them. The problems are twofold. First, some of these states are difficult to defend, and some may be simply indefensible. Second, many states in the area do not want to have to choose between aligning with either the United States or China; indeed, Indonesia, Malaysia, and Vietnam, among others, have strong traditions of nonalignment.[14] Despite these difficulties, any shift in the power balance toward China and its pro-hegemonic coalition would impel the United States and its allies and partners to consider adding Southeast Asian states to the anti-hegemonic coalition. Moreover, because of the greater danger such a powerful China and its coalition would pose, the United States might need to offer at least some of these states a security guarantee in order to provide them with the degree of assurance required to affiliate with the coalition in the face of such peril.

In light of these factors, the coalition would likely benefit by adding Indonesia, the largest state and economy in Southeast Asia and almost certainly the most defensible. Indonesia is located south of the Philippines, already a US ally, and thus to the rear of the US defense line. Moreover, with the exception of Borneo (which is unlikely to be key territory), Indonesia is located well to the south, below Malaysian Borneo and the Malay Peninsula. It is also an archipelago, which plays to the United States' advantages in the maritime arena. Even more, Indonesia is located just north of close US ally Australia, which has strong incentives to ensure the effective defense of its northern neighbor. This increases the probability that Indonesia's defense would invite the aid of other states. These factors also mean it would likely be reasonable for the United States to add Indonesia as an ally, if that proves necessary.

How the coalition should view the region's other states is less clear-cut.

Vietnam is a significant and growing economy with a capable military and a reputation for resolute self-defense. Its proximity to China and fierce independent streak will likely lead it to join an anti-hegemonic coalition without needing or even, given its tradition of eschewing alliances, wanting an alliance with the United States. This is a positive arrangement for the United States, which can and should still aid Vietnam's ability to defend itself. The question is, if China and its pro-hegemonic coalition grow in power and Vietnam becomes increasingly nervous about its vulnerability to China's focused strategy, would it make sense for the United States to ally with Hanoi? Vietnam's traversable land border with China makes much of its key territory difficult to defend against Beijing, especially given that the US military's advantages are particularly great in aerospace and maritime operations rather than on land. The United States should seek to avoid having to confront this dilemma by empowering Vietnam to defend itself. In any event, Washington should be very conservative about attaching its differentiated credibility to the effective defense of Vietnam. There would have to be a very potent benefit or need in order to match the gravity of this risk.

Malaysia and Singapore are wealthy, significant economies. The narrow neck of the Malay Peninsula gives both countries a significant degree of defensibility. Still, the peninsula is closer to the Asian mainland than Indonesia, making it more accessible to Chinese military power, especially if Thailand affiliates with Beijing or permits Chinese forces to cross or use its territory. The United States should therefore seek to bring these two important states into the anti-hegemonic coalition but be reluctant to extend an alliance guarantee to them. Brunei, given its wealth and location, surrounded by Malaysia's Sarawak territory, would likely fall into the same category.

Thailand is likely to be a significant swing state in the region. It is one of Southeast Asia's largest economies and centrally located; along with Vietnam, it sits between China and most of the maritime part of the region. Because of its wealth and strategic position, it would bring significant value to the anti-hegemonic coalition. But there is reason to be skeptical of Bangkok's willingness to join, and there are major risks to the United States of a full alliance relationship with Thailand. The two are technically allies now, but their relationship is generally understood to be considerably more ambiguous and thinner than Washington's relationship with Tokyo, Canberra, or even Manila. It is not entirely clear what Washington's defense obligations are if Thailand is attacked.[15]

First, Thailand has a historical tradition of accommodation rather than resistance. It accommodated the European imperial powers of the nineteenth and early twentieth centuries to preserve its autonomy and pursued a similar course toward imperial Japan in the Second World War.[16] This makes it unclear what policy Bangkok will pursue—with the anti-hegemonic coalition, with Beijing, or somewhere in between. Second, there are serious risks to a full-fledged US alliance with Thailand, if that is what is required to ensure its membership in the anti-hegemonic coalition. Thailand is separated from China only by weak Laos, Myanmar, and northern Vietnam. Accordingly, Thailand is relatively exposed to Chinese action along a land border, reducing the relative efficacy of US military forces. This makes an American alliance guarantee difficult to uphold. Thus, while the United States and other members of the anti-hegemonic coalition should seek to persuade Bangkok to join them, they should not be overly optimistic about Bangkok's doing so. Moreover, the United States should be very conservative about a full alliance relationship that obligates Washington to come to Thailand's defense.

Myanmar presents a strategic picture similar to Vietnam's, but from a lower power base. Myanmar has a strong tradition of independence and shares a long land border with China, but it is weaker than Vietnam, making its effective defense even harder. At the same time, however, Myanmar stands between China and the Indian Ocean; gaining use of Myanmar's territory could give Beijing reliable access to the Indian Ocean, with all its attendant advantages.[17] Accordingly, the United States and, given its proximity, India should be concerned about this and should seek to help Myanmar defend itself against Chinese action, but Washington should also be very conservative about extending an alliance guarantee to Yangon. As India grows in power, however, New Delhi might consider extending such an alliance guarantee, backed by US support.

Other states in Southeast Asia are already aligned with China or else too unimportant or too indefensible to make desirable additions to the anti-hegemonic coalition. Landlocked and weak Laos, for instance, will likely be unable to resist pressure from China, its direct neighbor along a land border.

Collective Defense

In addition to altering its defense perimeter, the United States can seek to integrate the efforts of its allies and partners toward the common goal of providing an effective defense of the most vulnerable US allies within the coalition—in other words, a true collective defense model. As noted before, the question is not whether this is desirable; the United States generally has an interest in its allies and partners collaborating to help defend other US allies, especially vulnerable ones. The question is how far to push the issue with allies and partners that may be resistant to doing so and that, in any case, may have limited ability to contribute to these efforts.

This issue is not highly relevant for most US allies and partners. It makes more sense for US allies in Europe to focus on defending Europe. Other countries outside Asia cannot project even negligible military power into the Western Pacific. And within Asia, most US allies and partners are better off ensuring their own effective defense because of their own limited capacity, military situation vis-à-vis China, or both. States like the Philippines, Vietnam, and Taiwan, which lack any meaningful capability to project power, will have their hands full ensuring they can contribute to their own effective defense. The same is probably true of Indonesia and Malaysia, if they joined the coalition. Singapore might be able to help a collective defense effort elsewhere, but its contribution would be small. South Korea has the ability to develop power projection forces but, as I will discuss later, should focus on providing for its own defense against North Korea and China.

As most states in the coalition will need to focus on their own defense, and because the United States has a critical interest in limiting the degree to which coalition members need to rely on it for their defense, Washington should provide all reasonable assistance to states seeking to defend themselves against Chinese attack or coercion, including those that are not US allies. The more stoutly these states can resist Chinese assault or coercion, the less likely they will be to fall under Beijing's sway and the less likely they are to need a formal

US alliance guarantee to participate in the coalition. Moreover, by providing all manner of defensive arms to these states, the United States and its allies and partners can demonstrate in the clearest way their interest in helping protect the sovereignty and independence of states in the region. It is unlikely that China will go to similar lengths, since doing so would undermine Beijing's ability to attain regional hegemony. This could only strengthen the coalition's hand in the regional competition with China.

This leaves Japan and Australia as states that could contribute significantly to the collective defense of a vulnerable ally such as Taiwan or the Philippines. Both are wealthy states with capable militaries that can develop relevant power projection capabilities.

Japan

Japan's role is critical. It is the world's third or fourth largest economy and at the very forefront of technological development. Yet it spends relatively little on defense. Given Japan's enormous unrealized military potential and geographic position along the US defense perimeter, it is simply vital that it increase its defense efforts.

Because of its location along the first island chain as the front line of the US defense perimeter within the anti-hegemonic coalition, Japan's first order of business is, alongside the United States and possibly other states such as Australia, to ensure the defense of Japan itself. Given the scale and sophistication of the Chinese military threat, Japan will now need to take a full role in its own defense in an integrated posture with the United States. This requires a significant change from its post–Second World War defense model, which entailed a high degree of demilitarization and an unequal reliance on the United States.

Given the size of the Japanese economy and its proximity to the most stressing scenarios for the US defense perimeter, however, Japan may also be able to allocate some efforts to preparing to aid the United States in mounting an effective defense of Taiwan, Japan's immediate neighbor to the south. This is not only of general utility to Japan, which is fundamentally reliant on the effective maintenance of the US alliance system in Asia, but also of direct military consequence for Japan. If China were able to subjugate Taiwan, it would gain unfettered access beyond the first island chain, substantially increasing Japan's vulnerability to Chinese military action. Tokyo can also plan to aid the US defense of the Philippines for comparable reasons, although those contributions are likely to be more attenuated given the greater distance of the Philippine archipelago from Japan.

Japan is, moreover, capable of this increased effort. It spends approximately 1 percent of its enormous GDP on defense—well below what the United States and China spend and far below what would reasonably be expected given Tokyo's own perception that it is seriously threatened by the growth of Chinese military power.[18] There is thus tremendous room for growth in Japan's contributions to defending both itself and the broader coalition.

Australia

Australia is a medium-sized but highly advanced economy with a significant military capability. It has a strong interest in a forward defense in the Western Pacific designed to sustain a functioning anti-hegemonic coalition. This is because, though it is distant from Taiwan and the Philippines, its fate is likely to be decided in the Western Pacific. A China that could dominate Southeast Asia would present the United States and any remaining coalition partners with a far more difficult power balance and consequently a far more painful, challenging, and risky effort to defend Australia. By leveraging bases in Southeast Asia, China could apply its focused strategy against Australia, presenting the United States with the exceptionally difficult military problem of helping to defend it. Although the United States did so in the Second World War, that defense was against a Japan that was far weaker relative to the United States than China would be. Australia thus has a strong interest in ensuring that the anti-hegemonic coalition checks China's focused and sequential strategy well before it reaches Australia's shores. The United States should therefore seek to enlist Canberra to prepare its forces to aid US efforts to defend the Philippines and Taiwan. Australia already appears to be moving in this direction.[19]

The Anti-Hegemonic Effort in Asia and Broader US Defense Strategy

As emphasized throughout this book, the key fundamental interest of the United States in the international arena is in preventing any other state from gaining hegemony over a key region of the world, and China in the Indo-Pacific is the only state that could plausibly pretend to this status in the foreseeable future. Preventing China from establishing such predominance must be the overriding priority for US strategy. If the United States and its allies and partners achieve this goal, other challenges will be manageable in an international system conducive to their interests; if they fail, all other challenges will pale in comparison to the consequences, and the management of those challenges will be subject to Chinese preferences rather than those of Americans and others in the coalition. This overriding interest must therefore be reflected across every aspect of the US armed forces and US defense planning, including the size, shape, composition, and readiness of the nation's armed forces, as well as the missions they are tasked to perform.

How, though, should this interest be related to and integrated with any other interests that the United States expects its armed forces to serve? This is a crucial question because, while China's pretensions to regional hegemony are America's primary geopolitical concern, they are not the only interest on which US defense strategy should focus.

Managing the Deadliest Threats

To return to the beginning of the book, Americans' core interests are in ensuring their security, freedom, and prosperity. Before they can address such goods as freedom and prosperity, however, they must first ensure their security from attacks that kill large numbers of Americans.

Perfect security is not the goal; it is neither possible nor consistent with the high value Americans attach to their freedom. Americans tolerate high murder and highway lethality rates rather than accept the consequences of policies that seek to eliminate them.[20] But there is a limit to the level of threat Americans will accept. Exactly where this limit falls is a matter of political debate because defending against threats involves trade-offs in terms of freedoms and resources. At a minimum, however, it is likely to mean securing the United States against attacks that kill hundreds and certainly thousands of Americans. The US defense establishment—and the national security establishment more broadly—should therefore ensure that the American people are adequately defended against this level of danger. What are these threats?

Pandemics

The most serious threat to human life is likely pandemic disease, as the Covid-19 pandemic has reminded us. It makes abundant sense for the American people to dedicate resources to ensuring a reasonable degree of protection from such diseases. Dealing with pandemics is not, however, principally a defense matter. Militaries are about the large-scale employment of lethal force; this has negligible utility against diseases that are neither susceptible to violent force nor intelligent—diseases cannot be coerced. Dealing with them, rather, is primarily a matter for public health—vaccines, medicine, hospital facilities, medical equipment, public hygiene, and the like. Military forces may assist in these functions, but doing so is not truly a military role unless such diseases are wielded deliberately by intelligent actors.

Moreover, pandemics do not put geopolitics on hold; power politics exists even during and after such outbreaks. They may even intensify geopolitical competition by distracting states' leaderships and changing power balances in ways that create opportunities for aggressive action. This means that, while effort and expense required to control the threat of pandemic disease may be very great, these efforts do not logically trade against national security requirements. Even if it may have fewer resources and less bandwidth for doing so, the United States will still need to plan for dealing with national security threats in a world of pandemic diseases.

Nuclear Deterrence

The most consequential plausible threat to the American people—in terms of the devastating consequences if it does happen—is the use of weapons of mass destruction against the United States. Any nation or entity that possesses a nuclear weapon could do the most grievous damage to the United States; it might also be able to achieve comparable damage with biological or possibly other novel weapons. The United States therefore needs a defense posture able to deal with the threat those who possess these weapons pose. Again, because perfect defense is impossible against the nearly infinite ways such weapons might be employed, deterrence is generally a critical element of any sensible strategy for dealing with the problem. And because of their unique destructiveness, promptness, and other advantages relative to biological weapons, nuclear weapons are a most suitable implement of deterrence against such a large-scale attack. Nonnuclear means of retaliation are also critical, however, to credibly deter lesser threats, given the political, reputational, and environmental problems a nuclear response could well generate.

In practice, this means that the United States should field a nuclear deterrent that can survive any plausible first strike, that is large and destructive enough in its effects to manifestly outweigh the benefits for any opponent of a large-scale attack, and that is discriminate enough to allow for effective employment in a limited war. The United States should ensure that its nuclear deterrent is sized and shaped to achieve this.

In particular, US nuclear forces should be able to destroy the most valued assets of any state that could wield such destructive force against Americans. This is important because it sets a relatively independent criterion for sizing and shaping US nuclear forces. Nuclear weapons ultimately deter and influence by the prospect of devastation of valued things. Naturally, divining what an opponent most values is an inherently subjective judgment, a matter of approximation, not of scientific certainty. Nonetheless, nuclear targeting has a long pedigree, and categories of such targets are well established in US strategic planning.[21] This means that American nuclear forces do not necessarily need to be greater or fewer than those of potential US opponents. Nor do all of them need to be ready on any given day. As long as they can survive, be mobilized, and achieve the effects designated, that level of effort should be sufficient.

A nuclear deterrent that meets this standard—especially one coupled with the conventional forces the United States would field under the defense strategy laid out in this book—would be well suited to deterring large-scale lethal attack by any even modestly rational actor. Any actor contemplating such an attack would face US armed forces capable of retaliating not only in the most destructive fashion but also discriminately, in ways adapted to the nature of the attack. This covers essentially all the relevant actors in the world.

Counterterrorism

But what of potential attackers whose rationality is not always susceptible to this type of deterrence? States very rarely fall into this category. A state, by definition, is an organized entity that has something it values and holds—territory and its citizenry. It essentially always has something that can be threatened, making it susceptible to coercion. States may value things differently, but they always care about something. This means that US nuclear and conventional military power offers a solid basis on which to deal with any state.

Individuals and groups, especially smaller groups, are not always so rational. Some people and groups may be willing to do enormous damage against Americans even knowing they will suffer grievous retaliation. We usually call these people terrorists. But the United States is not concerned to this degree with *all* terrorists. Rather, it is worried about those who might plausibly kill significant numbers of Americans, especially in international terrorist attacks.

This is, however, a relatively limited subset of terrorists. Many, if not most, of the world's terrorist organizations see little benefit to killing significant numbers of Americans, and whatever benefits they do see they consider less weighty than the costs and risks of undertaking such attacks. Groups like the Kurdistan Workers' Party, Basque Fatherland and Liberty, and the radical remnants of the Irish Republican Army tend to direct their violence toward local targets rather than the United States, both because they see striking at local targets as more likely to result in progress toward their goals and because attacking the United States is likely to bring down its wrath and risks worsening rather than improving the prospects of their achieving their goals. Even groups such as Hezbollah that have attacked Americans have often done so at least partly for local political reasons.[22]

Moreover, even among those groups that may see benefit in killing significant numbers of Americans, including through attacks on the United States itself—groups like al-Qaeda, the Islamic State of Iraq and Syria (ISIS), and their offshoots or affiliates—there are a number of factors limiting their interest and ability in doing so. Few such groups actually have or could realistically obtain the capability for a large strike. This is in significant part because any international terrorist attack is difficult to pull off. Law enforcement and intelligence services, international travel barriers, and restrictions on the availability of weaponry present significant barriers. Most terrorist organizations lack the personnel, resources, and sophistication required to overcome such obstacles and mount a large-scale attack. Inspiring attacks by individuals or smaller groups abroad can be easier, but those attacks also tend to be relatively small-scale.

A major terrorist attack on the United States is still possible, however, so continued vigilance is required to ensure that al-Qaeda, ISIS, and their potential successors are prevented from executing such an attack. But in an era of intensifying competition between the United States and China, that vigilance must be coupled with deliberate thinking about measures that not only deny terrorist organizations the ability to kill significant numbers of Americans but also allow for the strengthening of the US ability to defend allies in Asia against China.

There are opportunities to do this. The first is through coercion. Most terrorist organizations value something that the United States or others can damage or destroy, and they are therefore likely to be susceptible to coercion. So long as the United States can credibly threaten the things these organizations hold most dear, it should be able to persuade them not to try to kill significant numbers of Americans.[23] This should be possible even in the case of groups that may seek to kill significant numbers of Americans and may even have the ability to do so—or a credible chance of obtaining such an ability—so long as those groups have other interests or equities that they care about more than killing significant numbers of Americans. Such interests could include the lives of their leadership, control of territory, or certain political equities. So long as the United States can hold those targets at risk or otherwise influence them, there is reason to believe that these groups may be coercible. Moreover, it may not be necessary to coerce a whole group; rather, if parts of such groups can be deterred or coerced, that may be enough to hobble an attempted attack.

Importantly, this holds true not only for terrorist organizations whose motivations are immanent but also for those whose aims are transcendental; even these latter groups typically have earthly possessions or other interests that can be threatened. It is true as well of organizations that use suicide attacks. Although these groups might encourage or even order their foot soldiers to use such tactics, that does not necessarily mean that the organization's leaders or the groups as a whole are willing to sacrifice themselves in order to achieve their objectives. So long as they have something they value more than killing significant numbers of Americans, they should be coercible.

One cannot, however, predict with certainty that coercion will work against terrorist organizations considering attacks on Americans. There are and will be cases where deterrence simply will not work. Millenarian groups like Aleph (formerly known as Aum Shinrikyo) may be so focused on extramundane considerations that they are very difficult to coerce. And even in cases where a group's leadership might be susceptible to coercion, their subordinates may be less so and may act on their own.

The United States should therefore maintain the ability to prevent those organizations from planning, preparing for, and executing an attack to kill significant numbers of Americans, including by force if necessary.[24] Moreover, the United States should not be passive; aggressively targeting terrorist groups is often an effective method to keep them on their back foot.

But critically, the United States must do so as economically as possible so that the US military can protect the American people from international terrorism while simultaneously maintaining—or if necessary, restoring—a sufficiently powerful military capability against China in Asia. The United States has made progress in this regard over the past twenty years, including by shifting away from large-scale military interventions—which do not solve the terrorism problem and may make it worse—to smaller-footprint operations exploiting standoff capabilities and close cooperation with local partners to degrade or destroy terrorist organizations that have or may be able to secure an ability to kill significant numbers of Americans.[25] The United States should prioritize refining these more economical methods in order to sufficiently degrade or defeat terrorist threats using the least expensive and smallest number of forces possible. There has been some valuable work on how to do so, but more is needed to develop, refine, and implement such a more economical approach.[26]

The outlines of such an approach are discernible. The United States should first enable and incentivize local and regional actors to take the lead in the fight against terrorists operating out of these actors' own or proximate territory. In places where local and regional actors lack the resolve or ability to sufficiently degrade terrorists operating in their territory even with American help and encouragement, however, the United States must be prepared to act itself. But it should prioritize employing more cost-effective means to collect and analyze intelligence on terrorist groups, conduct strikes against them, and enable and execute limited ground operations against terrorist targets. This more economical approach should be feasible because terrorists lack the resources of a state like China. The United States does not need stealth aircraft to conduct strikes against terrorist groups or the highest-quality unmanned systems to conduct intelligence, surveillance, and reconnaissance against them. Rather, it can use more tailored, less expensive capabilities. These capabilities—such as light-attack aircraft and lower-cost unmanned aerial vehicles—should be treated as distinct from the broader set of conventional military capabilities the United States must develop and use, in combination with its nuclear forces, to deter or defeat Chinese aggression; capabilities for the counterterrorism mission should be developed specifically to deal with this threat, with a special focus on economy, rather than being a subset of conventional force operations. These military efforts must be coupled with continued development of law enforcement, intelligence, diplomatic, and other nonmilitary capabilities, in cooperation with other like-minded nations, to improve their shared ability to identify and intercept foreign attacks before they arrive on US shores or anywhere else where significant numbers of Americans might be vulnerable.[27]

Last, it is important to recognize in this context that much of the US force structure allocated to the Middle East in the past two decades has not been focused on preventing terrorist attacks on the United States as such. Rather, many—if not most—of these forces have been engaged in regime change operations against Iraq, in the nation-building and pacification efforts that followed, or in deterring Iran from attacking American interests. Some US forces in Afghanistan have been focused on counterterrorism, but others have concentrated on broader nation-building and pacification efforts. This means that the legacy US force presence in the Middle East is not the baseline for counterterrorism operations. This force could be smaller, likely significantly so, if scoped more narrowly on counterterrorism.

The Core Missions of the US Armed Forces

The core missions of the US armed forces should be to ensure an effective defense of allies in the anti-hegemonic coalition against China, maintain an effective nuclear deterrent, and deter or prevent large-scale lethal attacks against Americans, including terrorist attacks. In simplified terms, this breaks the US armed forces down into the nuclear arsenal, conventional forces, and the military counterterrorism enterprise. The nuclear arsenal and the counterterrorism enterprise are relatively self-contained demands that require only a relatively modest share of US defense efforts and resources. Over the 2020s, recapitalizing the US nuclear arsenal is expected to consume approximately 5–7 percent of the total defense budget. The United States spends something on the order of 15 percent of the defense budget on the counterterrorism enterprise—a significant fraction, but valuable given the importance of the mission.[28]

This means that the great bulk of US defense effort and resources go to the conventional forces, which are the primary mechanism for American deterrent and defense activities. While plenty of attention goes to the costs and demands on the other two missions, the main question for the nation in practical terms is what it should demand of its conventional forces. These are not purely military questions. Especially because of the expense involved, they are fundamentally political questions relating to how much importance the country is prepared to place on its defense. The Covid-19 pandemic and its economic consequences only throw these questions into sharper relief.

I have argued in this book that the United States should ensure that its conventional forces are able to effectively defend—in concert with other allies and partners—any US ally, however vulnerable. Because China is by far the most powerful state in the international system other than the United States and because the Indo-Pacific is the world's most important region, achieving this goal in the Indo-Pacific must be the priority for US conventional and, to the degree they are implicated, nuclear forces. The United States should therefore spend enough on defense to meet this standard.

The Issue of Simultaneity

The main question that follows for conventional force planning, then, is: Once this criterion has been satisfied, how much does the nation want to prepare for additional and particularly simultaneous contingencies? That is, what does the nation expect its military to do *in addition and at the same time* that it is conducting an effective denial defense of Taiwan or another threatened ally in the Western Pacific? This is important because simultaneity is a primary driver of the size, shape, and composition of military forces. If the nation believes that it can deal with threats sequentially, then it can address additional threats *after* having addressed the primary threat. But if it judges that it must be prepared to deal with multiple threats simultaneously, the armed forces must be sized, shaped, and postured accordingly.

Simultaneity is important because wars might break out concurrently, whether independently from one another or because, with the United States engaged elsewhere, other potential attackers see an opportunity. The United States simultaneously fought Germany and Japan in the Second World War, effectively requiring two separate sets of forces; conversely, it addressed what it considered a violation of the Monroe Doctrine in Mexico *after* the Civil War, deploying federal forces that had just defeated the Confederacy to pressure the French to withdraw from Mexico.[29] Britain wrestled with this issue in the years before the First World War. In the late nineteenth century, Britain faced multiple rivals in several theaters of its far-flung empire—not only Germany in Europe but France in Africa, the United States in the Western Hemisphere, Russia in

Central Asia, and Japan in East Asia—and conducted its military planning accordingly. In the years leading up to war, however, London increasingly recognized the primacy of the threat from imperial Germany. It settled its disputes around the world with each of its other rivals and altered the size, shape, and composition of its armed forces to focus on the threat from Germany in Europe.[30]

Once the United States has established that it can conduct an effective denial defense of Taiwan, sustain the nuclear deterrent, and maintain an effective counterterrorism enterprise, it is prudent for the United States to do two things. First, it should make *some* provision for a simultaneous conflict in one particular scenario: between NATO and Russia in Eastern Europe. This is the only plausible scenario in the contemporary international environment in which the United States, if it did not act simultaneously, might be unable to defeat a plausible adversary's theory of victory against an ally.[31] Second, the United States should maintain missile defenses sufficient to defeat an intercontinental missile attack by any state other than Russia or China.

No other contingency is sufficiently pressing to distract America's attention from these core missions. North Korea, Iran, Venezuela, and Cuba all have serious differences with the United States and some ability to do it harm. But each has substantial assets that can be attacked by the United States, which is far more powerful than any of them. This is a very strong basis for deterrence.

None of them, moreover, can present a plausible theory of victory against a US ally because none combines a survivable nuclear arsenal with conventional forces able to seize and hold any ally's key territory in the face of plausible resistance. There is thus no strict need for the United States to address the conventional threat from any of them simultaneously with conducting a denial defense of Taiwan. Once it has finished dealing with China in Asia, the United States and any engaged allies and partners could readily dislodge these states' forces from any gains and, if necessary, wreak tremendous punitive damage on them.

This is evident from an analysis of their military positions. North Korea, Iran, Venezuela, Cuba, and any other plausibly hostile states lack military forces that can even pretend to be able to conquer US allies. They therefore present no remotely conceivable scenario that might require handling simultaneously with an effective defense of Taiwan.

North Korea

North Korea has a large conventional military, but it is antiquated, even decrepit.[32] It should be expected to present exceptionally formidable resistance to an assault into North Korea. The United States, however, has no compelling strategic interest in conquering North Korea or changing its government. Although Washington might wish for a different form of government there, this desire is not a sufficiently compelling reason to justify an invasion.

The United States does, on the other hand, have an interest in the defense of its ally, South Korea. As discussed previously, the United States should retain its alliance with South Korea, and its differentiated credibility is therefore at stake in that nation's effective defense.

South Korea can, however, defend itself from a North Korean invasion on its own or with modest US support. South Korea has an economy of approximately two trillion dollars (PPP) and spends roughly 2.5 percent of its GDP on defense, in absolute terms more than twenty-five times what North Korea spends; the South Korean military also benefits from an advanced economy and access to US equipment and expertise.[33]

Because of this, South Korea could almost certainly defeat a North Korean invasion on its own. It could defend itself better, at lower cost and risk, with more significant US support—but the question is how much the United States strictly *needs* to contribute simultaneously to this effort alongside an extremely stressing war with China over Taiwan. The answer is that South Korea could essentially hold out on its own. Once the United States had prevailed against China, it could allocate resources to help defend South Korea against North Korea, but this effort should not detract from the US ability to defend Taiwan or another US ally—including South Korea itself—from China's focused strategy. The same logic would apply if a conflict with North Korea broke out while the United States was at peace with China; in this case Washington should ensure that its efforts against North Korea did not detract from its ability to meet this same standard. To emphasize, this would not be a *good* outcome, given the damage North Korea could inflict on parts of South Korea, but it would allow the United States to meet its basic commitments to US allies threatened by an exceptionally powerful China—including South Korea itself.

The main problem, however, is that North Korea has nuclear weapons. It could use these to threaten South Korea or even Japan and, absent an effective counter, might be able to use these weapons to coerce Seoul or Tokyo. Although the United States would benefit from the ability to preempt North Korea's nuclear forces, this would almost certainly be exceptionally difficult, if not practically impossible, to pull off.[34]

The United States, South Korea, and Japan do, though, have the option of relying on the US nuclear arsenal to deter North Korean attack. It is better for all three allies, however, if the United States is able to respond to any North Korean nuclear use without itself being vulnerable to a North Korean nuclear attack.

This is not merely a selfish US interest, assuming that all three states share a powerful interest in avoiding the need for South Korea or Japan to acquire an independent nuclear arsenal. In the event that North Korea could strike at the United States and sought to coerce Seoul or Tokyo, the United States would have to weigh its interest in defending South Korea and Japan from North Korea against its own enormous interest in avoiding nuclear attack. Moreover, American interests regarding North Korea are limited. On its own, North Korea cannot present a primary strategic challenge to America's core interest in preventing another state's hegemony over a key region, since Pyongyang has no prayer of being able to achieve hegemony in Asia. The cardinal strategic challenge North Korea poses is in its ability to weaken the anti-hegemonic coalition against China or if it becomes directly linked to China, as it was in 1950. If South Korea's or Japan's commitment or contributions to the anti-hegemonic coalition were weakened because of North Korea, then important US interests would suffer. This interest is, however, considerably more indirect than the threat posed by China.

As a result, the asymmetry of interests between North Korea and the United States over the Korean Peninsula could thus become significant. This is especially so because North Korea appears to have a very high pain tolerance; the government displays little regard for its subjects' well-being, raising the amount of damage and narrowing the set of targets the United States would need to be able to hold at risk in order to effectively deter or coerce Pyongyang. If North Korea could credibly threaten the United States with nuclear attack, a situation might arise in which North Korea could attempt a significant but still limited act of coercion or aggression against South Korea or Japan and seek to deter a sufficiently firm US response by threatening a nuclear strike against the United States itself, whether directly or as a result of things "getting out of hand" as a result of a forceful US response. The benefits of responding might appear too modest to Americans to justify risking such a painful consequence, potentially enabling North Korea to coerce South Korea or Japan. Seoul or Tokyo might find this situation exceptionally unsatisfying, jeopardizing relations with the United States and even their active participation in the anti-hegemonic coalition itself.

For these reasons, the United States—and South Korea and Japan, because of their reliance on an American nuclear deterrent—are all better off if Washington can confidently deny North Korea the ability to hit the United States with a nuclear weapon. In that circumstance, North Korea is likely to judge a US commitment to defend Japan and South Korea as more credible and thus is more likely to be deterred from precipitating such a course of action. The US ability to deny North Korea such an ability can involve a number of steps, including nonkinetic left-of-launch efforts. Realistically, however, the United States cannot be sure that preemptive measures will work, and it does not want to be forced to choose between acting either preemptively and comprehensively or not at all, since preemption heightens both the risk of error and the chance the United States will be seen as the aggressor.

Missile defenses, which try to deny missile attack once an opponent has launched them and thereby shown its intent, are therefore highly valuable. If the United States can confidently use missile defenses to deny North Korea the ability to attack America, Pyongyang's leverage over the United States, South Korea, and Japan will be distinctly limited, leaving all three states better off.

This is consistent with efforts to provide defenses for South Korea and Japan as well. Realistically, however, it will be much harder, if not impossible, to provide a perfect defense for them, given North Korea's much larger inventory of shorter-range missiles. Seeking a perfect defense would not only fail but consume far too large a proportion of Japan's and South Korea's defense efforts. Ultimately, Japan and South Korea are better off coupling limited missile defenses for their respective territories with reliance on US extended nuclear deterrence and an effective missile shield for the United States against North Korea.

The problem is that missile defenses are expensive and have an unfavorable cost-exchange ratio. They offer little prospect of blocking a large and sophisticated attack, such as could be launched by Russia or China. This means that a modest North Korean missile arsenal is manageable, but if Pyongyang's arsenal expands substantially and modernizes, it will cause a geometric rather than arithmetic increase in US costs and difficulties, which will trade against the US ability to defeat a Chinese assault against an ally in the Western Pacific.[35]

The United States should undertake an integrated approach to managing this problem. First, it should seek to inhibit as much as possible the maturation and growth of North Korea's long-range missile and nuclear arsenals. An important part of this may be linking the development of North Korea's arsenal with Chinese support and ensuring that China is properly incentivized to eliminate or at least minimize Pyongyang's access to the technology and other resources needed for this effort.[36] Second, the United States should seek to improve its missile defense systems while bending the cost curve back toward its favor, if possible.[37] Third, the United States and others can seek to engage North Korea diplomatically to try to stem the growth of its nuclear and missile arsenals.

If this integrated effort fails and North Korea's arsenal grows markedly, American missile defense costs may become so heavy as to jeopardize other core missions. In this case, the United States and its allies will have to weigh several courses of action. One is to rely more on US nuclear deterrence alongside missile defenses. It is important to remember that these defenses—like any defenses—do not need to be perfect to have an effect, though imperfection has far more severe consequences in nuclear than conventional war. Additionally, the United States and its allies might seek to tie North Korea's actions even more closely to China's, linking Beijing's interests much more closely to how Pyongyang behaves so as to discourage China from enabling North Korea's nuclear and missile programs.

If these courses prove insufficient and the costs threaten to detract from US core defense missions, the United States and its allies would have to consider friendly proliferation to South Korea, Japan, or both. Independent or semi-independent nuclear arsenals in Seoul's or Tokyo's hands would defeat North Korea's ability to exploit any divergence between its own willingness to run risks and US resolve. South Korea or Japan would then have their own means to retaliate against a North Korean nuclear attack, and the North is too poor to build the strike and missile defense architecture to block a South Korean or Japanese response. Such friendly proliferation would no doubt send out tremendous strategic reverberations, not least to China but also globally. These significant costs would have to be weighed against those of the alternative.

The point for US defense strategy is that, if affordable, on top of its core missions the United States should seek to maintain missile defenses sufficient to deny a North Korean ability to strike the United States with a nuclear weapon.

Iran

There is no need for the United States to address a threat from Iran simultaneously to conducting a denial defense of Taiwan and maintaining its strategic deterrent, counterterrorism enterprise, and missile defenses. Iran's conventional military is large and would present a formidable opponent if the United States wished to invade and occupy Iran, but doing so is not necessary to any US strategic interest and would almost certainly be a monumental and expensive mistake as well as a likely failure. Iran's conventional forces, meanwhile, do not pose a very significant threat of being able to seize the territory of such US regional partners as Kuwait, Saudi Arabia, and the United Arab Emirates. Their forces alone would stand a decent chance of repelling an Iranian invasion of one of these states. More to the point, even if Iranian forces did seize partner territory, US forces hold a commanding mastery over Iran's with respect to the Gulf states' territory and could readily expel and devastate any Iranian forces *after* defeating China over, for instance, Taiwan.[38] The United States could couple this expulsion of Iranian occupying elements with a punishing retaliatory campaign, which would add a large cost to Iran on top of the denial of its objectives. The same logic would hold true if a conflict with Iran broke out while the United States was at peace with China. But, as with North Korea, in such circumstances the United States should be sure that any efforts against Iran did not compromise its ability to defend Taiwan or another US ally in Asia.

Although Iran also possesses or directs substantial proxy and other unconventional forces able to strike at and harass US partners, these forces could not seize partner territory in any way that the United States could not reverse after having prevailed in a Taiwan contingency—and it is critical to emphasize that this is the standard US forces must meet, not ending Iranian strikes or harassment. That said, the United States can seek to mitigate its partners' vulnerability to such strikes or harassment through, for instance, the sale of missile defenses, hardening equipment, and training in dispersal. It can also encourage other states—especially those outside of Asia, such as the United Kingdom, France, and other European states—to play a larger role in helping regional partners defend themselves from Iranian strikes and harassment.

Iranian acquisition of a nuclear arsenal would complicate but not fundamentally change this calculus. The United States and other states rightly strive mightily to prevent Iran from acquiring a nuclear weapon. So long as the United States has the ability to defend its own territory against Iran's ability to deliver such a weapon, American resolve to respond to Iranian employment of any nuclear weapons it might attain is likely to be high—and thus its extended nuclear deterrent credible. In such a circumstance, the United States could retaliate with devastating force against Iran if it used nuclear weapons against, for instance, Israel or Saudi Arabia. Accordingly, if Iran were to obtain nuclear weapons, the United States should, as in the case of North Korea, take all reasonable and affordable steps to ensure that it possesses sufficient defenses to deny Iran any offensive benefit from such acquisition. It should especially deny Iran the ability to hit the United States with a nuclear weapon; cost permitting, these defenses would ideally be added to rather than combined with any defenses allocated toward North Korea.

Russia

The one scenario for which the United States might reasonably make provision for simultaneous action is a potential Russian attack on NATO member states in Eastern Europe. The reason is twofold. First, unlike any potential US adversary other than China, Russia does have a plausible way by which it could seize and hold the key territory of a US ally even in the face of US resistance. Second, Europe is one of the key regions of the world.

The fundamental stake at issue for the United States is denying Russia or any other state hegemony over Europe. No state—including Russia—has any realistic prospect of attaining predominance over Europe for the foreseeable future, in part because there is already an anti-hegemonic alliance there: NATO. The United States therefore has a potent interest in the maintenance of this alliance and thus in the effective defense of its member states.

NATO has, however, grown much larger than is necessary to achieve the goal of denying another state regional hegemony over Europe. Today it encompasses most of the European continent, including all of its large states except for Russia and Ukraine. Measured solely by membership, it boasts much more

than a favorable regional balance of power in Europe vis-à-vis Russia, something closer to an overwhelming preponderance. It could be considerably
smaller and still fulfill the fundamental task of denying another state hegemony
over Europe.

This means that, from an American point of view, NATO could lose members
and still perform its core function. Some NATO states, moreover, are difficult
to defend. But the critical issue is that withdrawing alliance commitments is
much more problematic than never making them in the first place. Accordingly,
withdrawing commitments from some NATO states would surely have significant reverberations; even more, failing to mount an effective defense of member states could undermine the alliance's differentiated credibility, possibly
enough to cause it to fissure or even break apart.

Consequently, although the alliance has room to give in terms of its power
margin over Russia, it also must consider the implications of withdrawing commitments from existing members. The question, then, is whether existing member states can be defended at a tolerable cost while the United States and other
allies are fighting or preparing to fight a war in the Pacific, and consistent with
the primary US interest in upholding the anti-hegemonic coalition in Asia. If
they can be defended under those conditions, it makes sense to keep the alliance
in its current form. If they cannot, it would be more sensible to redraw NATO's
defense perimeter to be consistent with this standard.

This is a pointed question because although Russia's precise intentions with
respect to NATO are unclear, there do appear to be circumstances in which Moscow might be willing to use military force against the alliance. Russia has been
willing to use military force against other states in recent years, including in
Ukraine since 2014. And Moscow regards NATO as hostile, a mechanism for
spreading Western ascendancy into Russia's traditional zone and a means of
weakening and even dismembering the country. Moscow accordingly appears to
want to weaken the alliance or even break it apart. Undermining NATO, Moscow appears to assess, would lessen the political and military threat the West
poses to Russia's sovereign integrity as well as open up space for Russia to exercise more influence, and possibly hegemonic control, in what Moscow views
as its "near abroad."[39] By seizing and holding allied territory, Moscow could undercut the alliance's differentiated credibility and move toward this goal.

Russia's plausible theory of victory against NATO is a fait accompli strategy
rooted in its proximity to the alliance's easternmost members and its possession

of sophisticated conventional forces as well as a large and varied nuclear arsenal. It does not have the practical ability to seize and hold noncontiguous NATO territory in the face of allied opposition; Moscow could not plausibly project such power across a resistant Ukraine or the Black Sea to seize and hold, for instance, Romania or Bulgaria.

Northeastern NATO is different. Here Russia directly borders the Baltic states and Poland, and Moscow enjoys a substantial local conventional military superiority over the Baltics and possibly at least parts of Poland. This is due to several factors. One is the weakness of the small Baltic states, whose militaries pale in comparison to Russia's. A second is geography. These countries occupy a narrow strip of territory sandwiched between Russia and the Baltic Sea; forces placed there are more vulnerable to attack—especially surprise attack—from Russia. A third is the thinness of the broader allied defense posture in Eastern NATO, a result of the alliance's decisions not to build up its defense posture in the states NATO added after the Soviet Union's collapse. Although NATO has strengthened its defenses in the east in recent years, Russia still may be able to generate local superiority, and possibly a significant degree of it.[40]

As a consequence, Russia could rapidly move its conventional forces into the Baltic states, very likely overrunning NATO forces and conceivably doing so very quickly. Russian forces could then harden and fortify their positions, integrating them with neighboring Russian battle networks in Russia proper as well as the Kaliningrad exclave, raising the costs of a NATO counterattack from the west. If allied forces are ill prepared to engage the Russians quickly, such a counterattack could take substantial time to mount, especially in the context of a simultaneous US conflict with China. And any such delayed counterassault would almost certainly need to be large and ferocious in order to expel the entrenched Russian defenders from their positions. Russian forces would have had substantial time to develop sophisticated and resilient defenses using the natural advantages of the ground and the closeness of Russia's own territory.[41]

Moscow could not, however, rely solely on its conventional forces for such a gambit to work. Russia is enormously overmatched in conventional forces by the North Atlantic Alliance, and even by the United States alone. Russian conventional forces would be formidable and extract a high cost in a purely conventional defense, but Moscow has to expect that this effort would almost certainly fail. Given the stakes, NATO—and possibly such friendly nonmembers as Sweden and Finland—would almost certainly follow through on the liberation of the occupied member states if only conventional forces were at issue.

Nuclear forces would therefore be key to any Russian theory of victory. Russia's nuclear weapons, which rival those of the United States in size and sophistication and exceed them in variety and applicability to the battlefield, could enable Moscow to threaten to inflict costs on the alliance far out of proportion to the stakes at issue. But as discussed previously, the primary challenge to employing nuclear weapons for coercive leverage in situations of mutual vulnerability is that their use must appear plausibly sensible in light of the nuclear retaliation that can be expected to follow. If using these weapons seems clearly irrational in light of these consequences, then the threat of their employment will not appear very credible and thus is unlikely to matter much.

But Russian use of its nuclear weapons *could* appear sensible and thus credible if the conflict unfolded in a certain way. Because of NATO's preponderance of power over Russia and because of the scale of the counterassault the alliance would have to mount to eject entrenched Russian forces from Eastern NATO territory, Russia would need to dedicate a great proportion—perhaps the bulk—of its forces, and certainly its best, to defend what it had just taken. To defeat and eject such an entrenched Russian force, NATO would very likely have to overwhelm it. Yet in doing so, the alliance could plausibly seem to imperil Moscow's ability to defend Russia proper, given the proximity of the Baltics and eastern Poland to key Russian territory.

Once the alliance had broken the back of Russia's forces in Eastern Europe and possibly Western Russia, what, Moscow might wonder, would stop them from going farther, perhaps exploiting Russia's defeat by dictating political terms that would infringe on Russia's own sovereignty, at least as Moscow understood it? NATO might deny any such aspirations, but would Moscow believe such protestations, especially given that war aims can so readily change during a conflict? To Russian decision-makers—and to those wondering how they might act—such a set of circumstances might appear to make deliberate nuclear escalation a less unattractive option for Russian decision-makers than conventional defeat and relying on the alliance's clemency. In a sense, the strength of Russia's strategy would lie in its weakness—its vulnerability if its forces defending its gains in the Baltics and Eastern Poland were to be ejected. Without this fundamental weakness, Russia's threat to escalate would not, paradoxically, seem so credible.[42]

Given these realities, in the face of an allied counterassault Moscow might credibly threaten to escalate to nuclear employment against NATO. Russia might pick any number of different strategies and targets from the enormous menu of options afforded by its nuclear arsenal, but the basic logic would likely be what is commonly referred to, at least in the West, as an *escalate to de-escalate* (or *escalate to terminate*) strategy.[43] Under this logic, Russia would seek to prevail by daring the West to follow it up the nuclear ladder while eroding NATO's conventional military advantages through selective nuclear employment. In such circumstances, NATO would face a most powerful incentive to stop. As discussed earlier, while there is no precedent for such a situation, it seems most likely that it would resolve by forces halting more or less in place—which would mean a Russian victory, with major repercussions for the alliance.

Fortunately for the United States and NATO, there is a clear way to defeat Russia's theory of victory, and the alliance has a superabundance of resources to do so. This is not primarily about nuclear forces. Russia's nuclear forces are very large; even if Moscow were willing to reduce them, the reduction is unlikely to diminish its ability to use the arsenal for an escalate to terminate strategy in these circumstances.

The critical element in Russia's theory of victory that NATO can most readily redress is its local conventional force advantages, and specifically its ability to seize and hold allied territory. Assuming that nuclear brinkmanship contests are most likely to end in a halt in place, the crucial thing is to ensure that Moscow cannot seize and hold allied territory. This is the sine qua non of Russia's theory of victory; without an ability to hold allied territory, Moscow's escalate to terminate strategy would not gain it much.

Accordingly, the alliance needs a force posture that can deny a Russian fait accompli against the Baltics and Eastern Poland. This means allied and partner forces that can contest a Russian assault from the outset of hostilities and, most important, not allow Russia the let-up that it could use to consolidate its hold on any seized territory. NATO allies could use either one of the denial options laid out previously to achieve this goal; that said, given the topography—including the lack of major land features between Russian and allied territory—denying Russia the ability to consolidate its hold on seized territory is likely to be more attractive. The key, however, is to ensure the ability to sustain a denial defense such that, at a minimum, the Russians would have to mount a much larger assault to try to overcome it, reducing their probability of success in the first place but also undercutting their contention that they would be acting defensively and thus the credibility of any nuclear threats they might issue. This would undermine their theory of victory.

Properly postured and readied ground and air forces as well as their key enablers are likely to be crucial for achieving this standard. Such forces need not be postured far forward or fixed in place like a new Maginot Line. Rather, a growing body of analysis suggests that they can be mobile and flexible—indeed, this will make them more resilient and survivable—but they need to be ready to move forward swiftly to contest Russian advances. Fortunately, the United States and NATO as a whole have made considerable progress in recent years in rectifying gaps in their defense posture in the East through more realistic and larger exercises, improved readiness, and posture enhancements.[44]

This strategy, however, needs to be considered in a broader context. Russia poses a serious threat to NATO, but this threat is both more tractable and less consequential than the threat China poses in the Indo-Pacific. Accordingly, the United States should give the first priority to making sure it is able to mount an effective defense of Taiwan or another ally in the Western Pacific above any efforts to defend Eastern NATO. It should make provision to help defend Eastern NATO *only* once it is assured that its denial defense of an ally in the Western Pacific will succeed.

It also means that, should a war break out with Russia in Europe, the United States should be sure that it maintains the ability to conduct a denial defense of Taiwan or another ally against China in the Western Pacific. This is critical because Beijing might take advantage of the opportunity afforded by a war in Europe to advance toward regional hegemony by conducting attacks on one or more US allies in Asia. Because China is so much more formidable and its actions are so much more consequential, the United States must ensure that it can defeat China's theory of victory *even* if Russia has acted first.

Indeed, the most stressing variant of such a simultaneous war scenario—and thus the one most relevant to the development, posturing, and readying of the force—would likely be a simultaneous conflict with China and Russia in which the Russia conflict emerged first, since Moscow's claims to be acting defensively and thus reasonably would ring far hollower if it attacked NATO while the United States was engaged in a war with China. Such a move would be likely to appear opportunistic rather than forced on Moscow; it would thus very likely legitimate a much fiercer and resolute NATO response, diminishing any

Russian theory of victory that relied on a perception of Moscow's reasonableness and defensive goals.

A contingency in which conflict with Russia broke out first, followed by war with China, thus presents the most serious challenge to US defense planning. This contingency is manageable, though, for one reason in particular: the NATO allies, as well as other states concerned by the potential for a Russian attack, such as Finland and Sweden, have the wherewithal to address it.[45] In simplest terms, these countries are together overwhelmingly richer, larger, and stronger than Russia, and if adequately prepared, they could readily defeat a Russian assault into NATO with much less American involvement than they currently depend on. America's NATO allies constitute almost fifteen times the GDP of Russia and spend four times what Moscow allocates to defense.[46] Even providing a substantial discount because of European demilitarization after the Cold War and Russia's cohesion as a unitary actor, non-US NATO still enjoys a very significant power advantage over Moscow. These countries along with plausible European partners could readily supply most if not the great proportion of the forces needed for an effective denial defense of Eastern NATO. Indeed, increased defense efforts by Poland alone in recent years promise to diminish Moscow's ability to conduct a successful fait accompli strategy in the East.[47]

Much of the issue in Europe is really about Germany. Germany is, as noted earlier, by far Europe's largest economy and its most important state. Yet it spends a small fraction—in 2018, 1.2 percent of GDP—on defense, and what it does spend yields little military capability that would be relevant to a contest with Russia. This is a historical anomaly—since 1989, not 1945. In 1988, a West Germany two-thirds the size of the current Federal Republic fielded twelve divisions along its border with East Germany, with three more in ready reserve. Today the reunited nation can barely field a pale shadow of that force.[48] Germany is therefore highly capable of contributing a great deal more to NATO's collective defense than it currently does, and given its wealth and sophistication, its doing so would make an enormous difference. If Germany today provided even a fraction of the capability that a smaller West Germany provided for alliance defense in 1988, the Russian fait accompli strategy would be seriously dented, if not denied. This would also allow smaller states to integrate their forces into Germany's within NATO; for instance, Danish, Dutch, Belgian, Italian, and even British and French contributions would benefit from being able to interoperate with more significant German forces.

A more robust effort by Germany and other relevant European states would enable a sound strategic approach by the United States and its allies to simultaneous conflicts against China in Asia and Russia in Europe. In these circumstances, European and whatever US forces could reasonably be made available might be able to halt a Russian assault against Eastern NATO outright; but, if not, these forces could focus on blunting a Russian attack, forcing Moscow to mount a larger campaign to succeed and keeping the fight going sufficiently to deny Moscow's attempt at a fait accompli. Once the United States had defeated the Chinese attack on a US ally in the Western Pacific and achieved a level of assurance that it could free up forces from that conflict, the United States could swing those forces to help defend the alliance and eject Russian forces from whatever ground they had gained.

This approach assumes that other European NATO allies will assume a considerably greater role in Eastern member states' defense. This is not a question of capacity; Europe is fully capable of assuming a much greater fraction of collective defense for NATO. It is a matter of will. NATO Europe, which maintained a stout military during the Cold War, substantially demilitarized after the collapse of the Soviet Union because it faced no meaningful threat. Now, however, Russia poses a significant threat to the alliance in the East, while the United States must focus on its essential role as the external cornerstone balancer on China and the Indo-Pacific.

But will they? Europeans—or at least some Europeans, including important ones like the Germans—should ultimately be willing to do so. Europe's reduction in defense effort after the Cold War was logical. Increased defense spending in this period would not have materially increased Europeans' security. The collapse of the USSR removed the main threat to NATO European security, and in its wake, the United States elected to sustain higher levels of defense spending and maintained an enormous military advantage over any plausible opponent, including Russia.

But conditions have changed. Russia has restored its ability to use military force against European NATO and has demonstrated its willingness to use its armed forces to take and hold territory and undermine neighboring states. China, meanwhile, is rapidly growing in military capability; dealing with it will by necessity absorb a greater share of US attention and resources.

In this context, Europeans have a choice. They can continue to spend little on defense, calculating that the Russians are not sufficiently dangerous to justify greater exertions or that NATO's Eastern states can safely be lost without too much decrement to the security of the Alliance's traditional core members. Or they might wager that the Americans are bluffing about greater burden-sharing, as they have in the past; a European decision not to do more might therefore be a calculated decision to free ride, based on the Europeans' confidence in Washington's unwavering commitment to their security.

Regardless of the rationale, a decision to avoid increased defense effort by Europeans would carry substantial costs and risks. Most pointedly, the United States might very well not fill the gap in Eastern NATO left by any European unwillingness to strengthen their own defense efforts. Indeed, my argument in this book is that the United States *should not* plug these gaps. If China succeeds in its focused and sequential strategy in Asia, it can establish hegemony over the world's most important region. If Russia succeeds in a fait accompli in Eastern Europe, it will call NATO into question and open the East to Moscow's predominance, but it will not be able to dominate the wealthiest parts of the continent.

Thus if compelled to face such a choice by European unwillingness to shoulder more of the defense burden, the United States must first ensure an effective defense of its allies in the anti-hegemonic coalition against China. And to do so effectively it must not spend too much on defense, since this could impair its economic prospects, the foundation of its long-term strength and thus its security. This puts a cap on how much the United States can allocate to European defense on top of its efforts in Asia. In such a situation, Washington might well then pursue the same tack the Europeans themselves had previously taken, assuming that in such a circumstance Germany would rearm to defend itself against a more powerful and emboldened Russia, which would deny Russia's ability to move farther west.

This would, of course, be an awful outcome. It would imperil European stability and could reopen the continent to an aggressive, overt form of power politics it has not seen in decades. A better choice for Europeans would be to spend more on defense and spend it more effectively, developing forces that, along with US elements, can effectively deny a Russian fait accompli attempt against Eastern NATO. Much preliminary evidence suggests that Europe is moving slowly and fitfully in this direction. Germany, however, remains the major outlier, and it should be the primary focus of US and Allied efforts to reconcile its obligations with its defense efforts.

Eastern NATO can, then, be effectively defended at a reasonable cost by a combination of greater European investment and adapted efforts and posture within NATO. This means that there are insufficient grounds to risk the alliance's cohesion by expelling the Baltic states from NATO. Doing so would signal a serious weakness at the core of NATO and would be more costly than beneficial.

At the same time, US strategy should focus on setting the conditions for a different relationship with Russia. The United States and the anti-hegemonic coalition would benefit substantially if Russia does not become too closely aligned with China and would benefit even more if Moscow inclined more toward the coalition. Enabling such a shift in the US-Russia relationship is compatible with more effective defenses against Russian action in the West, so long as it is clear that the US and allied strategy is focused on fortifying NATO's *defensive* position in Europe. To that point, the military strategy laid out here emphasizes the defense of NATO territory through a limited war—*not* the development or deployment of forces to invade Russia, forcibly change its government, decapitate its leadership, or disarm its strategic forces. By making clear both US restraint and the futility of trying to undermine NATO, this approach should reduce Moscow's interest in focusing its attention and efforts westward and allow it to take a clearer view of the substantial threat to its autonomy from China. This does not demand a full rapprochement or alignment of Moscow's perspective with those of the United States and Europe; it requires only a shift in balance and approach. Even a Russia that adopted a more moderate, less threatening position toward Europe while focusing more on checking Chinese power would be a significant boon to the anti-hegemonic coalition in Asia.[49]

Ultimately, issues of simultaneity highlight the fundamental question of how much resources to dedicate to national defense. Strategies and strategic choices cost money; in Bernard Brodie's phrase, they wear a dollar sign.[50] More ambitious strategies are generally more expensive. It is possible that the nation will agree to provide substantial additional resources for defense beyond the 3–4 percent of GDP allocated in recent decades.[51] Such an increase may be prudent if international circumstances materially worsen, particularly if China significantly increases its spending on military forces.

The nation's defense strategy should not, however, demand unusually high levels of spending on the military unless they are truly necessary. Even on strategic grounds, outside of research and development, money spent on defense is generally not invested as productively as it might be if invested in the civil economy; it is better for the nation's long-term strength—including military might—for spending to go elsewhere.[52] Moreover, money used for defense is not consumed by the citizenry, and if the purpose of US strategy is to promote not only Americans' security but their freedom and prosperity as well, Americans should not be unduly inhibited from allocating as much of the fruit of their work as feasible to consumption, charity, social services, or other purposes.

This means that the US defense establishment should seek to prune as many noncritical missions and activities as possible before demanding significant additional resources. Significant additional resources may be necessary to achieve the core necessary missions of the US armed forces, especially if China increases its own spending on the PLA. But the US government should first ensure that the money already allocated to it is spent as efficiently and rationally as possible. This means ceasing to buy or do things that do not clearly and efficiently contribute to one of the critical missions of the US armed forces outlined earlier.

What If the Strategy Is Too Much to Bear?

This book focuses on how America and its allies and partners can prevent China from realizing its goal of regional hegemony. What if, however, the demands of the approaches laid out here are too much for Americans to bear?

This could happen for several reasons.

Perhaps the most straightforward is that Americans may not be convinced that taking a leading role in denying another state hegemony over a distant region, however key, is worth the sacrifice and risk entailed. Such a development is more likely the stronger China is, since an effective defense of vulnerable allies in the anti-hegemonic coalition would then be more difficult as well as more costly and risky for the United States. It is therefore critical that the United States and others in the anti-hegemonic coalition maintain their economic vitality as much as possible in order to avoid such an outcome.

Americans are also more likely to turn away from this effort if other coalition members—especially allies, given the particular demands this strategy levies on America for their effective defense—do not pull their weight, whether through tending to their own defense, aiding others', or both. This situation would also increase the demands on Americans, who might begin to ask themselves—not unjustly—whether the effort is worth the costs and risks, if people in the region itself do not fear Chinese dominance enough to strive to counteract it. If the nations Americans are preparing to defend at such great risk can survive Chinese hegemony over their region, this might be seen to lend strength to the argument that perhaps Americans can too. A reasonably equitable sharing of burdens among the coalition states—and especially US allies within it—is therefore essential. Given Japan's importance, position, and very low levels of defense spending, this issue is especially pointed for Tokyo. Its decisions on this matter are likely to have outsized implications for the entire anti-hegemonic coalition.

That said, America has a far greater interest in denying China's regional hegemony than in equity among alliance members. It is the divergence in gravity between these interests that makes efforts to promote equitable burden-sharing so difficult and yet so important.[53] The less allies do, however, the more they will test not only the resilience of America's commitment to denying China hegemony over Asia but its ability to do so. China will almost certainly be so powerful that even with a very high degree of American effort and focus, a much greater effort from states like Japan will be essential. Moreover, states do not always make the best decisions; lassitude by other coalition members, especially allies, will tempt Americans to make an ill-advised decision to disengage from Asia or simply not commit enough to the effort, to the detriment of all who share this profound interest.

For the same reason, the United States must avoid becoming entangled in peripheral wars that sap American will and power, exhausting the US public and making the contest in the central theater of Asia even more direly competitive. Americans are more likely to decide that the benefits are not worth the costs and risks in such circumstances. Accordingly, it is crucial that the United States use its military instrument judiciously. Americans' strength and resolve should be husbanded for the primary challenges, above all China in the Western Pacific, lest they flag or be weakened beyond what is necessary for success in the central theater. Calls to use military force for anything but these primary challenges should thus receive a highly skeptical review and generally be resisted.

Friendly Nuclear Proliferation

If the American people do not want to make the effort needed for an effective defense of their allies, they have two options: they can accept Chinese regional hegemony or tolerate (or even encourage) some proliferation of nuclear weapons to US allies and partners. I outlined the demerits of the first earlier.

Some of the demerits of the second are well known. A world in which more states have nuclear weapons is probably a considerably more dangerous one. Although some prominent scholars have argued that general nuclear proliferation would produce a more stable world, this idea has had little purchase outside the academy.[54] A world in which many states have nuclear weapons might contribute to deterrence among them, but it would also contain more, and more complex, relationships among nuclear weapons states, more opportunities for accident or error, and more drivers for cataclysm. Whereas general proliferation might promote some level of stability, then, it would come at an extraordinarily high level of risk.

And widespread proliferation might not prove as stabilizing as these scholars have suggested, because it might not be quite as potent a deterrent as its advocates think. It is true that nuclear weapons introduce a fundamentally different level of caution for any prospective attacker, but they do not wholly suspend the rules of logic and reason. States that have nuclear weapons facing a nuclear-armed opponent know that the surest way to invite the most devastating nuclear blow is to launch a nuclear attack. They have the most powerful reasons to avoid such an outcome, even when their territorial integrity is at stake. In other words, even a state at risk of invasion has the strongest incentives to avoid a nuclear reprisal; occupation or even conquest, especially if partial, may be preferable to destruction. This is especially so when a small state faces a large one, such as China, that has a larger and more sophisticated arsenal and likely significant missile defense capabilities.[55] This dynamic is only more pronounced when what is at stake is the partial loss of territory or autonomy; nuclear war may be a tenable option when the alternative is total devastation or enslavement, but less so when it means the loss of a few provinces or submission to hegemony.[56] Nuclear weapons are not, therefore, a panacea. Their proliferation would complicate and hamper China's ability to establish hegemony over the Indo-Pacific but would not necessarily defeat it.

That said, selective nuclear proliferation might, rather than supplant the anti-hegemonic coalition's defense, strengthen it, in particular by making the binding strategy more effective. This could be especially relevant if China were able to attain commanding conventional military superiority over the coalition or important parts of it. In such an eventuality, a binding strategy confined to conventional forces might not suffice, since China might be able to overcome even a consolidated coalition conventional defense and pick apart its members.

Coalition members might then turn to the United States to compensate for this conventional military inferiority with the threat of first use of its nuclear forces. Because China would have immense ability to respond to US first use with nuclear reprisals against the United States itself, however, Americans would have the most powerful reasons for restraint. China might reckon that it could induce US nuclear restraint while salami-slicing away Washington's Asian allies and partners.

Selective nuclear proliferation to such states as Japan, South Korea, Australia, and even Taiwan might help bridge the gap between regional conventional defeat and US willingness to employ its nuclear forces, especially at scale. In this world, Chinese victory in a conventional war against the United States and its allies might transgress the interests of one of these nuclear-armed regional allies enough to prompt its nuclear use against China to defend its territory. That would likely trigger a Chinese response, including against US forces fighting alongside those of the embattled ally, which in turn would be more likely to catalyze American nuclear use to prevent the full collapse of its allies' position. Such a posture would likely make the anti-hegemonic coalition's deterrent posture more formidable. Indeed, selective nuclear proliferation of this sort to the United Kingdom and France is judged by many to have contributed to NATO's deterrent posture during the Cold War, when the Soviets enjoyed conventional superiority in Europe. This is, in fact, NATO's official stance.[57]

Nonetheless, the perils of proliferation make this option a last resort. Far preferable is an effective conventional defense backed by, but not primarily reliant on, the nuclear forces of the United States. That standard will be hard and costly to attain, and it will require sustained focus and discipline—but the alternatives are worse.

12

A Decent Peace

THIS IS A BOOK ABOUT WAR: what it would look like and how to wage it to prevail. Its unabashed aim is to give the United States and those who ally and partner with it a strategy for doing just that.

But it is written in the hope of peace. War is a great evil. It visits death, destruction, and suffering on civilians old and young, as well as on people in the military ranks who no more deserve to die than anyone else.

Americans and those who league with them could try to avoid risking such evils by forfeiture of the just goods they rightly prize—their security, freedom, and prosperity. But giving up these great goods would be a greater wrong than trying to secure them. So Americans and those aligned with them are right to strive for the kind of peace that respects these just interests: a decent peace.

Yet a decent peace is a paradox. It is not a naturally generating phenomenon but a willed and created thing. Not all people or states are wholly pacific, nor do they all see things the same way. Some long only for peace, but others are fearful, jealous, ambitious, or domineering enough that they are prepared to fight to get their way. Wanting a good peace is not the same thing as achieving it.[1] Hence the old saw that the best way to preserve peace is to prepare for war.

The depth of what that truism demands is often lost. It is one thing to prepare in some technical sense for war—to buy weapons or raise troops. But those weapons and troops must be readied and, if necessary, employed in ways that convince those fearful, ambitious, or domineering states that the game is not worth the candle and that they are better off accepting a tolerable peace than suffering defeat or intolerable loss. Such employment can only be the result of reckoning with what a war would look like and deliberate, hard thought about how to fare well enough in it.

Peace, then, does not come from some unfocused readiness to be unpeaceful but only from a willingness to imagine and consider what a war would actually be like. Only from this basis can a way to act in such a war be charted out, a way that will show others contemplating violating a decent peace that it is not worth the cost and risk. Thus that decent peace we seek is the product of a reckoning with the unpeaceful. For the armed forces, this means a warlike temperament and professionalism, a willingness to train and act always as if they are on the brink of war to refine and show their readiness. For leaders and strategists, it is the willingness to think that war is always possible and something which they are prepared to embark on, combined with the moral imagination to contemplate the terrible in order to avoid it. Those who treasure a decent peace must act this way, because a refusal to countenance conflict is as—indeed perhaps more—likely as bellicosity to lead to war.

As for the strategy I have laid out here, the proof of its ultimately peaceful intentions is this: it does not ask of anyone, including China, anything that they cannot nobly and with dignity give. This is a book about war, but it is about fighting a war to prevent China or anyone else from dominating a key region of the world. It is not anti-Chinese but is written with very high respect for China and long personal and familial experience with it. All it asks of China is that it leave aside any pretensions to hegemony over Asia. China could proudly live in a world in which this strategy had succeeded; it would be one of the greatest nations of the world, and its preferences and views would command respect. It would not be able to dominate, but neither would the United States or anyone else be able to dominate it.

Success for this strategy would be a decent equilibrium for all. For the United States, the result would be an Asia with which it could trade and interact without having to obtain a by your leave from Beijing—and with it, the likelihood of a secure, free, and prosperous future. For China, it would be a world in which it was honored and respected. For the peoples of the region, it would mean the autonomy and independence for which they have striven so mightily since freedom from colonial rule.

This might very well be a tense peace, but it would be peace all the same, and consistent with America's security, freedom, and prosperity. In the world produced by the success of this strategy, it is entirely plausible that the

United States and China would never come to blows, despite the structural tendencies pressing hard in that direction. But this good outcome would be the result of America's preparedness to countenance sacrificing peace in order to preserve it.

NOTES

Preface

1. Charles Krauthammer, "The Unipolar Moment," *Foreign Affairs* 70, no. 1 (1990/91): 23–33, doi:10.2307/20044692.
2. This remark is often attributed to Napoleon, though it may be apocryphal. See Isaac Stone Fish, "Crouching Tiger, Sleeping Giant," *Foreign Policy,* January 19, 2016, https://foreignpolicy.com/2016/01/19/china_shakes_the_world_cliche/. That said, Xi Jinping himself has tellingly made reference to it. See Teddy Ng and Andrea Chen, "Xi Jinping Says World Has Nothing to Fear from Awakening of 'Peaceful Lion,'" *South China Morning Post,* March 28, 2014, https://www.scmp.com/news/china/article/1459168/xi-says-world-has-nothing-fear-awakening-peaceful-lion.
3. A selection of recent important works on grand strategy would include: Robert Jervis, *American Foreign Policy for a New Era* (New York: Routledge, 2005); Christopher Layne, *The Peace of Illusions: American Grand Strategy from 1940 to the Present* (Ithaca, NY: Cornell University Press, 2006); Stephen G. Brooks and William C. Wohlforth, *World Out of Balance: International Relations and the Challenge of American Primacy* (Princeton, NJ: Princeton University Press, 2008); Aaron L. Friedberg, *A Contest for Supremacy: China, America, and the Struggle for Mastery in Asia* (New York: W. W. Norton, 2011); Hal Brands, *What Good Is Grand Strategy? Power and Purpose in American Statecraft from Harry S. Truman to George W. Bush* (Ithaca, NY: Cornell University Press, 2014); Colin S. Gray, *Strategy and Defense Planning: Meeting the Challenge of Uncertainty* (New York: Oxford University Press, 2014); Henry Kissinger, *World Order* (New York: Penguin, 2014); Barry R. Posen, *Restraint: A New Foundation for U.S. Grand Strategy* (Ithaca, NY: Cornell University Press, 2014); Hal Brands, *Making the Unipolar Moment: U.S. Foreign Policy and the Rise of the Post–Cold War Order* (Ithaca, NY: Cornell University Press, 2016); Anne-Marie Slaughter, *The Chessboard and The Web: Strategies of Connection in a Networked World* (New Haven: Yale University Press, 2017); Thomas J. Wright, *All Measures Short of War: The Contest for the 21st Century and the Future of American Power* (New Haven: Yale University Press, 2017); John Lewis

Gaddis, *On Grand Strategy* (New York: Penguin, 2018); Robert Kagan, *The Jungle Grows Back: America and Our Imperiled World* (New York: Alfred A. Knopf, 2018); John J. Mearsheimer, *The Great Delusion: Liberal Dreams and International Realities* (New Haven: Yale University Press, 2018); Stephen M. Walt, *The Hell of Good Intentions: America's Foreign Policy Elite and the Decline of U.S. Primacy* (New York: Farrar, Straus and Giroux, 2018); Michael E. O'Hanlon, *The Senkaku Paradox: Risking Great Power War over Small Stakes* (Washington, DC: Brookings Institution Press, 2019); Patrick Porter, "Advice for a Dark Age: Managing Great Power Competition," *Washington Quarterly* 42, no. 1 (Spring 2019): 7–25, doi:10.1080/0163660X.2019.1590079; and Rebecca Lissner and Mira Rapp-Hooper, *An Open World: How America Can Win the Contest for Twenty-First Century Order* (New Haven: Yale University Press, 2020).

4. Calculations of military expenditure by country (2018 USD) using Stockholm International Peace Research Institute, "SIPRI Military Expenditure Database" (Stockholm: SIPRI, 2019), https://www.sipri.org/databases/milex; and US Defense Intelligence Agency*, China Military Power: Modernizing a Force to Fight and Win,* DIA-02-1706-085 (Washington, DC: Defense Intelligence Agency, 2019), 20, https://www.dia.mil/Portals/27/Documents/News/Military%20Power%20Publications/China_Military_Power_FINAL_5MB_20190103.pdf. For official US government assessments, see US Department of Defense, *Summary of the 2018 National Defense Strategy of the United States of America: Sharpening the American Military's Strategic Edge* (Washington, DC: US Department of Defense, January 2018), https://dod.defense.gov/Portals/1/Documents/pubs/2018-National-Defense-Strategy-Summary.pdf. See also Eric Edelman et al., *Providing for the Common Defense: The Assessment and Recommendations of the National Defense Strategy Commission* (Washington, DC: United States Institute for Peace, 2018), v, https://www.usip.org/sites/default/files/2018-11/providing-for-the-common-defense.pdf.

5. Alfred, Lord Tennyson, *In Memoriam* (1850; repr., New York: Cambridge University Press, 2013), 80.

Chapter 1. The Purposes of American Strategy

1. For official statements, see White House, *National Security Strategy* (Washington, DC: White House, May 2010), 14–40, https://obamawhitehouse.archives.gov/sites/default/files/rss_viewer/national_security_strategy.pdf; White House, *National Security Strategy* (Washington, DC: White House, February 2015), 7–22; White House, *National Security Strategy of the United States of America* (Washington, DC: White House, 2017), 3–4; and Eric Edelman et al., *Providing for the Common Defense: The Assessment and Recommendations of the National Defense Strategy Commission* (Washington, DC: United States Institute for Peace, 2018), 4, https://www.usip.org/sites/default/files/2018-11/providing-for-the-common-defense.pdf. See also the remarks of Senator Josh Hawley, "Rethinking America's Foreign Policy Consensus" (Center for a New American Security, Washington, DC, November 12, 2019), https://www.hawley.senate.gov/senator-hawleys-speech-rethinking-americas-foreign-policy-consensus. For scholarly work, see, e.g., Hans J. Morgenthau, *The Purpose of American Politics* (New York:

Alfred A. Knopf, 1960), 3–42; Eugene V. Rostow, *A Breakfast for Bonaparte: U.S. National Security Interests from the Heights of Abraham to the Nuclear Age* (Washington, DC: National Defense University Press, 1993); Commission on America's National Interests, *America's National Interests* (Cambridge, MA: Center for Science and International Affairs, July 1996), https://www.belfercenter.org/sites/default/files/legacy/files/americas_interests.pdf; Samuel P. Huntington, "The Erosion of American National Interests," *Foreign Affairs* 76, no. 5 (September/October 1997): 28–49, doi:10.2307/20048198; and Robert J. Art, *A Grand Strategy for America* (Ithaca, NY: Cornell University Press, 2003).

2. My arguments are rooted in the kind of approach typified by Thucydides, *The Landmark Thucydides: A Comprehensive Guide to the Peloponnesian War,* ed. Robert B. Strassler (New York: Simon and Schuster, 1996); Thomas Hobbes, *Leviathan,* with selected variants from the Latin edition of 1668, ed. and intro. Edwin Curley (Indianapolis, IN: Hackett, 1994); Alexander Hamilton, James Madison, and John Jay, *The Federalist Papers,* ed. Ian Shapiro (New Haven: Yale University Press, 2009); Edward Hallett Carr, *The Twenty Years' Crisis, 1919–1929: An Introduction to the Study of International Relations,* 2nd ed. (New York: Harper and Row, 1964); Nicholas J. Spykman, *America's Strategy in World Politics: The United States and the Balance of Power* (1942; repr., New York: Routledge, 2017); Hans J. Morgenthau, *Politics among Nations: The Struggle for Power and Peace,* 7th ed. (New York: McGraw-Hill Education, 2005); Robert Gilpin, *War and Change in World Politics* (Cambridge: Cambridge University Press, 1981); Robert Gilpin, "The Richness of the Tradition of Political Realism," in *Neorealism and Its Critics,* ed. Robert O. Keohane (New York: Columbia University Press, 1986), 287–304; and Richard K. Betts, "The Realist Persuasion," *National Interest,* no. 139 (2015): 45–55, https://www.jstor.org/stable/44028493.

3. See, e.g., Jacob L. Heim and Benjamin M. Miller, *Measuring Power, Power Cycles, and the Risk of Great-Power War in the 21st Century* (Santa Monica, CA: RAND Corporation, 2020), https://doi.org/10.7249/RR2989; Lowy Institute, *Asia Power Index 2019* (Sydney, Australia: Lowy Institute, 2019), https://power.lowyinstitute.org/downloads/Lowy-Institute-Asia-Power-Index-2019-Pocket-Book.pdf; and International Futures (IF) modeling system, version 7.45 (Denver, CO: Frederick S. Pardee Center for International Futures, Josef Korbel School of International Studies, University of Denver, August 2019), https://pardee.du.edu/. The United States ranks second behind China, however, in the standard Composite Index of National Capability, using the National Military Capabilities (v5.0) dataset (2012). David J. Singer, Stuart Bremer, and John Stuckey, "Capability Distribution, Uncertainty, and Major Power War, 1820–1965," in *Peace, War, and Numbers,* ed. Bruce Russett (Beverly Hills, CA: Sage, 1972), 19–48. For an accounting of national power that is considerably more sanguine about the United States' ability to deal with China, see Michael Beckley, "The Power of Nations: Measuring What Matters," *International Security* 42, no. 2 (Fall 2018): 7–44, https://doi.org/10.1162/isec_a_00328.

4. World Bank, "GDP, PPP (Current International $)—South Asia, East Asia & Pacific, World" (Washington, DC: World Bank, accessed June 17, 2020), https://data.worldbank.org/indicator/NY.GDP.MKTP.PP.CD?locations=8S-Z4-1W; US Department of Defense, *Indo-Pacific Strategy Report: Preparedness, Partnerships, and Promoting a Networked*

Region (Washington, DC: US Department of Defense, July 1, 2019), 2, https://media.defense.gov/2019/Jul/01/2002152311/-1/-1/1/DEPARTMENT-OF-DEFENSE-INDO-PACIFIC-STRATEGY-REPORT-2019.PDF. As a late 2012 US assessment concluded, by 2030, "Asia will have surpassed North America and Europe combined in terms of global power, based upon GDP, population size, military spending, and technological investment. China alone will probably have the largest economy, surpassing that of the United States, a few years before 2030." US National Intelligence Council, *Global Trends 2030: Alternative Worlds* (Washington, DC: Office of the Director of National Intelligence, December 2012), iv, https://www.dni.gov/files/documents/GlobalTrends_2030.pdf. Indeed, measured in Purchasing Power Parity, China's economy has already surpassed America's. World Bank, "GDP, PPP (Current International $)—China, United States" (Washington, DC: World Bank, accessed June 22, 2020), https://data.worldbank.org/indicator/NY.GDP.MKTP.PP.CD?locations=CN-US. For a comparison of the size of the US and Chinese economies surveying different sources and methods, see Andrew Willige, "The World's Top Economy: The US vs China in Five Charts," *World Economic Forum,* December 5, 2016, https://www.weforum.org/agenda/2016/12/the-world-s-top-economy-the-us-vs-china-in-five-charts/.

5. World Bank, "GDP, PPP (Current International $)—European Union, United Kingdom, Russian Federation, Switzerland, Norway, North Macedonia, Bosnia and Herzegovina, Serbia, Albania, Montenegro, Belarus, Ukraine, Moldova, World" (Washington, DC: World Bank, accessed June 17, 2020), https://data.worldbank.org/indicator/NY.GDP.MKTP.PP.CD?locations=EU-GB-RU-CH-NO-MK-BA-RS-AL-ME-BY-UA-MD-1W.

6. World Bank, "GDP, PPP (Current International $)—United States, World" (Washington, DC: World Bank, accessed June 17, 2020), https://data.worldbank.org/indicator/NY.GDP.MKTP.PP.CD?locations=1W-US. According to one standard measure, the United States represents 13.9 percent of global power using indicators of military expenditure, military personnel, energy consumption, iron and steel production, urban population, and total population. Singer, Bremer, and Stuckey, "Capability Distribution, Uncertainty, and Major Power War."

7. World Bank, "GDP, PPP (Current International $)—Iraq, Iran, Islamic Rep., Saudi Arabia, United Arab Emirates, Oman, Kuwait, Bahrain, Qatar, World" (Washington, DC: World Bank, accessed June 17, 2020), https://data.worldbank.org/indicator/NY.GDP.MKTP.PP.CD?locations=IQ-IR-SA-AE-OM-KW-BH-QA-1W.

8. According to the Organization of Petroleum Exporting Countries (OPEC), the Persian Gulf is home to roughly 42 percent of the world's oil resources and 40 percent of its natural gas reserves. OPEC, *Annual Statistical Bulletin 2018* (Vienna: OPEC, 2018), 60, 112.

9. Excluding the Persian Gulf countries, the remaining region represents only 2 percent of global GDP. World Bank, "GDP, PPP (Current International $)—Middle East and North Africa, World" (Washington, DC: World Bank, accessed June 17, 2020), https://data.worldbank.org/indicator/NY.GDP.MKTP.PP.CD?locations=ZQ-1W.

10. Singer, Bremer, and Stuckey, "Capability Distribution, Uncertainty, and Major Power War." Latin America collectively represents 8 percent of global GDP. World Bank, "GDP, PPP (Current International $)—Latin America & Caribbean, World" (Washington, DC: World Bank, accessed June 22, 2020), https://data.worldbank.org/indicator/NY.GDP.MKTP.PP.CD?locations=ZJ-1W.

11. World Bank, "GDP, PPP (Current International $)—Sub-Saharan Africa, World" (Washington, DC: World Bank, accessed June 22, 2020), https://data.worldbank.org/indicator/NY.GDP.MKTP.PP.CD?locations=ZG-1W.

12. Central Asia and the Caucasus collectively represent just 2.7 percent of global GDP, less than that of sub-Saharan Africa, with a collective Composite Index of National Capability score of .0072, less than that of Egypt. Weak governance and other challenges are expected to inhibit growth and development in these states. World Bank, "GDP, PPP (Current International $)—GDP, PPP (Current International $)—Kazakhstan, Kyrgyz Republic, Tajikistan, Turkmenistan, Uzbekistan, Afghanistan, Armenia, Azerbaijan, Georgia, Turkey" (Washington, DC: World Bank, accessed June 22, 2020), https://data.worldbank.org/indicator/NY.GDP.MKTP.PP.CD?locations=KZ-KG-TJ-TM-UZ-AM-AZ-GE-TR-AF; Singer, Bremer, and Stuckey, "Capability Distribution, Uncertainty, and Major Power War"; US National Intelligence Council, *Global Trends 2030,* 32, 48, 52.

13. For the logic of this analysis, see H. J. Mackinder, "The Geographical Pivot of History," *Geographical Journal* 23, no. 4 (April 1904): 421–437; Spykman, *America's Strategy in World Politics;* and John Lewis Gaddis, *George F. Kennan: An American Life* (New York: Penguin Press, 2011), 331–332. For an overview, see Ronald O'Rourke, *Defense Primer: Geography, Strategy, and U.S. Force Design* (Washington, DC: Congressional Research Service, March 17, 2020, updated November 5, 2020), https://crsreports.congress.gov/product/pdf/IF/IF10485.

14. Winston Churchill to Lord Haldane, May 6, 1912, quoted in Randolph S. Churchill, *Winston S. Churchill,* vol. 2, *Young Statesman, 1901–1914* (London: Heinemann, 1967), 588. For a similar assessment of the importance of primary theater based on a review of a number of historical case studies, see A. Wess Mitchell, *Strategic Sequencing: How Great Powers Avoid Two-Front Wars* (Cambridge, MA: Belfer Center for Science and International Affairs, forthcoming).

15. John Lewis Gaddis, *Strategies of Containment: A Critical Appraisal of American National Security Policy during the Cold War,* rev. ed. (Oxford: Oxford University Press, 2005), 28–29; Gaddis, *George F. Kennan,* 331–332. This strategic principle has endured. See, e.g., Stephen M. Walt, "The Case for Finite Containment: Analyzing U.S. Grand Strategy," *International Security* 14, no. 1 (Summer 1989): 5–49, doi:10.2307/2538764; and Robert J. Art, "A Defensible Defense: America's Grand Strategy after the Cold War," *International Security* 15, no. 4 (Spring 1991): 5–53, doi:10.2307/2539010. For an emphasis on the deep roots and continuity of this anti-hegemonic approach in US foreign policy, see John J. Mearsheimer and Stephen M. Walt, "The Case for Offshore Balancing: A Superior U.S. Grand Strategy," *Foreign Affairs* 95, no. 4 (July/August 2016): 70–83, doi:10.2307/43946934.

16. The definition of *hegemony* given in the *Oxford English Dictionary* is: "Political, economic, or military predominance or leadership, esp. by one member of a confederacy or union over other states." *Oxford English Dictionary,* 3rd ed. (Oxford: Oxford University Press: 2014), s.v. "hegemony, n.," https://www.oed.com/view/Entry/85471. Given that the word covers a broad and nebulous scope, scholarly definitions vary. See discussions in Robert O. Keohane, *After Hegemony: Cooperation and Discord in World Political Economy* (Princeton, NJ: Princeton University Press, 1984), 45; Hedley Bull, *The*

Anarchical Society: A Study of Order in World Politics, 4th ed. (London: Red Globe Press, 2012), 209; Gilpin, *War and Change,* 29, as well as Robert Gilpin, *The Political Economy of International Relations* (Princeton, NJ: Princeton University Press, 1987), 73, and Robert Gilpin, *Global Political Economy: Understanding the International Economic Order* (Princeton, NJ: Princeton University Press, 2001), 99; and John J. Mearsheimer, *The Tragedy of Great Power Politics* (New York: W. W. Norton, 2001), 40. The definition provided by the *Oxford English Dictionary* for *predominance* is "the fact or property of predominating (in later use, especially in terms of quantity or number); preponderance, prevalence; prevailing or superior influence, power, or authority; an instance of this." *Oxford English Dictionary,* 3rd ed. (Oxford: Oxford University Press, 2007), s.v. "predominance, n."

17. See, e.g., the statement of the US Department of Defense: "The Indo-Pacific is the single most consequential region for America's future." US Department of Defense, *Indo-Pacific Strategy Report,* 1.

18. World Bank, "GDP, PPP (Current International $)—China, World" (Washington, DC: World Bank, accessed June 17, 2020), https://data.worldbank.org/indicator/NY.GDP.MKTP.PP.CD?end=2018&locations=CN-1W&start=1990&type=shaded&view=chart; Heim and Miller, *Measuring Power;* Lowy Institute, *Asia Power Index 2019;* International Futures (IF) modeling system; and Singer, Bremer, and Stuckey, "Capability Distribution, Uncertainty, and Major Power War."

19. Singer, Bremer, and Stuckey, "Capability Distribution, Uncertainty, and Major Power War."

20. As the US Department of Defense assessed in June 2019: "As China continues its economic and military ascendance, it seeks Indo-Pacific regional hegemony in the near-term and ultimately global preeminence in the long-term." US Department of Defense, Indo-Pacific Strategy Report, 8. See also US Department of the Navy, Advantage at Sea: Prevailing with Integrated All-Domain Naval Power (Washington, DC: US Department of the Navy, December 2020), 4, https://media.defense.gov/2020/Dec/16/2002553074/-1/-1/1/TRISERVICESTRATEGY.PDF. For scholarly appraisals, see Jennifer Lind, "Life in China's Asia: What Regional Hegemony Would Look Like," *Foreign Affairs* 97, no. 2 (March/April 2018): 71–82, https://www.foreignaffairs.com/articles/china /2018-02-13/life-chinas-asia; Liza Tobin, "Xi's Vision for Transforming Global Governance: A Strategic Challenge for Washington and Its Allies," *Texas National Security Review* 2, no. 1 (November 2018): 155–166, http://dx.doi.org/10.26153/tsw/863; Oriana Skylar Mastro, "The Stealth Superpower: How China Hid Its Global Ambitions," *Foreign Affairs* 98, no. 1 (January/February 2019): 31–39, https://www.foreignaffairs.com/ articles/china/china-plan-rule-asia; Nadège Rolland, *China's Vision for a New World Order,* NBR Special Report no. 83 (Seattle, WA: National Bureau of Asian Research, January 2020), 47–51, https://www.nbr.org/publication/chinas-vision-for-a-new-world-order/; *Hearing on a "China Model": Beijing's Promotion of Alternative Global Norms and Standards, before the U.S.-China Economic and Security Review Commission,* 116th Cong. (2020) (statement of Daniel Tobin, Faculty Member, China Studies, National Intelligence University and Senior Associate (Non-Resident), Freeman Chair in China Studies, Center for Strategic and International Studies), https://www.uscc.gov/sites/default/files/testimonies/SFR%20for%20USCC%20TobinD%2020200313.pdf; and Nadège

Rolland, *An Emerging China-Centric Order: China's Vision for a New World Order in Practice,* NBR Special Report no. 87 (Seattle, WA: National Bureau of Asian Research, August 2020), https://www.nbr.org/publication/an-emerging-china-centric-order-chinas-vision-for-a-new-world-order-in-practice/. For a contrary view, see, e.g., *Hearing on a "World-Class" Military: Assessing China's Global Military Ambitions, before the U.S.-China Economic and Security Review Commission,* 116th Cong. 12 (2019) (statement of M. Taylor Fravel, Arthur and Ruth Sloan Professor of Political Science, Massachusetts Institute of Technology), https://www.uscc.gov/sites/default/files/Fravel_USCC%20Testimony_FINAL.pdf.

21. World Bank, "GDP, PPP (Current International $)—European Union, United Kingdom, Russian Federation, Switzerland, Norway, North Macedonia, Bosnia and Herzegovina, Serbia, Albania, Montenegro, Belarus, Ukraine, Moldova, World" (Washington, DC: World Bank, accessed June 17, 2020), https://data.worldbank.org/indicator/NY.GDP.MKTP.PP.CD?locations=EU-GB-RU-CH-NO-MK-BA-RS-AL-ME-BY-UA-MD-1W.

22. World Bank, "GDP, PPP (Current International $)—Russian Federation, Germany, France, United Kingdom, Italy" (Washington, DC: World Bank, accessed June 17, 2020), https://data.worldbank.org/indicator/NY.GDP.MKTP.PP.CD?locations=RU-DE-FR-GB-IT.

23. Singer, Bremer, and Stuckey, "Capability Distribution, Uncertainty, and Major Power War."

24. A similar view of what is at issue was expressed by the US government. See US Department of Defense, *Indo-Pacific Strategy Report,* 4. For the most lucid contemporary statement of this foundational logic, see Evan Braden Montgomery, *In the Hegemon's Shadow: Leading States and the Rise of Regional Powers* (Ithaca, NY: Cornell University Press, 2016). Cf. Joshua Shifrinson, "The Rise of China, Balance of Power Theory, and US National Security: Reasons for Optimism?," *Journal of Strategic Studies* 42, no. 2 (2020): 175–216, doi:10.1080/01402390.2018.1558056.

25. Gilpin, *Political Economy of International Relations,* 76–77.

26. See Robert D. Blackwill and Jennifer M. Harris, *War by Other Means: Geoeconomics and Statecraft* (Cambridge, MA: Belknap Press of Harvard University Press, 2016), 93–128; Markus Brunnermeier, Rush Doshi, and Harold James, "Beijing's Bismarckian Ghosts: How Great Powers Compete Economically," *Washington Quarterly* 41, no. 3 (Fall 2018): 161–176, https://doi.org/10.1080/0163660X.2018.1520571; and, for a review of the extensive official and expert literature on this point, U.S-China Economic and Security Review Commission, *2019 Report to Congress of the U.S-China Economic and Security Review Commission, One Hundred Sixteenth Congress, First Session* (Washington, DC: U.S.-China Economic and Security Review Commission, November 2019), 33–104, 169–191.

27. See, e.g., Edward N. Luttwak, "From Geopolitics to Geo-Economics: Logic of Conflict, Grammar of Commerce," *National Interest,* no. 20 (Summer 1990): 17–23, https://www.jstor.org/stable/42894676. For a recent contribution, see Henrique Choer Moraes and Mikael Wigell, "The Emergence of Strategic Capitalism: Geoeconomics, Corporate Statecraft and the Repurposing of the Global Economy," FIIA Working Paper 117 (Helsinki: Finnish Institute of International Affairs, September 30, 2020), https://www.fiia.fi/en/publication/the-emergence-of-strategic-capitalism.

28. For conceptual arguments, see Robert Gilpin, *U.S. Power and Multinational Corporation: The Political Economy of Foreign Direct Investment* (New York: Basic Books, 1975), 79–84, as well as Gilpin, *War and Change,* 134–137; Eli F. Heckscher, *The Continental System: An Economic Interpretation* (Oxford: Clarendon Press, 1922); Jacob Viner, *The Customs Union Issue* (1950; repr., New York: Oxford University Press, 2014), esp. 125–126; Ikuhiko Hata, "Continental Expansion, 1905–1941," in *The Cambridge History of Japan,* vol. 6, *The Twentieth Century,* ed. Peter Duus (New York: Cambridge University Press, 2005), 299–302; and Michael Kaser, *Comecon: Integration Problems of the Planned Economies* (London: Oxford University Press, 1965).

29. Jeffrey A. Frankel, *Regional Trading Blocs in the World Economic System* (Washington, DC: Institute for International Economics, 1997), 35–47; Jeffrey A. Frankel, "Globalization of the Economy," NBER Working Paper no. 7858 (Cambridge, MA: National Bureau of Economic Research, August 2000): esp. 13–19, https://www.nber.org/papers/w7858.pdf; Dani Rodrik, "How Far Will International Economic Integration Go?," *Journal of Economic Perspectives* 14, no. 1 (Winter 2000): 177–186, http://www.jstor.com/stable/2647061; Daron Acemoglu and Pierre Yared, "Political Limits to Globalization," *American Economic Review: Papers and Proceedings* 100 (May 2010): 83–88, https://www.jstor.org/stable/27804968/; Jeffrey Frieden et al., *After the Fall: The Future of Global Cooperation,* Geneva Reports on the World Economy no. 14 (Geneva: International Center for Monetary and Banking Studies, July 2012); Michael J. Mazarr et al., *Measuring the Health of the Liberal International Order* (Santa Monica, CA: RAND Corporation, 2017), 49–64, https://doi.org/10.7249/RR1994.

30. See, e.g., Gilpin, *Political Economy of International Relations,* 294–296; Pier Carlo Padoan, "Regional Agreements as Clubs: The European Case," in *The Political Economy of Regionalism,* ed. Edward D. Mansfield and Helen V. Milner (New York: Columbia University Press, 1997), 107–133; Kenneth A. Froot and David B. Yoffie, "Trading Blocs and the Incentives to Protect: Implications for Japan and East Asia," in *Regionalism and Rivalry: Japan and the United States in Pacific Asia,* ed. Jeffrey A. Frankel and Miles Kahler (Chicago: University of Chicago Press, 1993), 125–158; Edward D. Mansfield and Helen V. Milner, "The New Wave of Regionalism," *International Organization* 53, no. 3 (Summer 1999): 589–627, https://www.jstor.org/stable/2601291; and Gilpin, *Global Political Economy,* 348.

31. Stephen D. Krasner, "State Power and the Structure of International Trade," *World Politics* 28, no. 3 (April 1976): 318–319, 321–322, doi:10.2307/2009974. See also Peter J. Katzenstein, "International Relations and Domestic Structures: Foreign Economic Policies of Advanced Industrial States," *International Organization* 30, no. 1 (Winter 1976): 1–45, https://www.jstor.org/stable/2706246.

32. Gilpin, *War and Change,* 150–152.

33. For official expressions of these concerns, see William P. Barr, "Remarks on China Policy" (Gerald R. Ford Presidential Museum, Grand Rapids, MI, July 16, 2020), https://www.justice.gov/opa/speech/attorney-general-william-p-barr-delivers-remarks-china-policy-gerald-r-ford-presidential; and Office of the Secretary of Defense, *Annual Report to Congress: Military and Security Developments involving the People's Republic of China 2020,* 9-A3DFCD4 (Washington, DC: US Department of Defense, August 11, 2020), 11–17, https://media.defense.gov/2020/Sep/01/2002488689/-1/-1/1/2020-

DOD-CHINA-MILITARY-POWER-REPORT-FINAL.PDF. For recent analyses of Chinese industrial policy, see, among others, Jean-Christophe Defraigne, "China's Industrial Policy," Short Term Policy Brief 81 (Brussels: Europe China Research and Advice Network, June 2014), https://eeas.europa.eu/archives/docs/china/docs/division_ ecran/ecran_is103_paper_81_chinas_industrial_policy_jean-christophe_defraigne_ en.pdf; Ernest Liu, "Industrial Policies in Production Networks," *Quarterly Journal of Economics* 134, no. 4 (2019): 1883–1948, doi:10.1093/qje/qjz024; Loren Brand and Thomas G. Rawski, eds., *Policy, Regulation, and Innovation in China's Electricity and Telecom Industries* (New York: Cambridge University Press, 2019); Panle Jia Barwick, Myrto Kalouptsidi, and Nahim Bin Zahur, "China Industrial Policy: An Empirical Evaluation," NBER Working Paper no. 26075 (Cambridge, MA: National Bureau of Economic Research, September 2019), https://www.nber.org/papers/w26075; and, for a synopsis, "Free Exchange: China's Industrial Policy Has Worked Better Than Critics Think," *Economist,* January 2, 2020, https://www.economist.com/finance-and-economics/2020/01/02/chinas-industrial-policy-has-worked-better-than-critics-think.

34. Chad P. Brown, "Should the United States Recognize China as a Market Economy?," (Washington, DC: Peterson Institute for International Economics, December 2016), 4, https://www.piie.com/publications/policy-briefs/should-united-states-recognize-china-market-economy; Mark Wu, "The 'China Inc.' Challenge to Global Trade Governance," *Harvard International Law Journal* 57, no. 2 (Spring 2016): 261–324, https://ssrn.com/ abstract=2779781. For a review of the issues, see also Wayne M. Morrison, "China-U.S. Trade Issues," RL33536 (Washington, DC: Congressional Research Service, July 30, 2018), 30–54, https://crsreports.congress.gov/product/pdf/RL/RL33536.

35. See Kurt M. Campbell and Ely Ratner, "The China Reckoning: How Beijing Defied American Expectations," *Foreign Affairs* 97, no. 2 (March/April 2018): 60–70, https:// www.foreignaffairs.com/articles/china/2018-02-13/china-reckoning.

36. For a study of how normative preferences inform the political, socioeconomic, and commercial dimensions of hegemonic orders, see Charles A. Kupchan, "The Normative Foundations of Hegemony and the Coming Challenge to Pax Americana," *Security Studies* 23, no. 2 (2014): 219–257, https://doi.org/10.1080/09636412.2014.874205.

37. Indeed, a recent study has found that dominant powers revise international orders to exclude a perceived threat and limit that threat's influence within the order. Kyle M. Lascurettes, *Orders of Exclusion: Great Powers and the Strategic Sources of Foundational Rules in International Relations* (New York: Oxford University Press, 2020).

38. For example, intra-alliance trading blocs formed during the Cold War to enhance the Free World's economic power while denying gains from trade to its rival and limiting concomitant security externalities. See, among others, David Allen Baldwin, *Economic Statecraft* (Princeton, NJ: Princeton University Press, 1985), 235–249; Michael Mastanduno, "Strategies of Economic Containment: U.S. Trade Relations with the Soviet Union," *World Politics* 37, no. 4 (June 1985): 503–531, https://www.jstor.org/stable/2010342; Joanne Gowa, *Allies, Adversaries, and International Trade* (Princeton, NJ: Princeton University Press, 1994); and Sebastian Rosato, *Europe United: Power Politics and the Making of the European Community* (Ithaca, NY: Cornell University Press, 2011).

39. The classic treatment of trade dependency and bargaining power is Albert O. Hirschman, *National Power and the Structure of Foreign Trade* (Berkeley: University of California Press, 1945). For recent work on coercive dependency, see Henry Farrell and Abraham L. Newman, "Weaponized Interdependence: How Global Economic Networks Shape State Coercion," *International Security* 44, no. 1 (Summer 2019): 42–79, https://doi.org/10.1162/ISEC_a_00351.

40. See "Appendix 2: Chinese Influence Activities in Select Countries," in *China's Influence and American Interests: Promoting Constructive Vigilance,* rev. ed., ed. Larry Diamond and Orville Schell (Stanford, CA: Hoover Institution Press, 2019), 164–170. See also the remarks of Malcolm Turnbull, "Countering Chinese Influence Activities in Australia" (Center for Strategic and International Studies, Washington, DC, July 15, 2020), https://www.csis.org/events/online-event-countering-chinese-influence-activities-australia.

41. See, e.g., Peter Mattis and Matthew Brazil, *Chinese Communist Espionage: An Intelligence Primer* (Annapolis, MD: Naval Institute Press, 2019).

42. See, e.g., Evan Braden Montgomery, "Breaking Out of the Security Dilemma: Realism, Reassurance, and the Problem of Uncertainty," *International Security* 31, no. 2 (Fall 2006): 151–185, https://www.jstor.org/stable/4137519.

43. For an argument emphasizing the global dimension of geopolitical competition rather than the primacy of the regional challenge, cf. Hal Brands and Jake Sullivan, "China Has Two Paths to Global Domination," *Foreign Policy,* May 22, 2020, https://foreignpolicy.com/2020/05/22/china-superpower-two-paths-global-domination-cold-war/.

Chapter 2. The Favorable Regional Balance of Power

1. Daniel Goffman, *The Ottoman Empire and Early Modern Europe* (Cambridge, UK: Cambridge University Press, 2002), 111.

2. See, e.g., White House, *National Security Strategy* (Washington, DC: White House, February 2015), 22.

3. For a close analog, see Gilpin's discussion of hegemonic war. Robert Gilpin, "The Theory of Hegemonic War," *Journal of Interdisciplinary History* 18, no. 4 (Spring 1988): 592, doi:10.2307/204816.

4. See, e.g., John Lewis Gaddis, *Strategies of Containment: A Critical Appraisal of American National Security Policy during the Cold War,* rev. ed. (Oxford: Oxford University Press, 2005); Marc Trachtenberg, *History and Strategy* (Princeton, NJ: Princeton University Press, 1991); and Francis J. Gavin, *Nuclear Statecraft: History and Strategy in America's Atomic Age* (Ithaca, NY: Cornell University Press, 2014).

5. See Kenneth N. Waltz, *Theory of International Politics* (Reading, MA: Addison-Wesley, 1979), 125–126; Stephen M. Walt, *The Origins of Alliances* (Ithaca, NY: Cornell University Press, 1987), esp. 17–21, 27–32; Robert Jervis and Jack Snyder, eds., *Dominoes and Bandwagons: Strategic Beliefs and Great Power Competition in the Eurasian Rimland* (New York: Oxford University Press, 1991); and Glenn H. Snyder, *Alliance Politics* (Ithaca, NY: Cornell University Press, 1997), 18, 158–161. For an argument that states will inevitably balance against China's rise, see Edward N. Luttwak, *The Rise of China vs. the Logic of Strategy* (Cambridge, MA: Harvard University Press, 2012).

6. Nicholas J. Spykman, *America's Strategy in World Politics: The United States and the Balance of Power* (1942; repr., New York: Routledge, 2017), 66–67, 80–81; George F. Kennan, *American Diplomacy*, 30–32; John J. Mearsheimer, *The Tragedy of Great Power Politics* (New York: W. W. Norton, 2001), 236.

7. See, e.g., Peter Harrell et al., *China's Use of Coercive Economic Measures* (Washington, DC: Center for a New American Security, June 2018), esp. 9–10, https://www.cnas.org/publications/reports/chinas-use-of-coercive-economic-measures.

8. For conceptual treatments, see Mancur Olson Jr. and Richard Zeckhauser, *An Economic Theory of Alliances* (Santa Monica, CA: RAND Corporation, 1966), https://www.rand.org/pubs/research_memoranda/RM4297.html. See also Mancur Olson, *The Logic of Collective Action: Public Goods and the Theory of the Groups* (Cambridge, MA: Harvard University Press, 1971); and Todd Sandler and Keith Hartley, "Economics of Alliances: The Lessons for Collective Action," *Journal of Economic Literature* 39 (September 2001): 869–896, https://www.jstor.org/stable/2698316.

9. For a classic discussion, see Henry Kissinger, *Diplomacy* (New York: Simon and Schuster, 1994), 103–136. See also Glenn H. Snyder, *Deterrence and Defense: Toward a Theory of National Security* (Ithaca, NY: Cornell University Press, 1961), 57; and John J. Mearsheimer, *Conventional Deterrence* (Ithaca, NY: Cornell University Press, 1983), 56–58.

10. Indeed, it is usually an anti-hegemonic coalition that has the incentive to launch a preventive war. See Dale C. Copeland, *The Origins of Major War* (Ithaca, NY: Cornell University Press, 2000), 10–55.

11. See, e.g., Kurt M. Campbell and Jake Sullivan, "Competition without Catastrophe: How America Can Both Challenge and Coexist with China," *Foreign Affairs* 98, no. 5 (September/October 2019): 104, https://www.foreignaffairs.com/articles/china/competition-with-china-without-catastrophe.

12. Important works on the causes of war include Kenneth N. Waltz, *Man, the State, and War: A Theoretical Analysis* (New York: Columbia University Press, 1954); Bernard Brodie, *War and Politics* (New York: Macmillan, 1973), 276–340; Geoffrey Blainey, *The Causes of War,* 3rd ed. (New York: Free Press, 1988); A. F. K. Organski and Jacek Kugler, *The War Ledger* (Chicago: University of Chicago Press, 1981); Robert I. Rotberg and Theodore L. Rabb, eds., *The Origins and Prevention of Major Wars* (New York: Cambridge University Press, 1989); Donald Kagan, *On the Origins of War and the Preservation of Peace* (New York: Doubleday, 1994); Michael E. Brown et al., eds., *Theories of War and Peace* (Cambridge, MA: MIT Press, 1998); Stephen Van Evera, *Causes of War: Power and the Roots of Conflict* (Ithaca, NY: Cornell University Press, 1999); and Jack S. Levy and William R. Thompson, *Causes of War* (Chichester, UK: Wiley-Blackwell, 2010). For a survey, see Greg Cashman, *What Causes War? An Introduction to Theories of International Conflict,* 2nd ed. (Lanham, MD: Rowman and Littlefield, 2014).

13. Office of the Secretary of Defense, *Annual Report to Congress: Military and Security Developments Involving the People's Republic of China 2020,* 9-A3DFCD4 (Washington, DC: US Department of Defense, August 11, 2020), esp. 38–121, https://media.defense.gov/2020/Sep/01/2002488689/-1/-1/1/2020-DOD-CHINA-MILITARY-POWER-REPORT-FINAL.PDF; US Defense Intelligence Agency, *China Military Power: Modernizing a Force to Fight and Win,* DIA-02-1706-085 (Washington, DC:

Defense Intelligence Agency, 2019), 23–51, https://www.dia.mil/Portals/27/Documents/News/Military%20Power%20Publications/China_Military_Power_FINAL_5MB_20190103.pdf; and Eric Heginbotham et al., *The U.S.-China Military Scorecard: Forces, Geography, and the Evolving Balance of Power, 1996–2017* (Santa Monica, CA: RAND Corporation, 2015), 23–41, https://www.jstor.org/stable/10.7249/j.ctt17rw5gb. See also Thomas Shugart and Javier Gonzales, *First Strike: China's Missile Threat to U.S. Bases in Asia* (Washington, DC: Center for a New American Security, July 2017), https://www.cnas.org/publications/reports/first-strike-chinas-missile-threat-to-u-s-bases-to-asia.

14. The cornerstone balancer concept is distinct from that of an "offshore balancer." Some proponents of the "offshore balancing" school argue for a large-scale retrenchment from Eurasia, but my argument is most similar to those variants that are prepared to countenance significant engagement abroad under certain conditions, especially when a state threatens to establish hegemony over a key region. The primary and critical difference between this view and mine, however, is this camp's relative sanguinity about regional states coming and staying together in a coalition to balance an aspiring hegemon, as well as their confidence that the United States can always come in later to rectify the situation at reasonable cost and risk. Their priority focus is therefore burden shifting rather than cornerstone balancing. In effect, premised as it is on the idea that balancing coalitions are likely to form and cohere, this offshore balancing approach seeks to maximize the degree to which it can shift burdens to local balancing states. For example, John Mearsheimer and Stephen Walt argued in an influential 2016 *Foreign Affairs* piece: "In essence, the aim is to remain offshore as long as possible, while recognizing that it is sometimes necessary to come onshore. If that happens, however, the United States should make its allies do as much of the heavy lifting as possible and remove its own forces as soon as it can . . . forcing other states to pull their own weight. . . . If the [United States] is forced to fight another great power, better to arrive late and let other countries bear the brunt of the costs. . . . Taken together, these steps would allow the United States to markedly reduce its defense spending." John J. Mearsheimer and Stephen M. Walt, "The Case for Offshore Balancing: A Superior U.S. Grand Strategy," *Foreign Affairs* 95, no. 4 (July/August 2016): 74, 78, 83, doi:10.2307/43946934. My view is much less sanguine about the prospects for balancing against China in Asia and for a favorable military balance in Asia—hence the focus of this book. By contrast to this camp's sanguinity, I emphasize the critical and active—not "offshore," which heavily connotes aloofness—role of the cornerstone balancer in forming, sustaining, and protecting the anti-hegemonic coalition. For additional selections from the offshore balancer school, representing variations on key themes, see, e.g., Barry R. Posen and Andrew L. Ross, "Competing Visions for U.S. Grand Strategy," *International Security* 21, no. 3 (Winter 1996/97), doi:10.2307/2539272; Eugene Gholz, Daryl G. Press, and Harvey M. Sapolsky, "Come Home, America: The Strategy of Restraint in the Face of Temptation," *International Security* 21, no. 4 (Spring 1997): 5–48, doi:10.2307/2539282; Christopher Layne, "From Preponderance to Offshore Balancing: America's Future Grand Strategy," *International Security* 22, no.1 (Summer 1997): 86–124, https://muse.jhu.edu/article/446821; Christopher Layne, *The Peace of Illusions: American Grand Strategy from 1940 to the Present* (Ithaca, NY: Cornell University Press, 2006); Barry R.

Posen, *Restraint: A New Foundation for U.S. Grand Strategy* (Ithaca, NY: Cornell University Press, 2014); and Jasen J. Castillo, "Passing the Torch: Criteria for Implementing a Grand Strategy of Offshore Balancing," in *New Voices in American Grand Strategy* (Washington, DC: Center for a New American Security, 2019), 23–35, https://www.cnas.org/publications/reports/new-voices-in-grand-strategy.

15. Edward C. Keefer, *Harold Brown: Offsetting the Soviet Military Challenge, 1977–1981* (Washington, DC: Historical Office, Office of the Secretary of Defense, 2017), 322–339.

16. This logic for American intervention beyond its own sphere also helps explain another puzzle: why the United States has not provoked more balancing itself by states in regions outside North and Central America, especially by powerful states in Europe and Asia. Part of this is that the United States is highly secure in its own area and thus has limited reasons to seek to expand its hegemonic zone beyond its own region. Moreover, doing so would be difficult; the other wealthy parts of the world are far distant and developed, and it is difficult and expensive to attempt to project and sustain hegemonic power over long distances. The United States therefore has not, with the exception of the Philippines in the first part of the twentieth century, sought to establish hegemony over or control of populated and developed areas beyond North and Central America. This solid and credible basis for restraint is almost certainly a primary reason why the United States has not triggered heavy counterbalancing. For arguments on this point, see, e.g., Stephen G. Brooks and William C. Wohlforth, "Hard Times for Soft Balancing," *International Security* 30, no. 1 (Summer 2005): 72–108, https://www.jstor.org/stable/4137459; and Keir A. Lieber and Gerard Alexander, "Waiting for Balancing: Why the World Is Not Pushing Back," *International Security* 30, no. 1 (Summer 2005): 109–139, https://www.jstor.org/stable/4137460.

17. World Bank, "GDP, PPP (Current International $)—Japan, China" (Washington, DC: World Bank, accessed June 17, 2020), https://data.worldbank.org/indicator/NY.GDP.MKTP.PP.CD?locations=JP-CN; David J. Singer, Stuart Bremer, and John Stuckey, "Capability Distribution, Uncertainty, and Major Power War, 1820–1965," in *Peace, War, and Numbers,* ed. Bruce Russett (Beverly Hills, CA: Sage, 1972), 19–48.

18. World Bank, "GDP, PPP (Current International $)—India, China" (Washington, DC: World Bank, accessed June 17, 2020), https://data.worldbank.org/indicator/NY.GDP.MKTP.PP.CD?locations=IN-CN; Singer, Bremer, and Stuckey, "Capability Distribution, Uncertainty, and Major Power War"; Charles Wolf Jr., *China and India, 2025: A Comparative Assessment* (Santa Monica, CA: RAND Corporation, 2011), 37–51, https://www.rand.org/pubs/monographs/MG1009.html.

19. The combined Composite Index of National Capability score for the prospective coalition is .15; that of China, Pakistan, and Cambodia is .23. The combined economic strength of China, Pakistan, and Cambodia could thus be well over 40 percent larger than a prospective coalition without US participation. Singer, Bremer, and Stuckey, "Capability Distribution, Uncertainty, and Major Power War."

20. National Security Council, "U.S. Strategic Framework for the Indo-Pacific," (Washington, DC: White House, 2018), 4, https://www.whitehouse.gov/wp-content/uploads/2021/01/IPS-Final-Declass.pdf; US Department of Defense, *Indo-Pacific Strategy Report: Preparedness, Partnerships, and Promoting a Networked Region* (Washington, DC: US Department of Defense, July 1, 2019), 48, https://media.defense.gov/2019/

Jul/01/2002152311/-1/-1/1/DEPARTMENT-OF-DEFENSE-INDO-PACIFIC-STRAT-EGY-REPORT-2019.PDF. See also Michael R. Pompeo, "Opening Remarks at Quad Ministerial" (Iikura Guest House, Tokyo, October 6, 2020), https://www.state.gov/secretary-michael-r-pompeo-opening-remarks-at-quad-ministerial/.

21. For an especially lucid analysis of such an effort, see Ashley J. Tellis, *Balancing without Containment: An American Strategy for Managing China* (Washington, DC: Carnegie Endowment for International Peace, 2014), https://carnegieendowment.org/files/balancing_without_containment.pdf.

22. For a survey of links among likely coalition states, see Richard Fontaine et al., *Networking Asian Security: An Integrated Approach to Order in the Pacific* (Washington, DC: Center for a New American Security, June 19, 2017), https://www.cnas.org/publications/reports/networking-asian-security; and Scott W. Harold et al., *The Thickening Web of Asian Security Cooperation: Deepening Defense Ties among U.S. Allies and Partners in the Indo-Pacific* (Santa Monica, CA: RAND Corporation, 2019), https://doi.org/10.7249/RR3125. For more recent developments, see Mark T. Esper, "Defense Secretary Addresses Free and Open Indo-Pacific" (Asia-Pacific Center for Security Studies, Honolulu, HI, August 26, 2020), https://www.defense.gov/Newsroom/Transcripts/Transcript/Article/2328124/defense-secretary-addresses-free-and-open-indo-pacific-at-apcss-courtesy-transc/source/GovDelivery/; Stephen Biegun, "Remarks at the U.S.-India Strategic Partnership Forum" (U.S.-India Strategic Partnership Forum, Washington, DC, August 31, 2020), https://www.state.gov/deputy-secretary-biegun-remarks-at-the-u-s-india-strategic-partnership-forum/; Hiroyuki Akita and Eri Segiura, "Pompeo Aims to 'Institutionalize' Quad Ties to Counter China," *Nikkei Asia,* October 6, 2020, https://asia.nikkei.com/Editor-s-Picks/Interview/Pompeo-aims-to-institutionalize-Quad-ties-to-counter-China; Stephen Biegun, "Remarks by Deputy Secretary Biegun" (Ananta Centre India-U.S. Forum, New Delhi, October 12, 2020), https://www.state.gov/remarks-by-deputy-secretary-stephen-e-biegun/; Katrina Manson, "Washington Looks to Five Eyes to Build Anti-China Coalition," *Financial Times,* June 3, 2020, https://www.ft.com/content/5c4d6c5c-b1b1-42fc-b779-0697bc0a33b9; Lindsey W. Ford and Julian Gewirtz, "China's Post-Coronavirus Aggression Is Reshaping Asia," *Foreign Policy,* June 18, 2020, https://foreignpolicy.com/2020/06/18/china-india-aggression-asia-alliances/; Angela Dewan, "US Allies Once Seemed Cowed by China. Now They're Responding with Rare Coordination," *CNN,* July 15, 2020, https://www.cnn.com/2020/07/14/world/china-world-coordinate-response-intl/index.html; Derek Grossman, "The Quad Is Poised to Become Openly Anti-China Soon," *RAND Blog,* July 28, 2020, https://www.rand.org/blog/2020/07/the-quad-is-poised-to-become-openly-anti-china-soon.html; David A. Andelman, "Trump Is Assembling a Coalition of the Willing against China," *CNN,* August 11, 2020, https://www.cnn.com/2020/08/11/opinions/trump-administration-china-andelman-opinion/index.html; and "No Drunken Sailors: America Musters the World's Biggest Naval Exercise," *Economist,* August 16, 2020, https://www.economist.com/international/2020/08/16/america-musters-the-worlds-biggest-naval-exercise.

23. Evan Braden Montgomery, *In the Hegemon's Shadow: Leading States and the Rise of Regional Powers* (Ithaca, NY: Cornell University Press, 2016), 54–74.

24. World Bank, "GDP, PPP (Current International $)—Iran, Islamic Rep., Middle East & North Africa" (Washington, DC: World Bank, accessed June 17, 2020), https://data. worldbank.org/indicator/NY.GDP.MKTP.PP.CD?locations=IR-ZQ; Singer, Bremer, and Stuckey, "Capability Distribution, Uncertainty, and Major Power War."

25. US Defense Intelligence Agency, *Russia Military Power: Building a Military to Support Great Power Aspirations,* DIA-11-1704-161 (Washington, DC: US Defense Intelligence Agency, 2017), 42–43, 58–70, https://www.dia.mil/Portals/27/Documents/News/Military%20Power%20Publications/Russia%20Military%20Power%20Report%202017. pdf.

26. Brazil represents 2.4 percent of global wealth, the largest in Central and South America by a significant margin. Mexico trails Brazil at 2 percent. No other state in the region represents more than 1 percent of global wealth. Brazil and Mexico's Composite Index of National Capability scores are .025 and .015, respectively, which are larger than France's but far below the United States'. Singer, Bremer, and Stuckey, "Capability Distribution, Uncertainty, and Major Power War"; World Bank, "GDP, PPP (Current International $)— Brazil, Mexico, World" (Washington, DC: World Bank, accessed June 22, 2020), https:// data.worldbank.org/indicator/NY.GDP.MKTP.PP.CD?end=2018&locations =1W-BR-MX&start=1990&view=chart.

27. Moreover, no state in sub-Saharan Africa represents more than 1 percent of global wealth, the highest being Nigeria at 0.8 percent, followed by South Africa at 0.6 percent, and then by Kenya and Tanzania, both just over 0.1 percent. These four largest economies in the region have a collective Composite Index of National Capability score of just .2, slightly higher than Portugal. World Bank, "GDP, PPP (Current International $)—Nigeria, South Africa, Kenya, Tanzania, World" (Washington, DC: World Bank, accessed June 22, 2020), https://data.worldbank.org/indicator/NY.GDP.MKTP.PP.CD?end=2018&locations= NG-ZA-KE-TZ-1W&start=1990&view=chart; Singer, Bremer, and Stuckey, "Capability Distribution, Uncertainty, and Major Power War"; US National Intelligence Council, *Global Trends 2030: Alternative Worlds* (Washington, DC: Office of the Director of National Intelligence, December 2012), 8, 14, 22, 50, https://www.dni.gov/files/documents/ GlobalTrends_2030.pdf.

Chapter 3. Alliances and Their Effective, Credible Defense

1. See Thomas J. Christensen and Jack Snyder, "Chain Gangs and Passed Bucks: Predicting Alliance Patterns in Multipolarity," *International Organization* 44, no. 2 (Spring 1990): 140, https://www.jstor.org/stable/2706792; Kenneth N. Waltz, *Theory of International Politics* (Reading, MA: Addison-Wesley, 1979), 167. Cf. Tongfi Kim, "Why Alliances Entangle but Seldom Entrap States," *Security Studies* 20, no. 3 (July 2011): 350–377, doi:10.1080/09636412.2011.599201; and Michael Beckley, "The Myth of Entangling Alliances: Reassessing the Security Risks of U.S. Defense Pacts," *International Security* 39, no. 4 (Spring 2015): 7–48.

2. See Office of the Secretary of Defense, *Annual Report to Congress: Military and Security Developments Involving the People's Republic of China 2020,* 9-A3DFCD4 (Washington, DC: US Department of Defense, August 11, 2020), esp. 76–89, https://media.

defense.gov/2020/Sep/01/2002488689/-1/-1/1/2020-DOD-CHINA-MILITARY-POWER-REPORT-FINAL.PDF.

3. See, e.g., H. D. Schmidt, "The Idea and Slogan of 'Perfidious Albion,' " *Journal of the History of Ideas* 14, no. 4 (October 1953): 604–616. Thanks to Wess Mitchell for this allusion.

4. Snyder, *Alliance Politics,* 45. There is an enormous literature on alliances. See, among others, Robert Osgood, *Alliances and American Foreign Policy* (Baltimore: Johns Hopkins University Press, 1968); George Liska, *Nations in Alliance: The Limits of Interdependence* (Baltimore: Johns Hopkins University Press, 1968); Stephen M. Walt, *The Origins of Alliances* (Ithaca, NY: Cornell University Press, 1987); James D. Morrow, "Arms versus Allies: Tradeoffs in the Search for Security," *International Organization* 47, no. 2 (1993): 207–233, https://www.jstor.org/stable/2706889; David A. Lake, *Entangling Relations* (Princeton, NJ: Princeton University Press, 1999); Brett Ashley Leeds, "Alliance Reliability in Times of War: Explaining State Decisions to Violate Treaties," *International Organization* 57, no. 4 (Autumn 2003): 801–827, https://www.jstor.org/stable/3594847; Jeremy Pressman, *Warring Friends: Alliance Restraint in International Politics* (Ithaca, NY: Cornell University Press, 2008); Stephen M. Walt, "Alliances in a Unipolar World," *World Politics* 61, no. 1 (2009): 86–120, https://www.jstor.org/stable/40060222; Matthew Fuhrmann and Todd S. Sechser, "Signaling Alliance Commitments: Hand-Tying and Sunk Costs in Extended Nuclear Deterrence," *American Journal of Political Science* 58, no. 4 (2014): 919–935; Paul Poast, *Arguing about Alliances: The Art of Agreement in Military-Pact Negotiations* (Ithaca, NY: Cornell University Press, 2019); and Mira Rapp-Hooper, *Shields of the Republic: The Triumph and Peril of America's Alliances* (Cambridge, MA: Harvard University Press, 2020).

5. For discussions, see James D. Fearon, "Signaling Foreign Policy Interests: Tying Hands versus Sinking Costs," *Journal of Conflict Resolution* 41, no. 4 (February 1997): 68–90, https://doi.org/10.1177/0022002797041001004; and Fuhrmann and Sechser, "Signaling Alliance Commitments."

6. Taiwan Relations Act (Public Law 96-8, 22 U.S.C. 3301 et seq.); and Susan V. Lawrence and Wayne M. Morrison, *Taiwan: Issues for Congress,* R44996 (Washington, DC: Congressional Research Service, October 30, 2017), 7–13 https://crsreports.congress.gov/product/pdf/R/R44996. See also Nancy Bernkopf Tucker, *Strait Talk: United States–Taiwan Relations and the Crisis with China* (Cambridge, MA: Harvard University Press, 2009); and Richard C. Bush, *A One-China Policy Primer* (Washington, DC: Brookings Institution, March 2017), https://www.brookings.edu/wp-content/uploads/2017/03/one-china-policy-primer.pdf.

7. See, e.g., Hugh White, *How to Defend Australia* (Melbourne: La Trobe University Press, 2019).

8. See, e.g., Richard L. Armitage and Victor Cha, "The 66-year Alliance between the U.S. and South Korea Is in Deep Trouble," *Washington Post,* November 22, 2019, https://www.washingtonpost.com/opinions/the-66-year-alliance-between-the-us-and-south-korea-is-in-deep-trouble/2019/11/22/63f593fc-0d63-11ea-bd9d-c628fd48b3a0_story.html; and Germelina Lacorte, "Duterte Says America Will Never Die for PH," *Inquirer,* August 2, 2015, https://globalnation.inquirer.net/126835/duterte-to-military-attaches-ph-not-out-for-war-china-should-just-let-us-fish-in-seas.

9. Victor D. Cha, "Powerplay: Origins of the U.S. Alliance System in Asia," *International Security* 34, no. 3 (Winter 2009/10): 158–196, https://www.jstor.org/stable/40389236.

10. For a description of these tensions, see Brad Glosserman and Scott A. Snyder, *The Japan–South Korea Identity Clash: East Asian Security and the United States* (New York: Columbia University Press, 2015).

11. On India, see C. Raja Mohan, "India between 'Strategic Autonomy' and 'Geopolitical Opportunity,'" *Asia Policy,* no. 15 (January 2013): 21–25, https://www.jstor.org/stable/24905202; and Ashley J. Tellis, *India as a Leading Power* (Washington, DC: Carnegie Endowment for International Peace, April 2016), 3–6, https://carnegieendowment.org/2016/04/04/india-as-leading-power-pub-63185. On Vietnam, see Scott W. Harold et al., *The Thickening Web of Asian Security Cooperation: Deepening Defense Ties among U.S. Allies and Partners in the Indo-Pacific* (Santa Monica, CA: RAND Corporation, 2019), 251–256, 283–284, https://doi.org/10.7249/RR3125.

12. For an official position on the need for flexibility and modest expectations about alliance formation, see Stephen Biegun, "Remarks at the U.S.-India Strategic Partnership Forum" (U.S.-India Strategic Partnership Forum, Washington, DC, August 31, 2020), https://www.state.gov/deputy-secretary-biegun-remarks-at-the-u-s-india-strategic-partnership-forum/.

13. Leslie H. Gelb and Richard K. Betts, *The Irony of Vietnam: The System Worked* (1979; repr., Washington, DC: Brookings Institution Press, 2016), 180.

14. US Department of State, "Overseas Bases: The Strategic Role of Iceland," Research Study (Washington, DC: Bureau of Intelligence and Research, US Department of State, August 14, 1972, declassified December 31, 1981).

15. P. W. J. Riley, *The Union of England and Scotland: A Study in Anglo-Scottish Politics of the 18th Century* (Manchester, UK: Manchester University Press, 1978).

16. For an eloquent argument that a liberal China should be the goal for US strategy, see Aaron L. Friedberg, *A Contest for Supremacy: China, America, and the Struggle for Mastery in Asia* (New York: W. W. Norton, 2011).

17. For a discussion, see Robert Jervis, "Domino Beliefs and Strategic Behavior," in *Dominoes and Bandwagons: Strategic Beliefs and Great Power Competition in the Eurasian Rimland,* ed. Robert Jervis and Jack Snyder (New York: Oxford University Press, 1991), 20–50.

18. For example, Robert Jervis, "Was the Cold War a Security Dilemma?," *Journal of Cold War Studies* 3, no. 1 (Winter 2001): 36–60, www.muse.jhu.edu/article/9175.

19. John Lewis Gaddis, *Strategies of Containment: A Critical Appraisal of American National Security Policy during the Cold War,* rev. ed. (Oxford: Oxford University Press, 2005), esp. 83–88, 95–98, 136–145.

20. Edward Gibbon, *The History of the Decline and Fall of the Roman Empire,* vol. 1 (1776; repr., New York: Harper and Brothers, 1905), ch. 3, sec. 2, 316.

21. Tobin, "Xi's Vision for Transforming Global Governance." See also Rushabh Doshi, "The Long Game: Chinese Grand Strategy after the Cold War" (Ph.D. diss., Harvard University, 2019).

22. Daryl G. Press, *Calculating Credibility: How Leaders Assess Military Threats* (Ithaca, NY: Cornell University Press, 2005), 163n2.

23. Ted Hopf, *Peripheral Visions: Deterrence Theory and American Foreign Policy in the Third World, 1965–1990* (Ann Arbor: University of Michigan Press, 1994); Jonathan Mercer, *Reputation and International Politics* (Ithaca, NY: Cornell University Press, 1996).

24. See, e.g., Geoffrey Parker, "Early Modern Europe," in *The Laws of War: Constraints on Warfare in the Western World,* ed. Michael Howard, George J. Andreopoulos, and Mark R. Shulman (New Haven: Yale University Press, 1994), 40–55.

25. A recent study argues that states evaluate an ally's reliability by monitoring the ally's behavior for convergence in interests. Iain D. Henry, "What Allies Want: Reconsidering Loyalty, Reliability, and Alliance Interdependence," *International Security* 44, no. 4 (Spring 2020): 45–83, https://doi.org/10.1162/ISEC_a_00375.

26. See Benjamin Graham, *The Intelligent Investor: A Book of Practical Counsel,* 3rd ed. (New York: Harper and Row, 1985); and Jonathan Berk and Peter DeMarzo, *Corporate Finance,* 3rd ed. (Boston: Pearson Education, 2014), 312.

27. For such an acknowledgment, see 38th Commandant of the Marine Corps (Gen. David. H. Berger), *Commandant's Planning Guidance* (Washington, DC: United States Marine Corps, July 17, 2019), 3, https://www.hqmc.marines.mil/Portals/142/Docs/%2038th%20 Commandant%27s%20Planning%20Guidance_2019.pdf; and US Department of the Navy, Advantage at Sea: Prevailing with Integrated All-Domain Naval Power (Washington, DC: US Department of the Navy, December 2020), 9, https://media.defense. gov/2020/Dec/16/2002553074/-1/-1/1/TRISERVICESTRATEGY.PDF.

28. See, e.g., "America's Public Pension Plans Make Over-Optimistic Return Assumptions," *Economist,* February 9, 2019, https://www.economist.com/finance-and-economics/2019 /02/09/americas-public-pension-plans-make-over-optimistic-return-assumptions.

29. J. Baxter Oliphant, "The Iraq War Continues to Divide the U.S. Public, 15 Years after It Began," Pew Research Center, March 19, 2018, https://www.pewresearch.org/fact-tank/2018/03/19/iraq-war-continues-to-divide-u-s-public-15-years-after-it-began/.

30. John F. Kennedy, "Inaugural Address" (Washington, DC, January 20, 1961), https:// www.jfklibrary.org/learn/about-jfk/historic-speeches/inaugural-address.

31. See, e.g., US Department of State, "U.S. Collective Defense Arrangements" (Washington, DC: US Department of State, undated, archived content), https://2009-2017.state. gov/s/l/treaty/collectivedefense//index.htm.

32. Jennifer Kavanagh, *U.S. Security-Related Agreements in Force since 1955: Introducing a New Database* (Santa Monica, CA: RAND Corporation, 2014), 21–28, https://www. rand.org/pubs/research_reports/RR736.html.

33. Charles Krauthammer, "The Unipolar Moment," *Foreign Affairs* 70, no. 1 (1990/91): 23–33, doi:10.2307/20044692; Francis Fukuyama, *The End of History and the Last Man* (New York: Free Press, 1992). Fukuyama's argument is more nuanced than commonly appreciated. Fukuyama did not argue that war was impossible; rather, he anticipated that the Hegelian conclusion of humanity's ideological evolution could in fact invite Nietzsche's "immense wars of the spirit." Fukuyama, *End of History,* 328–339. The common reception of the idea, however, emphasized the notion that major conflict was a thing of the past.

34. See, e.g., White, House, *The National Security Strategy of the United States of America* (Washington, DC: White House, September 2002), https://history.defense.gov/

Portals/70/Documents/nss/nss2002.pdf; White House, *The National Security Strategy of the United States of America* (Washington, DC: White House, March 2006), https://history.defense.gov/Portals/70/Documents/nss/nss2006.pdf; and US Department of Defense, *Quadrennial Defense Review Report* (Washington, DC: US Department of Defense, February 6, 2006), https://history.defense.gov/Portals/70/Documents/quadrennial/QDR2006.pdf.

35. Aaron L. Friedberg, "Competing with China," *Survival* 60, no. 3 (June–July 2018): 7–64, doi:10.1080/00396338.2018.1470755.

36. For American commitments in Afghanistan and Iraq, see James Dobbins et al., *After the War: Nation-Building from FDR to George W. Bush* (Santa Monica, CA: RAND Corporation, 2008), 85–133, https://www.rand.org/pubs/monographs/MG716.html.

37. Thomas Alan Schwartz, *Lyndon Johnson and Europe: The Shadow of Vietnam* (Cambridge, MA: Harvard University Press, 2003), esp. 140–142.

38. Edward Wong, "Americans Demand a Rethinking of the 'Forever War,'" *New York Times,* February 2, 2020, https://www.nytimes.com/2020/02/02/us/politics/trump-forever-war.html; Mark Hannah, *Worlds Apart: U.S. Foreign Policy and American Public Opinion* (New York: Eurasia Group Foundation, February 2019), https://egfound.org/wp-content/uploads/2019/02/EGF-WorldsApart-2019.pdf.

39. For comparable discussions, see Paul K. Huth, "Reputations and Deterrence: A Theoretical and Empirical Assessment," *Security Studies* 7, no. 1 (Autumn 1997): 72–99, doi:10.1080/09636419708429334; and Frank P. Harvey and John Mitton, *Fighting for Credibility: U.S. Reputation and International Politics* (Toronto: University of Toronto Press, 2017). For more expansive views of the importance of credibility, see Alex Weisiger and Keren Yarhi-Milo, "Revisiting Reputation: How Past Actions Matter in International Politics," *International Organization* 69, no. 2 (March 2015): 472–495, https://www.jstor.org/stable/24758122; and Hal Brands, Eric S. Edelman, and Thomas G. Mahnken, *Credibility Matters: Strengthening American Deterrence in an Age of Geopolitical Turmoil* (Washington, DC: Center for Strategic and Budgetary Assessments, 2018), https://csbaonline.org/uploads/documents/Credibility_Paper_FINAL_format.pdf. For a discussion of these issues, see Dale C. Copeland, "Do Reputations Matter?," *Security Studies* 7, no. 1 (Autumn 1997): 33–71, doi:10.1080/09636419708429333.

40. A number of scholars have found that leaders and governments use a state's reputation to make inferences about the state's behavior in a variety of contexts. Mark J. C. Crescenzi, "Reputation and Interstate Conflict," *American Journal of Political Science* 51, no. 2 (April 2007): 382–396, https://www.jstor.org/stable/4620072; Barbara F. Walter, *Reputation and Civil War: Why Separatist Conflicts Are So Violent* (Cambridge: Cambridge University Press, 2009); Gregory D. Miller, *The Shadow of the Past: Reputation and Military Alliances before the First World War* (Ithaca, NY: Cornell University Press, 2012); Danielle L. Lupton, "Signaling Resolve: Leaders, Reputations, and the Importance of Early Interaction," *International Interactions* 44, no. 1 (2018): 59–87, doi:10.7591/j.ctvq2w564.6.

41. There is an extensive literature on the relative role of stakes and military power in determining the outcome of conflicts and crises. See, e.g., Robert Powell, "The Theoretical Foundations of Strategic Nuclear Deterrence," *Political Science Quarterly* 100, no. 1 (Spring 1985): 76–96, https://www.jstor.org/stable/2150861; and Todd S. Sechser and

Mathew Fuhrmann, *Nuclear Weapons and Coercive Diplomacy* (Cambridge: Cambridge University Press, 2017), 32–33, 50–51.

42. For instance, despite Argentina's threat to invoke the Rio Treaty during the Falklands crisis, the United States sided instead with its NATO ally, Great Britain. Lawrence Freedman, *The Official History of the Falklands Campaign,* vol. 2, *War and Diplomacy* (Abingdon, UK: Routledge, 2005), 119.

43. See, e.g., Bennett Ramberg, "The Precedents for Withdrawal: From Vietnam to Iraq," *Foreign Affairs* 88, no. 2 (March/April 2009): 2–8, ww.jstor.org/stable/20699489; and Hopf, *Peripheral Visions,* 36.

44. Fact patterns are a "concise description of all the occurrences of circumstance of a particular case, without any discussion of their consequences under the law." Jeffrey Lehman and Shirelle Phelps, *West's Encyclopedia of American Law,* 2nd ed., vol. 7 (Detroit, MI: Thomson/Gale, 2005), 114; Henry Campbell Black, *Black's Law Dictionary,* rev. 4th ed. (St. Paul, Minn.: West, 1968), 345, 561, 1184; Grant Lamond, "Precedent and Analogy in Legal Reasoning," Stanford Encyclopedia of Philosophy, June 20, 2006, https://plato.stanford.edu/entries/legal-reas-prec/.

Chapter 4. Defining the Defense Perimeter

1. The idea of maintaining a "defensive perimeter" against the Soviets gained traction in the United States by the late 1940s. George Kennan played a central role in these discussions, advocating first "confront[ing] the Russians with unalterable counterforce at every point where they show signs of encroaching" and later for a more focused approach to containing Soviet expansion. These approaches have been referred to as "perimeter defense" and "strongpoint defense," respectively. John Lewis Gaddis, *Strategies of Containment: A Critical Appraisal of American National Security Policy during the Cold War,* rev. ed. (Oxford: Oxford University Press, 2005), 56–57.

2. US Defense Intelligence Agency, *Iran Military Power: Ensuring Regime Survival and Securing Regional Dominance,* DIA_Q_00055_A (Washington, DC: US Defense Intelligence Agency, 2019), 12, https://www.dia.mil/Portals/27/Documents/News/Military%20Power%20Publications/Iran_Military_Power_LR.pdf.

3. Richard C. Bush, *A One-China Policy Primer* (Washington, DC: Brookings Institution, March 2017), https://www.brookings.edu/wp-content/uploads/2017/03/one-china-policy-primer.pdf.

4. Dwight Eisenhower expressed a similar logic in 1945: "I have considered the effect on the enemy should Sweden enter the war, and conclude that if she should do so, and was able to hold her own without Allied support other than by air, it would be to our advantage. *But in no circumstances do we wish to accumulate further commitments which would divert effort from the main front."* Alfred D. Chandler Jr., ed., *The Papers of Dwight David Eisenhower: The War Years,* vol. 4 (Baltimore: Johns Hopkins University Press, 1970), 2433, emphasis in original.

5. Snyder, *Alliance Politics,* 45.

6. See George Liska, *Nations in Alliance: The Limits of Interdependence* (Baltimore: Johns Hopkins University Press, 1968), 60–66; Robert O. Keohane and Joseph S. Nye, *Power*

and Interdependence: World Politics in Transition (Boston: Little, Brown, 1977), 55; and G. John Ikenberry, "Institutions, Strategic Restraints, and the Persistence of American Postwar Order," *International Security* 23, no. 3 (Winter 1998/99): 67–71, doi:10.2307/2539338.

7. See, e.g., Johannes Kadura, *The War after the War: The Struggle for Credibility during America's Exit from Vietnam* (Ithaca, NY: Cornell University Press, 2016).

8. Freedom House, *Freedom in the World 2019* (Washington, DC: Freedom House, February 2019), 14, https://freedomhouse.org/report/freedom-world/2019/democracy-retreat.

9. See, e.g., Samuel P. Huntington, *The Third Wave: Democratization in the Late Twentieth Century* (Norman: University of Oklahoma Press, 1991), esp. 91–98.

10. Similar views appear to be widely shared within NATO. See, e.g., Robin Emmott and Sabine Siebold, "NATO Split on Message to Send Georgia on Membership Hopes," *Reuters,* November 27, 2015, https://www.reuters.com/article/us-nato-georgia/nato-split-on-message-to-send-georgia-on-membership-hopes-idUSKBN0TG1HP20151127.

11. The combined Composite Index of National Capability score of Australia, India, and Japan is .119; China's score is .218. Moreover, China far exceeds all three in disaggregated rankings of economic resources, wealth, and "economic capability," the metric designed by political scientist Michael Beckley. David J. Singer, Stuart Bremer, and John Stuckey, "Capability Distribution, Uncertainty, and Major Power War, 1820–1965," in *Peace, War, and Numbers,* ed. Bruce Russett (Beverly Hills, CA: Sage, 1972), 19–48; Lowy Institute, *Asia Power Index 2019* (Sydney, Australia: Lowy Institute, 2019), 4, 38–39, https://power.lowyinstitute.org/downloads/Lowy-Institute-Asia-Power-Index-2019-Pocket-Book.pdf; and Beckley, "Power of Nations," 11.

12. On regional power and growth projections, see Lowy Institute, *Asia Power Index 2019;* Organisation for Economic Cooperation and Development (OECD), *Economic Outlook for Southeast Asia, China and India 2020: Rethinking Education for the Digital Era,* preliminary version (Paris: OECD, November 2019), https://www.oecd.org/dev/economic-outlook-for-southeast-asia-china-and-india-23101113.htm; World Bank, *East Asia and Pacific Economic Update: Weathering Growing Risks* (Washington, DC: World Bank Group, October 2019), https://openknowledge.worldbank.org/handle/10986/32482.

13. On Cambodia, see Tanner Greer, "Cambodia Wants China as Its Neighborhood Bully," *Foreign Policy,* January 5, 2017, https://foreignpolicy.com/2017/01/05/cambodia-wants-china-as-its-neighborhood-bully/. On Pakistan, see, e.g., Harry I. Hannah, "The Great Game Moves to Sea: The Indian Ocean Region," *War on the Rocks,* April 1, 2019, https://warontherocks.com/2019/04/the-great-game-moves-to-sea-tripolar-competition-in-the-indian-ocean-region/; and Maria Abi-Habib, "China's 'Belt and Road' Plan in Pakistan Takes a Military Turn," *New York Times,* December 19, 2018, https://www.nytimes.com/2018/12/19/world/asia/pakistan-china-belt-road-military.html.

Chapter 5. Military Strategy in Limited Wars

1. For varying definitions, see, among others, Arthur F. Lykke Jr., "Defining Military Strategy," *Military Review* 69, no. 5 (May 1989): 3; Richard K. Betts, "Is Strategy an Illusion?," *International Security* 25, no. 2 (Fall 2000): 5, doi:10.1162/016228800560444;

Edward N. Luttwak, *Strategy: The Logic of War and Peace,* 2nd ed. (Cambridge, MA: Belknap Press of Harvard University Press, 2001), 2; and Colin S. Gray, *The Future of Strategy* (Cambridge: Polity, 2015), 23.

2. See, e.g., Michael Geyer, "German Strategy in the Age of Machine Warfare, 1914–1945," in *Makers of Modern Strategy from Machiavelli to the Nuclear Age,* ed. Peter Paret, Gordon A. Craig, and Felix Gilbert (Princeton, NJ: Princeton University Press, 1986), 527–597.

3. See, e.g., John Keegan, *A History of Warfare* (New York: Alfred A. Knopf, 1993), 379–385.

4. As then secretary of defense James Schlesinger remarked in 1974, "All wars since 1945 have been non-nuclear wars shadowed by the nuclear presence. The threat to use nuclear weapons has remained, for the most part, in the background, but belligerents and neutrals alike have known that, like the big stick in the closet, it was there." James R. Schlesinger, *Annual Defense Department Report FY 1975* (Washington, DC: Government Printing Office, 1974), 25, https://history.defense.gov/Portals/70/Documents/annual_reports/1975_DoD_AR.pdf. Paul Nitze made a similar point earlier: "The situation is analogous to a game of chess. The atomic queens may never be brought into play; they may never actually take one of the opponent's pieces. But the position of the atomic queens may still have a decisive bearing on which side can safely advance a limited-war bishop or even a cold war pawn." Paul H. Nitze, "Atoms, Strategy and Policy," *Foreign Affairs* 32, no. 2 (January 1956): 195, doi:10.2307/20031154.

5. As the US Department of Defense assessed in August 2020, "The anticipated changes to the capacity, capability, and readiness of China's nuclear forces in the coming years seem likely to outpace potential developments by any adversary that could plausibly threaten China's ability to retaliate against a first strike." Office of the Secretary of Defense, *Annual Report to Congress: Military and Security Developments Involving the People's Republic of China 2020,* 9-A3DFCD4 (Washington, DC: US Department of Defense, August 11, 2020), 86, https://media.defense.gov/2020/Sep/01/2002488689/-1/-1/1/2020-DOD-CHINA-MILITARY-POWER-REPORT-FINAL.PDF.

6. See, e.g., Dale C. Copeland, *The Origins of Major War* (Ithaca, NY: Cornell University Press, 2000), esp. 1–78, 147–175.

7. Indeed, "effective restraint of war" is a tenet of China's strategic concept of active defense. Office of the Secretary of Defense, *Annual Report to Congress,* 28. This also appears to inform PLA campaign planning. See, e.g., Edmund J. Burke et al., *People's Liberation Army Operational Concepts* (Santa Monica, CA: RAND Corporation, 2020), 8, https://doi.org/10.7249/RRA394-1.

8. For the standard overview of the evolution of this strain of strategic thinking, see Lawrence Freedman and Jeffrey Michaels, *The Evolution of Nuclear Strategy,* 4th ed. (New York: Palgrave Macmillan, 2019). See also Marc Trachtenberg, "Strategic Thought in America, 1952–1966," *Political Science Quarterly* 104, no. 2 (Summer 1989): 301–334, doi:10.2307/2151586.

9. Francis J. Gavin, *Nuclear Statecraft: History and Strategy in America's Atomic Age* (Ithaca, NY: Cornell University Press, 2014), 57–74.

10. Peter Hayes, Lyuba Zarsky, and Walden Bello, *American Lake: Nuclear Peril in the Pacific* (New York: Penguin Books, 1986), 57–59.

11. The conceptual literature on limited war is extensive. See, e.g., Robert E. Osgood, *Limited War: The Challenge to American Strategy* (Chicago: University of Chicago Press, 1957); Bernard Brodie, "The Meaning of Limited War" (Santa Monica, CA: RAND Corporation, 1958), https://www.rand.org/pubs/research_memoranda/RM2224.html; Thomas Schelling, "Nuclear Weapons and Limited War" (Santa Monica, CA: RAND Corporation, 1959), www.rand.org/pubs/research_memoranda/RM2510.html; Klaus E. Knorr and Thornton Reed, eds., *Limited Strategic War* (New York: Praeger, 1962); Morton H. Halperin, *Limited War in the Nuclear Age* (New York: Wiley, 1963); Herman Kahn, *On Escalation: Metaphors and Scenarios* (New York: Praeger, 1965); Henry A. Kissinger, *Nuclear Weapons and Foreign Policy* (New York: W. W. Norton, 1969); and Robert E. Osgood, "The Reappraisal of Limited War," *Adelphi Papers* 9, no. 54: Problems of Modern Strategy, Part I (1969): 41–54, https://doi.org/10.1080/05679326908448127. For some of its impact, see Stephen Peter Rosen, "Vietnam and the American Theory of Limited War," *International Security* 7, no. 2 (Fall 1982): 83–113, doi:10.2307/2538434.

12. On war termination, see Thomas C. Schelling, *Arms and Influence* (1966; repr., New Haven: Yale University Press, 2008), esp. 204–220; and Fred Charles Iklé, *Every War Must End,* 2nd ed. (1971; repr., New York: Columbia University Press, 2005).

13. See Robert A. Pape, *Bombing to Win: Air Power and Coercion in* War (Ithaca, NY: Cornell University Press, 1996), 254–313.

14. See Wallace J. Thies, *When Governments Collide: Coercion and Diplomacy in the Vietnam Conflict, 1964–1968* (Berkeley: University of California Press, 1980), esp. 82–93.

15. General Omar Bradley noted that the Chinese "have not used air against our front line troops, against our lines of communication in Korea, our ports; they have not used air against our bases in Japan or against our naval force." Bradley reasoned, "We are fighting under rather favorable rules for ourselves." Quoted in H. W. Brands, *The General vs. the President: MacArthur and Truman at the Brink of Nuclear War* (New York: Doubleday, 2016), 365. See also Morton H. Halperin, "The Limiting Process in the Korean War," *Political Science Quarterly* 78, no. 1 (March 1963): 13–39, doi:10.2307/2146665; Alexander L. George and Richard Smoke, *Deterrence in American Foreign Policy: Theory and Practice* (New York: Columbia University Press, 1974), 188–189; Richard Ned Lebow, *Between Peace and War: The Nature of International Crisis* (Baltimore: Johns Hopkins University Press, 1981), 148–228; and Thomas J. Christensen, *Useful Adversaries: Grand Strategy, Domestic Mobilization, and Sino-American Conflict, 1947–1958* (Princeton, NJ: Princeton University Press, 1996), 138–193.

16. Roger Dingman, "Atomic Diplomacy during the Korean War," *International Security* 13, no. 3 (Winter 1988/89): 66, doi:10.2307/2538736.

17. See, e.g., Wayne Thompson, *To Hanoi and Back: The United States Air Force and North Vietnam, 1966–1973* (Washington, DC: Air Force History and Museums Program, United States Air Force, 2000), 255–259.

18. See, e.g., Max Hastings, *Vietnam: An Epic Tragedy, 1945–1975* (New York: HarperCollins, 2018), 689–725.

19. For Schelling's discussion of the idea of a mutual "focal point," see Thomas C. Schelling, *The Strategy of Conflict* (1960; repr., Cambridge, MA: Harvard University Press, 1980), 57.

20. As Schelling wrote: "The power hurt is bargaining power. To exploit it is diplomacy—vicious diplomacy, but diplomacy." Schelling, *Arms and Influence,* 2.

21. As Helmuth von Moltke the Elder described, strategy is an *Aushilfe,* or an offset that compensates for material weakness. See foreword to Carl von Clausewitz, *Vom Kriege* (Berlin: Ferd. Dümmlers, 1911), cited in A. Wess Mitchell, *The Grand Strategy of the Habsburg Empire* (Princeton, NJ: Princeton University Press, 2018), 11.

22. Classic accounts of resolve and brinkmanship include Schelling, *Arms and Influence,* 92–125; Richard K. Betts, *Nuclear Blackmail and Nuclear Balance* (Washington, DC: Brookings Institution Press, 1987), 14–15; Robert Jervis, *The Meaning of the Nuclear Revolution: Statecraft and the Prospect of Armageddon* (Ithaca, NY: Cornell University Press, 1989), 193–201; and Charles L. Glaser, *Analyzing Strategic Nuclear Policy* (Princeton, NJ: Princeton University Press, 1990), 35–37.

23. Max Hastings, *Retribution: The Battle for Japan, 1944–45* (New York: Alfred A. Knopf, 2008), 283.

24. James M. McPherson, *Battle Cry of Freedom: The Civil War Era* (New York: Oxford University Press, 1988), 263, 267, 271–275.

25. See, e.g., Schlesinger, *Annual Defense Department Report,* 4.

26. See, e.g., Leon V. Sigal, *Fighting to a Finish: The Politics of War Termination in the United States and Japan, 1945* (Ithaca, NY: Cornell University Press, 1988).

Chapter 6. The Importance of Focusing on an Opponent's Best Strategies

1. For a discussion of the concept of "theory of victory," see especially Brad Roberts, *The Case for U.S. Nuclear Weapons in the 21st Century* (Stanford, CA: Stanford University Press, 2014); and Brad Roberts, *On Theories of Victory, Red and Blue* (Livermore, CA: Center for Global Security, Lawrence Livermore National Laboratory, June 2020), https://cgsr.llnl.gov/content/assets/docs/CGSR-LivermorePaper7.pdf.

2. For more recent contributions on the causes of the First World War, see, e.g., Steven E. Miller, Sean M. Lynn-Jones, and Stephen Van Evera, eds., *Military Strategy and the Origins of the First World War: An International Security Reader,* rev. and expanded ed. (Princeton, NJ: Princeton University Press, 1991); Dale C. Copeland, *The Origins of Major War* (Ithaca, NY: Cornell University Press, 2000); and Kier A. Lieber, "The New History of World War I and What It Means for International Relations Theory," *International Security* 32, no. 2 (Fall 2007): 155–191, https://www.jstor.org/stable/30133878. The seminal study of the Cuban Missile Crisis is Graham T. Allison and Philip Zelikow, *Essence of Decision: Explaining the Cuban Missile Crisis,* 2nd ed. (New York: Pearson, 1999). See also James G. Blight and David A. Welch, *On the Brink: Americans and Soviets Reexamine the Cuban Missile Crisis* (New York: Hill and Wang, 1989).

3. See, e.g., Ian Kershaw, *Fateful Choices: Ten Decisions That Changed the World, 1940–1941* (New York: Penguin Press, 2007).

4. Richard J. Heuer Jr., "Nosenko: Five Paths to Judgment," in *Inside CIA's Private World: Declassified Articles from the Agency's Internal Journal, 1955–1992,* ed. H. Bradford Westerfield (New Haven: Yale University Press, 1995).

5. See, e.g., Peter Mattis and Matthew Brazil, *Chinese Communist Espionage: An Intelligence Primer* (Annapolis: MD: Naval Institute Press, 2019).

6. See, e.g., Brian Bond, *Britain, France, and Belgium, 1939–1940,* 2nd ed. (Newark, NJ: Brassey's, 1990), 35–54.

7. For the Civil War, see James M. McPherson, *Battle Cry of Freedom: The Civil War Era* (New York: Oxford University Press, 1988), 537. For the Second World War, see Chris Bellamy, *Absolute War: Soviet Russia in the Second World War* (London: Pan Books, 2007), 498.

8. Carl von Clausewitz, *On War,* ed. and trans. Michael Howard and Peter Paret (Princeton, NJ: Princeton University Press 1976, revised 1989), 101, 117.

9. See, e.g., Christopher Andrew and Vasili Mitrokhin, *The Sword and the Shield: The Mitrokhin Archive and the Secret History of the KGB* (New York: Basic Books, 1985); Christopher Andrew and Vasili Mitrokhin, *The World Was Going Our Way: The KGB and the Battle for the Third World* (New York: Basic Books, 2005); and John G. Hines, Ellis M. Mishulovich, and John F. Shull, "Soviet Intentions, 1965–1985: An Analytical Comparison of U.S.-Soviet Assessments during the Cold War," OSD-Net Assessment Contract #MDA903-92-C-0147 (McLean, VA: BDM Federal, September 22, 1995), 68–71, https://nsarchive2.gwu.edu/NSAEBB/NSAEBB426/docs/25.%20Series%20of%20 six%20Interviews%20with%20Dr.Tsygichko%20by%20John%20G.%20Hines-begin-ning%20December%2010,%201990.pdf.

10. General Joseph Dunford Jr., "From the Chairman: Maintaining a Boxer's Stance," *Joint Force Quarterly* 86, no. 3 (2017): 2–3, https://ndupress.ndu.edu/Publications/Arti-cle/1218381/from-the-chairman-maintaining-a-boxers-stance/.

11. Richard K. Betts, *Surprise Attack: Lessons for Defense Planning* (Washington, DC: Brookings Institution Press, 1982), 34–42.

12. See P. K. Rose, "Two Strategic Intelligence Mistakes in Korea, 1950: Perceptions and Reality," *Studies in Intelligence* 45, no. 5 (Fall/Winter 2001): 57–65, https://www.cia.gov/library/center-for-the-study-of-intelligence/csi-publications/csi-studies/studies/fall_winter_2001/article06.html.

13. See Walter E. Kaegi, *Byzantium and the Early Islamic Conquests* (New York: Cambridge University Press, 1992), 73; Edward Luttwak, *The Grand Strategy of the Byzantine Empire* (Cambridge, MA: Belknap Press of Harvard University Press, 2011), 33.

14. Ernest R. May, *Strange Victory: Hitler's Conquest of France* (New York: Hill and Wang, 2000), 348–362.

15. The classic study is Roberta Wohlstetter, *Pearl Harbor: Warning and Decision* (Stanford, CA: Stanford University Press, 1962). For a revisionist view, see Erik J. Dahl, *Intelligence and Surprise Attack: Failure and Success from Pearl Harbor to 9/11 and Beyond* (Washington, DC: Georgetown University Press, 2013).

16. National Commission on Terrorist Attacks upon the United States, *The 9/11 Commission Report: Final Report of the National Commission on Terrorism Attacks upon the United States* (New York: W. W. Norton, 2004), 254–278.

17. See, e.g., Nora Bensahel, "Darker Shades of Gray: Why Gray Zone Conflicts Will Become More Frequent and Complex," Foreign Policy Research Institute, February, 13, 2017, https://www.fpri.org/article/2017/02/darker-shades-gray-gray-zone-conflicts-will-become-frequent-complex/; and Michael E. O'Hanlon, *China, the Gray Zone, and Contingency Planning at the Department of Defense and Beyond* (Washington, DC: Brookings Institution, September 2019), https://www.brookings.edu/research/china-the-gray-zone-and-con-tingency-planning-at-the-department-of-defense-and-beyond/.

18. For a review of these factors, see, e.g., Alan S. Blinder, Andrew W. Lo, and Robert M. Solow, eds., *Rethinking the Financial Crisis* (New York: Russell Sage Foundation, 2013).

19. For the classic account, see Edward Hallett Carr, *The Twenty Years' Crisis, 1919–1929: An Introduction to the Study of International Relations,* 2nd ed. (New York: Harper and Row, 1964).

20. Special thanks to Alex Velez-Green for this insight.

21. See, e.g., Keith B. Payne, *The Great American Gamble: Deterrence Theory and Practice from the Cold War to the Twenty-First Century* (Fairfax, VA: National Institute Press, 2008).

22. For a recent official statement of this long-standing policy, see US Department of Defense, *Nuclear Posture Review* (Washington, DC: US Department of Defense, 2018), vii, https://dod.defense.gov/News/SpecialReports/2018NuclearPostureReview.aspx. For a broader recent history, see Roberts, *Case for U.S. Nuclear Weapons.*

23. See, e.g., John Lewis Gaddis, "The Long Peace: Elements of Stability in the Postwar International System," *International Security* 10, no. 4 (Spring 1986): 99–142, doi:10.2307/2538951.

Chapter 7. Beijing's Best Strategy

1. Quansheng Zhao, *Interpreting Chinese Foreign Policy: The Micro-Macro Linkage Approach* (Hong Kong: Oxford University Press, 1996), 53–54. See, e.g., Daniel Tobin, *How Xi Jinping's "New Era" Should Have Ended U.S. Debate on Beijing's Ambitions* (Washington, DC: Center for Strategic and International Studies, May 2020), https://www.csis.org/analysis/how-xi-jinpings-new-era-should-have-ended-us-debate-beijings-ambitions; Tanner Greer, "China's Plans to Win Control of the Global Order," *Tablet,* May 17, 2020, https://www.tabletmag.com/sections/news/articles/china-plans-global-order; Bonnie S. Glaser and Mathew P. Funaiole, "The 19th Party Congress: A More Assertive Chinese Foreign Policy," *Interpreter* (Lowy Institute), October 26, 2017, https://www.lowyinstitute.org/the-interpreter/19th-party-congress-more-assertive-chinese-foreign-policy; and Rush Doshi, "Hu's to Blame for China's Foreign Assertiveness," Brookings Institution, January 22, 2019, https://www.brookings.edu/articles/hus-to-blame-for-chinas-foreign-assertiveness/.

2. See Nadège Rolland, ed., *Securing the Belt and Road Initiative: China's Evolving Military Engagement along the Silk Roads,* NBR Special Report #80 (Seattle, WA: National Bureau of Asian Research, September, 2019), esp. 1, 8, 10–12, https://www.nbr.org/wp-content/uploads/pdfs/publications/sr80_securing_the_belt_and_road_sep2019.pdf; Xi Jinping, "Remarks by President Obama and President Xi of the People's Republic of China in Joint Press Conference" (Washington, DC: White House, September 25, 2015), https://obamawhitehouse.archives.gov/the-press-office/2015/09/25/remarks-president-obama-and-president-xi-peoples-republic-china-joint; and Michael R. Pompeo, "P.R.C. National People's Congress Proposal on Hong Kong National Security Legislation," press statement (Washington, DC: US Department of State, May 27, 2020), https://www.state.gov/prc-national-peoples-congress-proposal-on-hong-kong-national-security-legislation/.

3. See, e.g., Robert A. Pape, "Why Economic Sanctions Still Do Not Work," *International Security* 23, no.1 (Summer 1998): 66–77, doi:10.2307/2539263; and Michael Singh, "Conflict with Small Powers Derails U.S. Foreign Policy: The Case for Strategic Discipline," *Foreign Affairs,* August 12, 2020, https://www.foreignaffairs.com/articles/north-america/2020-08-12/conflict-small-powers-derails-us-foreign-policy.

4. See, e.g., U.S.-China Economic and Security Review Commission, *2019 Report to Congress* (Washington, DC: U.S.-China Economic and Security Review Commission, November 2019), esp. 136–152, https://www.uscc.gov/sites/default/files/2019-11/2019%20 Annual%20Report%20to%20Congress.pdf; Keith Johnson and Robbie Gramer, "The Great Decoupling," *Foreign Policy,* https://foreignpolicy.com/2020/05/14/china-us-pandemic-economy-tensions-trump-coronavirus-covid-new-cold-war-economics-the-great-decoupling/; Rana Foroohar, "Coronavirus Is Speeding Up the Decoupling of Global Economies," *Financial Times,* February 23, 2020, https://www.ft.com/content/5cfea02e-549f-11ea-90ad-25e377c0ee1f; and Laura Silver, Kat Devlin, and Christine Huang, "Unfavorable Views of China Reach Historic Highs in Many Countries," Pew Research Center, October 6, 2020, https://www.pewresearch.org/global/2020/10/06/unfavorable-views-of-china-reach-historic-highs-in-many-countries/.

5. Marc Ozawa, ed., "The Alliance Five Years after Crimea: Implementing the Wales Summit Pledges" (Rome: Research Division, NATO Defense College, December 2017), http://www.ndc.nato.int/news/news.php?icode=1406; Lawrence S. Kaplan, *The United States and NATO: The Formative Years* (Lexington: University Press of Kentucky, 1984), esp. 8–11.

6. See, e.g., Chinese Taiwan Affairs Office and Information Office of the State Council, "The Taiwan Question and Reunification of China" (Taiwan Affairs Office and Information Office of the State Council, People's Republic of China, August 1993), china.org. cn/english/7953.htm. China has passed legislation codifying its "reunification policy" toward Taiwan, including by so-called nonpeaceful means. Susan V. Lawrence and Wayne M. Morrison, *Taiwan: Issues for Congress,* R44996 (Washington, DC: Congressional Research Service, October 30, 2017), 40–41, https://crsreports.congress.gov/ product/pdf/R/R44996.

7. Xi Jinping, "Secure a Decisive Victory in Building a Moderately Prosperous Society in All Respects and Strive for the Great Success of Socialism with Chinese Characteristics for a New Era" (19th National Congress of the Communist Party of China, Beijing, October 18, 2017), 21, xinhuanet.com/english/download/Xi_Jinping's_report_at_19th_ CPC_National_Congress.pdf. For more, see *Hearing on U.S.-China Relations in 2019: A Year in Review, before the U.S.-China Economic and Security Review Commission,* 116th Cong. esp. 1–2 (2019) (statement of Bonnie Glaser, Senior Advisor and Director, China Power Project, Center for Strategic and International Studies), https://www.uscc. gov/sites/default/files/Panel%20III%20Glaser_Written%20Testimony.pdf.

8. National Security Council, "U.S. Strategic Framework for the Indo-Pacific," (Washington, DC: White House, 2018), 7, https://www.whitehouse.gov/wp-content/uploads/2021 /01/IPS-Final-Declass.pdf; Lawrence Eagleburger, "Taiwan Arms Sales," cable to James Lilley (Washington, DC: White House, July 10, 1982), https://www.ait.org.tw/wp-content/uploads/sites/269/State-cable-of-1982-07-10-200235.pdf; and George Shultz, "Assurances for Taiwan," cable to James Lilley (Washington, DC: US Department of

State, August 17, 1982), https://www.ait.org.tw/wp-content/uploads/sites/269/State-ca-ble-of-1982-08-17-200235-1.pdf. On declassification of these cables, US Assistant Secretary of State for East Asian and Pacific Affairs David R. Stilwell stated: "We have changed nothing about these longstanding policies. What we are doing, though, is making some important updates to our engagement with Taiwan to better reflect these policies and respond to changing circumstances." Stilwell, "The United States, Taiwan, and the World: Partners for Peace and Prosperity" (Washington, DC: Heritage Foundation, August 31, 2020), https://www.state.gov/The-United-States-Taiwan-and-the-World-Partners-for-Peace-and-Prosperity/. See also Kathrin Hille, Demetri Sevastopulo, and Katrina Manson, "US Declassifies Taiwan Security Assurances," *Financial Times,* August 31, 2020, https://www.ft.com/content/24e87b4b-b146-4ea8-a9b2-9f801af21ea6.

9. National Security Council, "U.S. Strategic Framework for the Indo-Pacific," (Washington, DC: White House, 2018), 7, https://www.whitehouse.gov/wp-content/uploads/2021/01/IPS-Final-Declass.pdf; see also the comparisons of a US defense of Taiwan from 1996 to 2017 in Eric Heginbotham et al., *The U.S.-China Military Scorecard: Forces, Geography, and the Evolving Balance of Power, 1996–2017* (Santa Monica, CA: RAND Corporation, 2015), 23–41, https://www.jstor.org/stable/10.7249/j.ctt17rw5gb.

10. Ralph Cossa, former president of CSIS Pacific Forum and one of the most knowledgeable and well-connected experts on Asia security issues, related the following: "Based on hundreds, if not thousands, of discussions with Korean, Japanese, and other Asian officials and security specialists, I am convinced that the credibility of U.S. alliances in Asia and elsewhere hinges upon the credibility of the de facto U.S. defense commitment to Taiwan. Were the U.S. to fail to come to Taiwan's assistance in the event of an unprovoked attack by the Mainland, U.S. allies would lose faith in our alliances and seek other means of insuring their survival, be it an independent nuclear capability or seeking accommodation with Beijing. U.S. allies are comfortable with a degree of strategic ambiguity, especially since they don't want to publicly commit to lining up against China, but look to Taiwan as the proof in the pudding/canary in the coalmine." Ralph Cossa, email message to author, August 25, 2020. See also Richard Haass and David Sacks, "American Support for Taiwan Must Be Unambiguous: To Keep the Peace, Make Clear to China That Force Won't Stand," *Foreign Affairs,* September 2, 2020, https://www.foreignaffairs.com/articles/united-states/american-support-taiwan-must-be-unambiguous; Paul Dibb, "Taiwan Could Force Us into an ANZUS-Busting Choice," *Australian,* August 4, 2020, https://www.theaustralian.com.au/commentary/taiwan-could-force-us-into-an-anzusbusting-choice/news-story/02d38e6d3164ecff1e965b16f85a93f3; and Russell Hsiao, "Fortnightly Review," in *Global Taiwan Brief* 5, no. 18 (September 23, 2020), http://globaltaiwan.org/wp-content/uploads/2020/09/GTB-PDF-5.18.pdf.

11. Survey data of thought leaders in Asia indicate that allies and partners believe the United States would take considerable risk in defending Taiwan from Chinese aggression. Michael J. Green et al., "Survey Findings: U.S. Allies and Partners," Mapping the Future of U.S. China Policy (CSIS), October 13, 2020, https://chinasurvey.csis.org/groups/allies-and-partners/.

12. Jim Thomas, John Stillion, and Iskander Rehman, *Hard ROC 2.0: Taiwan and Deterrence through Protraction* (Washington, DC: Center for Strategic and Budgetary Assessments, 2014), 5–10, https://csbaonline.org/research/publications/hard-roc-2-0-taiwan-and

-deterrence-through-protraction; Office of the Secretary of Defense, *Annual Report to Congress: Military and Security Developments Involving the People's Republic of China 2020,* 9-A3DFCD4 (Washington, DC: US Department of Defense, August 11, 2020), 164–166, https://media.defense.gov/2020/Sep/01/2002488689/-1/-1/1/2020-DOD-CHINA-MILITARY-POWER-REPORT-FINAL.PDF. See also Ian Easton, *The Chinese Invasion Threat: Taiwan's Defense and American Strategy in Asia* (Arlington, VA: Project 2049 Institute, 2017).

13. A 2015 study projected that by 2017 the United States would lack major advantage in all nine dimensions of cross-strait military competition; indeed, the United States would suffer disadvantage in two key dimensions, air base defense and surface warfare, and find itself at parity in four others. Moreover, in their assessment trends would worsen for the United States beyond 2017. Heginbotham et al., *U.S.-China Military Scorecard,* 318.

14. Office of the Secretary of Defense, *Annual Report to Congress,* esp. 58–62; US Defense Intelligence Agency, *China Military Power: Modernizing a Force to Fight and Win,* DIA-02–1706–085 (Washington, DC: Defense Intelligence Agency, 2019), esp. 33–36, https://www.dia.mil/Portals/27/Documents/News/Military%20Power%20Publications/China_Military_Power_FINAL_5MB_20190103.pdf. See also David Lague, "China Expands Its Amphibious Forces in Challenge to U.S. Supremacy beyond Asia," *Reuters,* July 20, 2020, https://www.reuters.com/investigates/special-report/china-military-amphibious/.

15. See Thomas Lum, *The Republic of the Philippines and U.S. Interests,* R43498 (Washington, DC: Congressional Research Service, April 5, 2012), 14–18, https://crsreports.congress.gov/product/pdf/R/R43498; Bureau of East Asian and Pacific Affairs, "U.S. Relations with the Philippines," Bilateral Relations Fact Sheet (Washington, DC: US Department of State, January 21, 2018), https://www.state.gov/u-s-relations-with-the-philippines/; and *Hearing on U.S. Pacific Command Posture, before the Subcommittee on Defense, Committee on Appropriations, U.S. House of Representatives,* 114th Cong. 12 (2016) (statement of ADM Harry B. Harris Jr., USN, Commander, US Pacific Command), https://docs.house.gov/meetings/AP/AP02/20160414/104762/HHRG-114-AP02-Wstate-HarrisA-20160414.pdf.

16. Denny Roy, *Return of the Dragon: Rising China and Regional Security* (New York: Columbia University Press, 2013), 115–122; Scott W. Harold et al., *The Thickening Web of Asian Security Cooperation: Deepening Defense Ties among U.S. Allies and Partners in the Indo-Pacific* (Santa Monica, CA: RAND Corporation, 2019), 256–260 https://doi.org/10.7249/RR3125; Huong Le Thu, "Rough Waters Ahead for Vietnam-China Relations" (Washington, DC: Carnegie Endowment for International Peace, September 30, 2020), https://carnegieendowment.org/2020/09/30/rough-waters-ahead-for-vietnam-china-relations-pub-82826.

17. Arthur M. Schlesinger Jr., *A Thousand Days: John F. Kennedy in the White House* (Boston: Houghton Mifflin, 1965), 339; Secretary of Defense Robert M. Gates, "Secretary of Defense Speech" (United States Military Academy, West Point, NY, February 25, 2011), https://archive.defense.gov/Speeches/Speech.aspx?SpeechID=1539.

18. Association of Southeast Asian Nations (ASEAN), *Investing in ASEAN, 2013/2014* (Jakarta: ASEAN, 2013), 6, https://www.usasean.org/system/files/downloads/Investing-

in-ASEAN-2013-14.pdf; ASEAN, *Investing in ASEAN, 2019/2020* (Jakarta: ASEAN, 2019), 5, https://asean.org/storage/2019/10/Investing_in_ASEAN_2019_2020.pdf.

19. Thomas Schelling described brute force as an alternative to coercion: "There is a difference between taking what you want and making someone give it to you." Thomas C. Schelling, *Arms and Influence* (1966; repr., New Haven: Yale University Press, 2008), 1–18.

20. B. H. Liddell Hart, *The Strategy of Indirect Approach* (London: Faber and Faber, 1941), revised as *Strategy,* 2nd rev. ed. (New York: Meridian, 1991).

21. Giulio Douhet, *Command of the Air,* trans. Dino Ferrari (Maxwell AFB, AL: Air University Press, 2019), 53.

22. For a summary of these courses of action, see Office of the Secretary of Defense, *Annual Report to Congress,* 113.

23. I am grateful to Yashar Parsie for help in formulating this logic. Schelling, *Arms and Influence,* 69–91, 100, 174–184. See also Robert J. Art, "To What Ends Military Power?," *International Security* 4, no. 4 (Spring 1980): 7–10, doi:10.2307/2626666; and David E. Johnson, Karl P. Mueller, and William H. Taft, *Conventional Coercion across the Spectrum of Operations: The Utility of U.S. Military Forces in the Emerging Security Environment* (Santa Monica, CA: RAND Corporation, 2003), 14, https://www.rand.org/pubs/monograph_reports/MR1494.html.

24. For empirical assessments, see, among others, Walter J. Petersen, "Deterrence and Compellence: A Critical Assessment of Conventional Wisdom," *International Studies Quarterly* 30, no. 3 (September 1986): 269–294, https://doi.org/10.2307/2600418; Richard Ned Lebow, "Thucydides and Deterrence," *Security Studies* 16, no. 2 (April–June 2007): 163–188, https://doi.org/10.1080/09636410701399440; Todd S. Sechser, "Militarized Compellent Threats, 1918–2001," *Conflict Management and Peace Science* 28, no. 4 (September 2011): 377–401, https://doi.org/10.1177/0738894211413066; Todd S. Sechser and Mathew Fuhrmann, *Nuclear Weapons and Coercive Diplomacy* (Cambridge: Cambridge University Press, 2017); and Alexander B. Downes, "Step Aside or Face the Consequences: Explaining the Success and Failure of Compellent Threats to Remove Foreign Leaders," in *Coercion: The Power to Hurt in International Politics,* ed. Kelly M. Greenhill and Peter Krause (New York: Oxford University Press, 2018), 93–116.

25. Schelling, *Arms and Influence,* 70–75; Thomas C. Schelling, *The Strategy of Conflict* (1960; repr., Cambridge, MA: Harvard University Press, 1980), 196, emphasis in original. See also Glenn Herald Snyder and Paul Diesing, *Conflict among Nations: Bargaining, Decision Making, and System Structure in International Crises* (Princeton, NJ: Princeton University Press, 1977), 24–25; Robert A. Pape, *Bombing to Win: Air Power and Coercion in War* (Ithaca, NY: Cornell University Press, 1996), 6; Robert Jervis, *The Meaning of the Nuclear Revolution: Statecraft and the Prospect of Armageddon* (Ithaca, NY: Cornell University Press, 1989), 29–35; and Oran R. Young, *Politics of Force: Bargaining during International Crises* (Princeton, NJ: Princeton University Press, 1969), 337–361.

26. Demosthenes, *Orations,* vol. 1, trans. J. H. Vince (Cambridge, MA: Harvard University Press, 1930), 417.

27. Daniel Kahneman and Amos Tversky, "Prospect Theory: An Analysis of Decision under Risk," *Econometrica* 47, no. 2 (March 1979): 263–291, doi:10.2307/1914185; Robert

Jervis, "Political Implications of Loss Aversion," *Political Psychology* 13, no. 2 (June 1992): 187–204, doi:10.2307/3791678; Jack S. Levy, "Loss Aversion, Framing, and Bargaining: The Implications of Prospect Theory for International Conflict," *International Political Science Review* 17, no. 2 (April 1996): 179–195, https://doi.org/10.1177 /019251296017002004; Gary Schaub Jr., "Deterrence, Compellence, and Prospect Theory," *Political Psychology* 25, no. 3 (2004): 389–411, https://www.jstor.org/stable/379254; Jonathan Mercer, "Prospect Theory and Political Science," *Annual Review of Political Science* 8, no. 1 (2005): 1–21, doi:10.1146/annurev.polisci.8.082103.10491. See also Snyder and Diesing, *Conflict among Nations, 25.*

28. For a doctrinal treatment, see US Air Force, "Practical Design: The Coercion Continuum," in *Annex 3-0: Operations and Planning* (Maxwell AFB, AL: Curtis E. LeMay Center for Doctrine Development and Education, Air University, November 4, 2016), https://www.doctrine.af.mil/Portals/61/documents/Annex_3-0/3-0-D15-OPS-Coercion-Continuum.pdf. For a recent survey, see Tami Davis Biddle, "Coercion Theory: A Basic Introduction for Practitioners," *Texas National Security Review* 3, no. 2 (Spring 2020), http://dx.doi.org/10.26153/tsw/8864.

29. Pape, *Bombing to Win,* 21–25.

30. Karl P. Mueller, "The Essence of Coercive Air Power: A Primer for Military Strategists," *Royal Air Force Air Power Review* 4, no. 3 (Autumn 2001): 6, https://www.airuniversity. af.edu/Portals/10/ASPJ/journals/Chronicles/mueller.pdf.

31. See "Punishment" in US Air Force, "Practical Design."

32. Whether or to what degree punishment alone is likely to compel enemy surrender has been the subject of debate for many years. The debate itself has focused primarily on nations' use of airpower to achieve coercive victories, but its findings are logically extensible to other forms of military punishment involving cost imposition. For seminal contributions to the debate, see Pape, *Bombing to Win;* Robert A. Pape, "The Limits of Precision-Guided Air Power," *Security Studies* 7, no. 2 (Winter 1997/98): 93–114, https:// doi.org/10.1080/09636419708429343; Barry D. Watts, "Ignoring Reality: Problems of Theory and Evidence in Security Studies," *Security Studies* 7, no. 2 (Winter 1997/98): 115–171, https://doi.org/10.1080/09636419708429344; John Warden, "Success in Modern War," *Security Studies* 7, no. 2 (Winter 1997/98): 172–190, https://doi. org/10.1080/09636419708429345; Robert A. Pape, "The Air Force Strikes Back: A Reply to Barry Watts and John Warden," *Security Studies* 7, no. 2 (Winter 1997/98), 191–214, https://doi.org/10.1080/09636419708429346; Karl Mueller, "Strategies of Coercion: Denial, Punishment, and the Future of Air Power," *Security Studies, 7, no. 3 (Spring 1998):* 182–228, https://doi.org/10.1080/09636419808429354; Daniel L. Byman and Matthew C. Waxman, "Kosovo and the Great Air Power Debate," *International Security,* 24, no. 4 (Spring 2000): 5–38, https://www.jstor.org/stable/2539314; and Michael Horowitz and Dan Reiter, "When Does Aerial Bombing Work? Quantitative Empirical Tests, 1917–1999," *Journal of Conflict Resolution* 45, no. 2 (April 2001): 147–173: https://www.jstor. org/stable/3176274. For historical studies of coercive airpower, see Morale Division, United States Strategic Bombing Survey, *The Effects of Strategic Bombing on German Morale,* 2 vols. (Washington, DC: Government Printing Office, December 1946, May 1947); Morale Division, United States Strategic Bombing Survey, *The Effects of Strategic Bombing on Japanese Morale* (Washington, DC: Government Printing

Office, June 1947); Ronald Schaffer, *Wings of Judgement: American Bombing in World War II* (New York: Oxford University Press, 1985); Kenneth P. Werrell, "The Strategic Bombing of Germany in World War II: Costs and Accomplishments," *Journal of American History* 73, no. 2 (December 1986): 702–713, https://doi.org/10.2307/1902984; Mark Clodfelter, *The Limits of Air Power: The American Bombing of North Vietnam* (New York: Free Press, 1989); Stephen T. Hosmer, *Psychological Effects of U.S. Air Operations in Four Wars, 1941–1991: Lessons for U.S. Commanders* (Santa Monica, CA: RAND Corporation, 1996), https://www.rand.org/pubs/monograph_reports/MR576.html; and Tami Davis Biddle, *Rhetoric and Reality in Air Warfare: The Evolution of British and American Ideas about Strategic Bombing, 1914–1945* (Princeton, NJ: Princeton University Press, 2002), esp. 214–288. For studies of coercive maritime blockades, see Mancur Olson Jr., *The Economics of Wartime Shortage: A History of British Food Supplies in the Napoleonic Wars and in World Wars I and II* (Durham, NC: Duke University Press, 1963); Hein E. Goemans, *War and Punishment: The Causes of War Termination in the First World War* (Princeton, NJ: Princeton University Press, 2000); John J. Mearsheimer, *The Tragedy of Great Power Politics* (New York: W. W. Norton, 2001), 83–137; Paul Kennedy, *The Rise and Fall of British Naval Mastery,* 2nd ed. (New York: Humanity Books, 1986), 299–322; Philip A. Crowl, "Alfred Thayer Mahan: The Naval Historian," in *Makers of Modern Strategy: From Machiavelli to the Nuclear Age,* ed. Peter Paret, Gordon A. Craig, and Felix Gilbert (Princeton, NJ: Princeton University Press, 1986), 444–477; Michael A. Glosny, "Strangulation from the Sea? A PRC Submarine Blockade of Taiwan," *International Security* 28, no. 4 (Spring 2004): 125–160, https://www.jstor.org/stable/4137451; and Erik Sand, "Desperate Measures: The Effects of Economic Isolation on Warring Powers," *Texas National Security Review* 3, no. 2 (Spring 2020), https://tnsr.org/2020/04/desperate-measures-the-effects-of-economic-isolation-on-warring-powers/.

33. Robert A. Pape, "Why Japan Surrendered," *International Security* 18, no. 2 (Fall 1993): 154–201, doi:10.2307/2539100; Ward Wilson, "The Winning Weapon? Rethinking Nuclear Weapons in Light of Hiroshima," *International Security* 31, no. 4 (Spring 2007): 162–179, https://www.jstor.org/stable/4137569.

34. Robert A. Pape Jr., "Coercive Air Power in the Vietnam War," *International Security* 15, no. 2 (Fall 1990): 103–146, doi:10.2307/2538867; Earl H. Tolford Jr., *SETUP: What the Air Force Did in Vietnam and Why* (Maxwell AFB, AL: Air University Press, 1991), 283–288, https://media.defense.gov/2017/Apr/07/2001728434/-1/-1/0/B_0040_TILFORD_SETUP.PDF; Conrad C. Crane, *American Airpower Strategy in Korea, 1950–1953* (Lawrence: University of Kansas Press, 2000); William W. Momyer, *Airpower in Three Wars: WWII, Korea, Vietnam* (Maxwell AFB, AL: Air University Press, 2003), https://www.airuniversity.af.edu/Portals/10/AUPress/Books/B_0089_MOMYER_AIRPOWER.pdf; and Clodfelter, *Limits of Air Power.*

35. Stephen T. Hosmer, *The Conflict over Kosovo: Why Milosevic Decided to Settle When He Did* (Santa Monica, CA: RAND Corporation, 2001), 114, 123, https://www.rand.org/pubs/monograph_reports/MR1351.html. See also Horowitz and Reiter, "When Does Aerial Bombing Work?"

36. Adam Smith, quoted in Ernst Campbell Messner and Ian Simpson Ross, eds., *The Glasgow Edition of the Works and Correspondence of Adam Smith,* vol. 6, *Correspondence,* 2nd ed. (Oxford: Oxford University Press, 2014), 262n3.

37. Hosmer, *Conflict over Kosovo,* 40–47.

38. For overviews of Chinese strategic thinking about Taiwan, see Tai Ming Cheung, "Chinese Military Preparations against Taiwan over the Next 10 Years," in *Crisis in the Taiwan Strait,* ed. James R. Lilley and Chuck Downs (Washington, DC: National Defense University and American Enterprise Institute, 1997), 45–72; Allen S. Whiting, "China's Use of Force, 1950–96, and Taiwan," *International Security* 26, no. 2 (Fall 2001): 124–131, https://www.jstor.org/stable/3092124; Thomas J. Christensen, "Posing Problems without Catching Up: China's Rise and Challenges for U.S. Security Policy," *International Security* 25, no. 4 (Spring 2001): 14–21, https://www.jstor.org/stable/3092132; Robert S. Ross, "Navigating the Strait: Deterrence, Escalation Dominance, and U.S.-China Relations," *International Security* 27, no. 2 (Fall 2002): 54–56, https://www.jstor.org/stable/3092143; Brad Roberts, "The Nuclear Dimension: How Likely? How Stable?," in *Assessing the Threat: The Chinese Military and Taiwan's Security,* ed. Michael D. Swaine et al. (Washington, DC: Carnegie Endowment for International Peace, 2007), 213–242; *Chinese Political and Military Thinking regarding Taiwan and the East and South China Seas, before the U.S.-China Economic and Security Review Commission,* 115th Cong. (2017) (statement of Timothy R. Heath, Senior International/Defense Researcher, RAND Corporation), https://www.rand.org/pubs/testimonies/CT470.html; and Peter Gries and Tao Wang, "Will China Seize Taiwan? Wishful Thinking in Beijing, Taipei, and Washington Could Spell War in 2019," *Foreign Affairs,* February 15, 2019, https://www.foreignaffairs.com/articles/china/2019-02-15/will-china-seize-taiwan.

39. Consistent very large majorities of the Taiwan public prefer some form of maintaining the status quo; in a 2019 survey only 1.4 percent favored unification with the Mainland as soon as possible, with 8.9 percent favoring the status quo now and unification later. ROC Mainland Affairs Council, "Percentage Distribution of the Questionnaire for the Routine Survey on the 'Public Views on Current Cross-Strait Issues' " (Taipei: Mainland Affairs Council, Republic of China, October 24, 2019), 2, https://ws.mac.gov.tw/001/Upload/297/relfile/8010/5823/ef1a8650-abae-4b61-8da5-6bb00e5053e7.pdf. At the same time, 69.8 percent of respondents supported the proposition that, when Taiwan's freedom and democracy are challenged and when the ROC's existence and development are threatened, the people of Taiwan must stand up and defend themselves. ROC Mainland Affairs Council, "Public Opinion on the Cross-Strait Relations in the Republic of China" (Taipei: Mainland Affairs Council, Republic of China, October 24, 2019), 2, https://ws.mac.gov.tw/001/Upload/297/relfile/8010/5823/dd8e265f-c130-4278-8a0c-348ab8296672.pdf; ROC Mainland Affairs Council, "Public View on Current Cross-Strait Relation (October 24–28, 2018)" (Taipei: Mainland Affairs Council, Republic of China, November 1, 2018), 3, https://ws.mac.gov.tw/001/Upload/297/relfile/8010/5674/ca75e10c-bb7c-4cc2-a1bc-eb8ec78ed336.pdf.

40. Benjamin S. Lambeth, *The Transformation of American Air Power* (Ithaca, NY: Cornell University Press, 2000), 15–16. See also James G. Hershberg and Chen Jian, "Reading and Warning the Likely Enemy: China's Signals to the United States about Vietnam in 1965," *International History Review* 27, no. 1 (March 2005): 47–84, https://www.jstor.org/stable/40110654.

41. Former secretary of defense James N. Mattis colorfully improved on this famous line commonly attributed to Napoleon in the context of the 2004 Battle of Fallujah when he

remarked: "If you're going to take Vienna, take [expletive] Vienna." Jim Mattis and Bing West, *Call Sign Chaos: Learning to Lead* (New York: Random House, 2019), 129.

42. For instance, Dan Altman calculated that, between 1918 and 2016, there were thirteen examples of coerced territorial cessions; in the same period, there were 112 direct land-grabs, 82 of them after 1945. Dan Altman, "By Fait Accompli, Not Coercion: How States Wrest Territory from Their Adversaries," *International Studies Quarterly* 61, no. 4 (December 2017): 885–886, https://doi.org/10.1093/isq/sqx049.

43. Pape, *Bombing to Win,* 88.

44. See David G. Chandler, *The Campaigns of Napoleon* (New York: Macmillan, 1966), esp. xxxiii-xxxvi, 511, 600; and Williamson Murray and Allan R. Millet, *A War to Be Won: Fighting the Second World War* (Cambridge, MA: Belknap Press of Harvard University Press, 2000), 83–89, 236–240.

45. Josh. 6:1–27.

46. See, e.g., Barry S. Strauss, "The War for Empire: Rome versus Carthage," in *Great Strategic Rivalries: From the Classical World to the Cold War,* ed. James Lacey (New York: Oxford University Press, 2016), 97–100; Flavius Josephus, "The Wars of the Jews, or The History of the Destruction of Jerusalem," in *The Complete Works of Flavius Josephus, the Celebrated Jewish Historian [. . .],* trans. William Whiston (Chicago: Thompson and Thomas, 1901), 498–709.

47. Iñigo Olalde et al., "The Genomic History of the Iberian Peninsula over the Past 8000 Years," *Science* 363 (2019): 1230–1235, doi:10.1126/science.aav4040.

48. See, e.g., Henry A. Kissinger: *A World Restored: Metternich, Castlereagh, and the Problem of Peace, 1812–1822* (Boston: Houghton Mifflin, 1957), 98, 155.

49. See, e.g., Henry Kissinger, *Diplomacy* (New York: Simon and Schuster, 1994), 424; John Lewis Gaddis, *Strategies of Containment: A Critical Appraisal of American National Security Policy during the Cold War,* rev. ed. (Oxford: Oxford University Press, 2005), 37; and Walter Isaacson and Evan Thomas, *The Wise Men: Six Friends and the World They Made* (New York: Simon and Schuster, 1986), 34.

50. See, e.g., Paul Kecskemeti, *Strategic Surrender: The Politics of Victory and Defeat* (Santa Monica, CA: RAND Corporation, 1958), 5–6, 8–9, https://www.rand.org/pubs/reports/R308.html.

51. See, e.g., Williamson Murray and Wayne Wei-Siang Hsieh, *A Savage War: A Military History of the Civil War* (Princeton, NJ: Princeton University Press, 2016), 504–505.

52. See, e.g., Julian Jackson, *The Fall of France: The Nazi Invasion of 1940* (New York: Oxford University Press, 2003), 143–182.

53. See, e.g., David Stevenson, *With Our Backs to the Wall: Victory and Defeat in 1918* (Cambridge, MA: Harvard University Press, 2011), 161–169.

54. See Shlomo Aronson, *Conflict and Bargaining in the Middle East* (Baltimore: Johns Hopkins University Press, 1978), 178–179.

55. Lawrence Freedman, *The Official History of the Falklands Campaign,* vol. 2, *War and Diplomacy* (Abingdon, UK: Routledge, 2005), esp. 1–12.

56. For legal-historical accounts of this status, see Ian Brownlie, *International Law and the Use of Force by States* (Oxford: Clarendon Press, 1963), 19–21; and James Crawford, *The Creation of States in International Law,* 2nd ed. (New York: Oxford University Press, 2006), 282–328.

57. See Paul W. Schroeder, *The Transformation of European Politics, 1763–1848* (Oxford: Clarendon Press, 1994), 371–395.

58. See Mark Mazower, *Hitler's Empire: How the Nazis Ruled Europe* (New York: Penguin Press, 2008), esp. 102–136.

59. See, e.g., Stephen A. Carney, *The U.S. Army Campaigns of the Mexican War: The Occupation of Mexico, May 1846–July 1848* (Center for Military History, U.S. Army, 2005), https://history.army.mil/html/books/073/73-3/index.html.

60. Geoffrey Wawro, *The Franco-Prussian War: The German Conquest of France in 1870–1871* (New York: Cambridge University Press, 2003), 246.

61. Barry E. Carter, Allen S. Weiner, and Duncan B. Hollis, *International Law,* 7th ed. (New York: Wolters Kluwer, 2018), 450–451.

62. See Alexander L. George, "The Cuban Missile Crisis," in *Avoiding War: Problems of Crisis Management,* ed. Alexander L. George (Boulder, CO: Westview, 1991), 227, 382–383, 549–550, 553–554; Schelling, *Arms and Influence,* 1–30, 44–45; Alexander L. George and Richard Smoke, *Deterrence in American Foreign Policy: Theory and Practice* (New York: Columbia University Press, 1974), 536–540; Glenn Herald Snyder and Paul Diesing, *Conflict among Nations: Bargaining, Decision Making, and System Structure in International Crises* (Princeton, NJ: Princeton University Press, 1977), esp. 227; Stephen Van Evera, "Offense, Defense, and the Causes of War," *International Security* 22, no. 4 (Spring 1998): 10, doi:10.2307/2539239; Van Jackson, "Tactics of Strategic Competition: Gray Zone, Redlines, and Conflicts before War," *Naval War College Review* 70, no. 3 (Summer 2017): 39–61, https://digital-commons.usnwc.edu/nwc-review/vol70/iss3/4/; and Ahmer Tarar, "A Strategic Logic of the Military Fait Accompli," *International Studies Quarterly* 60, no. 4 (December 2017): 743, https://doi.org/10.1093/isq/sqw018.

63. NATO planners encountered this challenge in preparing a defense of the North German Plain. See contemporary accounts in Paul Bracken, "Urban Sprawl and NATO Defence," *Survival* 18, no. 6 (1976): 254–260, https://doi.org/10.1080/00396337608441648; Drew Middleton, "Urban Sprawl on the North German Plain Forces NATO to Rethink Its Strategy against a Soviet Invasion," *New York Times,* February 20, 1977, https://www.nytimes.com/1977/02/20/archives/urban-sprawl-on-the-north-german-plain-forces-nato-to-rethink-its.html; James H. Polk, "The North German Plain Attack Scenario: Threat or Illusion?," *Strategic Review* 8, no. 3 (Summer 1980): 60–66; and John J. Mearsheimer, *Conventional Deterrence* (Ithaca, NY: Cornell University Press, 1983), 179–181.

64. US Army, *ADP 3-0: Operations* (Washington, DC: US Department of the Army, July 31, 2019), esp. 2-1, https://armypubs.army.mil/epubs/DR_pubs/DR_a/pdf/web/ARN18010_ADP%203-0%20FINAL%20WEB.pdf.

65. See, e.g., Billy Fabian et al., *Strengthening Deterrence on NATO's Eastern Front* (Washington, DC: Center for Strategic and Budgetary Assessments, 2019), esp. 17–28, https://csbaonline.org/research/publications/strengthening-the-defense-of-natos-eastern-frontier.

66. Uri Bar-Joseph, *The Watchmen Fell Asleep: The Surprise of Yom Kippur and Its Sources* (Albany: State University of New York Press, 2005).

67. Lawrence and Morrison, *Taiwan,* 16, 23; Richard C. Bush, *A One-China Policy Primer* (Washington, DC: Brookings Institution, March 2017), 21n4, https://www.brookings.edu/wp-content/uploads/2017/03/one-china-policy-primer.pdf.

68. For official expressions of concern about China and its employment of the fait accompli, see *Review of the FY2020 Budget Request for the Dept. of Defense, before the Subcommittee on Defense, Committee on Appropriations, United States Senate,* 116th Cong. 3 (2019) (statement of Patrick M. Shanahan, Acting Secretary of Defense), https://www.appropriations.senate.gov/imo/media/doc/05.08.19-Shanahan%20Testimony.pdf; US Department of Defense, Indo-Pacific Strategy Report: Preparedness, Partnerships, and Promoting a Networked Region (Washington, DC: US Department of Defense, July 1, 2019), 18, https://media.defense.gov/2019/Jul/01/2002152311/-1/-1/1/DEPARTMENT-OF-DEFENSE-INDO-PACIFIC-STRATEGY-REPORT-2019.PDF; and US Department of the Navy, Advantage at Sea: Prevailing with Integrated All-Domain Naval Power (Washington, DC: US Department of the Navy, December 2020), 5, https://media.defense.gov/2020/Dec/16/2002553074/-1/-1/1/TRISERVICESTRATEGY.PDF. See also Michèle A. Flournoy, "How to Prevent a War in Asia: The Erosion of American Deterrence Raises the Risk of Chinese Miscalculation," *Foreign Affairs,* July 18, 2020, https://www.foreignaffairs.com/articles/united-states/2020-06-18/how-prevent-war-asia.

69. For arguments emphasizing that China's ambitions are limited, see Lyle J. Goldstein, *Meeting China Halfway: How to Defuse the Emerging US-China Rivalry* (Washington, DC: Georgetown University Press, 2015); Jeffrey A. Bader, *A Framework for U.S. Policy toward China* (Washington, DC: Brookings Institution, March 2016), 6, https://www.brookings.edu/research/a-framework-for-u-s-policy-toward-china-2/; Paul Heer, "Understanding the Challenge from China," Open Forum (The Asan Forum), April 3, 2018, http://www.theasanforum.org/understanding-the-challenge-from-china/; *Hearing on a "World-Class" Military: Assessing China's Global Military Ambitions, before the U.S.-China Economic and Security Review Commission,* 116th Cong. 12 (2019) (statement of M. Taylor Fravel, Arthur and Ruth Sloan Professor of Political Science, Massachusetts Institute of Technology), https://www.uscc.gov/sites/default/files/Fravel_USCC%20Testimony_FINAL.pdf; and Fareed Zakaria, "The New China Scare: Why America Shouldn't Panic about Its Latest Challenger," *Foreign Affairs* 100, no. 1 (January/February 2020): 59–62, https://www.foreignaffairs.com/articles/china/2019-12-06/new-china-scare.

70. Karine Varley, *Under the Shadow of Defeat: The War of 1870–71 in French Memory* (London: Palgrave Macmillan, 2008).

71. Thomas, Stillion, and Rehman, *Hard ROC 2.0;* Office of the Secretary of Defense, *Annual Report to Congress,* 164–166. See also Easton, *Chinese Invasion Threat.*

72. See, e.g., the unfavorable trendlines in a Spratly Islands scenario outlined in Heginbotham et al., *U.S.-China Military Scorecard,* 318, 338–342.

Chapter 8. A Denial Defense

1. For a conceptual description, see Herman Kahn, *On Escalation: Metaphors and Scenarios* (New York: Praeger, 1965), 289–291. For a case advocating US military dominance, see, e.g., *The Impact of National Defense on the Economy, Diplomacy, and International Order, before the Armed Services Committee, U.S. House of Representatives,* 115th Cong. 2–3 (2018) (statement of Hal Brands, Henry A. Kissinger Distinguished Professor, Johns Hopkins-SAIS, Senior Fellow, Center for Strategy and Budgetary Assessments),

https://csbaonline.org/research/publications/statement-before-the-house-armed-services
-committee-the-impact-of-national-.

2. Eric Heginbotham et al., *The U.S.-China Military Scorecard: Forces, Geography, and the Evolving Balance of Power, 1996–2017* (Santa Monica, CA: RAND Corporation, 2015), 332–334, https://www.jstor.org/stable/10.7249/j.ctt17rw5gb.

3. Stockholm International Peace Research Institute, *SIPRI Yearbook: Armaments, Disarmament and International Security* (Stockholm: SIPRI, various years), cited in World Bank, "Military Expenditure (% of GDP)—United States, China" (Washington, DC: World Bank, accessed June 4, 2020), https://data.worldbank.org/indicator/MS.MIL.XPND.GD.ZS?locations=US-CN; Office of the Secretary of Defense, *Annual Report to Congress: Military and Security Developments Involving the People's Republic of China 2020,* 9-A3DFCD4 (Washington, DC: US Department of Defense, August 11, 2020), 139–140, https://media.defense.gov/2020/Sep/01/2002488689/-1/-1/1/2020-DOD-CHINA-MILITARY-POWER-REPORT-FINAL.PDF. Some analysts estimate that the PLA's defense expenditure is significantly larger when measured by purchasing power parity. Frederico Bartels, *China's Defense Budget in Context: How Under-Reporting and Differing Standards and Economies Distort the Picture* (Washington, DC: Heritage Foundation, March 2020), https://www.heritage.org/asia/report/chinas-defense-budget-context-how-under-reporting-and-differing-standards-and-economies; Peter Robertson, "China's Military Might Is Much Closer to the US Than You Probably Think," *Conversation,* October, 1, 2019, https://theconversation.com/chinas-military-might-is-much-closer-to-the-us-than-you-probably-think-124487.

4. US Department of Defense, *Summary of the 2018 National Defense Strategy: Sharpening the American Military's Strategic Edge* (Washington, DC: US Department of Defense, January 2018), https://dod.defense.gov/Portals/1/Documents/pubs/2018-National-Defense-Strategy-Summary.pdf.

5. The Joint Staff, *Description of the National Military Strategy 2018* (Washington, DC: Joint Chiefs of Staff, July 2019), https://www.jcs.mil/Portals/36/Documents/Publications/UNCLASS_2018_National_Military_Strategy_Description.pdf. See also T. X. Hammes, *An Affordable Defense of Asia* (Washington, DC: Atlantic Council, June 2020), https://www.atlanticcouncil.org/in-depth-research-reports/report/an-affordable-defense-of-asia/.

6. Elbridge Colby and David Ochmanek, "How the United States Could Lose a Great-Power War," *Foreign Policy,* October 29, 2019, https://foreignpolicy.com/2019/10/29/united-states-china-russia-great-power-war/; R. W. Komer, "Horizontal Escalation Paper," Memorandum for the Secretary of Defense, I-35354-80 (Washington, DC: Office of the Undersecretary of Defense for Policy, US Department of Defense, October 9, 1980), https://www.archives.gov/files/declassification/iscap/pdf/2010073-doc1.pdf; Robert Komer, *Maritime Strategy or Coalition Defense?* (Cambridge, MA: Abt Books, 1984), esp. 70–73; Michael Fitzsimmons, "Horizontal Escalation: An Asymmetric Approach to Russian Aggression?," *Strategic Studies Quarterly* 13, no. 1 (Spring 2019): 95–133, https://www.airuniversity.af.edu/Portals/10/SSQ/documents/Volume-13_Issue-1/Fitzsimmons.pdf.

7. See Glenn H. Snyder, *Deterrence and Defense: Toward a Theory of National Security* (Ithaca, NY: Cornell University Press, 1961), 14–16. See also A. Wess Mitchell, "The

Case for Deterrence by Denial," *American Interest,* August 12, 2015, https://www.the-american-interest.com/2015/08/12/the-case-for-deterrence-by-denial/; and Elbridge Colby and Jonathon F. Solomon, "Avoiding Becoming a Paper Tiger: Presence in a Warfighting Defense Strategy, *Joint Force Quarterly* 82, 3rd Quarter (2016): 24–32, https://ndupress.ndu.edu/Portals/68/Documents/jfq/jfq-82/jfq-82_24–32_Colby-Solomon.pdf.

8. Air Chief Marshal Hugh Dowding quoted in Robert Wright, *Dowding and the Battle of Britain* (London: Corgi, 1970), 146, in turn quoted in Colin Gray, "Dowding and the British Strategy of Air Defense, 1936–1940," in *Successful Strategies: Triumphing in War and Peace from Antiquity to the Present,* ed. Williamson Murray and Richard Hart Sinnreich (Cambridge: Cambridge University Press, 2014), 241.

9. Carl von Clausewitz, *On War,* ed. and trans. Michael Howard and Peter Paret (Princeton, NJ: Princeton University Press, 1976, revised 1989), 348. See also Harold A. Winters et al., *Battling the Elements: Weather and Terrain in the Conduct of War* (Baltimore: Johns Hopkins University Press, 1998), 1–4; and Colin Gray, "The Continued Primacy of Geography," *Orbis* 40, no. 2 (Spring 1996): 247–259, doi:10.1080/01402399908437759.

10. Andrew F. Krepinevich Jr., *Archipelagic Defense: The Japan-U.S. Alliance and Preserving Peace and Stability in the Western Pacific* (Tokyo: Sasakawa Peace Foundation, 2017), 46–51, https://www.spf.org/en/global-data/SPF_20170810_03.pdf; Toshi Yoshihara and James R. Holmes, *Red Star over the Pacific: China's Rise and the Challenge to U.S. Maritime Strategy,* 2nd ed. (Annapolis, MD: Naval Institute Press, 2018).

11. US Army, *FM 3-90: Tactics* (Washington, DC: US Department of the Army, July 2001), B-14, https://usacac.army.mil/sites/default/files/misc/doctrine/CDG/cdg_resources/manuals/fm/fm3_90.pdf.

12. Edward C. O'Dowd, *Chinese Military Strategy in the Third Indochina War: The Last Maoist War* (New York: Routledge, 2007), 46–50.

13. John J. Mearsheimer, *The Tragedy of Great Power Politics* (New York: W. W. Norton, 2001), 114–128; Nicholas J. Spykman, *America's Strategy in World Politics: The United States and the Balance of Power* (1942; repr., New York: Routledge, 2017), 392–393.

14. Office of the Secretary of Defense, *Annual Report to Congress: Military Power of the People's Republic of China, 2008* (Washington, DC: US Department of Defense, 2008), 44, https://www.hsdl.org/?view&did=483904; Office of the Secretary of Defense, *Annual Report to Congress: Military and Security Developments Involving the People's Republic of China 2020,* 9-A3DFCD4 (Washington, DC: US Department of Defense, August 11, 2020), 114, https://media.defense.gov/2020/Sep/01/2002488689/-1/-1/1/2020-DOD-CHINA-MILITARY-POWER-REPORT-FINAL.PDF; Theodore L. Gatchel, *At Water's Edge: Defending against the Modern Amphibious Assault* (Annapolis, MD: Naval Institute Press, 1996), 7, 207.

15. Paul S. Dull, *A Battle History of the Japanese Imperial Navy (1941–1945)* (Annapolis, MD: Naval Institute Press, 1978), 35–40.

16. Robert E. Ball and Charles N. Calvano, "Establishing the Fundamentals of a Surface Ship Survivability Design Discipline," *American Society of Naval Engineers* 106, no. 1 (1994): 72, https://calhoun.nps.edu/handle/10945/61577.

17. For an overview of stealth and aircraft survivability, see, e.g., Committee on Future Air Force Needs for Survivability, Air Force Studies Board, Division on Engineering and

Physical Sciences, National Research Council of the National Academies, *Future Air Force Needs for Survivability* (Washington, DC: National Academies Press, 2006), 9–15.

18. Jonathan F. Solomon, "Maritime Deception and Concealment: Concepts for Defeating Wide-Area Oceanic Surveillance-Reconnaissance-Strike Networks," *Naval War College Review* 66, no. 4 (Autumn 2013): 87–116, https://digital-commons.usnwc.edu/cgi/viewcontent.cgi?article=1413&context=nwc-review; Bryan Clark and Timothy A. Walton, *Transforming the U.S. Surface Fleet for Decision-Centric Warfare* (Washington, DC: Center for Strategic and Budgetary Assessments, 2019), 28–30, https://csbaonline.org/research/publications/taking-back-the-seas-transforming-the-u.s-surface-fleet-for-decision-centric-warfare.

19. See, e.g., Gatchel, *At Water's Edge,* 1–9.

20. Stephen Biddle*, Military Power: Explaining Victory in Modern Battle* (Princeton, NJ: Princeton University Press, 2004), 44–46; US Army*, ATP 2-01.3: Intelligence Preparation of the Battlefield* (Washington, DC: US Department of the Army, March 2019), 4-40, https://home.army.mil/wood/application/files/8915/5751/8365/ATP_2-01.3_Intelligence_Preparation_of_the_Battlefield.pdf.

21. See US Army, *FM: 3-21.8 (FM 7-8): The Infantry Rifle Platoon and Squad* (Washington, DC: US Department of the Army, March 2007), 8-62, 8-143–8-144, https://www.globalsecurity.org/military/library/policy/army/fm/3-21-8/l; and Robert A. Pape, *Bombing to Win: Air Power and Coercion in War* (Ithaca, NY: Cornell University Press, 1996), 174–210.

22. See, e.g., John W. McGillvray Jr., "Stealth Technology in Surface Warships," *Naval War College Review* 47, no. 1 (Winter 1994): 28–19, https://www.jstor.org/stable/44642486. See also Timothy A. Walton, Ryan Boone, and Harrison Schramm, *Sustaining the Fight: Resilient Maritime Logistics for a New Era* (Washington, DC: Center for Strategic and Budgetary Assessments, 2019), 47, 57, 94–97, https://csbaonline.org/research/publications/sustaining-the-fight-resilient-maritime-logistics-for-a-new-era.

23. See also Paul McLeary, "In War, Chinese Shipyards Could Outpace US in Replacing Losses; Marine Commandant," *Breaking Defense,* June 17, 2020, https://breakingdefense.com/2020/06/in-war-chinese-shipyards-can-outpace-us-in-replacing-losses/.

24. Stephen E. Ambrose, *D-Day: June 6, 1944: The Climactic Battle of World War II* (New York: Simon and Schuster, 1994), 239, 252.

25. See, e.g., Barry D. Watts, *The Evolution of Precision Strike* (Washington, DC: Center for Strategic and Budgetary Assessments, 2013), https://csbaonline.org/research/publications/the-evolution-of-precision-strike.

26. Mark Gunzinger and Bryan Clark, *Sustaining America's Precision Strike Advantage* (Washington, DC: Center for Strategic and Budgetary Assessments, 2015), 8, https://csbaonline.org/research/publications/sustaining-americas-precision-strike-advantage; A. J. C. Lavelle, ed., *The Tale of Two Bridges and the Battle for the Skies over North Vietnam* (Washington, DC: Office of Air Force History, United States Air Force, 1985), 85, cited in Barry D. Watts, *Six Decades of Guided Munitions and Battle Networks: Progress and Prospects* (Washington, DC: Center for Strategic and Budgetary Assessments, March 2007), 187, https://csbaonline.org/research/publications/six-decades-of-guided-munitions-and-battle-networks-progress-and-prospects; Robert O. Work and Shawn Brimley, *20YY: Preparing for War in the Robotic Age* (Washington, DC: Center

for a New American Security, January 2014), 10–16, https://www.jstor.org/stable/resrep06442.

27. Gunzinger and Clark, *Sustaining America's Precision Strike Advantage,* 48–55.

28. Curtis E. LeMay Center for Doctrine Development and Education, "Dynamic Targeting and the Tasking Process," in *Annex 3-60: Targeting* (Maxwell AFB, AL: US Air Force, updated March 15, 2019), https://www.doctrine.af.mil/Portals/61/documents/Annex_3-60/3-60-D17-Target-Dynamic-Task.pdf.

29. Gunzinger and Clark, *Sustaining America's Precision Strike Advantage*, 13–15; *Hearing on a Review of Defense Innovation and Research Funding, before the Subcommittee on Defense, Committee on Armed Services, U.S. Senate,* 115th Cong. 2–3 (2017) (Statement of William B. Roper Jr., Director, Strategic Capabilities Office), https://www.appropriations.senate.gov/hearings/a-review-defense-innovation-and-research-funding.

30. Alan J. Vick et al., *Aerospace Operations against Elusive Ground Targets* (Santa Monica, CA: RAND Corporation, 2001), esp. 1–56, https://www.rand.org/pubs/monograph_reports/MR1398.html; James Acton, "Escalation through Entanglement: How the Vulnerability of Command-and-Control Systems Raises the Risks of an Inadvertent Nuclear War," *International Security* 43, no. 1 (Summer 2018): 75, https://doi.org/10.1162/isec_a_00320; Charles L. Glaser and Steve Fetter, "Should the United States Reject MAD? Damage Limitation and U.S. Nuclear Strategy toward China," *International Security* 41, no. 1 (Summer 2016): 63–70, https://doi.org/10.1162/ISEC_a_00248; Christopher J. Bowie, "Destroying Mobile Ground Targets in an Anti-Access Environment" (Rosslyn, VA: Northrop Grumman Analysis Center, December 2001).

31. In the vicinity of the Taiwan Strait (that is, in the PLA's Eastern and Southern Theater Commands), China is estimated to have thirty-seven tank landing ships/amphibious transport dock and twenty-two medium landing ships; it is estimated to have four hundred military transport aircraft but fewer than 10 percent of its airlift fleet carry payloads above 27,000 kilograms. Office of the Secretary of Defense, *Annual Report to Congress* (2020), 165–166; International Institute for Strategic Studies, *The Military Balance,* vol. 120 (London: International Institute for Strategic Studies, 2020), 263–264, 266.

32. For estimates about numbers of targets in a Taiwan scenario and a Baltic scenario, respectively, see David A. Shlapak et al., *A Question of Balance: Political Context and Military Aspects of the China-Taiwan Dispute* (Santa Monica, CA: RAND Corporation, 2009), 104, https://www.rand.org/pubs/monographs/MG888.html; and Scott Boston et al., *Assessing the Conventional Force Imbalance in Europe: Implications for Countering Russian Local Superiority* (Santa Monica, CA: RAND Corporation, 2018), 9, https://www.rand.org/pubs/research_reports/RR2402.html. I am grateful to David Ochmanek for this standard.

33. For a similar logic, albeit with some different permutations and conclusions, see Stephen Biddle and Ivan Oelrich, "Future Warfare in the Western Pacific: Chinese Antiaccess/Area Denial, U.S. AirSea Battle, and Command of the Commons in East Asia," *International Security* 41, no. 1 (Summer 2016): 23, doi:10.1162/ISEC_a_00249.

34. Martin van Creveld, *Military Lessons of the Yom Kippur War: Historical Perspectives* (Beverly Hills, CA: Sage, 1975), esp. 11–20.

35. United States Strategic Bombing Survey (Pacific), Naval Analysis Division, *The Campaigns of the Pacific War* (Washington, DC: Government Printing Office, 1946), https://

www.ibiblio.org/hyperwar/NHC/NewPDFs/USAAF/United%20States%20Strate-gic%20Bombing%20Survey/USSBS%20Campaigns%20of%20Pacific%20War.pdf.

36. See, e.g., Williamson Murray and Wayne Wei-Siang Hsieh, *A Savage War: A Military History of the Civil War* (Princeton, NJ: Princeton University Press, 2016), 167–191.

37. Murray and Hsieh, 260–261; Russell F. Weigley, *The American Way of War: A History of United States Military Strategy and Policy* (Bloomington: Indiana University Press, 1973), 114–118.

38. John B. Lundstrom, *The First South Pacific Campaign: Pacific Fleet Strategy, December 1941–June 1942* (Annapolis, MD: Naval Institute Press, 1976).

39. See, among others, James M. McPherson, *Battle Cry of Freedom: The Civil War Era* (New York: Oxford University Press, 1988), 654–662; and John Keegan, *The American Civil War: A Military History* (New York: Vintage Books, 2009), 195–196.

40. US Army, *ADP 3-90: Offense and Defense* (Washington, DC: US Department of the Army, July 31, 2019), 1-5, 4-6, 4-50, 4-55, https://fas.org/irp/doddir/army/adp3_90.pdf.

41. See John Keegan, *The First World War* (New York: Alfred A. Knopf, 1998), 408–414.

42. See, e.g., Philip J. Haythornthwaite, *Gallipoli, 1915: Frontal Assault on Turkey* (London: Osprey, 1991), 39–40, 48, 57, 64–66.

43. See, e.g., Patrick Sullivan and Jesse W. Miller Jr., *The Geography of Warfare* (1983; New York: Routledge, 2015), 63–64.

44. US Army, *ADP 3-90*, 4-51–4-53; US Army, *FM 3-90*, 8-37–8-42.

45. US Army, *FM 3-90-1: Offense and Defense*, vol. 1 (Washington, DC: US Department of the Army, March 2013), 7–34, http://www.bits.de/NRANEU/others/amd-us-archive/fm3-90-1C2%2815%29.pdf; US Army, *FM 3-90*, 3-28–3-109.

46. See, e.g., John J. Mearsheimer, *Conventional Deterrence* (Ithaca, NY: Cornell University Press, 1983), 43, 74, 125–126.

47. See, e.g., Biddle, *Military Power,* esp. 48–49; B. H. Liddell Hart, *Strategy,* 2nd rev. ed. (New York: Meridian, 1991); Elbridge Colby, *Masters of Mobile Warfare* (Princeton, NJ: Princeton University Press, 1943); and Edward Luttwak, *The Grand Strategy of the Roman Empire: From the First Century CE to the Third,* rev. ed. (Baltimore: Johns Hopkins University Press, 2016), 146–149. Cf. John J. Mearsheimer, "Maneuver, Mobile Defense, and the NATO Central Front," *International Security* 6, no. 3 (Winter 1981/82): 104–122, https://www.jstor.org/stable/253860.

48. Naval Analysis Division, United States Strategic Bombing Survey (Pacific), *The Campaigns of the Pacific War,* 320–321, 325–326; George W. Garand and Truman R. Strobridge, *History of U.S. Marine Corps Operations in World War II,* vol. 4, *Western Pacific Operations* (Washington, DC: Historical Division, US Marine Corps, 1971), 456–457, https://www.marines.mil/News/Publications/MCPEL/Electronic-Library-Display/Article/1151105/history-of-the-us-marine-corps-operations-in-world-war-ii-western-pacific-opera/.

49. Barry S. Strauss, *The Trojan Wars: A New History* (New York: Simon and Schuster, 2006), 65–66.

50. Allen F. Chew, *Fighting the Russians in Winter: Three Case Studies* (Fort Leavenworth, KS: Combat Studies Institute, US Army Command and General Staff College, December 1981); Lawrence Freedman, *Strategy: A History* (New York: Oxford University Press, 2013), 78–81.

51. Bryan I. Fugate, *Operation Barbarossa: Strategy and Tactics on the Eastern Front, 1941* (Novato, CA: Presidio Press, 1984), 40–50; John Keegan, *The Second World War* (New York: Penguin Books, 1990), 182–185.

52. Biddle, *Military Power,* 49; Freedman, *Strategy,* 198–201.

53. US Army, *FM 100-5: Operations* (Washington, DC: Headquarters, Department of the Army, 1982), 7-1-7-2, http://cgsc.cdmhost.com/cdm/ref/collection/p4013coll9/id/48; John L. Romjue, *From Active Defense to AirLand Battle: The Development of Army Doctrine, 1973–1982* (Fort Monroe, VA: US Army Training and Doctrine Command, June 1984), https://www.tradoc.army.mil/Portals/14/Documents/Command%20History/Command%20History%20Publications/From%20Active%20Defense%20to%20Air-Land%20Battle.pdf; Bernard W. Rogers, "Follow-On Forces Attack: Myths and Realities," *NATO Review,* no. 6 (December 1984): 1–9; US Congress, Office of Technology Assessment, *New Technology for NATO: Implementing Follow-On Forces Attack,* OTA-ISC-309 (Washington, DC: Government Printing Office, June 1987), https://www.hsdl.org/?view&did=446427.

54. See, among others, Bruce A. Elleman, *Modern Chinese Warfare, 1795–1989* (New York: Routledge, 2001), 284–294.

Chapter 9. Limited War after an Effective Denial Defense

1. See John Speed Meyers, "Mainland Strikes and U.S. Military Strategy towards China: Historical Cases, Interviews, and a Scenario-Based Survey of American National Security Elites" (PhD diss., Pardee RAND Graduate School, 2019), https://doi.org/10.7249/RGSD430.

2. See, e.g., Alison A. Kaufman and Daniel M. Hartnett, *Managing Conflict: Examining Recent PLA Writings on Escalation Control* (Washington, DC: CNA, February 2016), https://apps.dtic.mil/dtic/tr/fulltext/u2/1005033.pdf; Burgess Laird, *War Control: Chinese Writings on the Control of Escalation in Crisis and Conflict* (Washington, DC: Center for a New American Security, April 2017), https://www.cnas.org/publications/reports/war-control; and Fiona S. Cunningham and M. Taylor Fravel, "Dangerous Confidence? Chinese Views on Nuclear Escalation," *International Security* 44, no. 2 (Fall 2019): 61–109, https://doi.org/10.1162/isec_a_00359. On Chinese air defense networks, see Eric Heginbotham et al., *The U.S.-China Military Scorecard: Forces, Geography, and the Evolving Balance of Power, 1996–2017* (Santa Monica, CA: RAND Corporation, 2015), 97–131, https://www.jstor.org/stable/10.7249/j.ctt17rw5gb.

3. For cases favoring selective economic decoupling, see *Hearing to Receive Testimony on China and Russia, before the Armed Services Committee, United States Senate,* 116th Cong. (2019) (statement of Ely Ratner, Executive Vice President and Director of Studies, Center for a New American Security), https://www.armed-services.senate.gov/imo/media/doc/Ratner_01-29-19.pdf; and Charles W. Boustany Jr. and Aaron L. Friedberg, *Partial Disengagement: A New Strategy for Economic Competition with China* (Seattle, WA: National Bureau of Asian Research, November 2019), https://www.nbr.org/wp-content/uploads/pdfs/publications/sr82_china-task-force-report-final.pdf. See also Julian Gewirtz, "The Chinese Reassessment of Interdependence," *China Leadership Monitor,* June 1, 2020, https://www.prcleader.org/gewirtz.

4. See, e.g., Michael Pettis, "China Cannot Weaponize Its U.S. Treasury Bonds" (Washington, DC: Carnegie Endowment for International Peace, May 28, 2019), https://carnegieendowment.org/chinafinancialmarkets/79218.

5. See, e.g., Caitlin Talmadge, "Would China Go Nuclear? Assessing the Risk of Chinese Nuclear Escalation in a Conventional War with the United States," *International Security* 41, no. 4 (Spring 2017): 50–92, https://doi.org/10.1162/ISEC_a_0027.

6. Carl von Clausewitz, *On War,* ed. and trans. Michael Howard and Peter Paret (Princeton, NJ: Princeton University Press, 1976, revised 1989), 370.

7. See Thomas Schelling's Nobel Prize lecture, "An Astonishing Sixty Years: The Legacy of Hiroshima," in *Arms and Influence* (1966; repr., New Haven: Yale University Press, 2008), 287–303.

8. US Department of Defense, *Nuclear Posture Review* (Washington, DC: US Department of Defense, 2018), 54–55, https://dod.defense.gov/News/SpecialReports/2018Nuclear PostureReview.aspx.

9. See John K. Warden, *Limited Nuclear War: The 21st Century Challenge for the United States* (Livermore, CA: Center for Global Security, Lawrence Livermore National Laboratory, July 2018), https://cgsr.llnl.gov/content/assets/docs/CGSR_LP4-FINAL.pdf.

10. See, e.g., Brad Roberts, *The Case for U.S. Nuclear Weapons* (Stanford, CA: Stanford University Press, 2014), 171.

11. Thomas C. Schelling, *The Strategy of Conflict* (1960; repr., Cambridge, MA: Harvard University Press, 1980), 57; and Rober Jervis, *The Meaning of the Nuclear Revolution: Statecraft and the Prospect of Armageddon* (Ithaca, NY: Cornell University Press, 1989), 31.

12. I am grateful to Alex Velez-Green for this point.

13. See especially Andrew F. Krepinevich Jr., *Protracted Great-Power War: A Preliminary Assessment* (Washington, DC: Center for a New American Security, February 2020), https://www.cnas.org/publications/reports/protracted-great-power-war. For Chinese thinking on this issue, see M. Taylor Fravel, *Active Defense: China's Military Strategy since 1949* (Princeton, NJ: Princeton University Press, 2019), 49–50, 65, 67.

14. See, e.g., David G. Chandler, *The Campaigns of Napoleon* (New York: Macmillan, 1966), 321–325.

15. Christopher M. Clark, *Iron Kingdom: The Rise and Downfall of Prussia, 1600–1947* (Cambridge, MA: Belknap Press of Harvard University Press, 2006), 204–206.

16. Emma Chanlett-Avery, *A Peace Treaty with North Korea?,* R45169 (Washington, DC: Congressional Research Service, April 19, 2018), https://crsreports.congress.gov/product/pdf/R/R45169. Find a summary of Russo-Japanese relations in Ministry of Foreign Affairs of Japan, Ministry of Foreign Affairs of the Russian Federation, "Preface," in *Joint Compendium of Documents on the History of Territorial Issue between Japan and Russia* (Tokyo: Ministry of Foreign Affairs of Japan, September 1992), https://www.mofa.go.jp/region/europe/russia/territory/edition92/preface.html.

17. I am grateful to Alex Velez-Green for this point.

18. See, e.g., Talmadge, "Would China Go Nuclear?," 54–55.

19. See, e.g., National Security Decision Memorandum 242, "Policy for Planning the Employment of Nuclear Weapons" (Washington, DC: National Security Council, 1974), https://fas.org/irp/offdocs/nsdm-nixon/nsdm_242.pdf; Presidential Directive/NSC-59,

"Nuclear Weapons Employment Policy" (Washington, DC: White House, July 25, 1980), https://fas.org/irp/offdocs/pd/pd59.pdf; Office of the Secretary of Defense, *Policy Guidance the Employment of Nuclear Weapons* (Washington, DC: US Department of Defense, October 1980), https://www.archives.gov/files/declassification/iscap/pdf/2013-111-doc01.pdf; and Walter Slocombe, "The Countervailing Strategy," *International Security* 5, no. 4 (Spring 1981): 18–27, https://www.jstor.org/stable/2538711.

20. US Department of Treasury, "Suggested Post-Surrender Program for Germany," September 1, 1944, in *Foreign Relations of the United States, Conference at Quebec, 1944,* ed. Richardson Dougall et al. (Washington, DC: Government Printing Office, 1972), document 77, https://history.state.gov/historicaldocuments/frus1944Quebec/d77.

21. See, e.g., Robert A. Pape, *Bombing to Win: Air Power and Coercion in War* (Ithaca, NY: Cornell University Press, 1996), 90, 257; and Michael Horowitz and Dan Reiter, "When Does Aerial Bombing Work? Quantitative Empirical Tests, 1917–1999," *Journal of Conflict Resolution* 45, no. 2 (April 2001): esp. 156, https://www.jstor.org/stable/3176274.

22. See, e.g., Forrest E. Morgan et al*., Dangerous Thresholds: Managing Escalation in the 21st Century* (Santa Monica, CA: RAND Corporation, 2008), 169–170, https://www.rand.org/pubs/monographs/MG614.html; and John Speed Meyers, "Mainland Strikes and U.S. Military Strategy towards China: Historical Cases, Interviews, and a Scenario-Based Survey of American National Security Elites" (PhD diss., Pardee RAND Graduate School, 2019), https://doi.org/10.7249/RGSD430.

23. For seminal scholarly formulations of compellence, see, among others, Thomas C. Schelling, *Arms and Influence* (1966; repr., New Haven: Yale University Press, 2008), 69–91; Robert J. Art, "To What Ends Military Power?," *International Security* 4, no. 4 (Spring 1980): 7–10, doi:10.2307/2626666; and Pape, *Bombing to Win,* esp. 4–8. See also Robert J. Art and Kelly M. Greenhill, "Coercion: An Analytical Overview," in *Coercion: The Power to Hurt in International Politics,* ed. Kelly M. Greenhill and Peter Krause (New York: Oxford University Press, 2018), 5–6, 13–22; and Tami Davis Biddle, "Coercion Theory: A Basic Introduction for Practitioners," *Texas National Security Review* 3, no. 2 (Spring 2020), http://dx.doi.org/10.26153/tsw/8864.

24. See Krepinevich Jr., *Protracted Great-Power War,* 23–27, 34–35.

25. See Piers Mackesy, *The War for America, 1775–1783* (1964; repr., Lincoln: University of Nebraska Press, 1993), esp. 435–436.

26. See, e.g., Geoffrey Jukes, *The Russo-Japanese War, 1904–1905* (Oxford: Osprey, 2002), 76.

27. US Department of Defense, *Summary of the 2018 National Defense Strategy: Sharpening the American Military's Strategic Edge* (Washington, DC: US Department of Defense, January 2018), 6, https://dod.defense.gov/Portals/1/Documents/pubs/2018-National-Defense-Strategy-Summary.pdf; David Ochmanek, *Restoring U.S. Power Projection Capabilities: Responding to the 2018 National Defense Strategy* (Santa Monica, CA: RAND Corporation, July 2018), 8, https://www.rand.org/pubs/perspectives/PE260.html; *Hearing to Receive Testimony on China and Russia, before the Armed Services Committee, United States Senate,* 116th Cong. (2019) (statement of Elbridge A. Colby), https://www.armed-services.senate.gov/imo/media/doc/Colby_01-29-19.pdf; Elbridge Colby, "How to Win America's Next War," *Foreign Policy* no. 232 (Spring 2019): 48, https://foreign-policy.com/2019/05/05/how-to-win-americas-next-war-china-russia-military-infrastruc-

ture/; Christopher M. Dougherty, *Why America Needs a New Way of War* (Washington, DC: Center for a New American Security, June 2019), 33.

Chapter 10. The Binding Strategy

1. Edward S. Miller, *War Plan Orange: The U.S. Strategy to Defeat Japan, 1897–1945* (Annapolis, MD: Naval Institute Press, 1991), 223–232.

2. See, e.g., David Ochmanek, "Wisdom and Will? American Military Strategy in the Indo-Pacific" (Sydney: United States Studies Centre, University of Sydney, November 28, 2018), esp. 10–11, https://www.ussc.edu.au/analysis/american-military-strategy-in-the-indo-pacific.

3. I am grateful to Alex Velez-Green for this formulation.

4. See Bryan Clark and Jesse Sloman, *Advancing beyond the Beach: Amphibious Operations in an Era of Precision Weapons* (Washington, DC: Center for Strategic and Budgetary Assessments, 2016), esp. 5–14, https://csbaonline.org/research/publications/advancing-beyond-the-beach-amphibious-operations-in-an-era-of-precision-wea.

5. *Hearing to Receive Testimony on Reshaping the U.S. Military, before the Committee on Armed Services United States Senate,* 115th Cong. 3 (2017) (statement of David Ochmanek, Senior International/Defense Researcher, RAND Corporation), https://www.armed-services.senate.gov/imo/media/doc/Ochmanek_02-16-17.pdf; Christopher M. Dougherty, *Why America Needs a New Way of War* (Washington, DC: Center for a New American Security, June 2019).

6. See Maury Klein, *A Call to Arms: Mobilizing America for World War II* (New York: Bloomsbury, 2013). On industrial surge capacity in great power competition, see Andrew Krepinevich, *Defense Investment Strategies in an Uncertain World* (Washington, DC: Center for Strategic and Budgetary Assessments, 2008), https://csbaonline.org/research/publications/defense-investment-strategies-in-an-uncertain-world.

7. Office of the Under Secretary of Defense for Acquisition and Sustainment, Office of the Deputy Assistant Secretary of Defense for Manufacturing and Industrial Base Policy, *Fiscal Year 2017 Annual Industrial Capabilities: Report to Congress* (Washington, DC: US Department of Defense, March 2018), 81–87, https://www.businessdefense.gov/Portals/51/Documents/Resources/2017%20AIC%20RTC%2005-17-2018%20-%20Public%20Release.pdf?ver=2018-05-17-224631-340.

8. Marc Levinson, *U.S. Manufacturing in International Perspective,* R42135 (Washington, DC: Congressional Research Service, February 21, 2018), 2, https://crsreports.congress.gov/product/pdf/R/R42135.

9. For examination of the role of such forces, see Jim Thomas and Chris Dougherty, *Beyond the Ramparts: The Future of U.S. Special Operations Forces* (Washington, DC: Center for Strategic and Budgetary Assessments, 2013), https://csbaonline.org/research/publications/beyond-the-ramparts-the-future-of-u-s-special-operations-forces.

10. See, e.g., Richard B. Frank, *Guadalcanal: The Definitive Account of the Landmark Battle* (New York: Penguin Books, 1992).

11. Caitlin Talmadge, "Would China Go Nuclear? Assessing the Risk of Chinese Nuclear Escalation in a Conventional War with the United States," *International Security* 41, no.

4 (Spring 2017): 50–92, https://doi.org/10.1162/ISEC_a_0027; James Acton, "Escalation through Entanglement: How the Vulnerability of Command-and-Control Systems Raises the Risks of an Inadvertent Nuclear War," *International Security* 43, no. 1 (Summer 2018): 56–99, https://doi.org/10.1162/isec_a_00320.

12. Carl von Clausewitz, *On War*, ed. and trans. Michael Howard and Peter Paret (Princeton, NJ: Princeton University Press, 1976, revised 1989), 106.

13. The baseline for such an approach is considerable. One 2019 survey found that, absent any other factors, if China invaded Taiwan, 76 percent of Americans would support recognizing Taiwan's independence; 64 percent would support economic sanctions against China; 55 percent would support deploying US military assets to the region; 42 percent would support a no-fly zone to destroy Chinese aircraft; and 39 percent would support committing US ground troops to Taiwan's defense. Reagan Foundation, "U.S. National Survey of Defense Attitudes" (Washington, DC: Ronald Reagan Foundation, October 24–30, 2019), 11, https://www.reaganfoundation.org/media/355278/regan-national-defense-survey-2019-topline.pdf.

14. Thucydides, *The Landmark Thucydides: A Comprehensive Guide to the Peloponnesian War*, ed. Robert B. Strassler (New York: Simon and Schuster, 1996), 1.76, 43.

15. Clausewitz, *On War*, 80, 86.

16. Stephen M. Walt, *The Origins of Alliances* (Ithaca, NY: Cornell University Press, 1987), esp. 24–26.

17. For a signal example, see Winston Churchill, *The Second World War*, vol. 2, *Their Finest Hour* (1949; repr., Boston: Houghton Mifflin, 1985), 231.

18. *Thumos* is a Greek concept expressing spiritedness. There is not a precise term for it in English, though it bears resemblance to the now somewhat archaic use of the word *passions*. It is distinct from what we normally understand by the term *emotional*. Thumotic impulses are more akin to what might be termed the "higher" but not strictly instrumentally rational motives—the desire for honor and glory, the *libido dominandi,* and the like. See Plato, *The Republic of Plato,* trans. Allan Bloom, 2nd ed. (New York: Basic Books, 1991), 4.439e, 199, 449n33; Saint Augustine, *Concerning the City of God against the Pagans,* trans. Henry Bettenson (London: Pelican Books, 1972); and Albert O. Hirschman, *The Passions and the Interests: Political Arguments for Capitalism before Its Triumph* (Princeton, NJ: Princeton University Press, 1977), esp. 7–20. Indeed, scholarly research has identified "standing"—something akin to honor—as a primary or secondary motive of war in sixty-two cases and "revenge" in eleven cases from 1648 to the present era. See Richard Ned Lebow, *Why Nations Fight: Past and Future Motives for War* (Cambridge: Cambridge University Press, 2010). See also David A. Welch, *Justice and the Genesis of War* (Cambridge: Cambridge University Press, 1993).

19. Bradley A. Thayer, *Darwin and International Relations: On the Evolutionary Origins of War and Ethnic Conflict* (Lexington: University Press of Kentucky, 2004).

20. See, e.g., Martin Gilbert, *The First World War: A Complete History* (New York: Henry Holt, 1994).

21. See, e.g., Clausewitz, *On War*, 127. For contemporary discussion, see, e.g., Joint Chiefs of Staff, *Joint Publication 3-0: Joint Operations* (Washington, DC: US Department of Defense, January 17, 2017, updated October 22, 2018), III-38, VIII-19, https://www.jcs.mil/Portals/36/Documents/Doctrine/pubs/jp3_0ch1.pdf?ver=2018-11-27-160457-910.

See also Ben Connable et al., *Will to Fight: Analyzing, Modeling, and Simulating the Will to Fight of Military Units* (Santa Monica, CA: RAND Corporation, 2018), https://www.rand.org/pubs/research_reports/RR2341.html.

22. James M. McPherson, *Battle Cry of Freedom: The Civil War Era* (New York: Oxford University Press, 1988), 274, 318; Doris Kearns Goodwin, *Team of Rivals: The Political Genius of Abraham Lincoln* (New York: Simon and Schuster, 2005), 335–348.

23. David Hackett Fisher, *Paul Revere's Ride* (New York: Oxford University Press, 1994), 261–281.

24. See G. W. T. Omond, "Belgium, 1830–1839," in *The Cambridge History of British Foreign Policy, 1783–1919,* vol. 2, *1815–1866,* ed. Adolphus William War and George Peabody Gooch (Cambridge: Cambridge University Press, 2011), 160; and Michael Brook, "Britain Enters the War," in *The Coming of the First World War*, ed. Robert John Weston Evans and H. Pogge Von Strandmann (Oxford: Oxford University Press, 2001), 148.

25. Paul W. Schroeder, *The Transformation of European Politics, 1763–1848* (Oxford: Clarendon Press, 1994), 670–691; Zara S. Steiner and Keith Neilson, *Britain and the Origins of the First World War,* 2nd ed. (Basingstoke, UK: Palgrave Macmillan, 2003), 233; Larry Zuckerman, *The Rape of Belgium: The Untold Story of World War One* (New York: New York University Press, 2004), 1, 43.

26. Frederick C. Schneid, *The Second War of Italian Unification, 1859–1861* (Oxford: Osprey, 2012), 27–28.

27. Scott D. Sagan, "The Origins of the Pacific War," *Journal of Interdisciplinary History* 18, no. 4 (Spring 1988): 893–922, https://www.jstor.org/stable/204828.

28. Franklin Roosevelt, "Address to Congress Requesting a Declaration of War with Japan" (United States Capitol, Washington, DC, December 8, 1941), https://www.loc.gov/resource/afc1986022.afc1986022_ms2201/?st=text&r=0.004,-0.152,0.793,0.391,0.

29. Quoted in Steven Englund, *Napoleon: A Political Life* (Cambridge, MA: Harvard University Press, 2004), 105. See also Clausewitz, *On War,* 185.

30. Joel Ira Holwitt, *"Execute against Japan": The U.S. Decision to Conduct Unrestricted Submarine Warfare* (College Station: Texas A&M University Press, 2009), 139–149.

31. Richard Overy, *Why the Allies Won* (New York: W. W. Norton, 1997), 11–13.

32. US Department of Defense, *Indo-Pacific Strategy Report: Preparedness, Partnerships, and Promoting a Networked Region* (Washington, DC: US Department of Defense, July 1, 2019), 23–24, https://media.defense.gov/2019/Jul/01/2002152311/-1/-1/1/DEPARTMENT-OF-DEFENSE-INDO-PACIFIC-STRATEGY-REPORT-2019.PDF.

33. I am especially grateful to Alex Velez-Green for this point.

34. Narushige Michishita, Peter M. Swartz, and David F. Winkle, *Lessons of the Cold War in the Pacific: U.S. Maritime Strategy, Crisis Prevention, and Japan's Role* (Washington, DC: Wilson Center, May 2016), 8, https://www.wilsoncenter.org/sites/default/files/media/documents/publication/lessons_of_the_cold_war_in_the_pacific.pdf, cited in Ashley Townshend and Brendan Thomas-Noone with Matilda Steward, *Averting Crisis: American Strategy, Military Spending and Collective Defence in the Indo-Pacific* (United States Studies Centre, University of Sydney, August 2019), 62–64, https://united-states-studies-centre.s3.amazonaws.com/uploads/9e7/e52/ff4/9e7e52ff4c698816393349716d6d61e5f4566606/Averting-crisis-American-strategy-military-spending-and-collective-defence-in-the-Indo-Pacific.pdf. See also Ashley Townshend et al.,

Bolstering Resilience in the Indo-Pacific: Policy Options after COVID-19 (Sydney: United States Studies Centre, University of Sydney, June 2020), 13–14, https://www.ussc.edu.au/analysis/bolstering-resilience-in-the-indo-pacific-policy-options-for-aus-min-after-covid-19.

35. William L. Shirer, *The Rise and Fall of the Third Reich: A History of Nazi Germany* (1960; repr., New York: Simon and Schuster, 2011), 286–290.

36. See, e.g., David G. Chandler, *The Campaigns of Napoleon* (New York: Macmillan, 1966), 739–749; and A. Wess Mitchell, *The Grand Strategy of the Habsburg Empire* (Princeton, NJ: Princeton University Press, 2018), 194–224.

37. See, e.g., McPherson, *Battle Cry of Freedom,* esp. 309, 312, 768–771; Gilbert, *First World War,* esp. 437, 511, 514–515; Michael Howard, *The Franco-Prussian War: The German Invasion of France, 1870–1871,* 2nd ed. (London: Routledge, 2005), 352–357; Carter Malkasian, *The Korean War: 1950–1953* (Oxford: Osprey, 2001), 27–29; and William Stueck, "The Korean War," in *The Cambridge History of the Cold War,* ed. Melvyn P. Leffler and Odd Arne Westad (Cambridge: Cambridge University Press, 2010), 277–278.

38. Michael J. Green, *By More Than Providence: Grand Strategy and American Power in the Asia Pacific since 1783* (New York: Columbia University Press, 2017), esp. 199–207; H. W. Brands, *Bound to Empire: The United States and the Philippines* (New York: Oxford University Press, 1992), 20–38; and Philip Zelikow, "Why Did America Cross the Pacific? Reconstructing the U.S. Decision to Take the Philippines, 1898–99," *Texas National Security Review* 1, no. 1 (November 2017): 36–67, https://doi.org/10.15781/.

39. See, e.g., the Soviet Bloc's "Seven Days to the Rhine" exercise. Kyle Mizokami, "Revealed: How the Warsaw Pact Planned to Win World War Three in Europe," *National Interest,* July 2, 2016, https://nationalinterest.org/feature/revealed-how-the-warsaw-pact-planned-win-world-war-three-16822. For a history of Warsaw Pact plans, see Vojtech Mastny, Sven G. Holtsmark, and Andreas Wenger, eds., *War Plans and Alliances in the Cold War: Threat Perceptions in the East and West* (London: Routledge, 2006).

40. Charles Esdaile, *Napoleon's Wars: An International History, 1801–1815* (London: Allen Lane, 2007), 249–251; Ramon Hawley Myers, Mark R. Peattie, and Ching-Chih Chen, *The Japanese Colonial Empire, 1895–1945* (Princeton, NJ: Princeton University Press, 1998); Norman M. Naimark, *The Russians in Germany: A History of the Soviet Zone of Occupation, 1945–1949* (Cambridge, MA: Belknap Press of Harvard University Press, 1995); Jean-Louis Panné et al., *The Black Book of Communism: Crimes, Terror, Repression,* trans. Jonathan Murphy (Cambridge, MA: Harvard University Press, 1999), 33–456.

41. Protocol Additional to the Geneva Conventions of 12 August 1949, and Relating to the Protection of Victims of International Armed Conflicts (Protocol I), art. 58, August 6, 1977, U.N.T.C. 17512; Protocol Additional to the Geneva Conventions of 12 August 1949 and Relating to the Protection of Victims of Non-International Armed Conflicts (Protocol II), art. 13, August 6, 1977, U.N.T.C. 17513; US Department of Defense, *Department of Defense Law of War Manual* (Washington, DC: Office of the General Counsel, US Department of Defense, June 2015), §5.6.1.2, 209, https://dod.defense.gov/Portals/1/Documents/pubs/DoD%20Law%20of%20War%20Manual%20-%20June%202015%20Updated%20Dec%202016.pdf?ver=2016-12-13-172036-190.

42. US Department of Defense, *Department of Defense Law of War Manual,* §2.2, 52–53, §2.2.2.2, 55–56.

43. James S. Corum, *The Luftwaffe: Creating the Operational Air War, 1918–1940* (Lawrence: University Press of Kansas, 1997), 7, 198–199, 327n72.

44. See B. H. Liddell Hart, *History of the Second World War* (New York: G. P. Putnam's Sons, 1970), 66–68, 594.

45. See, e.g., Michael Warner, *The Office of Strategic Services: America's First Intelligence Agency* (Langley, VA: CIA History Staff, Center for the Study of Intelligence, Central Intelligence Agency, May 2000); M. R. D. Foot, *SOE in France: An Account of the Work of the British Special Operations Executive in France, 1940–1944* (London: Her Majesty's Stationery Office, 1966).

46. See, e.g., Denis Judd, *Empire: The British Imperial Experience from 1765 to the Present* (New York: Basic Books, 1996), 258–272; and Richard English, *Armed Struggle: The History of the IRA* (Oxford: Oxford University Press, 2003), 187–227.

47. See, e.g., Alistair Horne, *A Savage War of Peace: Algeria, 1954–1962* (London: Macmillan, 1972).

48. ROC Mainland Affairs Council, "Summarized Results of the Public Opinion Survey on the 'Public's View on the President's Inaugural Address and Related Cross-Strait Issues'" (Taipei: Mainland Affairs Council, Republic of China, May 31, 2020), https://ws.mac.gov.tw/001/Upload/297/relfile/8010/5920/203aeeaf-e762-4ee8-a1c2-0c7cc0d3245e.pdf. See also James T. Areddy and William Mauldin, "Outrage over China's Treatment of Hong Kong Galvanizes the West," *Wall Street Journal,* July 15, 2020, https://www.wsj.com/articles/outrage-over-chinas-treatment-of-hong-kong-galvanizes-the-west-11594805405.

49. See Paul Kennedy, *The Rise and Fall of the Great Powers: Economic Change and Military Conflict from 1500 to 2000* (New York: Random House, 1987), 100–115.

50. See, e.g., White House, *United States Strategic Approach to the People's Republic of China* (Washington, DC: White House, May 2020), https://www.whitehouse.gov/wp-content/uploads/2020/05/U.S.-Strategic-Approach-to-The-Peoples-Republic-of-China-Report-5.20.20.pdf. For an example of China's more open pursuit of grand aims, see Xi Jinping, "Secure a Decisive Victory in Building a Moderately Prosperous Society in All Respects and Strive for the Great Success of Socialism with Chinese Characteristics for a New Era" (19th National Congress of the Communist Party of China, Beijing, October 18, 2017), 21, xinhuanet.com/english/download/Xi_Jinping's_report_at_19th_CPC_National_Congress.pdf. See also Elizabeth C. Economy, *The Third Revolution* (New York: Oxford University Press, 2018).

51. See Karen M. Sutter, Andres B. Schwarzenberg, and Michael D. Sutherland, *COVID-19: China Medical Supply Chains and Broader Issues,* R46304 (Washington, DC: Congressional Research Service, April 6, 2020), esp. 9–21, https://crsreports.congress.gov/product/pdf/R/R46304.

52. David Kahn, *Seizing the Enigma: The Race to Break the German U-Boat Codes, 1939–1943,* rev. ed. (Annapolis, MD: Naval Institute Press, 2012).

53. Herman Kahn, *On Escalation: Metaphors and Scenarios* (New York: Praeger, 1965), 289–291.

54. Fred Anderson, *Crucible of War: The Seven Years' War and the Fate of Empire in British North America* (New York: Random House, 2000), 504–506.

55. For a superb exploration of this issue, see German Federal Minister of Defence, *White Paper 1983: The Security of the Federal Republic of Germany* (Bonn: German Federal Government, 1983).

56. For my assessment of this history, including citations, see Elbridge A. Colby, "The United States and Discriminate Nuclear Options in the Cold War," in *On Limited Nuclear War in the 21st Century,* ed. Jeffrey A. Larsen and Kerry M. Kartchner (Stanford, CA: Stanford University Press, 2014), 49–79.

57. For an excellent analysis of this, see Robert Komer, *Maritime Strategy or Coalition Defense?* (Cambridge, MA: Abt Books, 1984).

58. See, e.g., Eliot A. Cohen, "Toward Better Net Assessment: Rethinking European Conventional Balance," *International Security* 13, no. 1 (Summer 1988): 50–89, doi:10.2307/2538896.

59. Clausewitz, *On War,* 87.

Chapter 11. Implications

1. See, among others, Hugh White, *The China Choice: Why America Should Share Power* (Melbourne: Black, 2012); Christopher Layne, "Sleepwalking with Beijing," *National Interest,* no. 137 (May/June 2015): 37–45, https://www.jstor.org/stable/44028380; and Graham Allison, "The New Spheres of Influence: Sharing the Globe with Other Great Powers," *Foreign Affairs* 99, no. 2 (March/April 2020): 30–40, https://www.foreignaffairs.com/articles/united-states/2020-02-10/new-spheres-influence.

2. This definition resembles those in Barry R. Posen, *Restraint: A New Foundation for U.S. Grand Strategy* (Ithaca, NY: Cornell University Press, 2014), 1; and Hal Brands, *What Good Is Grand Strategy: Power and Purpose in American Statecraft from Harry S. Truman to George W. Bush* (Ithaca, NY: Cornell University Press, 2014), 3. On the concept of a paradigm, see Thomas S. Kuhn, *The Structure of Scientific Revolutions,* 4th ed. (Chicago: University of Chicago, 2012).

3. Stephen Peter Rosen, *Winning the Next War: Innovation and the Modern Military* (Ithaca, NY: Cornell University Press, 1991), 34–38. See also Barry R. Posen, *The Sources of Military Doctrine: France, Britain, and Germany between the World Wars* (Ithaca, NY: Cornell University Press, 1984); Williamson Murray and Allan R. Millett, eds., *Military Innovation in the Interwar Period* (New York: Cambridge University Press, 1996); and David E. Johnson, *Fast Tanks and Heavy Bombers: Innovation in the U.S. Army, 1917–1945* (Ithaca, NY: Cornell University Press, 1998).

4. US Department of Defense, *Summary of the 2018 National Defense Strategy: Sharpening the American Military's Strategic Edge* (Washington, DC: US Department of Defense, January 2018), https://dod.defense.gov/Portals/1/Documents/pubs/2018-National-Defense-Strategy-Summary.pdf. For a more detailed exposition of what the National Defense Strategy entailed, see *Hearing to Receive Testimony on China and Russia, before the Armed Services Committee, United States Senate,* 116th Cong. (2019) (statement of Elbridge A. Colby), https://www.armed-services.senate.gov/imo/media/doc/Colby

_01-29-19.pdf. For the Department's progress along these lines and challenges to further progress, see Mark T. Esper, "Implementing the National Defense Strategy: A Year of Success," US Department of Defense, July 2020, https://media.defense.gov/2020/Jul/17/2002459291/-1/-1/1/NDS-FIRST-YEAR-ACCOMPLISHMENTS-FINAL.PDF; and Govini, *The 2020 Federal Scorecard* (Rosslyn, VA: Govini, 2019), https://www.govini.com/wp-content/uploads/2020/06/Govini-2020-Federal-Scorecard.pdf.

5. See, e.g., Japanese Ministry of Defense, *National Defense Program Guidelines for FY 2019 and beyond* (Tokyo: Japanese Ministry of Defense, December 18, 2018), https://www.mod.go.jp/j/approach/agenda/guideline/2019/pdf/20181218_e.pdf; and Australian Department of Defence, *2020 Defence Strategic Update* (Canberra: Australian Government, July 2020), https://www.defence.gov.au/strategicupdate-2020/. See also Eric Heginbotham and Richard J. Samuels, "Active Denial: Redesigning Japan's Response to China's Military Challenge," *International Security* 42, no. 4 (Spring 2018): esp. 153–155, https://doi.org/10.1162/isec_a_00313; and Ashley Townshend and Brendan Thomas-Noone with Matilda Steward, *Averting Crisis: American Strategy, Military Spending and Collective Defence in the Indo-Pacific* (Sydney: United States Studies Centre, University of Sydney, August 2019), esp. 60–73, https://united-states-studies-centre.s3.amazonaws.com/uploads/9e7/e52/ff4/9e7e52ff4c698816393349716d6d61e5f4566606/Averting-crisis-American-strategy-military-spending-and-collective-defence-in-the-Indo-Pacific.pdf.

6. See, e.g., the comments of David Ochmanek in Richard Bernstein, "The Scary War Game Over Taiwan That the U.S. Loses Again and Again," *Real Clear Investigations,* August 17, 2020, https://www.realclearinvestigations.com/articles/2020/08/17/the_scary_war_game_over_taiwan_that_the_us_loses_again_and_again_124836.html. See also Christopher M. Dougherty, *Why America Needs a New Way of War* (Washington, DC: Center for a New American Security, June 2019), esp. 24.

7. National Security Council, "U.S. Strategic Framework for the Indo-Pacific," (Washington, DC: White House, 2018), 5, https://www.whitehouse.gov/wp-content/uploads/2021/01/IPS-Final-Declass.pdf. For examples of how Taiwan can do so, see, e.g., William S. Murray, "Revisiting Taiwan Defense Strategy," *Naval War College* 61, no. 3 (2008): 13–38, https://digital-commons.usnwc.edu/cgi/viewcontent.cgi?article=1814&context=nwc-review; and Jim Thomas, John Stillion, and Iskander Rehman, *Hard ROC 2.0: Taiwan and Deterrence through Protraction* (Washington, DC: Center for Strategic and Budgetary Assessments, 2014), https://csbaonline.org/research/publications/hard-roc-2-0-taiwan-and-deterrence-through-protraction.

8. See, e.g., Jonathan F. Solomon, "Demystifying Conventional Deterrence: Great Power Conflict and East Asian Peace," *Strategic Studies Quarterly* 7, no. 4 (Winter 2013): 117–157, https://www.jstor.org/stable/26270780; Andrew F. Krepinevich Jr., *Archipelagic Defense: The Japan-U.S. Alliance and Preserving Peace and Stability in the Western Pacific* (Tokyo: Sasakawa Peace Foundation, 2017), https://www.spf.org/en/global-data/SPF_20170810_03.pdf; Evan Braden Montgomery, *Reinforcing the Front Line: U.S. Defense Strategy and the Rise of China* (Washington, DC: Center for Strategic and Budgetary Assessments, 2017), https://csbaonline.org/research/publications/reinforcing-the-front-line-u.s.-defense-strategy-and-the-rise-of-china; David Ochmanek et al., *U.S. Military Capabilities and Forces for a Dangerous World; Readying the U.S.*

Military for Future Warfare, before the House Armed Services Committee, 115th Cong. (2018) (statement of Jim Thomas, Principal and Co-Founder, Telemus Group), https:// docs.house.gov/meetings/AS/AS00/20180130/106813/HfHRG-115-AS00-Wstate-Tho-masJ-20180130.pdf; David Ochmanek, *Restoring U.S. Power Projection Capabilities: Responding to the 2018 National Defense Strategy* (Santa Monica, CA: RAND Corporation, July 2018), https://www.rand.org/pubs/perspectives/PE260.html; Bryan Clark et al., *Regaining the High Ground at Sea: Transforming the U.S. Navy's Carrier Air Wing for Great Power Competition* (Washington, DC: Center for Strategic and Budgetary Assessment, December 2018), https://csbaonline.org/research/publications/regaining-the-high-ground-at-sea-transforming-the-u.s.-navys-carrier-air-wi; David Johnson, "An Army Caught in the Middle between Luddites, Luminaries, and the Occasional Looney," *War on the Rocks,* December 19, 2018, https://warontherocks.com/2018/12/an-army-caught-in-the-middle-between-luddites-luminaries-and-the-occasional-looney/; Jim Mitre, "A Eulogy for the Two-War Construct," *Washington Quarterly* 41, no. 4 (Winter 2019): 7–30, https://doi.org/10.1080/0163660X.2018.1557479; Billy Fabian et al., *Strengthening the Defense of NATO's Eastern Frontier* (Washington, DC: Center for Strategic and Budgetary Assessments, March 2019), https://csbaonline.org/research/ publications/strengthening-the-defense-of-natos-eastern-frontier; Thomas G. Mahnken et al., *Tightening the Chain: Implementing a Strategy of Maritime Pressure in the Western Pacific* (Washington, DC: Center for Strategic and Budgetary Assessments, May 2019), https://csbaonline.org/research/publications/implementing-a-strategy-of-mari-time-pressure-in-the-western-pacific; Mike Gallagher, "State of (Deterrence by) Denial," *Washington Quarterly* 42, no. 2 (Summer 2019): 31–45, https://doi.org/10.1080/0 163660X.2019.1626687; Dougherty, *Why America Needs a New Way of War;* Robert O. Work and Greg Grant, *Beating the Americans at Their Own Game: An Offset Strategy with Chinese Characteristics* (Washington, DC: Center for a New American Security, June 2019), https://www.cnas.org/publications/reports/beating-the-americans-at-their-own-game; Thomas P. Ehrhard, "Treating Pathologies of Victory: Hardening the Nation for Strategic Competition," in *2020 Index of U.S. Military Strength,* ed. Dakota L. Wood (Washington, DC: Heritage Foundation, 2019), 19–33, https://www.heritage.org/mili-tary-strength/topical-essays/treating-the-pathologies-victory-hardening-the-nation-stra-tegic; Townshend, Thomas-Noone, and Steward, *Averting Crisis;* Bryan Clark and Timothy A. Walton, *Taking Back the Seas: Transforming the U.S. Surface Fleet for Decision-Centric Warfare* (Washington, DC: Center for Strategic and Budgetary Assessments, December 2019), https://csbaonline.org/research/publications/taking-back-the-seas-transforming-the-u.s-surface-fleet-for-decision-centric-warfare; Miranda Priebe et al., *Distributed Operations in a Contested Environment: Implications for USAF Force Presentation* (Santa Monica, CA: RAND Corporation, 2019), https://www. rand.org/pubs/research_reports/RR2959.html; Andrew F. Krepinevich Jr., *Protracted Great-Power War: A Preliminary Assessment* (Washington, DC: Center for a New American Security, February 2020), https://www.cnas.org/publications/reports/protracted-great-power-war; Brendan Rittenhouse Green and Austin Long, "Conceal or Reveal? Managing Clandestine Military Capabilities in Peacetime Competition," *International Security* 44, no. 3 (Winter 2019/20): 48–83, https://doi.org/10.1162/ISEC_a_00367; Christian Brose, *The Kill Chain: Defending America in the Future of High-Tech Warfare*

(New York: Hachette, 2020); Bryan Frederick et al., *Understanding the Deterrent Impact of U.S. Overseas Forces* (Santa Monica, CA: RAND Corporation, 2020), https:// doi.org/10.7249/RR2533; Eric J. Wesley and Robert H. Simpson, "Expanding the Battlefield: An Important Fundamental of Multi-Domain Operations," Land Warfare Paper 131 (Arlington, VA: Association of the United States Army, April 2020), https://www. ausa.org/sites/default/files/publications/LWP-131-Expanding-the-Battlefield-An-Important-Fundamental-of-Multi-Domain-Operations.pdf; and David H. Berger, *Force Design 2030* (Washington, DC: US Marine Corps, March 2020), https://www.hqmc.marines.mil/Portals/142/Docs/CMC38%20Force%20Design%202030%20Report%20 Phase%20I%20and%20II.pdf?ver=2020-03-26-121328-460.

9. See Michael J. Green, *By More Than Providence: Grand Strategy and American Power in the Asia Pacific since 1783* (New York: Columbia University Press, 2017), 245–296, 321–322. See also Abraham M. Denmark, *U.S. Strategy in the Asian Century: Empowering Allies and Partners* (New York: Columbia University Press, 2020).

10. Andrew Rhodes, "The Second Island Cloud: A Deeper and Broader Concept for American Presence in the Pacific Islands," *Joint Force Quarterly* 95 (2019): 46–53, https:// ndupress.ndu.edu/Portals/68/Documents/jfq/jfq-95/jfq-95.pdf.

11. For a treatment of Sino-Indian strategic competition, see Daniel Kliman et al., *Imbalance of Power: India's Military Choices in an Era of Strategic Competition with China* (Washington, DC: Center for a New American Security, October 2019), https://www. cnas.org/publications/reports/imbalance-of-power.

12. See, e.g., Jacob Cohn, Adam Lemon, and Evan Braden Montgomery, *Assessing the Arsenals: Past, Present, and Future Capabilities* (Washington, DC: Center for Strategic and Budgetary Assessments, 2019), esp. 35–37, https://csbaonline.org/research/publications/Assessing_the_Arsenals_Past_Present_and_Future_Capabilities.

13. See Alexander Benard, *Swing Nations: How the United States Can Win against China across Asia and Africa* (Stanford, CA: Hoover Institution, forthcoming).

14. See, e.g., David Shambaugh, "U.S.-China Rivalry in Southeast Asia: Power Shift or Competitive Coexistence?," *International Security* 42, no. 4 (Spring 2018): 93–95, doi:10.1162/ISEC_a_00314; Murray Hiebert, *Under Beijing's Shadow: Southeast Asia's China Challenge* (Lanham, MD: Rowman and Littlefield, 2020); and Gregory B. Policy, *Rocks and Rules: America and the South China Sea* (New York: Oxford University Press, forthcoming).

15. Thailand has a thin alliance with the United States, a function of the multilateral 1954 Southeast Asia Treaty/Manila Pact (SEATO has since dissolved), the 1962 Thanat-Rusk communiqué, its 2003 Major Non-NATO Ally designation, and the 2012 Joint Vision Statement for the Thai-U.S. Defense Alliance. See Bureau of East Asian and Pacific Affairs, "U.S. Relations with Thailand," Bilateral Relations Fact Sheet (Washington, DC: US Department of State, October 21, 2019), https://www.state.gov/u-s-relations -with-thailand/; Emma Chanlett-Avery, Ben Dolven, and Wil Mackey, *Thailand: Background and U.S. Relations,* IF10253 (Washington, DC: Congressional Research Service, July 29, 2015), 1, 5–8, https://crsreports.congress.gov/product/pdf/IF/IF10253; and Thai Minister of Defense Sukumpol Suwanatat and Secretary of Defense Leon E. Panetta, "2012 Joint Vision Statement for the Thai-U.S. Defense Alliance" (Bangkok, November 15, 2012), https://archive.defense.gov/releases/release.aspx?releaseid=15685.

I am grateful to Rear Admiral Mark Montgomery, USN (Ret.), former director for operations at US Pacific Command, for clarifying Thailand's status vis-à-vis Washington.

16. For a history, see Chris Baker and Pasuk Phongpaichit, *A History of Thailand,* 2nd ed. (Melbourne: Cambridge University Press, 2009), 81–139.

17. For a brief overview, see Ian Storey, "China's 'Malacca Dilemma,'" *China Brief* (Jamestown Foundation) 6, no. 8 (April 12, 2006), https://jamestown.org/program/chinas-malacca-dilemma/.

18. Emma Chanlett-Avery, Caitlin Campbell, and Joshua A. Williams, *The U.S.-Japan Alliance,* RL33740 (Washington, DC: Congressional Research Service, updated June 13, 2019), 9, https://crsreports.congress.gov/product/pdf/RL/RL33740.

19. Australian Department of Defence, *2020 Defence Strategic Update.*

20. For a critique of the pursuit of perfect security in US foreign policy, see Patrick Porter, *The Global Village Myth: Distance, War, and the Limits of Power* (Washington, DC: Georgetown University Press, 2015).

21. For scholarly treatments, see, e.g., Desmond Ball and Jeffery Richelson, eds., *Strategic Nuclear Targeting* (Ithaca, NY: Cornell University Press, 1986); and Scott D. Sagan, *Moving Targets: Nuclear Strategy and National Security* (Princeton, NJ: Princeton University Press, 1989), esp. 10–98.

22. See, e.g., Augustus Richard Norton, *Hezbollah: A Short History,* updated ed. (Princeton, NJ: Princeton University Press, 2014), 27–46.

23. See, e.g., Paul K. Davis and Brian Michael Jenkins, *Deterring and Influence in Counterterrorism: A Component in the War on al Qaeda* (Santa Monica, CA: RAND Corporation, 2002), https://www.rand.org/pubs/monograph_reports/MR1619.html; Robert Trager and Dessislava Zagorcheva, "Deterring Terrorism: It Can Be Done," *International Security* 30, no. 3 (Winter 2005/06): 87–123, https://www.jstor.org/stable/4137488; and Daniel Byman, *A High Price: The Triumphs and Failures of Israeli Counterterrorism* (Oxford: Oxford University Press, 2011). For my earlier analysis of this issue, see Elbridge A. Colby, "Expanded Deterrence," *Policy Review* (June and July 2008), https://www.hoover.org/research/expanded-deterrence.

24. See Stephen Tankel, "A Resource-Sustainable Strategy for Countering Violent Extremist Organizations" (Washington, DC: Center for a New American Security, September 24, 2020), https://www.cnas.org/publications/commentary/a-resource-sustainable-strategy-for-countering-violent-extremist-organizations; and, for force structure implications, David Ochmanek et al., *U.S. Military Capabilities and Forces for a Dangerous World,* xv, 77–94.

25. See, e.g., Erik W. Goepner, "Learning from Today's War: Measuring the Effectiveness of America's War on Terror," *Parameters* 46, no. 1 (Spring 2016): 107–120, https://publications.armywarcollege.edu/pubs/3323.pdf.

26. See, e.g., *Hearing to Consider the Nomination of: General Mark A. Milley, USA for Reappointment to the Grade of General and to Be Chairman of the Joint Chiefs of Staff, before the Committee on Armed Services, United States Senate,* 116th Cong. 67 (2019) (Advance Policy Questions for Gen. Mark A. Milley, US Army, nominee for appointment to be Chairman of the Joint Chiefs of Staff), https://www.armed-services.senate.gov/imo/media/doc/Milley_APQs_07-11-19.pdf; and Melissa Dalton and Mara Karlin, "Toward a Smaller, Smarter Force Posture in the Middle East," *Defense One,* August 26, 2018,

https://www.defenseone.com/ideas/2018/08/toward-smaller-smarter-force-posture-middle-east/150817/.

27. I am especially grateful to Alex Velez-Green for his contributions to this section on counterterrorism, which largely reflects his analysis of how to deal with this challenge, and to Michael Leiter for his helpful comments on this section.

28. Michael Bennet, *Projected Costs of U.S. Nuclear Forces, 2019–2028* (Washington, DC: Congressional Budget Office, January 2019), 4, https://www.cbo.gov/publication/54914; Laicie Heeley et al., *Counterterrorism Spending: Protecting America While Promoting Efficiencies and Accountability* (Washington, DC: Stimson Center, May 2018), 13, https://www.stimson.org/2018/counterterrorism-spending-protecting-america-while-promoting-efficiencies-and-accountability/. The Stimson Center study included Overseas Contingency Operations (OCO) funding in its calculation of spending on counterterrorism; the OCO account included noncounterterrorism funding such as the European Deterrence Initiative.

29. See Office of the Historian, "French Intervention in Mexico and the American Civil War," Foreign Service Institute, US Department of State, https://history.state.gov/milestones/1861-1865/french-intervention.

30. As First Lord of the Admiralty Selborne put it: "The decisive battles . . . would certainly be fought in European waters. . . . If the British Navy were defeated in the Mediterranean and the Channel the stress of our position would not be alleviated by any amount of superiority in the Chinese seas. If, on the other hand, it were to prove supreme in the Mediterranean and the Channel, even serious disasters in Chinese waters would matter little. These considerations furnish, therefore, a sound argument for keeping our naval strength in Chinese waters as low as is compatible with the safety of the Empire." Quoted in Aaron L. Friedberg, *The Weary Titan: Britain and the Experience of Relative Decline, 1895–1905* (Princeton, NJ: Princeton University Press, 1988), 176. For an important study of the issue of strategic simultaneity, see A. Wess Mitchell, *Strategic Sequencing: How Great Powers Avoid Two Front Wars* (Cambridge, MA: Belfer Center for Science and International Affairs, forthcoming).

31. For an essential treatment of the simultaneity issue, see Mitre, "Eulogy for the Two-War Construct." For a different view, see Hal Brands and Evan Braden Montgomery, "One War Is Not Enough: Strategy and Force Planning for Great Power Competition," *Texas National Security Review* 3, no. 2 (Spring 2020), http://dx.doi.org/10.26153/tsw/8865; and *The Department of Defense's Role in Long-Term Major State Competition, before the Armed Services Committee, U.S. House of Representatives,* 116th Cong. 3 (2020) (statement of Thomas G. Mahnken, President and Chief Executive Officer, Center for Strategic and Budgetary Assessments), https://csbaonline.org/research/publications/statement-before-the-house-armed-services-committee-the-department-of-defenses-role-in-long-term-major-state-competition.

32. International Institute for Strategic Studies, *Military Balance,* 284–286.

33. World Bank, "GDP, PPP (Current International $)—Korea, Rep." (Washington, DC: World Bank, accessed June 17, 2020), https://data.worldbank.org/indicator/NY.GDP.MKTP.PP.CD?locations=KR; International Institute for Strategic Studies, *The Military Balance,* vol. 119 (London: International Institute for Strategic Studies, 2019), 515; Stockholm International Peace Research Institute, "Military Expenditure by Country, in

Constant (2017) US $m., 1988–2018" (Stockholm: SIPRI, 2019), 18, https://www.sipri.org/sites/default/files/Data%20for%20all%20countries%20from%201988%E2%80%932018%20in%20constant%20%282017%29%20USD%20%28pdf%29.pdf. Comparative data is for 2018, measured in constant (2017) USD.

34. See David Ochmanek and Lowell H. Schwartz, *The Challenge of Nuclear-Armed Regional Adversaries* (Santa Monica, CA: RAND Corporation, 2008), 53, https://www.rand.org/pubs/monographs/MG671.html; Committee on Conventional Global Strike Capability, National Research Council, *U.S. Conventional Prompt Global Strike: Issues for 2008 and Beyond* (Washington, DC: National Academies Press, 2008), 48–50; and Defense Science Board Task Force, *Time Critical Conventional Strike from Strategic Standoff* (Washington, DC: Office of the Under Secretary of Defense for Acquisition, Technology, and Logistics, US Department of Defense, March 2009), 81–84, https://dsb.cto.mil/reports/2000s/ADA498403.pdf.

35. Brad Roberts, "On the Strategic Value of Ballistic Missile Defense," *Proliferation Papers* (Institut Français des Relations Internationales), no. 50 (June 2014): 9–35, https://www.ifri.org/sites/default/files/atoms/files/pp50roberts.pdf.

36. For a similar view, see Isaac Stone Fish and Robert Kelly, "North Korea Is Ultimately China's Problem: How Washington Can Get Beijing to Step Up," *Foreign Affairs,* June 8, 2018, https://www.foreignaffairs.com/articles/china/2018-06-08/north-korea-ultimately-chinas-problem.

37. See, e.g., Kenneth E. Todorov, *Missile Defense: Getting to the Elusive "Right Side of the Cost Curve"* (Washington, DC: Center for Strategic and International Studies, April 2016), https://www.csis.org/analysis/missile-defense-getting-elusive-right-side-cost-curve.

38. Evan Braden Montgomery, "Primacy and Punishment: U.S. Grand Strategy, Maritime Power, and Military Options to Manage Decline," *Security Studies* 29, no. 4 (2020): 769–796, doi:10.1080/09636412.2020.1811463.

39. Jakub J. Grygiel and A. Wess Mitchell, *The Unquiet Frontier: Rising Rivals, Vulnerable Allies, and the Crisis of American Power* (Princeton, NJ: Princeton University Press, 2017), 8; President of the Russian Federation, "The Russian Federation's National Security Strategy," Russian Federation, trans. Instituto Español de Estudios Estratégicos (IEEE), December 31, 2015, http://www.ieee.es/Galerias/fichero/OtrasPublicaciones/Internacional/2016/Russian-National-Security-Strategy-31Dec2015.pdf.

40. Scott Boston et al., *Assessing the Conventional Force Imbalance in Europe: Implications for Countering Russian Local Superiority* (Santa Monica, CA: RAND Corporation, 2018), https://www.rand.org/pubs/research_reports/RR2402.html; Fabian et al., *Strengthening the Defense of NATO's Eastern Front,* 1–14.

41. David A. Shlapak and Michael W. Johnson, *Reinforcing Deterrence on NATO's Eastern Flank* (Santa Monica, CA: RAND Corporation, 2016), 6, 8, https://www.rand.org/pubs/research_reports/RR1253.html; Dougherty, *Why America Needs a New Way of War,* 34–35. See North Atlantic Treaty Organization, "NATO Readiness Initiative" (Brussels: NATO, June 2018), https://www.nato.int/nato_static_fl2014/assets/pdf/pdf_2018_06/20180608_1806-NATO-Readiness-Initiative_en.pdf; and North Atlantic Treaty Organization, "NATO: Ready for the Future: Adapting the Alliance (2018–2019)"

(Brussels: NATO, November 2019), https://www.nato.int/nato_static_fl2014/assets/pdf/pdf_2019_11/20191129_191129-adaptation_2018_2019_en.pdf.

42. For a seminal treatment on the paradoxical logic of strategy, see Edward N. Luttwak, *Strategy: The Logic of War and Peace,* 2nd ed. (Cambridge, MA: Belknap Press of Harvard University Press, 2001).

43. US Department of Defense, *Nuclear Posture Review* (Washington, DC: US Department of Defense, 2018), 8, 30, https://dod.defense.gov/News/SpecialReports/2018NuclearPostureReview.aspx. See also Alexander Velez-Green, *The Unsettling View from Moscow: Russia's Strategic Debate on a Doctrine of Pre-Emption* (Washington, DC: Center for a New American Security, April 2017), https://www.jstor.org/stable/resrep06406; Dave Johnson, *Russia's Conventional Precision Strike Capabilities, Regional Crises, and Nuclear Thresholds* (Livermore, CA: Center for Global Security Research, Lawrence Livermore National Laboratory, February 2018), https://cgsr.llnl.gov/content/assets/docs/Precision-Strike-Capabilities-report-v3-7.pdf.

44. See, among others, David A. Shlapak and Michael W. Johnson, *Reinforcing Deterrence on NATO's Eastern Flank*; *Testimony from Outside Experts on Recommendations for a Future National Defense Strategy, before the Committee on Armed Services, United States Senate,* 115th Cong. (2017) (statement of David Ochmanek, Senior International/Defense Researcher, RAND Corporation), https://www.armed-services.senate.gov/imo/media/doc/Ochmanek_11-30-17.pdf; and Fabian et al., *Strengthening the Defense of NATO's Eastern Front.*

45. For an excellent analysis of Sweden's contemporary strategic environment, see Johan Raeder, "The United States National Defense Strategy—Consequences for Swedish Defense Policy," *Royal Academy of Swedish War Sciences Proceedings and Journal,* no. 1 (2020): 7–23.

46. Calculation using North Atlantic Treaty Organization, "Defence Expenditure of NATO Countries (2012–2019)," PR/CP(2019)069 (Brussels: NATO, June 2019), 7–10, https://www.nato.int/nato_static_fl2014/assets/pdf/pdf_2019_06/20190625_PR2019-069-EN.pdf; and World Bank, "GDP (Current US$)—Russian Federation" (Washington, DC: World Bank, accessed December 7, 2019), https://data.worldbank.org/indicator/NY.GDP.MKTP.CD?locations=RU. Both figures are in 2015 USD.

47. See Polish Ministry of National Defence, *The Defence Concept of the Republic of Poland* (Warsaw: Polish Ministry of National Defence, 2017), https://www.gov.pl/web/national-defence/defenceconcept-publication.

48. Stockholm International Peace Research Institute, *SIPRI Yearbook: Armaments, Disarmament and International Security* (Stockholm: SIPRI, various years), cited in World Bank, "Military Expenditure (% of GDP)—Germany," (Washington, DC: World Bank, accessed December 8, 2019), https://data.worldbank.org/indicator/ms.mil.xpnd.gd.zs; Congressional Budget Office, *U.S. Ground Forces and the Conventional Balance in Europe* (Washington, DC: Congress of the United States, June 1988), 93, https://www.cbo.gov/sites/default/files/100th-congress-1987-1988/reports/doc01b-entire.pdf; and Michael Shurkin, *The Abilities of the British, French, and German Armies to Generate and Sustain Armored Brigades in the Baltics* (Santa Monica, CA: RAND Corporation, 2017), 10, https://www.rand.org/pubs/research_reports/RR1629.html.

49. For a similar view, see Andrew F. Krepinevich, *Preserving the Balance: A U.S. Eurasia Defense Strategy* (Washington, DC: Center for Strategic and Budgetary Assessments, 2017),28,https://csbaonline.org/research/publications/preserving-the-balance-a-u.s.-eurasia -defense-strategy.

50. Bernard Brodie, *Strategy in the Missile Age* (Santa Monica, CA: RAND Corporation, 1959), 358.

51. SIPRI, *SIPRI Yearbook,* cited in World Bank, "Military Expenditure (% of GDP)— United States" (Washington, DC: World Bank, accessed June 2, 2020), https:// data.worldbank.org/indicator/MS.MIL.XPND.GD.ZS?locations=US&start=2000; and Brendan W. McGarry, *FY2021 Defense Budget Request: An Overview* (Washington, DC: Congressional Research Service, February 20, 2020), 4, https://crsreports.congress.gov/ product/pdf/IN/IN11224.

52. For a survey of the literature on this topic, see Rati Ram, "Defense Expenditure and Economic Growth," in *Handbook of Defense Economics,* vol. 1, ed. Keith Hartley and Todd Sandler (Oxford: Elsevier, 1995), 251–274.

53. Mancur Olson Jr. and Richard Zeckhauser, *An Economic Theory of Alliances* (Santa Monica, CA: RAND Corporation, 1966), https://www.rand.org/pubs/research_memoranda/RM4297.html. See also Hedley Bull, "Strategy and the Atlantic Alliance: A Critique of United States Doctrine" (Princeton, NJ: Center for International Studies, Woodrow Wilson School of Public and International Affairs, Princeton University, 1964); Mancur Olson, *The Logic of Collective Action: Public Goods and the Theory of Groups* (Cambridge, MA: Harvard University Press, 1971); Francis A. Beer, *The Political Economy of Alliances* (Beverly Hills, CA: Sage, 1972); Todd Sander and Jon Cauley, "On the Economic Theory of Alliances," *Journal of Conflict Resolution* 19, no. 2 (1975): 330–348, https://doi.org/10.1177/002200277501900207; Todd Sandler, "Sharing Burdens in NATO," *Challenge* 31, no. 2 (March/April 1988): 29–35 https://www.jstor.org/ stable/40720487; Todd Sandler, "The Economic Theory of Alliances: A Survey," *Journal of Conflict Resolution* 37, no. 3 (September 1993): 446–483, https://www.jstor.org/ stable/174264; John R. Oneal and Paul F. Diehl, "The Theory of Collective Action and NATO Defense Burdens: New Empirical Tests," *Political Research Quarterly* 47, no. 2 (June 1994): 373–396, doi:10.2307/449016; and Anika Binnedijk and Miranda Priebe, *An Attack against Them All? Drivers of Decisions to Contribute to NATO Collective Defense* (Santa Monica, CA: RAND Corporation, 2019), https://www.rand.org/pubs/ research_reports/RR2964.html.

54. Scott D. Sagan and Kenneth N. Waltz, *The Spread of Nuclear Weapons: An Enduring Debate,* 3rd ed. (New York: W. W. Norton, 2013). For a rebuttal, see Richard K. Betts, "Universal Deterrence or Conceptual Collapse? Liberal Pessimism and Utopian Realism," in *The Coming Crisis: Nuclear Proliferation, U.S. Interests, and World Order,* ed. Victor A. Utgoff (Cambridge, MA: MIT Press, 2000), 65–66.

55. For a similar view, see James R. Schlesinger, "The Strategic Consequences of Nuclear Proliferation," in *Selected Papers on National Security, 1964–1968* (Santa Monica, CA: RAND Corporation, 1974), 3–11.

56. On the concept of the stability-instability paradox, see Glenn H. Snyder, "The Balance of Power and the Balance of Terror," in *The Balance of Power,* ed. Paul Seabury (San

Francisco: Chandler, 1965), 185–201. See also Robert Jervis, *The Illogic of American Nuclear Strategy* (Ithaca, NY: Cornell University Press, 1984), 31.

57. See North Atlantic Treaty Organization, "Deterrence and Defense Posture Review," 2012 (063) (Brussels: NATO, May 2012), para. 10, https://www.nato.int/cps/en/natohq/official_texts_87597.htm.

Chapter 12. A Decent Peace

1. Hans J. Morgenthau, *Politics among Nations: The Struggle for Power and Peace,* 7th ed. (New York: McGraw-Hill Education, 2005).

INDEX

Active Defense doctrine, 168

Afghanistan: counterterrorism in, 260; scaling back commitments in, 60–61, 303n36; Soviet occupation of, 95; US differentiated credibility in Asia and, 60, 62–64; US military strategy in, 81

Africa: economic power in, 5–6, 299n27; potential for hegemonic state emerging in, 36–37; punishment approach in, 149; regional balance of power in, 36. *See also specific countries*

aggressiveness of opponent, 15, 50, 213–214

air forces: denial defense and, 155–156, 158–159, 273; limited war and, 307n15; in Persian Gulf, 35; punishment approach and, 315n32; recapture approach and, 198

AirLand Battle concept, 168

al-Qaeda, 104, 257

alliances, 38–64; architecture of, 239, 242; autonomy and, 40, 43, 46, 51, 54; bandwagoning and, 41; challenges to mounting an effective defense of, 47–53; commitments to, 42–43, 47, 49, 55, 66, 70, 242; credibility and, 53–64, 302n25; defense

perimeter and, 239–244; defined, 40–41; multilateral, 42, 44, 64, 232, 244; vulnerable states and, 39, 42, 45, 47, 54, 61, 67–68. *See also* anti-hegemonic coalition in general; effective defense of alliances

Altman, Dan, 318n42

ambiguity in defense perimeter, 67–68

ambition of opponent as source of resolve, 216–219

annexation, 134–136, 144–145

anti-hegemonic coalition in general: alliances in, 40–45; burden sharing within, 279; challenges of forming and sustaining, 19–23; coalition cornerstone balancer's importance for, 26–27; in Asia and implications for US defense strategy, 253–254

anti-hegemonic coalition in Asia: burden sharing within, 279; conquest approach and, 139–144; defense perimeter and, 67–69, 72, 242–243; failure of denial defense and, 193–194, 201–208, 213–227; fait accompli and, 139–144; preventive war and, 295n10; prospects for, 29–37; regional balance of power and, 16, 19–23.